Native Americans and the Law

Contemporary and Historical Perspectives on American Indian Rights, Freedoms, and Sovereignty

Series Editor

John R. Wunder
University of Nebraska-Lincoln

GARLAND PUBLISHING, INC.
New York & London
1996

Contents of the Series

1. Native American Law and Colonialism, Before 1776 to 1903
2. Constitutionalism and Native Americans, 1903–1968
3. The Indian Bill of Rights, 1968
4. Recent Legal Issues for American Indians, 1968 to the Present
5. Native American Cultural and Religious Freedoms
6. Native American Sovereignty

Native American Sovereignty

Edited with introductions by

John R. Wunder

University of Nebraska-Lincoln

GARLAND PUBLISHING, INC.

New York & London

1996

Library of Congress Cataloging-in-Publication Data

Native American sovereignty / edited with introductions by John R. Wunder.
p. cm. — (Native Americans and the law ; 6)
Includes bibliographical references.
ISBN 0-8153-3629-2
1. Indians of North America—Legal status, laws, etc. 2. Indians of North America—Government relations. 3. Indians of North America—Politics and government. I. Wunder John R. II. Series.
KF8205.N386 1996
342.73'0872—dc20 96-34704
[347.302872] CIP

Printed on acid-free, 250-year-life paper
Manufactured in the United States of America

Contents

Series Introduction

N. Scott Momaday, in his masterful *The Way to Rainy Mountain*, tells a story of a Kiowa family—a father, mother, and son. During one evening, while the father was resting inside their tipi, the mother was preparing a meal over the fire. She gave a piece of meat to her young son. He went outside to eat it, but soon came back in and asked for another piece. This happened three more times in succession, and when he came back once again he brought several enemies into the tipi. They told the Kiowa parents there were many other enemies nearby who also wanted food, but if they were fed now they would help the family against those other enemies and not harm them.

The father did not think this story was quite right, but he pretended to believe it. As his wife put a large amount of fatty meat on the fire to cook, he went outside the tipi and proceeded to hide the enemies' horses. He did not see any other enemies. Once the father was a short distance away, he sang in the voice of a bird. The mother knew now it was time to act, so she set fire to the fat and threw it all around upon those who were sitting nearby. While the enemies screamed, she grabbed up her little boy in her arms, ran outside the tipi, and without hesitating sprinted upstream to be reunited with her husband. As the Kiowa family escaped, they turned and saw the fire destroying all of their belongings and heard the cries of their enemies.[1] They thought of their terrifying duress they had so suddenly experienced, of their disastrous and sacrificial loss of their home, and of their forced removal. They also remembered their resistance and their survival.

* * * * *

Within this story are some of the characteristics that help to describe the legal relationship of Native Americans to law in the United States. Such traits include duress, disaster, removal, resistance, sacrifice, and survival. Each of these, among others, can be applied to a legal understanding of the past, present, and future. The relationship of American Indians to law, in particular to federal law, is one highlighted by ambiguity, confusion, and all too frequently imbalance. There are many colonial manifestations as well. No other group in the United States has been the subject of more litigation than Native Americans. Throughout the nineteenth and continuing into the twentieth century, these legal relationships have not been resolved and likely never will be. So litigious are the issues that the famous John Marshall decision, *Worcester v. Georgia* (1832), remains one of the most cited court decisions in United States legal history.[2] The fat, we might say, is constantly in the fire.

As Sidney Herring has pointed out in his recent book, *Crow Dog's Case*, there are two basic legal traditions at play in modern considerations of Native Americans and law. There are the constitutional and common law structures of the state and federal governments. But Indian tribes also have their own laws and customs that have evolved through time and have been practiced by succeeding generations. Although these traditions have been modified and attacked, most significantly in the twentieth century, they continue to be practiced. These legal traditions are very rich, reflecting the diversity of Native peoples in North America. Thus, federal Indian law is a conflict of laws exercised in theory, but seldom is Indian law analyzed in legal determinations outside of tribal courts. The history of Native Americans and law is the history of this curious duality inherent in two competing legal systems.[3]

These legal relationships are dynamic and frequently changing, as this six-volume collection of articles will show. For the first time, more than 70 scholarly essays concerning the legal history of Native Americans and law are offered. They represent a wide variety of expertise, including writings from Native leadership, practicing lawyers, legal scholars, anthropologists, and historians—a vast interdisciplinary wealth of authors who normally would not be bound together.

This anthology is divided into two sections. How the United States attempts, generally unsuccessfully, to make Native Americans fit within a federal legal framework is the primary theme of these essays. The first four volumes offer a historical survey of the development of Indian legal relationships within their communities and from without. Volume 1 covers the evolution of legal cultures among Native peoples from pre-1776 through an era of colonialism to 1903. Volume 2 next considers the first sixty years of the twentieth century built around the theme of constitutionalism. Here there is an emphasis on the intersection of the U.S. government and tribal law when so many legal changes were made. Of particular significance is Volume 3, the first collection of essays published on the Indian Bill of Rights, legislation passed by Congress and signed by President Lyndon Johnson that encompassed six sections of the Civil Rights Act of 1968. The last of the historical survey volumes, Volume 4, considers recent legal issues, from 1968 to the present. Included among those discussed are fishing and hunting rights, water law, zoning, the Indian Child Welfare Act of 1978, taxation, gaming, and repatriation.

The last two volumes of this series each stand on their own, representing important themes in Native American law. Volume 5 considers cultural and religious freedoms that have evolved from important legal confrontations between Native American societies and the United States government and from those legal decisions reached. Volume 6 offers assessments of the various legal nuances and meanings of sovereignty for Indian tribes. These two volumes also present the historical underpinnings of the exercise of cultural and religious freedoms and sovereignty rights entailed in today's legal arena.

* * * * *

The preparation of this collection involved the work of many people. I am most grateful for the scholarly expertise of Mark Ellis of the University of Nebraska-Lincoln, Department of History, and his help in this endeavor. In addition, the staff of the Center for Great Plains Studies at the University of Nebraska, notably Gretchen Walker and Linda Ratcliffe, were instrumental in the timely preparation of materials. While editing these six volumes, I held the position as Bicentennial Fulbright Chair in North American Studies at the Renvall Institute of the University of Helsinki, Finland, and there the assistance of its director, Eino Lyytinen, the Institute staff, and my Finnish students in American legal history and Native American history classes were indispensible. Thanks also go to Carole Puccino, Leo Balk, and the Garland staff for their careful and steadfast work on this intricate project.

NOTES

1. N. Scott Momaday, *The Way to Rainy Mountain* (Albuquerque: University of New Mexico Press, 1969), p. 44.
2. See John R. Wunder, *"Retained by The People": A History of American Indians and the Bill of Rights* (New York: Oxford University Press, 1994), 219, n. 25.
3. See Sidney L. Herring, *Crow Dog's Case: American Indian Sovereignty, Tribal Law, and United States Law in the Nineteenth Century* (New York: Cambridge University Press, 1994).

Volume Introduction

Sovereignty for Native Americans is defined in many ways. Sometimes it is seen as a question of military control. Ben Kindle wrote his Winter Count for the year 1791 and expressed in Oglala Sioux his definition: "We' mapi mak'o' 'kawih ahi'yayapi'" [Flag around the earth/they carry it along.] He was referring to the new United States nation.[1] Modern definitions have become more precise. Article I of the Montevideo Convention on the Rights and Duties of States defined a sovereign nation as having a permanent population, a definitive territory, a functioning government, and an ability to conduct relations with other states.[2] Vine Deloria Jr. sees sovereignty as dynamic and evolutionary. A sovereign nation, to Deloria, has the power to "determine its own course of action with respect to other nations," to control "sufficient territory and military strength," and "regulate one's own international functions in the field of domestic relations."[3]

At first European nations and then the United States made agreements with Native American nations. These agreements, *treaties*, became the basis for international relationships. Confrontations and wars ended with the signing of treaties, and alliances were concluded with treaties. Treaties helped calm cultural tensions. Treaties also required a meeting of minds, a contractual agreement, and a sense of fair play. Nation states continue to use this kind of agreement and recognize the power of treaty agreements.[4]

However, the treaty in American law with reference to United States-Indian agreements has been significantly altered. Supreme Courts cases, such as *Lone Wolf* v. *Hitchcock* (1903),[5] have denigrated the nature of these agreements. The Indian Claims Commission attempted to once and for all rectify past treaty violations, but even though this body functioned for nearly thirty years, it failed miserably. Treaty agreements remain an important aspect of Indian sovereignty discussions.

Given past relationships, do American Indian nations today retain sovereignty, whatever its form, under American law? The answer is unequivocal—Yes. In *Menominee Tribe of Indians* v. *United States* (1968),[6] the U.S. Supreme Court was asked to interpret the legal meaning of termination, arguably the greatest threat to Indian sovereignty. The Menominees of Wisconsin were terminated by federal statute, and they wished to retain past treaty hunting and fishing rights. The Court held that termination meant merely the loss of federal support services. It did not mean the legal abolition of the tribe. That was not possible as long as the Menominees continued to exist. Tribes, even those terminated, retained sovereignty.

Most Indian tribes today in the United States consider themselves nations with limited forms of sovereignty. The legal struggle for Native American nations is to eventually be in a position to control one's own economic, social, and political destiny. Indian tribes in the past were fully capable of making treaties, deciding what was in their own national interests, and operating legal systems within their nations. Many today continue to exercise these sovereign rights. Independent political autonomy, a goal of some Indian leaders, requires military strength and self-government, aspects of sovereignty that are beyond any current Indian nation's grasp. However, there are clearly degrees of sovereignty, home rule elements political scientists would say, that are achievable.

The following essays help define Native American sovereignty in today's world. They draw upon past legal experiences and project into the future. The collection begins with a brief definition of sovereignty as formulated by Kirke Kickingbird, Lynn Kickingbird, Charles J. Chibitty, and Curtis Berkey of the Institute for the Development of American Indian Law. This is followed by a consideration of the most important documents that show the relationships between Native American nations and the U.S. government. Finnish scholar Markku Henriksson has studied how treaties were handled by Congress, and Ward Churchill follows this selection with a consideration of current and future implications of the treaty relationships. David E. Wilkins then looks at the issue of federal plenary power in terms of treaties and the evolution of American case law.

The next group of essays interprets how the recent federal policy of Indian self-determination impacts the pursuit of Native American sovereignty. Vine Deloria Jr. first explores how self-determination meshes with sovereignty generally. Then Emma Gross traces the evolution of both concepts, and Russel Barsh attempts to formulate how self-determination will eventually foster the strengthening of Indian sovereignty. Ann McCullogh singles out tribal taxation powers as a very important aspect of the exercise of Indian sovereignty today. Annette Jaimes explains how federal interference in a tribe's ability to choose its own members is a basic infringement upon Indian sovereignty, and must be resisted.

The next three essays attempt to place historically the struggle for the exercise of any and all aspects of Native American sovereignty. Sidney L. Harring shows how the Creeks of Oklahoma in the early twentieth century attempted to retain control over their lands and avoid allotments in the face of significant legal and extra-legal obstacles. George Lubick then documents the important career of Peterson Zah, former Navajo Legal Services director and tribal chairman of the Navajos. Zah represents modern Indian leadership, legally educated and committed to the retention and expansion of tribal sovereignty. Much of the current struggle for Native American sovereignty has been handled by the legal warriors, those Indians together with sympathetic non-Indians who have brought the issues to the courts and legislatures throughout the United States. Linda Medcalf explains this development.

The last articles project the pursuit of sovereignty into the future. Rebecca L. Robbins considers how self-determination policies can impact future efforts at Indian governance. Glenn T. Morris explains how international law and international politics are fruitful avenues for taking the struggle for Native American sovereignty. And Vine Deloria Jr. and Clifford Lytle summarize how far the pursuit of sovereignty has come and what the future holds.

NOTES

1. See Martha Warren Beckwith, "Mythology of the Oglala Sioux," *Journal of American Folklore* 43 (1930): 399–442.
2. Roxanne Dunbar Ortiz, "Sources of Underdevelopment," in *Economic Development in American Indian Reservations*, ed. Roxanne Dunbar Ortiz (Albuquerque: University of New Mexico Native American Studies, 1979), 61. See also John R. Wunder, *"Retained by The People": A History of American Indians and the Bill of Rights* (New York: Oxford University Press, 1994), 8.
3. Vine Deloria Jr. "Self-Determination and the Concept of Sovereignty," in *Economic Development in American Indian Reservations*, ed. Roxanne Dunbar Ortiz. See also John R. Wunder, *"Retained by The People": A History of American Indians and the Bill of Rights* (New York: Oxford University Press, 1994), 8.
4. John R. Wunder, *"Retained by The People": A History of American Indians and the Bill of Rights* (New York: Oxford University Press, 1994), 17–18.
5. *Lone Wolf* v. *Hitchcock*, 187 US 553 (1903).
6. *Menominee Tribe of Indians* v. *United States*, 391 US 404 (1968).

FURTHER READING

American Indian Law Review, University of Oklahoma College of Law, Norman, Okla.

Russel Lawrence Barsh and James Youngblood Henderson, *The Road: Indian Tribes and Political Liberty* (Berkeley: University of California Press, 1980).

Vine Deloria Jr. and Clifford Lytle, *The Nations Within: The Past and Future of American Indian Sovereignty* (New York: Pantheon Books, 1984).

Indian Country Today (formerly *Lakota Times*), Rapid City, S.D.

Peter Iverson, ed., *The Plains Indians of the Twentieth Century* (Norman: University of Oklahoma Press, 1985).

L.G. Moses and Raymond Wilson, eds., *Indian Lives: Essays on Nineteenth- and Twentieth-Century Native American Leaders* (Albuquerque: University of New Mexico Press, 1985).

The NARF Legal Review (formerly *Announcements*, newsletter of the Native American Rights Fund), Boulder, Colo.

Roger Nichols, ed., *The American Indian: Past and Present*, 4th edition (New York: McGraw-Hill, 1992).

James S. Olson and Raymond Wilson, *Native Americans in the Twentieth Century* (Urbana: University of Illinois Press, 1984).

Rebecca L. Robbins, "The Forgotten American: A Foundation for Contemporary American Indian Self-Determination," *Wicazo Sa Review* 6 (Spring, 1990): 27–33.

Indian Sovereignty

Kirke Kickingbird Lynn Kickingbird
Charles J. Chibitty Curtis Berkey

We are of the same opinion with the people of the United States; you consider yourselves as independent people; we, as the original inhabitants of this country, and sovereigns of the soil, look upon ourselves as equally independent, and free as any other nation or nations.

–Joseph Brant, Mohawk

WHAT IS SOVEREIGNTY?

A. General Definition

"Sovereignty" is a difficult word to define. Sovereignty is a difficult word to define because it is intangible, it cannot be seen or touched. It is very much like an awesome power, a strong feeling, or the attitude of a people. What can be seen, however, is the *exercise* of sovereign powers.

Sovereignty is also difficult to define because the word has changed in meaning over the years. For our purposes, a good working definition of sovereignty is: THE SUPREME POWER FROM WHICH ALL SPECIFIC POLITICAL POWERS ARE DERIVED. Sovereignty is inherent; it comes from within a people or culture. It *cannot be given* to one group by another. Some people feel that sovereignty, or the supreme power, comes from spiritual sources. Other people feel that it comes from the people themselves.

Mike Myers, a Seneca consultant to the Institute for the Development of Indian Law, was recently asked to give his definition of sovereignty. He responded as follows:

> Ideally, sovereignty is the unrestricted right of groups of people to organize themselves in political, social and cultural patterns that meet their needs. It is the right of a people to freely define ways in which to use land, resources and manpower for their common good. Above all, sovereignty is the right of people to exist without external exploitation or interference.

Still other people believe that sovereignty is derived from the "law of nature." Some feel that it comes from the unique capabilities of a single ruler by whom the people consent to be governed. Whatever the case, sovereignty cannot be separated from people or their culture.

B. European Origins

The concept of sovereignty began in Europe around the time of the birth of Christ. Roman judges, drawing upon Greek philosophy, described *majestas* or sovereignty as the "proper authority by which people make laws."[1] Under the reign of Louis XIV, King of France (1643-1715), the concept of proper or supreme authority became associated with the word "sovereignty" which literally means rule or power above all else. During this period, sovereignty almost always meant the absolute power of a ruler—the king, queen, czar or emperor. Since sovereignty was said to come from God, kings ruled by "divine right." They were responsible only to God for their actions. The theory of *divine right of kings* was generally accepted because of the continual warfare and turmoil Europeans found themselves in during the 17th century. With a strong individual leader, stability was more easily maintained.

Toward the end of the 17th century, the large European empires were beginning to break up and the concept of nation-states evolved. Nations were made up of people of similar cultures, who shared similar attitudes toward life and who organized under a system of law and government. Many theories developed about where sovereignty came from. One was the divine right theory just discussed. Under this system a king who got his power from God was the absolute ruler and had a monopoly over the administration of justice.[2]

A second theory developed by the Englishman, John Locke (1632-1704), was that sovereignty evolves when the people of a nation consciously make a contract with a ruler or king to govern them. According to Locke, the people of a nation grant to a central government or ruler the power to govern them. At the same time, they reserve certain individual rights which no centralized government can take away.[3] One can see that the political theories of John Locke heavily influenced the founding fathers of the United States government.

A third theorist who greatly influenced European thought was the Frenchman, Jean Jacques Rousseau. Rousseau developed the "Social Contract" theory of sovereignty. This states that sovereignty is derived from an agreement among the people of a nation to combine their individuality into a General Will. Sovereignty, in other words, is the General Will or common interest which binds people together. It is sacred and absolute. According to Rousseau, the General Will consists of a sense of membership, a feeling of community and responsibility, and the actual participation of people in public affairs.

Although the modern concepts of sovereignty were formally developed and written about by European philosophers and political scientists, the ideas associated with sovereignty are part of many cultures. Throughout the world, people who live together, who come from similar cultural backgrounds, and who share common attitudes toward life feel they have the right to be sovereign. Thus, the word is used today to mean the special quality that nations have which enables them to govern themselves.

C. Sovereignty and Independence

Does sovereignty mean complete independence? Again in the *ideal* sense, sovereignty means the absolute or supreme power of a people to govern themselves, completely independent from interference by or involvement with other sovereign nations. Yet no nation in the world today is completely independent. Our industrialized world of mass communications, global transportation, and soaring populations makes national isolation virtually impossible. Economic and political considerations, such as the need for raw materials or military assistance, make nations dependent upon each other. In reality, the economic dependence of one nation on another often leads to political limitations as well. Consequently, even such large and powerful countries as the United States and the Soviet Union are limited in their capacity to act by the small oil-rich nations of the world. This dependence has been continually demonstrated during the energy crisis of recent years.

Examples of nations which have semidependent relationships with others are too numerous to list. According to international economic theory, it is neither possible nor desirable for a nation to be economically self-sufficient.[4] Consequently, nations rely on one another to provide many human and industrial needs such as grain, meat, minerals and oil. There are many nations of the world whose technology is such that they cannot yet compete effectively in the world trade market. Thus, they must rely on aid from other nations. India, for example, requires over one billion dollars in foreign aid annually. Nevertheless, while India may be less "powerful" than those nations which lend her support, she is a sovereign nation.

D. The International Recognition of Sovereignty

We have talked about nations being sovereign; we have talked about interdependence among nations; we have talked about economic and political power. One might then ask, "Isn't a nation's sovereignty dependent upon whether or not other nations of the world recognize it as sovereign?"

In theory, the answer to this question is "no." It has been a common practice for nations to refuse to "recognize" the existence of another nation because of the type of government the nation has or because of certain political actions taken by a nation. That nation's sovereignty, however, is no less real because other nations refuse to recognize its existence. The key is whether the people within the nation support its existence. The People's Republic of China is a good example of this. For almost thirty years the United States has refused to officially recognize the existence of the People's Republic of China. Yet it still exists; it is no less a reality.

But the recognition of a nation's sovereignty by other nations can strengthen the claim to sovereignty and alter in a positive way that nation's relations with the rest of the world. Certainly, if no other countries in the world will recognize a particular nation, it may have difficulty in providing for its people. But if it is accorded recognition as a sovereign, its stature among nations increases, it can trade its products in the world market, and it is subject to less interference in its internal affairs.

The problem with international recognition of sovereignty is that there is no generally accepted formula for determining which nations are in fact sovereign and no formula for when recognition should be given or withheld. People and governments often neglect to examine the basis for their conclusions about which nations are sovereign and which are not. If a nation in fact operates as a sovereign with the consent of its people that nation is a sovereign nation, whether it is recognized as such or not.

E. How is Sovereignty Related to Nations, Government, Politics?

Some people fall into the trap of equating sovereignty to nationhood, government or politics. While sovereignty, nationhood, government, and politics are related, it is important to remember that sovereignty is absolute and comes before nations, governments, and politics. In theory, sovereignty is the supreme power which binds a nation together. It cannot change. The manifestations of sovereignty (nations, governments, politics) can change and take on different forms from time to time.

Before we end our discussion about the meaning of sovereignty, let's briefly define these other terms which are frequently confused with sovereignty.

What is a Nation? The American Heritage Dictionary defines a nation as "a people, usually the inhabitants of a specific territory, who share common customs, origins, history and frequently language or related languages."[5] Webster's says that a nation is "a community of people composed of one or more nationalities and possessing a more or less defined territory and government."[6] Webster's also says that a nation is "a tribe or federation of tribes (as of American Indians)."[7]

What is Government? Government is the system or machinery through which a political unit or nation exercises its sovereignty.

What is Politics? Politics is the art of interpreting the will of the people and influencing the actions and functions of government.

What is Sovereignty, Again? Sovereignty is the supreme power from which all specific political powers are derived. Sovereignty is the inherent power that causes people to band together to form a nation and govern themselves.

F. What are the Powers Exercised by Sovereign Nations?

Sovereignty has the most meaning in a practical sense when we look at the sovereign powers exercised by a government. So the most basic power of a sovereign people is the power to select their own form of government.

What kind of government it is or how it functions does not affect the sovereignty of the nation. Throughout the world, democracies, monarchies, theocracies, and dictatorships all exercise sovereign powers to one extent or another.

The exact methods of governing also vary widely. Some governments operate under written constitutions, others under customary or spiritual laws handed down from generation to generation. Some have highly structured institutions, others have relatively simple, informal organizations. Many nations operate under a system which allows for orderly change in leaders and powers. A change in the form or procedures of government or in one of its institutions, however, does not affect the sovereignty of a nation.

In addition to the power to select a form of government, sovereign nations have many other powers necessary for self-government. Among these powers may be the following:

1. The power to make and enforce laws.
2. The power to define and regulate the use of its territory.
3. The power to determine membership or citizenship.
4. The power to regulate trade within its borders, among its members and between its members and those of other nations.
5. The power to impose and collect taxes.
6. The power to appropriate monies.
7. The power to regulate domestic relations (including marriage, divorce, adoption).
8. The power to regulate property.
9. The power to establish a monetary system.
10. The power to make war and peace.
11. The power to form alliances with foreign nations through treaties, contracts and agreements.

There is no magic formula about how many and which of these powers a nation must exercise in order to be sovereign. How and if a nation uses any or all of these powers is dependent on many things, including: (1) the will and needs of the people; (2) the history and religion of the people; (3) internal and external economics; (4) internal and external politics. A nation may be able to operate well, for example, without exercising the power to make war or print money. It may choose to have another nation exercise certain of the powers for it. Certainly, the greater number of powers a nation gives up or loses to another, the more interference it may expect in its internal affairs. But this does not necessarily mean that it has given up its sovereignty. Indeed, it would be a sovereign act for a nation to decide to give up some of its sovereign powers or to temporarily not exercise them. According to principles of international law, a nation may do this without losing its place in the family of nations.

A good example of a European nation giving up certain powers is San Marino. San Marino, one of the world's smallest nations, is located completely within the boundaries of Italy. In 1862, the tiny nation entered into a "treaty of peace and friendship" with Italy. By this treaty, Italy agreed to provide protection for San Marino, which has a land area of 23.5 square miles and a population of 20,000. In addition, San Marino receives financial assistance from Italy and uses the Italian lira as its monetary unit. In return, San Marino agreed to let Italy handle much of its international affairs. So San Marino gave up some of its powers in return for services and benefits which it felt were desirable for its people. San Marino is still a sovereign nation which enjoys a substantial amount of independence. In fact, it is a member of the International Court of Justice.

G. Are Indian Nations Sovereign?

Anthropologists estimate that at the time European explorers first arrived on the North American continent there were about one million Indians living in the area now comprising the United States.[8] They were organized into over 600 different tribes, bands, and groups and had thriving social, political, and cultural institutions.[9] Although they shared certain cultural characteristics and attitudes toward life, each group was distinct from the others.

Some, for example, had loosely structured governments in which local or band leaders exercised most of the political power. Others had hereditary systems of government in which governing power was passed from one generation to another. Some had individual leaders whose power flowed from religious sources.

Most Indian governments were democratic in the sense that power was spread among several individuals or institutions.

The Iroquois Confederacy was an example of a strong Indian governmental system. Formed as an alliance to keep peace among the Mohawks, Senecas, Oneidas, Cayugas, and Onondagas, the Confederacy eventually controlled half of the area east of the Mississippi River. The Confederacy's governing council was composed of representatives of member nations. It was given certain sovereign powers by the member nations. This arrangement permitted member nations to exercise all sovereign powers not delegated to the Confederacy, including the power of local self-government.[10]

All of the colonial powers and later the United States . . . recognized the sovereignty of Indian nations by entering into over 800 treaties with Indians.

This confederacy concept, where political power flowed *up* from a sovereign people through units of local government to a central government, was an extraordinary political achievement. The confederacy brought peace and stability to its members for over 200 years. And this was during a time when much of the rest of the world was in political and economic turmoil.

The democratic ideas which the Iroquois and other Indian nations had were new to western political theory.[11] But Thomas Jefferson and other writers of the U.S. Constitution recognized their value. In fact, some of the democratic ideas contained in the Constitution were borrowed from Indians.[12]

Additional evidence of the national character of Indian nations is found in the attitudes of Indian people. In 1838, the Cherokee people were facing eviction from their traditional lands by the United States government. In an attempt to prevent forced removal, the Cherokees passed a resolution defending their right to control their own affairs:

> The title of the Cherokee people to their lands is the most ancient pure, and absolute known to man; its date is beyond the reach of human record; its validity confirmed by possession and enjoyment antecedent to all pretense of claim by any portion of the human race. The free consent of the Cherokee people is indispensable to a valid transfer of the Cherokee title. The Cherokee people have existed as a distinct national community for a period extending into antiquity beyond the date and records and memory of man. These attributes have never been relinquished by the Cherokee people, and cannot be dissolved by the expulsion of the Nation from its territory by the power of the United States government.[13]

But regardless of the particular form of organization, all the Indian nations exercised the powers of sovereign nations. They recognized the sovereignty of one another by forming compacts, treaties, trade agreements and military alliances.

All of the colonial powers, and later the United States, also recognized the sovereignty of Indian nations by entering into over 800 treaties with Indians. Under international law, treaties are a means for sovereign nations to relate to each other, and the fact that Europeans and the United States made treaties with Indian nations demonstrates that they recognized the sovereignty of Indian nations.

In *Worcester v. Georgia,* the United States Supreme Court said that ". . . the very fact of repeated treaties with them recognizes [the Indians' right to self-government] and the settled doctrine of the law of nations is that a weaker power does not surrender its independence–its right to self-government–by associating with a stronger, and taking its protection."[14] The power of Indian nations to wage war was pointed out by the Supreme Court on several occasions as evidence of their sovereign character.[15] And when critics complained that Indian tribes were not "nations" in the European sense, the Court responded that:

> The words "treaty" and "nation" are words of our language, selected in our diplomatic and legislative proceedings, by ourselves, having each a definite and well understood meaning. We have applied them to Indians as we have applied them to other nations of the earth. They are applied to all in the same sense.[16]

While the exercise of sovereign powers by Indian governments has been restricted to some extent (see following section), there can be no doubt that the United States and other nations have recognized the inherent sovereignty of Indian nations and their right to self-government.[17]

H. What are the Sovereign Powers Exercised by Indian Nations?

Throughout the political history of Indian nations, the colonial powers, the United States and state governments, the struggle over which government may exercise sovereign powers in a particular situation has been crucial. Which government prevailed was sometimes determined

". . .Our nation was respected by all who came in contact with it, for we had the ability as well as the courage to defend and maintain our rights of territory, person and property against the world. . . ."

Black Hawk, Sac and Fox

by military power, and sometimes by political bargains in the form of treaties and agreements. The result of these struggles was that powers were dispersed among the various units of government.

The distribution of governmental powers between the federal government on the one hand and the original 13 states on the other hand was made in the U.S. Constitution. The states delegated certain powers to the federal government and retained others. Included in this delegation was the power to make treaties with Indian nations.

The distribution of governmental powers between the United States government and each Indian nation was somewhat similar. It may be viewed as a process of dividing up a bundle of sticks. Each stick represented a sovereign power. So there was a power to declare war, a power to impose taxes, a power to regulate property, and so forth. Originally the tribe held the entire bundle of sticks and so had complete power over the geographical area it controlled and the people living within that area. It was an absolute sovereign.

Over the decades and for various reasons, each tribe granted certain of those powers to the United States government in exchange for certain benefits and rights. This was done by treaty or agreement. In other cases some powers were taken from the tribe by war or coercion.

The point to remember is that all of the powers were once held *by the tribes,* not the U.S. government. Whatever powers the federal government may exercise over Indian nations it received from the tribe, not the other way around. This is important because if the United States gave sovereign powers *to* the Indian nations, then it could also take them away whenever and however it wanted to. Some people say this is the case.

The law is clear, however, that an Indian nation possesses all the inherent powers of any sovereign government except as those powers may have been qualified or limited by treaties, agreements, or specific acts of Congress.[18] Therefore, while tribes have lost some of the "sticks in the bundle" they retain all the rest. So they can and do exercise many sovereign powers.

Included among these inherent powers of Indian governments are the following:

1. The power to determine the form of government.
2. The power to define conditions for membership in the nation.
3. The power to administer justice and enforce laws.
4. The power to tax.
5. The power to regulate domestic relations of its members.
6. The power to regulate property use.

1. The Power to Determine Form of Government

As previously stated, the most important attribute of a sovereign people is the power to choose the form of government under which they wish to live. Since sovereignty means the power or authority to govern, and tribes are sovereign, they must be allowed to choose the manner and form by which they will govern.

Since 1832 the Supreme Court has been fairly consistent in acknowledging that Indian nations have the power to develop forms of self-government in accordance with their political and cultural history.[19] Many Indian nations have chosen to adopt governmental models similar to that of the United States. Others, such as the Six Nations Confederacy and the Pueblo tribes, for example, have chosen to retain their traditional forms of government. In *Pueblo of Santa Rosa v. Fall,*[20] the Supreme Court confirmed that tribes are not required to function under a "normal" constitutional government if they elect not to.

Other Supreme Court cases have said that since the states have no duties or responsibilities to Indian nations, they cannot levy taxes on Indian traders operating on Indian lands and thus interfere with the right of Indian self-government.[21]

Associated with this power to determine the form of government are the following rights:

a. The right to pass laws, interpret laws, and administer justice.
b. The right to define powers and duties of governmental officers.
c. The right to determine whether acts done in the name of the government are authoritative.
d. The right to define the manner in which governmental officers are to be selected and removed.

There are, however, certain federal constraints on *how* tribal governments function. Unlike all other governmental units in America and because of their unique status as sovereigns, Indian nations are not bound by the Bill of Rights in the U.S. Constitution. In 1968, however, Congress passed the Indian Bill of Rights,[22] which places on tribal governments and tribal courts restrictions similar but not exactly like those placed on the U.S. and state governments by the Constitution. Enactment of this law was met with resistance in the Indian community but it remains in force today. For a further discussion of this act and its provisions see Chapter II of this book.

2. The Power to Define Conditions for Membership in the Nation

An Indian government has, in most cases, complete authority to determine its membership. Standards for tribal membership may be established by custom, historical practice, written law, treaties with the United States, or agreements between Indian nations. Tribal governments have exercised this power by establishing procedures for:

a. Abandonment of membership.
b. Adoption of non-Indians.
c. Adoption of persons holding citizenship in another Indian nation.[23]

But the Secretary of Interior has, in certain circumstances, assumed authority to determine tribal membership. For example, by the Act of June 30, 1919,[24] Congress gave the Secretary power to draw up a final membership role for purposes of distributing tribal funds.

Unfortunately, the language of the Act is very broad: ". . . wherever *in his* (the Secretary's) *discretion* such actions would be *for the best Interests of the Indians*. . . " (emphasis added). Despite such broad authority, many court cases have held that an Indian nation has complete authority to determine all questions of membership unless there is express Congressional legislation to the contrary.[25] In an 1888 Opinion of the Attorney General it was emphasized that Indian people should determine membership for themselves, since they would ultimately participate in the benefits of that relationship.[26]

A 1927 case decided by the Court of Appeals of New York declared that the power of an Indian government to decide questions of membership comes from its status as a sovereign nation:

> . . .[T]he right to enrollment. . . depends upon the laws and usages of the Seneca Nation and is to be determined by that Nation for itself without interference or dictation from the supreme court of the state.
>
> The conclusion is inescapable that the Seneca tribe remains a separate nation; that its powers of self-government are retained with the sanction of the state, that the ancient customs and usages of the nation, except in a few particulars remain, unabolished, the law of the Indian land; that in its capacity of a sovereign nation, the Seneca Nation is not subservient to the orders and directions of the courts of New York State; that above all, the Seneca Nation retains for itself the power of determining who are Senecas, and in that respect it is above interference and dictation.[27]

In 1924 Congress passed an act which gave U.S. citizenship to all Indians living within the territorial limits of the United States.[28] While there can be no doubt that, according to U.S. law, all Indians are U.S. citizens, many Indians refuse to accept this grant of citizenship. They will not accept it because of the fear they would be forced to give up their citizenship in an Indian nation. The fear is not well-founded, however, since the concept of dual citizenship is well-established in both domestic and international law. Thus Indians can be U.S. citizens as well as citizens of an Indian nation. The courts have held that the 1924 Citizenship Act did not destroy the existence or sovereignty of Indian nations or their jurisdiction over tribal members.[29]

3. The Power to Administer Justice and Enforce Laws.

As sovereign governments, Indian nations generally have the power to: (1) make laws governing the conduct of persons, both Indians and non-Indians, within reservations;[30] (2) establish bodies such as tribal police forces and courts to enforce those laws and administer justice;[31] (3) exclude non-tribal members from the reservation;[32] and (4) regulate hunting, fishing, and gathering.[33]

The power of tribes to make their own laws has been recognized in a number of areas including domestic relations, taxation, and property use.[34] The power of Indian tribes to make and enforce laws also extends generally to the exercise of criminal jurisdiction over persons who commit crimes on the reservation.[35]

The power of a tribe to establish tribal courts is also firmly established in the law. In *Iron Crow v. Oglala Sioux Tribe,*[36] a federal court of appeals upheld the jurisdiction of a tribal court to punish members of the tribe for violating a tribal law and to enforce a tribal tax on non-Indians who leased land on the reservation. The court stated that the power of the tribe to establish courts to enforce its laws was not dependent upon any federal law, but was inherent in the tribe's sovereignty.

Another aspect of an Indian tribe's power to administer justice is its power over the extradition of persons accused of crimes. (Extradition is the surrender of a person accused of a crime to another government for trial.) A federal appeals court has upheld the power of a tribal government to determine whether or not it will extradite an Indian within its jurisdiction for trial in another state.[37] In that case, the court said that extradition was governed by tribal law, not the law of the state.

Although the power of Indian tribes to make and enforce their laws has been recognized as an aspect of Indian sovereignty, federal courts have said that this power is subject to limitation by treaty or express acts of Congress.[38] For example, three federal laws–the Major Crimes Act,[39] Public Law 280,[40] and the Indian Civil Rights Act[41]–limit the power of Indian tribes to make and enforce laws free from interference. The Major Crimes Act allows certain major crimes, including murder, rape, and robbery, to be tried in federal court even though the crimes occur on the reservation. Under Public Law 280, Congress has authorized certain states to assume civil and criminal jurisdiction over Indian reservations within those states. And under the Indian Civil Rights Act, tribal governments and courts must guarantee certain individual rights, such as right to trial by jury in criminal cases.

But to the extent that Congress has not expressly limited the exercise of power, Indian governments remain free to exercise their sovereign power to administer justice and enforce their own laws.

4. The Power to Tax

Generally, a tribe has the power to collect taxes from its members and from non-Indians residing on or doing business on the reservation, unless a treaty or act of Congress places restrictions on the exercise of that power. Like other sovereign powers, the power to tax is not a privilege or right given to Indian nations by the federal government. It is an inherent sovereign power.[42]

The power to tax has long been recognized by the federal government to include the power to tax both members of the nation and non-Indians within the reservation. A 1934 opinion of the Solicitor of the Interior Department states:

> Chief among the powers of sovereignty recognized as pertaining to an Indian tribe is the power of taxation. Except where Congress has provided otherwise, this

power may be exercised over members of the tribe and over non-members, so far as such non-members may accept privileges of trade, residence, etc., to which taxes may be attached as conditions.[43]

The federal courts have also upheld the taxation powers of Indian governments. Early court cases said that since Indian nations could exclude non-Indians from their territory, they could also set the terms, such as payment of a tax, under which non-Indians would be permitted to enter and conduct business within Indian territory.[44] Later cases have simply held that the power to tax is "an inherent attribute of tribal sovereignty which continues unless withdrawn or limited by treaty or by act of Congress. . . ."[45]

While few Indian governments exercise their power to tax, they still have that power.[46] Powers of sovereign governments are not given up by nonuse.[47] The power to tax may become much more important to Indian governments in the future as a means of providing services to its members, regulating non-Indian activities on the reservation, and preventing the imposition of state taxes within the reservation.[48]

5. The Power to Regulate Domestic Relations of Its Members

Power to govern the domestic relations of its members is another aspect of an Indian nation's inherent sovereignty.[49] Included in this power is the authority to make rules governing marriage, divorce, illegitimacy, adoption, guardianship, and support of family members.

Marriages in accordance with Indian laws or customs are just as valid as marriages in accordance with state laws and have been recognized as valid by federal statutes.[50] Even when Indian law and custom have permitted polygamy, the power of the tribe to approve such marriages has been upheld against state interference:

> We must either hold that there can be no valid Indian marriage, or we must hold that all marriages are valid which by Indian usage are [regarded as valid]. [The Indians] did not occupy their territory by our grace and permission, but by a right beyond our control. They were placed by the constitution of the United States beyond our jurisdiction, and we had no more right to control their domestic usages than those of Turkey or India.[51]

The power of an Indian nation to grant divorces, adoption, and guardianship according to tribal law has also been recognized by the courts.[52]

6. The Power to Regulate Property Use

Indian nations, as both sovereign governments and as landowners, generally have the power to regulate the use of property by their members and by non-Indians within their jurisdiction.[53] The courts have held that this is true except where that power has been limited by Congress or by constitutional provisions.[54] An Indian government may exercise its power to regulate property use in a variety of ways, such as *licensing* provisions, *zoning* laws and rules for the *inheritance* of property.

The United States Supreme Court stated in *United States* v. *Mazurie* that ". . . Indian tribes are unique aggregations possessing attributes of sovereignty over both their members *and their territory*. . . ."[55] In that case the Court upheld a criminal conviction for operating a bar on an Indian reservation without complying with the tribe's liquor licensing ordinance.

The power of Indian governments to regulate property use within the reservation through tribal zoning laws free from state interference has also been recognized, even in those states in which Public Law 280 applies.[56] In striking down the application of a county zoning ordinance within the Santa Rosa reservation, a federal court of appeals stated that ". . . extension of local jurisdiction is inconsistent with tribal self-determination and autonomy."[57]

Indian nations, as sovereigns, also have the power to regulate the inheritance of property of their members.[58] Originally this power was absolute[59] but it has been restricted somewhat by federal laws relating to the inheritance of restricted Indian lands.[60] Federal law does not, however, limit the power of Indian nations to govern the inheritance of unrestricted lands or personal property.

Conclusion

The above explanation of sovereign powers of Indian nations is not intended to be a complete list of powers. Nor is it intended to suggest that *all* tribes exercise *all* of these powers. The powers a particular nation does or does not exercise depends upon its history, its relationship with the United States, the status of its tribal government and the wishes of its people.

Many Indian people believe that Indian nations could and should return to the treaty-making process in their relationship with the United States. There is some basis for this belief because even though the United States Congress passed an act in 1871 prohibiting treaty-making between the United States and Indian nations,[61] it continued to make "agreements" with them for decades after that.

"Treaties" were negotiated by the Executive and ratified by the Senate. "Agreements" were negotiated also by the Executive but they were ratified by *both* the Senate and the House of Representatives. Legally though there is little difference between them. U.S. courts have recognized that the 1871 act merely changed the procedure for approving negotiated settlements with Indian nations.[62] "Treaties" and "agreements" have the same legal effect. Furthermore, the 1871 act did not alter the legal force of the treaties made before that act.[63]

Many Indian people believe that Indian nations could and should return to the treaty-making process in their relationship with the United States.

The last "agreement" made between an Indian nation and the United States government was in 1911. There is no reason, however, why the process of making agreements between Indian nations and the United States could not resume today. In fact, under Public Law 93-638 it has already resumed in a way.[64]

Some Indian people also say that Indian nations should resume making treaties with other nations of the world. While the power to do so may exist, some tribes have agreed in treaties to restrict their right to exercise it. For example, several treaties have been interpreted by the courts to mean that by accepting the "protection" of the United States, certain Indian nations have relinquished their powers to deal with other nations of the world. For example, in the Treaty with the Kaskaskias:

> The United States will take the Kaskaskia tribe under their immediate care and patronage, and will afford them a protection as effectual against the other Indian tribes and against all other persons whatever as is enjoyed by their own citizens. And the said Kaskaskia tribe do hereby engage to refrain from making war or giving any insult or offense to any foreign nation, without hav-

ing first obtained the appropriation and consent of the United States.[65]

The Supreme Court has given a similar interpretation to the Treaty of Hopewell between the Cherokee Nation and the United States:

> The undersigned Chiefs and Warriors, for themselves and all parts of the Cherokee nation, do acknowledge themselves and the said Cherokee nation, to be under the protection of the said United States of America, and of no other sovereign whosoever; and they also stipulate that the said Cherokee nation will not hold any treaty with any foreign power, individual state, or with individuals of any state.[66]

In other treaties Indian governments agreed to restrictions upon trade and the sale of lands. In some cases the restrictions were explicit and in others they were vague. In the Treaty of the Osage of November 10, 1808, the Osage nation gave up the right to:

> . . .(C)ede, sell or in any manner transfer their lands to any foreign power, or to citizens of the United States or inhabitants of Louisiana, unless duly authorized by the President of the United States to make the said purchase or accept the said cession on behalf of the government."[67]

Many treaties implied that regulation of trade was relinquished by the Indian nation with a phrase such as follows:

> It is agreed on the part of the Cherokees, that the United States shall have the sole and exclusive right of regulating their trade.[68]

Sometimes, Indian nations were prohibited from trading outside the boundaries of the United States as in the Treaty with the Nisqualli, Puyallup, etc. of December 26, 1854:

> The said tribes and bands finally agree not to trade at Vancouver's Island, or elsewhere out of the dominions of the United States; nor shall foreign Indians be permitted to reside in their reservations without consent of the superintendent or agent. . . .[69]

It is possible that a return to the treaty relationship or at least some variation of it, along with an accompanying recognition of sovereignty, is the only way to prevent non-Indian governments from interfering in the affairs of Indian nations. For example, in November, 1972, the Trail of Broken Treaties Caravan presented a paper to the U.S. government in which a call for the restoration of the treaty relationship was made. Central to the demands made in the 20-point paper was the insistence that the U.S. reopen treaty negotiations with Indian nations. The leaders of the Caravan pointed out that there is no valid reason why Indian nations cannot make treaties or reach agreements with the U.S. government today. Treaty-making could start again if Congress repealed the 1871 act. And Congress has never specifically prohibited the making of "agreements" with Indian governments. Both the U.S. government and Indian governments apparently have the legal capacity to reach new agreements which would clarify or redefine their relationship. New treaties or renegotiated old treaties would form the basis for a legal relationship in which Indian sovereignty would be preserved.

For further discussion of treaties and other issues facing Indian nations today, see Chapter III of this book.

NOTES

". . .It has been our wish to live here in this country peaceably, and do such things as may be for the welfare and good of our people. . . ."

Spotted Tail, Brule Sioux

INDIAN SOVEREIGNTY AND THE UNITED STATES GOVERNMENT

Chapter I explored the concept of sovereignty by providing a definition and a historical background under which use of the term was developed. We began to apply the concepts to Indian governments with the understanding that sovereignty in a modern context has a universal application to the nations of the world. This provided the opportunity to explore the potential impact of international law on Indian sovereignty and Indian governments.

Chapter II makes the transition from the general and international view of sovereignty to the specific impact of the laws of the United States upon Indian nations. The United States has pursued an anomalous course with respect to the recognition of the sovereignty of Indian governments. This course has combined the concepts of international law, the contention that the conduct of Indian affairs falls within the realm of the domestic laws of the United States, and a history of U.S. conduct that fluctuates from the highly morally principled to the most squalidly self-serving.

The United States Constitution gives the federal government rather than the states the responsibility for the conduct of Indian affairs. This chapter concentrates on the institutions of the United States government and their responses to the exercise of sovereign powers by Indian nations.

The chapter briefly discusses the powers of the three branches of the United States government: the President and his executive offices; the Congress; and the federal courts. Congress sets Indian policy, the President carries it out, and the courts review the actions of the other branches. How these functions interrelate, and how Indian nations are affected by the sometimes competing interests of the three branches is the subject of much of this chapter.

A. Sovereignty and the United States Congress

The United States Congress has played a major role in the continuing relationship between Indian nations and the U.S. government. This is clear from the fact that American Indians have been the subject of more federal legislation than any other single group in the United States.[70] Since 1790, when the first Indian Trade and Intercourse Act was adopted, Congress has approved more than 4,000 treaties, agreements, and statutes relating to Indian affairs.[71] Some of these represented good faith attempts by Congress to deal with Indians honorably.[72] Some were only thinly disguised measures designed to take Indian lands and destroy their governments.[73] Many have limited, directly or indirectly, the power of Indian nations to exercise their sovereign rights.

American Indians have been the subject of more federal legislation than any other single group in the United States.

According to federal court decisions, many of the powers of Congress to legislate in Indian affairs are found in the following provisions of the U.S. Constitution:

1. The power to regulate commerce with Indian nations.[74]
2. The power to ratify treaties with other governments.[75]
3. The power to make war.[76]
4. The power to provide for the general welfare.[77]
5. The power to admit new states into the union, which also includes the power to specify the conditions upon which new states will be admitted.[78]
6. The power over federal territories.[79]

Early in the relationship between Indian nations and the United States, Congress used the above-mentioned constitutional powers as justification for passing legislation and approving treaties to regulate trade with Indian nations and to maintain peace between Indians and non-Indians. Soon, however, Congress began to pass legislation which was designed to interfere with the internal affairs of

Indian nations and to control virtually every aspect of Indian life. This coincided to some extent with similar efforts by the United States to exercise broad control over many of the governments throughout the American continents.[80]

When the right of Congress to interfere with Indian self-government has been challenged, the U.S. courts have usually supported that right on the basis of any one of three rationales: the *political question* doctrine; the *guardian-ward relationship*; or the *plenary power* of Congress. For example, in the Supreme Court case of *Lone Wolf v. Hitchcock*,[81] Indians challenged an act of Congress which was passed in violation of a prior treaty with the Indian nation. The court upheld the law by stating that the power of Congress over Indian affairs was "absolute" and would not be reviewed by the federal courts because of the "political nature" of the relationship between Indian nations and the U.S. ("Political questions" are those which are to be decided by the legislative or executive branches of government rather than the courts.)

The courts have used the "guardian-ward" relationship or the "federal trust responsibility" to justify Congressional power in Indian affairs. This responsibility supposedly allows Congress extraordinary power to take actions to "protect" Indian nations.[82]

Relying on interpretations of the constitutional provisions listed above, the courts have said that the power of Congress in Indian affairs is *plenary* (full or complete). Under present law, Congressional power in Indian matters *is* great, but it is not *absolute*.[84] Nor could it be, because to some extent the doctrines of plenary power of Congress and inherent sovereignty of Indian nations are mutually exclusive. We have seen that one of the most basic principles underlying the rights and powers of Indian nations is that they retain all those original sovereign powers which have not been given up or taken away.[85] And we have seen that there are many such powers which they have not given up.[86] Therefore, to the extent that sovereign powers still reside with Indian nations, Congressional power over Indian governments is not absolute. Furthermore, the courts have said that Congressional power in Indian affairs is limited by the U.S. Constitution.[87]

1. Congressional Limitations on Exercise of Powers

The means by which Congress has limited Indian governmental powers have changed as often as the policies and motives have changed.[88]

Early acts were designed to prevent conflicts between white settlers and Indians, and to protect Indians from the whites. As hostilities continued, Congress believed that the best way to restore the peace was to socialize Indians in the ways of the whites through cultural assimilation. In the early years of U.S. policy this meant breaking up the Indian land base and reducing the authority of Indian governments by increasing their dependence on the United States. In modern times, the same assimilation policy has meant that Indian governments have been allowed to manage their affairs with a minimum of external control so long as they conform to U.S. standards of governmental practice.

Also underlying early Congressional intrusions into the affairs of Indians was the attitude that there are certain powers and functions with which an Indian government could not be trusted because the people were uncivilized. Even today, Congress has often taken the attitude that Indians are incapable of governing themselves without outside supervision. Interior Solicitor Nathan Margold wrote in 1934 that Congress intervenes "where the need for other types of governmental controls are clearly manifest."[89] In short, Congress often overreacts on the issue of Indian sovereignty and self-government.

Perhaps there are occasions where external controls are welcome by Indian governments. Too often, however, Congressional action has been prompted by political pressure from special interest groups who oppose the exercise of Indian sovereignty. In the short space of 80 years (1790-1870), Congress increased its role in Indian affairs from initially regulating trade with Indians to almost totally controlling all areas of Indian government. This was done primarily in response to pressures from settlers who wanted Indian lands.

The following sections highlight various pieces of legislation which have been used to restrict Indian governments in the exercise of their sovereign powers.

a. Indian Trade and Intercourse Act

Congressional acts conflicted with the principle of Indian sovereignty as early as 1790 with the enactment of the first Indian Trade and Intercourse Act.[90] Passed as a protective measure against incursions of white traders in Indian country,[91] the act operated to bring federal control over non-Indians on Indian land. The drafters of the first Trade and Intercourse Act relied on the theory that Indian sovereignty meant ". . . tribes should be considered as foreign nations and that tribal lands protected by treaty, even though situated within the boundaries of a state, should be considered as outside the limits of jurisdiction of the states."[92]

The stated purpose of the early Trade and Intercourse Acts[93] was to protect against unscrupulous white traders, control liquor traffic in Indian country, and provide a way to remove renegade white desperados from Indian country.[94] This was also attempted by Section 25 of the final Trade and Intercourse Act of 1834,[95] which read:

> Section 25. And be it Further Enacted that so much of the laws of the United States as provide for the punishment of crimes committed within the sole and exclusive jurisdiction of the United States, shall be in force in the Indian country. Provided: That same shall not extend to crimes committed by an Indian against the person or property of another Indian.

What occurred, however, was an extension of federal criminal jurisdiction to offenses involving non-Indians in Indian territory. The act also regulated land transactions in Indian country.[96]

The Trade and Intercourse Acts operated to restrict the exercise of Indian sovereign powers through the influence of the U.S. government in Indian country. These first steps set the pattern and established a foundation for later, broader intrusions upon Indian self-government, even though Congress apparently realized it had no right to do so.[97]

By the time the final Indian Trade and Intercourse Act was passed in 1834,[98] the exercise of sovereign powers by Indian nations had already been eroded considerably by other legislation.

b. Indian Removal Act of 1830

It is not an accident that today a majority of Indians are located west of the Mississippi River.

For a major portion of Indian-U.S. history, Congress yielded to public pressures to open up aboriginal Indian lands to white settlement. In the 1830's this was demonstrated by Congressional support of an Indian removal policy. Under this policy Indian nations situated in the eastern half of the United States were forced to leave their traditional lands for new lands west of the Mississippi River.

Congress officially endorsed this policy with enactment of the Indian Removal Act of 1830.[99] Officially a voluntary "exchange of lands,"[100] the act resulted in the involuntary removal of Indians to the unsettled western half of the continental United States. Indians were powerless to fight this policy in the legislature, but many nations chose to react in a more direct way. Forced to leave by the states, who wanted the lands for white settlement and for the valuable mineral and other natural resources, Indian nations became partially fragmented during this tumultuous period.

Although a purpose of westward removal was the resolution of the problems of state resistance to Indian sovereignty[101] and the jurisdictional struggle between Indian nations and states, the act seriously undermined the authority of Indian governments. Families and tribes were separated, some choosing to leave, others deciding to stay and fight. In many cases, the land "exchanged" was different in climate and fertility from the original land. Many nations also lost considerable numbers of people in the forced migration.

It is obvious that the powers of Indian governments were severely diminished by this policy. Additionally, removal precipitated a great number of treaty agreements, which often resulted in increased U.S. suppression of Indian governments.

In summary, westward removal was one of the root causes of the problems from which Indian nations suffer today.

c. Amendments to Treaties

One of the most important Congressional powers in international affairs is the power to revoke or change treaties without the consent of the other party. This is true whether the treaty is between the U.S. and the Soviet Union or between the U.S. and an Indian nation.[102] However, international law recognizes only a few instances where a treaty can be unilaterally changed without the consent of the other party.[103]

Congress has consistently changed Indian treaties without the consent of Indians. This is a clear violation of international legal principles. Yet U.S. courts have held that Congress may change or abrogate Indian treaties by Congressional act, just as a later Congressional act may repeal an earlier one.[104]

Congress has consistently changed Indian treaties without the consent of Indians.

Although the U.S. has revoked or changed Indian treaties, under international law these treaties in their original form are still binding today. U.S. courts, however, do not question the power of Congress to pass laws that conflict with treaties. But while the courts acknowledge the power to override treaties as absolute, they have also said that Congress has a moral duty to uphold treaty obligations and to make amends for any violations.

d. Appropriation Acts

Appropriation acts (money bills) are the way in which Congress actually gets the needed money into a specific program for a specified purpose.

Historically, attaching riders to appropriation acts has been a convenient means for Congress to enact special interest legislation which otherwise might not survive the legislative process. This fact holds true in Indian affairs legislation.

Perhaps the most infamous attachment (rider) to an appropriation act is that which ended treaty-making between Indian nations and the United States.[105] Another rider to an appropriation act in 1885 gave federal courts jurisdiction over seven major crimes in Indian territory.

This was known as the Major Crimes Act.[106]

These riders are a most unfair way of enacting major legislation affecting many of the basic rights and sovereign powers of Indian nations without allowing Indians the opportunity to object.

e. The Major Crimes Act

The Major Crimes Act[107] was passed by Congress in 1885 as a "rider" to an Indian appropriations bill. Before that time, Indian nations retained exclusive power to make criminal laws and punish Indians who committed crimes against other Indians in Indian country. The Supreme Court had recognized this power of Indian governments in *Ex Parte Crow Dog.*[108]

The Congress, however, passed the Major Crimes Act in order to limit the power of Indian nations to punish Indians who violated tribal law. Despite this clear violation of Indian sovereign rights, the Supreme Court upheld the legality of the Act.[109] The Major Crimes Act gave the U.S. courts jurisdiction over seven crimes, including murder, rape, and robbery, when those crimes were committed by an Indian against another Indian within Indian country. The Act has been changed so that today it covers fourteen crimes.[110] The effect of the Act has been to punish crimes committed by Indians in accordance with American ideas of law and justice rather than in accordance with Indian law and custom. Although some courts have interpreted this act as taking away Indian jurisdiction over the listed crimes, it is possible that *both* an Indian nation and the U.S. government have jurisdiction.[111]

f. General Allotment Act

The General Allotment Act,[112] passed by Congress in 1887, was one of many federal laws and agreements which allotted (divided) Indian lands among tribal members.[113]

"... The earth and myself are of one mind. The measure of the land and the measure of our bodies are the same...."

Chief Joseph, Nez Perce

These acts were some of the most destructive pieces of Indian legislation ever passed.

The allotment acts were intended to dissolve the Indian nations and assimilate Indians into American society by breaking up the tribal land base.[114] In passing these acts, Congress was influenced by public demands to open more Indian lands for settlement.

Under these acts, tribally-held lands were usually divided into 80 or 160 acre allotments for each member of the tribe living at that time.[115] These allotted lands were to be held in trust for the Indian allottees by the U.S. government for a period of twenty-five years.[116] During the trust period, the Indian allottee could not sell, lease, mortgage or give the land without the approval of agency officials. At the end of the trust period or when the Secretary of Interior determined that an Indian allottee was "competent" to manage his own affairs, the restrictions on the land were to be removed and the land would be owned by the Indian absolutely. The trust period could be (and has been) extended by federal administrators and Congress.[117]

Indian lands left over after each member of the tribe received his allotment were declared "surplus" and opened for settlement by non-Indians. Sometimes, land within the reservation was reserved for the tribe as a whole. Further allotment of Indian lands was stopped by the Indian Reorganization Act of 1934.[118]

The allotment acts affected the sovereignty of Indian nations in several ways. First, the acts weakened Indian governments by destroying the tribal land base and substituting American values such as private ownership of land. Second, the acts permitted increased administrative interference in the internal affairs of Indian nations.[119] Third, the acts reduced the amount of lands owned by Indians and made them less independent. A 1934 memorandum by B.I.A. Commissioner John Collier reported that as a result of the allotment acts more than 80 percent of the total value of land belonging to Indians had been lost:

> Through sales by the Government of the fictitiously designated "surplus" lands, through sales by allottees after the trust period had ended or had been terminated by administrative act, and through sales by the Government of heirship land. . . the total of Indian land holdings has been cut from 138,000,000 acres in 1887 to 48,000,000 acres in 1934 [nearly 20,000,000 of which were desert or semi-desert lands].[120]

g. Legislation Affecting the Five Civilized Tribes

In the 1890's Congress began a policy of terminating the national character and governments of the Five Civilized Tribes in what was then called Indian Territory (now Oklahoma).[121]

Under the Curtis Act[122] tribal lands were allotted, tribal courts were abolished, and Indian laws were declared unenforceable in federal courts. In 1906, Congress passed legislation which made the chiefs of the Five Tribes removable by the President, and provided for the sale of buildings owned by the Indian governments.[123] This law almost completely destroyed the Indian governments of the Five Civilized Tribes. It abolished tribal taxes, distributed the resources of the Five Tribes among their members, and provided that any tribal law had to be approved by the federal government. Once the Indian governments had been crippled, Congress acted to include the Indian Territory within the new state of Oklahoma.

The effect of this legislation was to severely limit the capability of the Five Civilized Tribes to exercise their sovereign powers. And it is probably the most obvious example of a deliberate effort by Congress to destroy the government of an Indian nation. A recent federal court case has made it clear, however, that these acts did not completely eliminate the Indian governments of the Five Tribes or their powers.[124]

h. The Indian Reorganization Act

The Indian Reorganization Act (IRA)[125] was "perhaps the most fundamental and far-reaching piece of legislation passed by Congress in this century."[126] The Act recognized tribal governments, placed some restraints on the exercise of federal power over Indians, and established programs to assist the economic development of Indian tribes.[127]

The I.R.A. was a recognition of Indian sovereignty, not a grant of power to the Indian nations from the U.S. government. Commissioner Collier stated:

> The powers of self-government possessed by Indian tribes are not derived from the Indian Reorganization Act. This Act is largely a recognition of the in-

herent powers of self-government which the tribes have always possessed. . . .[128]

The I.R.A. was a recognition of Indian sovereignty, not a grant of power to the Indian nations from the U.S. government.

Section 16 of the Act provided that any powers granted Indian nations under the I.R.A. were "[i]n addition to the powers vested in any Indian tribe or tribal council by existing law...."[129] The Interior Department interpreted the powers referred to in that section as "...those [inherent] powers of local self-government which have never been terminated by law or waived by treaty. . . ."[130]

Under the I.R.A., Indian nations were given the option of adopting tribal constitutions. The constitutions, however, were required to be approved by the Secretary of Interior so that Indian nations would adopt "American" forms of government![131] But Indian governments have not lost their sovereignty by either adopting I.R.A. constitutions or rejecting the I.R.A.

The I.R.A. also aided Indian sovereignty by stopping the allotment process,[132] providing for the purchase of additional lands for Indian nations,[133] recognizing the power of Indian governments to prevent the disposition of tribal lands and resources without Indian consent,[134] and providing economic aid to Indian governments.[135]

i. Public Law 280

Perhaps the most widely known and widely denounced federal Indian legislation in recent memory is Public Law 83-280.[136] Passed in 1953, P.L. 280 ushered in the "termination" phase of federal Indian affairs. It gave Wisconsin, Oregon, California, Minnesota, and Nebraska criminal and civil jurisdiction in Indian country and provided a mechanism whereby the states could assume permanent jurisdiction over Indian nations.

The law applied to most of the Indian land within the boundaries of those five states. The power given to these states did not include the power to tax, regulate, or decide the ownership or use of Indian property.

The statute also authorized other states to assume civil and criminal jurisdiction over Indian territory by making appropriate changes in their state constitutions or laws. In 1968 the law was amended to require the consent of Indian nations before states could assume jurisdiction.[137]

The criterion for applying P.L. 280 was whether or not the United States felt that certain Indian nations were capable of handling their own affairs. The U.S. excluded those tribes which had law and order organizations that functioned in a reasonably satisfactory manner. Termination of the federal relationship with the Menominees, Klamaths, and other Indian nations followed in short order.

By giving jurisdiction to the states without the consent of affected Indian nations, the United States was blatantly ignoring Indian sovereignty and in many cases, ignoring treaties. Unfortunately, the legality of P.L. 280 has never fully been questioned by U.S. courts.[138]

Although the termination period was relatively short-lived (lasting approximately 10 years), its effects have been long lasting.[139] A terminationist policy such as that underlying P.L. 280 is clearly harmful to the exercise of the sovereign powers of Indian nations.

j. Indian Civil Rights Act

The Indian Civil Rights Act of 1968[140] placed certain restrictions on the actions of Indian governments. These restrictions are similar to those placed upon the U.S. government and the states by the U.S. Constitution. According to the Act, no Indian tribe may:

a. Pass laws prohibiting free exercise of religion, restricting freedom of speech or of the press, peaceable assembly, and petition for redress of grievances.
b. Violate the right of individuals to be secure in their persons, houses and papers against unreasonable search and seizure, nor issue warrants without probable cause.
c. Subject any person to trial for the same offense twice.
d. Compel any person in a criminal trial to be a witness against himself.
e. Take any private property for public use without just compensation.
f. Deny any person charged with a criminal offense the right to speedy and public trial; to be informed of the nature and cause of the accusation; to be confronted with the witnesses against him and to obtain witnesses in his favor; and, at his own expense to have assistance of counsel.
g. Require excessive bail, impose excessive fines, inflict cruel and unusual punishment and impose a punishment greater than six months in jail or a fine of $500.
h. Deny any person equal protection of laws or deprive any person of liberty or property without due process of law.
i. Pass any bill of attainder or ex post facto law.
j. Deny any person a trial by jury of not less than six persons.

The imposition of these requirements placed restrictions on Indian governments which had not existed before. Congress has thus restricted the freedom of an Indian nation to maintain a governmental system consistent with its own laws and customs.

The actions of Indian governments often do not conform to U.S. ideas of how a government should operate. For example, in some tribal courts, persons appearing at trials are not entitled to representation by an attorney. In other Indian communities the government supports an established religion. Under the Indian Civil Rights Act, federal courts may have authority to force these governments to change their practices.

In the past, courts have recognized that provisions in the U.S. Constitution do not apply to Indian governments.[141] The courts have stated that Indian governments were not subject to constitutional requirements because they existed before the establishment of both the U.S. and the Constitution. These cases recognized the legitimate interest of Indian nations' remaining culturally and politically separate. A U.S. court, in upholding the Indian Civil Rights Act, stated that:

> The object of the Indian Civil Rights Act was to protect the individual members from arbitrary tribal action, but it was not intended that historic sovereignty of a tribe be abolished.[142]

In 1973 a U.S. court said that it was the intention of Congress that terms such as "due process" should be interpreted in the same way when applied to Indian nations as when applied to the United States.[143] Interpreting the act in this manner conflicts with Indian sovereignty and could have a harmful influence on Indian culture. Since 1973, however, other courts have held that a distinction must be maintained between the requirements imposed on an Indian government through the Indian Civil Rights Act and the requirements imposed on federal and state governments through the Bill of Rights and the Constitution.[144]

Today, the terms "due process" and "equal protection" as used in the Indian Civil Rights Act are being interpreted by the courts with due regard for the historical, governmental, and cultural values of Indian nations.[145] These terms do not always receive the same meanings they have come to represent under the U.S. Constitution. Although the Indian Civil Rights Act is a clear infringement on the sovereignty of Indian nations, the U.S. courts have lessened its effect by applying Indian standards for its application.

Conclusion

We have seen in this chapter that actions of the Congress of the United States have limited the right of Indian governments to exercise their sovereignty. However, the current policy of the United States is to take an expansive view of Indian governmental powers.

From the time of the founding of the United States until the early years of the 19th century, the federal government quite clearly recognized the power of Indian governments. During these early years of the United States, the Senate and House of Representatives each had a committee on Indian affairs. In 1946, the Senate and House reorganized their committee system and, in the mistaken belief that Indian lands were nothing more than a type of public land of the United States, gave responsibility for Indian affairs to the Committee on Public Lands, which was retitled in 1948 the Committee on Interior and Insular Affairs.

The actions of Indian governments often do not conform to U.S. ideas of how a government should operate.

In January of 1977, the Senate took steps to reorganize its committee system and establish a Select Committee on Indian Affairs. To a small degree the Senate has recognized the traditional importance and unique aspects of the relationship of the United States to American Indian governments. This committee has been established on a trial basis for two years. After two years the Senate will decide whether to continue with an independent committee on Indian affairs, or to place Indian affairs under another committee, as had been the practice between 1946 and 1976.

B. Sovereignty and the Executive Branch

The Office of the President and its various departments and agencies make up the executive branch of the federal government. The executive branch is responsible for implementing and enforcing the laws enacted by Congress. This involves a process of interpreting the laws, setting administrative policy, and devising regulations to guide the day-to-day operations of government.

While this explanation of what the executive branch does is simple, the process itself is not. It involves thousands of policy makers, bureaucrats, and technical people. It also involves truckloads of paperwork. How well the process works generally is perhaps a question which will never be answered, but it is clear that in Indian affairs the administration of federal laws leaves great room for improvement. Both the past and the present are littered with examples in which the administration of laws is inconsistent with Congressional intent, grossly inefficient, and damaging to the exercise of inherent sovereign powers and the right of self-government of Indian nations.

1. The Beginning of the Indian Bureaucracy

The primary agency charged with the responsibility of implementing legislation related to Indians is the Bureau of Indian Affairs (B.I.A.). It is located within the Department of Interior. The B.I.A. is one of the oldest bureaucracies in the U.S. government. Before 1824, administration of federal-Indian relations was the direct responsibility of the Secretary of War, because a special Indian department had not been established.

In 1824, a separate Indian Office was established within the War Department. With the creation of the Department of Interior in 1849, the Office of Indian Affairs (later changed to Bureau of Indian Affairs) was transferred to the new department. This reflected a change in U.S. Indian policy from treating Indian governments as separate nations to treating them as part of the United States.

To maintain peace on the frontier and to confine Indians on reservations, the Office of Indian Affairs developed an agency system. The Indian agency assumed responsibility for controlling Indian tribes within a prescribed geographical area. In the early days of the agency system, Indian agents served as ambassadors who negotiated treaties. Eventually, Indian agents exercised almost total control over every aspect of the tribe's political, economic, and social existence.

The agent often served as employer, landlord, policeman, judge, doctor, teacher, and relief administrator. Many agents sought to dissolve the Indian way of life by breaking up families and the tribal land base or by decreasing the authority of Indian governments. As early as 1834, a House of Representatives committee noted the growing power of Indian agents:

> The tribes are placed at too great a distance from the Government to enable them to make their complaints against the arbitrary acts of our agents heard; and it is believed they have had much cause of complaint. Hitherto they have suffered in silence. The agents being subject to no immediate control, have acted under scarcely any other responsibility than that of accountability for monies received. Although much is expected from the personal character of the agents, yet it is not deemed safe to depend entirely upon it.[146]

Agents were sometimes motivated by personal power and greed. Historical research reveals that many of them had economic interests in railroads, trading posts, and businesses which exploited Indian lands. Some became landowners and wealthy ranchers as a result of their position and power.[147]

Many of the abuses of the past have since been corrected due to federal legislation, judicial decisions, and a distribution of responsibilities to federal agencies other than the Bureau of Indian Affairs.[148] The most important improvements, however, have come about as a result of the actions and positive demands of Indian governments and people.

Yet today federal administrators still exercise broad discretion in dealing with Indian governments. This discretion presents numerous opportunities for a misuse of power and infringement on the sovereign powers of Indian nations. Historically, federal administrators have confused their power to manage the affairs of the U.S. government relating to Indian nations with the power to manage the internal affairs of Indian nations. The Supreme Court in 1832 responded to this by saying that interference in the internal affairs of Indian nations by federal administrators is inconsistent with Indian sovereignty:

> The only inference to be drawn from [federal laws and treaties] is that the United States considered the Cherokees as a nation. * * * To construe the expression "managing all their affairs" [in a treaty as meaning] a surrender of self-government, would be, we think, a perversion of their necessary meaning, and a departure

from the construction which has been universally put on them.[149]

The only way to prevent this "rule by a government department"[150] is for Indians to continue asserting their sovereign rights.

The sources of power for federal administrators in Indian affairs are too numerous and complex to explain in detail here.[151] But the following examples of where Congress has delegated enormous powers in Indian matters to executive branch administrators will illustrate how Indian sovereignty has and does suffer at the hands of the "federal administrators."

2. The B.I.A. Today

Several laws give the President and Commissioner of Indian Affairs general authority to "manage Indian affairs." The act of July 9, 1832[152] authorized the Commissioner of Indian Affairs to manage "all Indian affairs and all matters arising out of Indian relations."[153] The act of June 30, 1834 authorized the President to draw up regulations designed to implement "the various provisions of any act relating to Indian affairs . . . ."[154] These two laws have been cited in court cases to justify broad supervision of the conduct of Indian people.[155]

Many acts of Congress require the Bureau of Indian Affairs to draw up detailed regulations to implement and enforce the laws. For example, the Snyder Act of 1921, which is only one-half page in length, gave general authority to the B.I.A. to "direct, supervise, and expend monies as Congress may from time to time appropriate, for the benefit, care, and assistance of the Indians throughout the United States . . . ."[156]

By contrast, the volume of administrative regulations implementing this act and others is staggering. The BIA Manual consists of 42 Titles and 57 Supplements. In "loose-leaf form it covers one entire book shelf."[157] It is a "confusing, often contradictory, and generally inefficient compilation of policy and procedure ranging from generally adequate to absolutely unfathomable."[158] This incredible morass of government regulations often makes it easier for federal administrators to illegally interfere in the internal affairs of Indian nations.

3. Control Over Land and Property

Despite the fact that Indian nations possess the inherent power to regulate property use within their territory,[159] a number of federal laws limit the exercise of this power by giving federal officials a great deal of control over Indian lands.

Many of these laws were passed when the federal government was trying to dissolve the tribes and assimilate Indian people into United States society. Under those laws, Indian lands were allotted to (divided among) individual members of the tribes and certain restrictions were placed on the disposition of those lands.

Much administrative power over Indian lands stems from these allotment laws, most importantly the General Allotment Act of 1887.[160] These laws resulted in great losses of Indian lands. While the Indian Reorganization Act of 1934[161] prevents the further allotment of Indian lands, administrative power delegated under the allotment acts remains.

For example, the Secretary of Interior generally has the power to approve or disapprove the lease, sale, or gift of restricted Indian lands. He also has the power under the allotment laws to make rules and regulations for determining who inherits the land and property of Indian allottees who die. The Secretary also was given administrative power to sell allotted Indian lands when he found the heirs to be incapable of managing their own affairs.[162] The Secretary has delegated all of these powers to Bureau of Indian Affairs officials.

Administrative control of the Department of Interior also extends to lands held by Indian tribes under a federal law which requirės secretarial approval for the leasing or other disposition of tribal lands.[163] Administrative regulation over the sale of timber and exploitation of natural resources is also permitted by federal law.[164]

Administrative control over Indian lands can also be seen in the B.I.A.'s power to grant rights of way on Indian lands for construction of railroads, telegraph and telephone lines,[165] public highways,[166] pipelines,[167] and other purposes.[168] But federal law requires that no right of way be granted without the payment of adequate compensation[169] and without (usually) the consent of the Indian owners.[170]

In some cases, administrative control over Indian lands and property is limited by federal laws or court decisions.[171] But the Secretary of Interior and the B.I.A. still exercise far more control than is permitted by the concept of Indian sovereignty.[172]

4. The Federal Trust Responsibility Doctrine

The trust responsibility of the United States toward Indians is an important concept in U.S.-Indian relations. Simply stated, the trust responsibility is the legal obligation of the U.S. government to protect Indian lands, resources, and the right of self-government. In carrying out this obligation, the federal government must meet the highest standards of loyalty to the interests of Indians. Sound judgment must be exercised in protecting those interests.[173]

When properly carried out, the trust responsibility can be, and sometimes is, an aid to Indian nations seeking to: establish firm control over their natural resources and economies; strengthen their governments; and deal effectively with neghboring governments.

When misinterpreted, the trust responsibility has been used by the U.S. government to take Indian lands and resources, suppress their governments, and insult the dignity of Indian nations. Unfortunately, there are many examples of this.[174] As the American Indian Policy Review Commission stated in its recent report: "[Often Indians] find the federal trust responsibility being used as a tool (either deliberately or innocently) to deny them that control (over their own lives), to inject federal bureaucracy where there should be self-government, to encourage paternalism where cooperation or independence should prevail."[175]

For further discussion of this negative impact of the federal trust responsibility for Indians and suggestions on how it can be avoided, see the book entitled "Federal-Indian Trust Relationship" in this series.[176]

5. Control Over Indian Funds

U.S. courts have said that, under the doctrines of trust responsibility[177] and the plenary power of Congress,[178] the federal government has broad control over Indian monies. This control restricts the exercise of Indian sovereignty in the area of financial management.[179] The problem is compounded by the fact that the issues involved in control over tribal funds are both complex and confusing.[180] Very few people can wade through the vast array of laws, regulations, and internal administrative directives which restrict access to these funds by those most concerned with their productivity–Indian people.

Under the trust responsibility doctrine, the U.S. Government is theoretically held to an exacting standard of accountability.[181] As stated previously, under the trust responsibility, the B.I.A. must act in the best interests of Indian people when handling Indian funds. Should they fail to exercise this duty, the tribe may, and should, force the B.I.A. to fulfill its responsibility. The courts have consistently upheld such suits.[182]

The second problem, the B.I.A.'s broad discretion in managing Indian funds, is based upon several federal laws.[183] These laws, passed under the doctrine of the plenary power of Congress, allow a greater degree of control over Indian monies than may be desirable. Authority for these powers arises from such poorly decided cases as *Lone Wolf v. Hitchcock,*[184] which emphasized that Indian affairs revolved around the political question doctrine, and thus it was for the legislative branch (Congress), and not the judiciary (the courts), to decide those matters.

It should be noted that Indian nations have the potential for a greater degree of control over tribal funds than is currently being exercised.

Felix Cohen, in his *Handbook of Federal Indian Law,*[185] breaks down tribal funds into several major categories:[186]

a. Tribal funds with no B.I.A. control
b. Tribal funds with limited B.I.A. control (control is derived from specific authority in tribal constitutions)
c. Tribal *trust* funds under strict B.I.A. control.

Cases decided to date usually involve those trust funds under strict B.I.A. control where the Bureau has failed to properly invest these funds in the "best interests of the Indians."[187] By so doing, the B.I.A. has failed in its duty to the Indian owners of such funds and is therefore liable for breach of the trust responsibility.

A major point to remember is that set out in *Creek Nation v. U.S.*:[188]

> The Secretary of Interior has only such authority over the funds of Indian tribes as is (granted) in him by Congress. He cannot legally disburse and pay out Indian funds for purposes other than those authorized by law.[189]

It should be noted also that Indian nations have the potential for a greater degree of control over tribal funds than is currently being exercised.[190] Few tribes have taken advantage of the option to exercise more control, perhaps because the B.I.A. Branch of Investments has managed to obtain a favorable rate of interest on those Indian trust funds under its control.[191] Much more needs to be done before it can be said that Indian funds are being wisely managed in a manner consistent with the concept of Indian sovereignty.

6. Control Over Tribal Laws

Perhaps the best example of administrative control over Indian governments and interference with sovereign rights is the power of the Secretary of Interior and his delegated agents (usually the B.I.A.) to approve or disapprove laws passed by an Indian government.

A Congressional subcommittee investigating the rights of Indian people in 1964 stated that it "failed to uncover any federal statute which specifically requires Secretarial approval of tribal ordinances."[192] Despite this absence, the Secretary does in fact exercise a veto power over Indian governmental actions in many circumstances.[193] And this, of course, interferes with the right of Indian nations to self-government.

According to courts, the legal basis for this administrative control over Indian governments is found in (1) the federal-Indian trust relationship,[194] and (2) tribal constitutions. While the I.R.A. did not require that Secretarial approval be obtained before laws passed by an Indian government may be effective, many Indian constitutions written under the I.R.A. do require such approval. Such restrictions were often the result of efforts by local interest groups to control Indian nations. The effect of these constitutional provisions is that the Department of Interior continues to "supervise" Indian nations while allowing the appearance of self-government.

While in certain circumstances an Indian nation may feel that continuing this Secretarial approval power is in the best interests of its people, there are many cases in which it can be highly detrimental to Indian rights. As long as that power exists, true Indian self-government will not become a reality and sovereignty will be in jeopardy. To prevent this, Indians should consider the desirability of amending their constitutions so that the power of the Secretary of Interior to disapprove of tribal ordinances is either severely restricted or entirely abolished.[195]

7. The Courts and Bureaucratic Power

Generally, United States courts have permitted the exercise of broad control over Indian affairs by federal administrators. The primary criteria the courts have used in deciding whether agency officials have overstepped their authority have been the intent of the law under which they have exercised their authority, and whether their actions are arbitrary or capricious.

While the courts have allowed federal agencies much discretion, it is clear that administrative officials do not have unrestricted power. Instead, any power which officials exercise must be expressly granted by Congress.[196] And in determining whether power has been delegated to administrators by Congress, the courts have developed several rules which may limit administrative control over Indian affairs. Included in these are the rules that federal laws generally should be interpreted in favor of Indians and that the actions of federal officials must be consistent with the trust responsibility.[197]

For further discussion of the relationship between the courts, Congress and administrative agencies in Indian affairs, see Section C of this chapter.

C. Sovereignty and the U.S. Courts

The function of the United States courts is, in part, to interpret the laws passed by Congress and to determine the constitutionality of those laws and the legality of acts by federal officials under those laws. Therefore, laws and the actions of officials administering those laws, have sometimes been challenged in the federal courts when they interfered with the exercise of Indian sovereign rights.

Generally, the federal courts have permitted both the Congress and the President broad latitude in their powers to deal with Indian nations.[198] In some cases, the courts have limited the exercise of sovereignty by Indian nations because of the "plenary power" doctrine.[199] In other cases, the courts have applied the "political question" doctrine and have not inquired as to whether or not Congress acted within constitutional limits.[200]

But while the courts have generally upheld U.S. powers in Indian matters, they have also recognized the inherent sovereignty of Indian nations. The main principle that emerges from court decisions is that Indian governments may exercise all their inherent powers unless Congress has restricted the use of those powers or the Indian nations have voluntarily given up those powers in a treaty or agreement.

The courts have also developed rules for interpreting federal laws dealing with Indians which may limit interference with Indian sovereignty. For example, the courts have held that agreements with Indian nations should be interpreted in the way in which they were understood by the Indians and that federal laws should be interpreted in favor of the Indians, if possible.[201]

Some of the major U.S. court decisions dealing with the issue of Indian sovereignty are the following.

1. *Cherokee Nation v. Georgia* (1831)

The case of *Cherokee Nation v. Georgia*[202] was the first case in which the Supreme Court discussed the sovereign nature of Indian nations. In that case the Cherokee Nation requested the Supreme Court to prevent Georgia from imposing its state laws within the Cherokee Territory.

The Supreme Court, however, refused to accept the case because it found that the Cherokee Nation was not a "foreign state" which could sue Georgia in the U.S. courts.[203] The court, therefore, did not have jurisdiction over the case.

While the court held that the Cherokee Nation was not a *foreign* state, this did not mean that Indian nations were not sovereign states. Chief Justice Marshall agreed that the Cherokee Nation was a "state" because it was a "distinct political society . . .capable of managing its own affairs and governing itself."[204] Indian nations were "domestic, dependent nations" rather than foreign states, according to the court.

Although the Court in *Cherokee Nation v. Georgia* did not fully recognize Indian sovereignty, it did not deny the sovereignty of Indian nations.

2. *Worcester v. Georgia* (1832)

Georgia's attempt to impose its laws on the Cherokee Nation was challenged again one year later in the case of *Worcester v. Georgia.*[205] In that case, a non-Indian was arrested for living within Cherokee Territory without permission from the state authorities. He was convicted for violating a Georgia law that required such permission and was sentenced to four years at hard labor by a Georgia court. He appealed his conviction to the Supreme Court.

The Supreme Court overturned Worcester's conviction[206] and declared the state law unconstitutional. In reaching its decision, the court relied upon the constitutional doctrine that the regulation of Indian affairs was granted to the federal government rather than the states:

> [Georgia's laws] interfere forcibly with the relations between the United States and the Cherokee Nation, the regulation of which, according to the settled principles of our Constitution, are committed exclusively to the government of the union.[207]

The court recognized that Indian nations were "distinct political communities, having territorial boundaries, within which their authority is exclusive, and having a right to all the lands within those boundaries. . . ."[208] The sovereign nature of Indian nations had also been recognized by the federal government in treaties with the Indian nations, according to the court.[209] Since the Cherokee Nation retained its inherent sovereignty, the state of Georgia could not impose its laws over the Cherokee Nation. Instead, the relationship between the Cherokee Nation and citizens of the U.S. was strictly a matter between the Cherokees and the federal government.

Although the Supreme Court has sometimes ignored the sovereignty of Indian nations, its statement in *Worcester v. Georgia* is still referred to in cases today in support of the inherent sovereignty of Indian nations.[210]

3. *Ex Partė Crow Dog* (1883)

In 1883, an Indian known as Crow Dog assassinated another Indian known as Spotted Tail, who was chief of the Brule Sioux, within Sioux Territory. The Sioux Tribal Council punished Crow Dog according to tribal laws and customs, but the Territory of Dakota also arrested Crow Dog, tried him for murder, and sentenced him to death. Crow Dog challenged the jurisdiction of the federal Territorial Court and the Supreme Court held that only an Indian government could punish an Indian for committing a crime against another Indian.[211]

The main principle that emerges from court decisions is that Indian governments may exercise all their inherent powers unless Congress has restricted the use of those powers or the Indian nations have voluntarily given up those powers in a treaty or agreement.

Crow Dog's case is an example of the Supreme Court's recognition of Indian sovereignty. The court pointed out that under the 1834 Trade and Intercourse Act Indian nations retained authority over their domestic affairs, including the punishment of members of the tribe who violated tribal law. This sovereign power of Indian nations had not been surrendered by later treaties, according to the court.

The Supreme Court's decision in *Ex Parte Crow Dog* resulted in public outrage because non-Indians felt that Sioux laws did not punish Crow Dog severely enough. As a result, Congress passed the Major Crimes Act which authorized federal jurisdiction over certain crimes, including murder, rape, and robbery, committed by an Indian against another Indian in Indian territory. The effect of the Major Crimes Act, which was passed without the consent of the Indians, was to limit the exercise of Indian nations' sovereign power to make and enforce its own laws.[212]

4. *United States v. Kagama* (1886)

One year later, the validity of the Major Crimes Act was challenged in *United States v. Kagama.*[213] Kagama, an Indian, murdered another Indian on the Hoopa Reservation in California and was convicted of murder in a U.S. court under the Major Crimes Act. He claimed that the United States had no jurisdiction over the case because the Major Crimes Act was unconstitutional. The Supreme Court upheld federal jurisdiction and the power of Congress to apply federal laws in Indian territory.

In reaching its decision, the court relied on the "guardian-ward relationship" between the U.S. and Indian nations to support the power of Congress over Indian nations. The court also said that Indian nations were "dependent on the United States. .for their political rights" and denied that Indian nations were sovereign.[214] While the court recognized that Indian nations were "a separate people, with the power of regulating their internal and social relations,"[215] the effect of its decision was that Congress could interfere with the internal relations of Indian nations.

5. *Lone Wolf v. Hitchcock* (1903)

In the case of *Lone Wolf v. Hitchcock,*[216] the Supreme Court again ignored the sovereignty of Indian nations and upheld the "plenary power" of Congress over Indian affairs.

In 1867 the Comanches and Kiowas entered into a treaty with the United States known as the Treaty of Medicine Lodge.

The treaty established a reservation for the tribes and provided that any sale of tribal lands must have the approval of three-fourths of the adult male members of the tribes.

In 1892 an agreement for the sale of tribal lands was drafted between the Indian nations and the United States but was not approved by three-fourths of the adult male members as required by the treaty. Even though Congress knew that the agreement violated the treaty, the sale was approved.

The Indians sued the United States claiming that the agreement violated the Treaty of Medicine Lodge and that they had signed the agreement because of fraud. The Supreme Court upheld the action of Congress in violation of the treaty on the ground that Congress had "plenary power" in Indian affairs. The court stated:

> Plenary authority over the tribal relations of Indians has been exercised by Congress from the beginning, and the power has always been deemed a political one, not subject to be controlled by the judicial department of the government. * * * In any event, as Congress possessed full power in the matter, the judiciary cannot question or inquire into the motives which prompted the enactment of this legislation.[217]

By using the political question doctrine,[218] the court left Congress free to exercise whatever power it wished over Indian nations, free from restraint by the U.S. courts. It remained that way for several decades.

6. *Iron Crow v. Oglala Sioux Tribe* (1956)

The inherent sovereignty of Indian nations was recognized in *Iron Crow v. Oglala Sioux Tribe.*[219] In that case, members of the tribe asked a U.S. court to stop the Sioux Nation from enforcing two tribal laws in its Indian courts. One law made adultery a crime. The other law imposed a tax on persons who leased Indian lands for grazing. The U.S. court of appeals upheld the tribe's power to make and enforce its own laws.

The court said that Indian nations were recognized by the U.S. Constitution as sovereign governments which possessed "all the inherent rights of sovereignty" except where Congress had specifically restricted their powers. The inherent powers of Indian nations included both the power to make and enforce criminal laws and to tax. Neither of these powers had been limited by Congress and since the powers were *inherent,* no act of Congress was necessary to support those powers.

7. *Williams v. Lee* (1959)

In *Williams v. Lee*[220] a non-Indian who operated a store within the Navajo Nation sued an Indian customer in the Arizona state courts claiming that the Indian customer had not paid for goods sold to him on credit. The Indian appealed to the U.S. Supreme Court claiming that the state courts did not have jurisdiction over the case.

The court recognized that under treaties with the Navajos "the internal affairs of the Indians remained exclusively within the jurisdiction of whatever tribal governments existed," and that their sovereign power had not been limited by Congress. Since the Navajo tribal court exercised jurisdiction over suits by non-Indians against Indians arising on the reservation, the court held that "to allow the exercise of state jurisdiction here would undermine the authority of the tribal courts over Reservation affairs and hence would infringe on the right of the Indians to govern themselves."

8. *McClanahan v. Arizona Tax Commission* (1973)

In *McClanahan v. Arizona Tax Commission,*[221] the Supreme Court held that Arizona could not impose its state income tax on a reservation Indian who earned her entire income on the reservation. The court, however, treated the issue of Indian sovereignty in a somewhat different manner than other cases.

Although the court found that the case was really no different from the case of *Worcester v. Georgia*[222] in which the state attempted to impose its laws within Indian territory, it said that the sovereignty of Indian nations has been adjusted over the years to permit some state control over *non-Indians* on reservations.[223] The court also said that while early tax cases struck down state taxes on the basis of Indian sovereignty, ". . . the trend has been away from the idea of inherent Indian sovereignty as a bar to state jurisdiction. . . ."[224]

But it is clear that the court was not denying the sovereignty of Indian tribes. Instead it said that the federal government had recognized the Indian nations as sovereign and that Congress, not the states, has the responsibility for dealing with sovereign Indian nations.[225]

9. Other Recent Court Cases

Other recent court cases have also recognized the sovereign powers of Indian governments.

In the case of *Oliphant v. Schlie*[226] a U.S. court of appeals upheld Indian jurisdiction over non-Indians who committed crimes within the reservation. In that case, a non-Indian was arrested by Indian police on the reservation and charged with assaulting an officer and resisting arrest. He claimed that the Indian court had no jurisdiction over him, but the court held that the Indian government retained its power to punish persons violating tribal laws, since no treaty or law restricted that power. The court stated:

> Surely the power to preserve order on the reservation, when necessary by punishing those who violate tribal law, is a [necessary element] of the sovereignty that the Suquamish originally possessed.[227]

The Supreme Court in the case of *United States v. Mazurie*[228] also referred to Indian nations as possessing sovereign power over their members and territory. In that case the court upheld the conviction of a non-Indian for operating a bar in violation of a tribal liquor licensing law.

In *Tom v. Sutton*[229] a federal court of appeals upheld the conviction of an Indian before the tribal court. The court said that Indian nations have the power to enact their own laws and administer their own criminal justice system, except where that power is limited by Congress. Although the Indian Civil Rights Act placed some restrictions on the exercise of Indian governments' power of self-government, the court held that the restrictions of the federal law should be interpreted in line with *Indian* governmental and cultural values.[230]

Recent court cases have also supported Indian sovereignty by limiting state jurisdiction over Indians under Public Law 280.[231] For example, in *Santa Rosa Band of Indians v. Kings County*[232] a U.S. appeals court held that a county could not enforce its zoning laws within the reservation even though Public Law 280 had given civil jurisdiction over the reservation to the state. The court said that "extension of local jurisdiction is inconsistent with tribal self-determination and autonomy."[233] And in *Bryan v. Itasca County,*[234] the Supreme Court held that Public Law 280 does not permit a state to impose a personal property tax on reservation Indians.

While the U.S. courts have often not recognized Indian sovereignty, they have supported the sovereignty of Indian nations more consistently than either Congress or the executive administration.

NOTES

Put your house in order with respect to our people, so that we may continue to coexist in peace and friendship as our grandfathers and their grandfathers tried so hard to do. . . .

***If you want your children to do what is right, then it is up to you to set the example. . . .* —Resolution, Six Nations Iroquois Confederacy, March, 1973.**

INDIAN NATIONS TODAY

A. Introduction

The previous chapters of this book have briefly reviewed the law and history to demonstrate that today Indian nations are sovereign and do exercise many sovereign powers. They are not mere social organizations, any more than any other legitimate governmental unit is. They are not artificial creations of the United States government any more than the governments of foreign nations are. On the contrary, Indian governments are viable functioning political units which exercise inherent sovereign powers.

There are, of course, great differences among Indian nations in their abilities and desire to actually exercise their sovereign powers. Some have well-developed and sophisticated governmental institutions which function efficiently and exercise power wisely. Other Indian governments are in great need of technical assistance, training programs, and a stable source of funding in order to function to their full potential and serve the needs of their people. When we recognize that almost 83% of all "federally recognized tribes" have very small populations and limited resources,[235] it is readily apparent that the practical problems of exercising sovereign rights are formidable for many Indian nations. There are, however, modern developments which encourage optimism and confidence in the future of Indian nations.

There are basically two reasons why many Indian sovereign powers have not been fully exercised since the early 1800's:

(1) suppression by non-Indians; and (2) a reluctance on the part of many Indian governments to press for reforms and exercise the powers which they retain.

Historically, the non-Indian attitude toward Indian self-government was influenced by the pervasive belief that Indian culture, social institutions, and governmental forms were inferior to those of European immigrants. The hope was that after enough "education," the Indian would realize this, abandon his more traditional ways, and embrace non-Indian culture. This would eventually lead Indian governments to wither and disappear. As we have seen, a great deal of federal legislation throughout the 19th and early 20th centuries was designed to encourage this policy. But the survival of Indian nations today is resounding proof of the shortsightedness and lack of understanding inherent in that belief and the policies it nurtured.

Despite the ravages of history, there are approximately as many Indians in North America today as there were when Columbus landed, and they are growing faster in population than any other cultural group.

While the belief that Indian nations may disappear still lingers in the minds of some people, there has been a growing acceptance within the U.S. government in recent decades of the strength of Indian nations and their determination to re-establish meaningful control over their lives and resources. Despite the ravages of history, there are approximately as many Indians in North America today as there were when Columbus landed, and they are growing faster in population than any other cultural group.[236] In some ways their governments and social institutions are as strong as they were 200 years ago. Certainly Indian people are better educated and more capable of withstanding the pressures for conformity from their non-Indian neighbors. Recognition of these facts has encouraged the general trend of federal legislation, court decisions, and administrative actions over the last 10 years to support the strengthening of Indian self-government. Legislation such as the Indian Financing Act,[237] the Indian Self-Determination and Education Assistance Act,[238] amendments to the legislation authorizing the Farmers Home Administration,[239] amendments to Public Law 280,[240] the Alaska Native Claims Settlement Act,[241] and others are evidence of this trend. The many recent federal court decisions supporting the concept of Indian sovereignty also demonstrate this trend.[242] So the United States government seems to have totally abandoned its old policies of suppression of Indian governments and assimilation of their people for the more positive directions of "self-determination."

The other reason why Indian sovereign powers have not been fully exercised in this century is because of reluctance of the Indian people to do so. Perhaps because of a fear that the U.S. government will return to its policies of suppression and termination or perhaps because of an overall lack of confidence, Indian governments have not exercised many of the sovereign powers which they retain. But this also is changing. Today Indian nations are realizing that the best way to prevent interference in their internal affairs is to take firm control of those governmental functions which are crucial to their continued survival. An example of this increased awareness is the American Indian Declaration of Sovereignty adopted by the National Congress of American Indians in 1974. It is attached as an appendix to this book.

History has repeatedly confirmed that non-Indian governments are less likely to violate Indian sovereign rights where the Indian government has already firmly and fairly asserted its powers. This is true whether "bureaucratic imperialism,"[243] assertion of state jurisdiction on Indian reservations, or misuse of the "plenary power" of Congress is involved. Therefore, many Indian nations today are: drafting or revising their tribal codes; enacting hunting and fishing regulations; establishing and expanding their judicial systems; devising fair and efficient taxing plans to provide more dependable revenues for governmental activities; establishing a broad range of Indian business enterprises; increasing their capacities to deliver essential governmental services to their people; and taking steps to gain more control over Indian lands and resources. The list of areas in which Indians are asserting more sovereign rights is virtually endless, and there is every reason to think that the list will grow longer. The following pages contain just a sample of those governmental powers which Indian nations are exercising more and more today.[244]

Today Indian nations are realizing that the best way to prevent interference in their internal affairs is to take firm control of those governmental functions which are crucial to their continued survival.

B. Taxation

As discussed in Chapter I, Indian governments have the inherent power to tax persons and property within their jurisdiction.[245] The power to tax is "essential to the maintenance of any government."[246] This is especially true in the case of Indian nations today.

While some Indian governments have exercised their power of taxation in the past,[247] many Indian nations have chosen not to exercise their inherent power to tax.[248] Indian governments have often financed their governmental functions through tribal revenues from resources held in common by the tribe rather than through taxing their members directly.[249]

The exercise of Indian governments' power to tax, however, may become much more important for Indian nations today as a means of promoting their sovereignty. First, taxation by Indian governments would raise money needed by Indian nations to increase the governmental services provided to their members.[250] As Indian nations are financially able to undertake more governmental functions on their own, they should become less dependent on the federal and state governments. Second, taxation of non-Indian sources on the reservation by Indian governments might prevent state taxation of these same resources[251] and lessen state interference within their jurisdiction. Third, taxation by Indian governments would allow Indian nations to receive more income from the sale of their natural resources by supplementing often inadequate royalty payments.[252]

In each case, taxation by Indian governments can promote Indian sovereignty by making Indian nations more financially independent[253] and capable of undertaking more governmental services.

Indian governments seeking to exercise their power to tax may also face several problems. Taxation of only tribal members may be politically and economically impractical because of the poverty of many Indians.[254] Taxation of non-Indians would provide a better source of revenue for Indian governments but may also present problems. It is unclear whether the Indian Civil Rights Act would restrict an Indian government's taxation of only non-Indians.[255] But even if the Act is not a restriction, the federal government might try to limit the power of Indian governments to tax non-Indians through the power of the Secretary of Interior to approve or disapprove tribal laws[256] or through acts of Congress which would limit Indian sovereignty.

Despite these problems, Indian nations have imposed taxes on persons and property on the reservation. The Crow Nation of Montana has enacted a severance tax on coal produced within the reservation and on ceded lands in which the tribe retained mineral rights.[257] The tax is equal to 25% of the value of each ton of coal produced and is imposed on all persons, Indian or non-Indian, producing more than ten tons of coal per year. A civil fine of $500 is imposed for violations of the tax law. The Crow severance tax was recently approved by the Solicitor of the Interior Department. By the use of this tax, the Crows finally should be able to receive a fair compensation for their coal.

The Oglala Sioux Nation has also recently passed a comprehensive tax law.[258] Included in the tax law are a land sale tax, grazing permit preparation tax, land use tax, occupation tax, cigarette tax, and a retail sales, service, and use tax. Revenue from the land use tax was earmarked for the purchase of additional tribal lands. In some instances, the tribe has entered into agreements with the state for the collection of taxes. In 1975, the Oglala Sioux Nation derived $660,000 from tribal taxes, or 92% of its total tribal budget of $720,000.[259]

The power of Indian governments to tax is essential to the right of Indian self-government.[260] But it is also important that the tax laws of the state and federal governments recognize the right of Indian self-government. Therefore state laws which attempt to tax Indians or non-Indians on the reservation are inconsistent with the power of Indian governments to tax persons and property within their jurisdiction.[261] And federal tax laws which extend benefits to state and local governments should be amended to extend the same benefits to Indian governments.[262]

Indian governments should realize that the exercise of the power to tax involves disadvantages as well as advantages. They should be aware that their actions may be challenged by non-Indians, their own members, or the federal government. At the same time, Indian nations should recognize

When we let others destroy our own environment,. . . we destroy ourselves. For our own survival, we must teach the immigrant culture to love as we love, for we have been here thousands of years and theirs is but a short time.

Douglas Cardinal, 1972

the exercise of their taxing power is important in preserving the right to govern themselves.

C. Control Over Land and Natural Resources

Land has always occupied an important place in Indian cultures.

> Indians believed, and still believe, that because of the sacredness of the land it could not be owned, could not be partitioned, fenced and developed for one individual. Territories were looked upon in the context of tribal use over individual use.[263]

The land base and natural resources of Indian nations continue to be important today as a means of preserving Indian sovereignty. Through control over Indian lands and resources, Indian nations can regain a degree of economic self-sufficiency necessary to Indian self-determination.[264]

As discussed in Chapter I, Indian governments have the power to regulate the use of land and resources on their reservations as both sovereign governments and as landowners.[265] On a number of reservations, Indian governments are using this power to regulate property use through enacting zoning or licensing laws. Several recent court cases have held that even in Public Law 280 states, state and local authorities cannot impose their zoning ordinances on Indian reservations.[266]

Non-Indian governments, however, still challenge tribal zoning jurisdiction. Recently, when one county government in Washington attempted to approve commercial tourist development on coastal lands owned by non-Indians in the Quinault reservation, the Quinault government reacted by establishing a land use planning commission and enacting a comprehensive zoning law which prohibited commercial development on the coast.[267]

As Indian nations assert more control over their land and resources and achieve a greater degree of economic self-sufficiency, they will become financially able to undertake more governmental functions and reduce their dependence on non-Indian governments.

Probably the most important issue facing Indian nations today in this area is land consolidation and acquisition. The loss of the Indian land base through removal, cession, and allotment was enormous.[268] Despite provisions in the Indian Reorganization Act authorizing the acquisition of lands for Indian nations, little money was appropriated for the purchase of additional lands and the loss of Indian lands has continued.[269] In addition, much Indian land is unusable because of fractionated ownership of trust allotments under federal inheritance laws.

> With each generation, more and more heirs inherit interests in small parcels of land, and in some cases more than 100 individuals may hold interests in a 160 acre piece of land. * * * [As a result,] individuals continue to sell their allotments, lease them to non-Indians, or let them lie idle. Hence it is not surprising that non-Indian farmers cultivate about 63% of Indian agricultural lands and that Indian people believe that land consolidation and acquisition is important to their economic future.[270]

Some Indian nations have established land acquisition and consolidation programs.[271] A major problem, however, is lack of funds with which to purchase the lands. Loans to help Indian governments acquire and consolidate lands are available from the federal government under the Indian Financing Act.[272] But to further aid in the consolidation of Indian lands, it has been suggested that Indian governments rather than the federal government control the inheritance of restricted land.[273]

Indian nations today are also seeking to assert more control over the development of their natural resources.[274] The leasing of Indian lands for mineral development, which often resulted in inadequate income from the sale of tribal resources, has been replaced in some instances by more fair arrangements such as Indian development of resources, joint ventures, and negotiated contracts.[275]

For instance, the Blackfeet Nation has entered into a service contract with a non-Indian contractor for the development of the tribe's mineral resources.[276] The contractor has no ownership or lease interest in the lands or minerals. All production is owned by the tribe. The contractor furnishes the equipment, advances funds for exploration and production, and is repaid from production profits. The tribe receives a 1/6 royalty and 50% of the profits after the contractor's costs have been paid. Indian governments should realize, however, that while joint ventures, production-sharing and service contracts allow more Indian control over the development of an Indian nation's resources, they may also expose the tribe to greater economic risk.[277] Other Indian governments have negotiated for royalty rates based on the selling price of minerals rather than fixed royalty rates in order to achieve a more fair return on the sale of tribal resources.[278]

As Indian nations assert more control over their land and resources and achieve a greater degree of economic self-sufficiency, they will become financially able to undertake more governmental functions and reduce their dependence on non-Indian governments.

D. Law and Order and Indian Nations

Until recently, U.S.-Indian policy in the administration of law and order had evidenced little concern for Indian traditions, cultural values, and self-determination.[279] The dominant law and order influences on reservations have frequently been either the Bureau of Indian Affairs or other federal or state entities. But recent years have shown an important trend toward Indian nations regaining control over law and order systems on reservations.

To some extent, the federal government is retreating from a total imposition of its values on Indian justice systems. The Indian Reorganization Act of 1934[280] began the process by allowing some Indian nations to return to their traditional forms of government if they so desired. The Indian Civil Rights Act of 1968[281] also took some consideration of the interrelationship of religion and government[282] and the personalized judicial setting[283] of most Indian communities. Public Law 93-262, the Indian Financing Act of 1974,[284] and Public Law 93-638, the Indian Self-Determination and Education Assistance Act of 1975,[285] set the stage for increased economic independence for Indian people by allowing greater viability in financing Indian community operations.

As a result, stronger Indian law and order systems are evolving. As Indian nations regain confidence in their ability to administer these programs, new constitutions, bylaws, and law and order codes are being written. Some nations are asserting jurisdiction by tribal ordinance over non-Indians on reservation lands.[286] Others are making formal extradition agreements with surrounding local governments.[287] State and federal courts are accepting the concept of "full faith and credit" of the decisions of Indian courts as a right, not a favor.[288]

There are, to be certain, some problems arising with imposition of these expanded powers of self-government. Resistance by the states is the major one. Other problems are evident, such as decisions about cross-deputization of police, the question of choosing formal or informal extradition agreements, too much B.I.A. control in ratification of governing documents, gaining the general cooperation of surrounding non-Indian governments, and a low priority by the nation itself when dealing with law and order matters. All these problems slow down the process of returning to a form of law and order administration tailored to the unique situation of each Indian community.

As Indian nations gain more power and sophistication in controlling their internal affairs, positive changes will come quickly. But expanded federal financial assistance for these programs is overdue, as is the necessity for the U.S. government to step back and let Indian nations truly govern themselves.

E. Indian Self-Determination Act

Another hopeful point in the increasing push by Indians to exercise their sovereign rights is that, generally, recent federal legislation has been supportive.[289] The trend, in fact, has been to encourage and assist Indian nations in the exercise of self-government. An example is the Indian Self-Determination and Education Assistance Act.[290]

> **"[T]he Indian people will never surrender their desire to control their relationships both among themselves and with non-Indian governments, organizations and persons."**
>
> *Indian Self-Determination and Education Assistance Act, 1973*

In the Act, Congress flatly states that "the Indian people will never surrender their desire to control their relationships both among themselves and with non-Indian governments, organizations, and persons."[291] In explaining the regulations drafted to carry out the Act, the Bureau of Indian Affairs asserts that "the federal government is committed to accept and support tribal government judgments based on the needs and goals of their people."[292] Although neither the Congress nor the B.I.A. could bring themselves to use the term "Indian sovereignty," the statements above imply a recognition that Indians retain sovereign rights and that the policy of the U.S. government is to support that sovereignty.

The Act provides basically for four measures:

1. Authorizes direct money grants to Indian nations for the "strengthening or improvement of tribal government."
2. Establishes a procedure where the Bureau of Indian Affairs and the Indian Health Service are virtually required to allow Indian governments to take over control of certain programs delivering services to Indians.
3. Establishes a procedure in which Indian nations may set priorities for programs which are administered by the B.I.A.
4. Provides for Indian governments to borrow federal employees to assist in administering Indian service programs.

The Self-Determination Act is hardly a panacea for all of the problems facing Indian governments today. But it does signify that the U.S. government recognizes the legitimacy of Indian governments and their capabilities to govern. How well this act really works to strengthen Indian governments and diminish the influence of other governments on the reservation remains to be seen. It will depend on the willingness of federal bureaucrats to give up control over programs and funds and the willingness of Indian nations to accept control.

F. Treaties

1. Treaties Among Indian Nations

Indian nations have resumed the use of treaties to relate to each other in recent years.

Early in 1973, headmen of the Lakota Nation visited the Six Nations of the Iroquois Confederacy at Onondaga and requested help in resolving the conflict arising over the second siege of Wounded Knee. This request resulted in the creation of a treaty between the Lakota and the Six Nations in which the Six Nations pledged to support and act on behalf of the Lakota Nation in the interest of peace and tranquility.

The Comanche and Ute Nations are using a treaty to mend old wounds. Traditional enemies in the past, they are currently finalizing negotiations of friendship and trade between each other.

In the Pacific Northwest, Indian nations are currently in the process of negotiating treaties between each other in relation to the conduct and management of fishing rights in their traditional fishing places. In the past, these Indian governments would have looked to the Bureau of Indian Affairs to resolve such problems. But because they found that the involvement of the B.I.A. has often led to drawn-out resolutions of problems and federal interference in their internal affairs, they are seeking to solve problems among themselves through treaty-making.

2. Agreements Between Indian Nations and the United States

Many Indian people have criticized the tendency of the U.S. government to interfere in the internal matters of Indian nations. Some have suggested that the only way to prevent this intervention is for Indian nations to re-establish some process of making treaties or agreements with the U.S. For example, in late 1972, the Trail of Broken Treaties Caravan, which took over the Bureau of Indian Affairs building in Washington, D.C., called for the resumption of treaty-making as the basis for continuing relations between Indian governments and the U.S. Point Six of the 20-point Position Paper which the Caravan presented to the U.S. government stated:

> The Congress should enact a joint resolution declaring that, as a matter of public policy and good faith, all Indian people in the United States shall be considered to be in treaty relations with the Federal Government and governed by doctrines of such relationship.

As previously pointed out, there is probably no technical reason why Indian nations and the U.S. could not resume the process of making "agreements" which would define their relationship. Such agreements were made for decades after the U.S. Congress supposedly stopped the treaty-making mechanism in 1871.[293] On many reservations, a formal agreement might go far to clarify rights and duties, decide jurisdictional problems, and improve communication and understanding between the various governmental units involved.

3. International Recognition of Indian Sovereignty

Recently, Indian nations have also begun to exercise their sovereign rights by participating in international activities. For example, in 1974 the International Treaty Council was formed when chiefs, headmen, holy men and other tribal leaders from 98 American Indian nations met for ten days at the Standing Rock Sioux Reservation in North Dakota. The meeting, hosted by the Standing Rock Sioux Tribal Council, was the largest inter-tribal meeting of Indian people in the U.S. in this century. On February 10, 1977 the United Nations granted consultative status to the International Indian Treaty Council. This means that Indian people throughout the world will have a formal voice in the world's largest international forum.

"The will for self-determination. . .is an irreversible trend. . . that will eventually compel all of America . . .to recognize the dignity and human rights of Indian people."

Louis R. Bruce,
Commissioner of Indian Affairs,
1969-1973

In September, 1977 a conference on Discrimination Against the Indian People of the Americas will take place at the United Nations in Geneva under the U.N. Non-governmental Organization Sub-Committee on Racism and De-Colonization. This conference is being organized by the Institute for the Development of Indian Law and the International Indian Treaty Council.

Conclusion

A lengthy book could easily be devoted to the subject of "Indian Nations Today" and what they are doing to reassert their sovereign rights. Space limitations have limited this book to merely a brief examination of the nature of sovereignty, the types of sovereign powers which Indian nations exercise, and a suggestion of what lies ahead for us. Even this short review should be enough to show that Indian sovereignty is a far-reaching and vigorous reality today. As a former Commissioner of the Bureau of Indian Affairs stated: "[The] will for self-determination has become a vital component of the thinking of Indian leadership and the grassroots Indian on every reservation and in every city. It is an irreversible trend, a tide in the destiny of American Indians that will eventually compel all of America. . . to recognize the dignity and human rights of Indian people."[294] He also could have added that this will springs naturally from the sovereignty of the Indian people and their tenacious refusal to surrender it.

NOTES

Appendix

American Indian Declaration of Sovereignty

The National Congress of American Indians assembled at the Royal Inn in San Diego, California for the Thirty First Annual Convention during the period of October 21-25, 1974, hereby declares:

1. The Sovereign Aboriginal American Indian Nations and the United States of America, from time to time, subsequent to the year 1776 A.D., did negotiate and did enter into solemn treaties to exchange territorial rights for the mutual benefit and welfare of both parties to the negotiated treaties, and that,

2. The Sovereign Aboriginal American Indian Nations through said direct binding relations, whether written or implied by the sacred treaties, the Constitution of the United States of America, or by Executive, legislative, or judicial action, did believe and do hereby further declare that,

3. The Government of the United States of America in negotiating said solemn treaties, did recognize Aboriginal sovereignty and by its sacred honor, did agree to honor, preserve, protect and guarantee to other states and nations and to the Aboriginal Tribes and nations those inherent sovereign rights and powers of self-government and self-determination afforded every sovereign nation of the world, and

4. The government of the United States of America did accept an obligation to assume a Trust Responsibility to honor, enforce, preserve, protect, and guarantee, without interference, the inherent sovereign rights and powers of self-government to the recognized and specified Aboriginal American Indian Nations, and,

5. The government of the United States of America, by acceptance and assumption of Trust Responsibility, did obligate itself to provide and to establish the necessary Federal Governmental instrumentalities required to honor, enforce, preserve, protect, and fulfill the treaty obligations and the general constitutional obligations pursuant thereto, and

6. The government of the United States of America is, by the conditions of said treaties and other agreements, and by legislation, and by results of litigation, required to assist in the management, development, preservation, protection, and guarantee of sovereign status of all of the Exclusive rights of the Aboriginal American Indian Nations to their Aboriginal or Treaty Territorial Domain, to the assets of natural resources of the surface, subsurface, and above-surface, to include but not limited to, hunting, fishing rights, land, water, air, wild rice, minerals, and timber, and

7. The government of the United States of America is further required to insure adequate Federal facilities and services, to be staffed with sufficient professional and qualified technical personnel for Health, Education, Welfare, and personal services to be commensurate with the predominant society, and

8. The National Congress of American Indians hereby States that the Government of the United States of America, in performance and recognition of its treaty obligations and responsibilities, has Failed and Neglected:

a. To fully recognize inherent Aboriginal American Indian sovereignty and the rights and powers of self-government and self-determination, and

b. To provide and fulfill its Trust Obligations and Responsibilities to establish Independent Governmental Instrumentalities, free from conflicts of interest, to insure inherent rights and powers of self-government as guaranteed by the negotiated treaties with Aboriginal American Indian Nations, and

c. To honor, preserve, protect, and guarantee the Aboriginal American Indian Tribes and Nations' territorial integrity and other rights guaranteed by treaties which under article six of the Constitution of the United States of America is the supreme law of the land, and therefore,

9. The National Congress of American Indians *declares and hereby petitions* the Congress of the United States of America to initiate and implement immediate corrective legislation to:

a. Honor and recognize the sovereignty and rights of Aboriginal American Indian Tribes and Nations, whether they exist by treaty or non-treaty, and

b. Re-establish those independent Aboriginal American Indian Tribes and Nations which were terminated by executive order or legislative action without the consent of the Tribe or Nation, and

c. Establish a Single, Independent, Federal Governmental Instrumentality with Concurrence of the Majority of the Recognized Aboriginal American Indian Tribes and Nations, in order to implement and guarantee the treaty responsibilities and Trust Obligations of the United States of America under Article Six of the Constitution of Said Nation.

d. We, the assembled members of the National Congress of American Indians and of various tribes do hereby adopt this declaration and pledge our honor toward instituting its intent to the end that the Indian people shall enjoy the fruits of liberty, justice and the right to maintain their culture and religious heritage.

Certification

At a duly called meeting of the National Congress of American Indians held in San Diego, California, on October 24, 1974, the foregoing declaration was passed by a unanimous vote for passage of said declaration.

[s] Mel Tonasket,
President.

[s] Ernest L. Stevens,
First Vice President.

[s] Katherine Whitehorn,
Recording Secretary.

Notes

The following footnotes contain extensive citations to authority for statements and conclusions made in the text as well as suggestions for additional reading in selected areas. Since it is anticipated that many of the persons reading this book will be non-lawyers, the authors have taken the liberty of slightly modifying the style generally used in citing legal materials. In places we have inserted words or reversed the order of information in the cite in order to facilitate understanding.

The American Indian Policy Review Commission submitted its final report to the Congress on May 17, 1977. The eleven task forces of the Commission submitted their reports to the Commission in September, 1976. We have shortened the citations to these materials as follows: Final report of the Commission is cited as "A.I.P.R.C., Commission Report, (chapter or section)"; final report of a task force is cited as "A.I.P.R.C., Task Force No. 9, (page or chapter)."

We have also used a shortened form for other frequently cited materials. For example, Felix Cohen's *Handbook of Federal Indian Law* (Albuquerque, University of New Mexico Press, 1972) (reprint of 1940 ed.) is usually cited just as "Handbook of Federal Indian Law."

The term "Id." in a footnote refers the reader to the source cited in the immediately preceding footnote. For example, "Id. at 252" means the preceding source at page 252.

1 R.R. Palmer, *A History of the Modern World*, (New York: Knopf, 1962), p. 10.

2 Id. at 158.

3 Id. at 286.

4 Vine Deloria, Jr., *Behind the Trail of Broken Treaties*, (New York: Delacorte, 1974), p. 173.

5 *The American Heritage Dictionary of the English Language*, William Morris, ed., 1970.

6 *Webster's New Collegiate Dictionary*, Henry Bosley Wolf, ed., 1975.

7 Id.

8 J. Collier, *Indians of the Americas*, (New York: New American Library, 1947), p. 101.

9 Id.

10 F.S. Cohen, *Handbook of Federal Indian Law*, (Albuquerque: University of New Mexico Press, 1972) (reprint of 1940 ed.), p. 128-129.

11 Id.

12 Id.

13 *Indians of the Americas*, p. 124-125.

[14] 31 U.S. 515, 559-61 (1832).

[15] See, for example, *Montoya v. U.S.*, 180 U.S. 269 (1901); *Marks v. U.S.*, 161 U.S. 297 (1896). See also *Handbook of Indian Law*, p. 274; A. Debo, *A History of the Indians of the United States* (1970).

[16] *Worcester v. Georgia*, 31 U.S. 515, 559 (1832).

[17] *Handbook of Federal Indian Law*, p. 122; U.S. Department of Interior, Solicitor's Opinion, *Powers of Indian Tribes*, 55 I.D. 14 (1934).

[18] *Handbook of Indian Law*, p. 123. A.I.P.R.C., Commission Report, Chapter 3. Courts have held that the intent of Congress to limit the sovereign powers of Indian governments by legislation must be *clearly expressed* in the law in order to be effective. See *Menominee Tribe v. United States*, 391 U.S. 404 (1968).

[19] *Worcester v. Georgia*, 31 U.S. 515 (1832).

[20] 273 U.S. 315 (1927).

[21] In *Williams v. Lee*, 358 U.S. 217 (1959), a non-Indian trading post operator brought suit for non-payment of goods sold on credit to an Indian husband and wife. The trading post was located on reservation land, yet the trading post operator brought suit in Arizona State Court in lieu of Navajo Tribal Court. The lower court refused to dismiss for lack of jurisdiction. The Supreme Court held that the action should have been dismissed. The State had no right to infringe upon Indian sovereignty regarding self-government, since this right had neither been negotiated away by the tribe nor taken away through the plenary power of Congress.

In *Warren Trading Post v. Arizona Tax Commission*, 380 U.S. 685 (1965), the state of Arizona attempted to impose a 2% tax upon the gross sales of an Indian trading post located on reservation land and federally licensed under 25 U.S.C. § 261. The state court upheld imposition of such tax. The Supreme Court reversed, holding that since federal statutes and regulations control Indian traders, there was no basis upon which the state may intrude and levy such a tax. For a discussion of state jurisdictional problems on Indian reservations see: Indian Civil Rights Task Force, *Development of Tripartite Jurisdiction in Indian Country*, 22 Kansas L. Rev. 351 (1974).

[22] Act of April 11, 1968, Title II, 82 Stat. 77, 25 U.S.C. § 1302 *et. seq.*(1976 Supp.) For an excellent discussion of the impact of the Indian Civil Rights Act in Indian Country, see A.I.P.R.C., Commission Report, Chapter 5. The chapter analyzes pertinent case law and examines judicial construction of the act. Also see A.I.P.R.C., Task Force No. 2, pp. 27-37; A.I.P.R.C., Task Force No. 4, pp. 129-149; A.I.P.R.C., Task Force No. 9, pp. 37-45, 87-91, 323-330.

[23] *Smith v. Bonifer*, 154 F. 883; aff'd. 166 F. 846 (1909).

[24] 41 Stat. 9, 25 U.S.C. § 163.

[25] For a thorough discussion, see *Powers of Indian Tribes*, 55 I.D. 14, 32-40 (1934).

[26] 19 Op. Att'y Gen. 115 (1888).

[27] Id. at 116.

[28] 8 U.S.C.A. § 1401(a)(2).

[29] *Iron Crow v. Oglala Sioux Tribe,* 231 F.2d 89 (8th Cir. 1956); *Tom v. Sutton,* 553 F.2d 1101 (9th Cir. 1976).

[30] *Powers of Indian Tribes,* 55 I.D. 14, 56; *Oliphant v. Schlie,* 544 F.2d 1007 (9th Cir. 1976).

[31] *Iron Crow v. Oglala Sioux Tribe,* 231 F.2d 89 (8th Cir. 1956).

[32] *Powers of Indian Tribes,* 55 I.D. 14, 48 (1934).

[33] *Colville Tribe v. Washington,* 412 F.Supp. 651 (E.D. Wash. 1976); *Quechan Tribe v. Rowe,* 531 F.2d 408 (9th Cir. 1976).

[34] See pp. 10-12 of this chapter.

[35] *Oliphant v. Schlie,* 544 F.2d 1007 (9th Cir. 1976).

[36] 231 F.2d 89 (8th Cir. 1956).

[37] *Arizona ex. rel. Merrill v. Turtle,* 413 F.2d 683 (9th Cir. 1969).

[38] *Handbook of Federal Indian Law,* p. 123; *Powers of Indian Tribes,* 55 I.D. 14, 22 (1934).

[39] 18 U.S.C. § § 1153, 3242. This act is also discussed in Ch. II of this book at p. 20.

[40] 18 U.S.C. § 1162, 28 U.S.C. § 1360. This act is discussed in Ch. II, p. 22 of this book. See also 25 U.S.C. § § 232, 233 authorizing the assumption of civil and criminal jurisdiction over reservation Indians by the state of New York, and 18 U.S.C. § 3243 authorizing the state of Kansas to assert criminal jurisdiction over Indian reservations.

[41] 25 U.S.C. § 1302. See Ch. II, pp. 22-24.

[42] *Buster v. Wright,* 135 F. 947 (8th Cir. 1905); *Iron Crow v. Oglala Sioux Tribe,* 231 F.2d 89, 98 (8th Cir. 1956).

[43] *Powers of Indian Tribes,* 55 I.D. 14, 46 (1934).

[44] *Buster v. Wright,* 135 F. 947 (8th Cir. 1905).

[45] *Iron Crow v. Oglala Sioux Tribe,* 231 F.2d 89 (8th Cir. 1956); *Barta v. Oglala Sioux Tribe,* 259 F.2d 553 (8th Cir. 1958), *cert. den.* 385 U.S. 932 (1959). One limitation on the taxing power of Indian tribes may be found in the Indian Civil Rights Act, 25 U.S.C. § 1302, which subjects Indian tribes to the requirements of "equal protection" and "due process" in the exercise of their powers of self-government. Such requirements might be construed to prohibit discriminatory or confiscatory tribal taxes. See A.I.P.R.C.,

Commission Report, Ch. 5. The power of tribes to tax may also be found to be limited under some tribal constitutions adopted pursuant to the I.R.A. See A.I.P.R.C., Task Force No. 2, Appendix 14.

46 A.I.P.R.C., Commission Report, Ch. 5.

47 Cf. *Powers of Indian Tribes,* 55 I.D. 14, 28 (1934).

48 Under the decision in *Williams v. Lee,* 358 U.S. 217 (1959) state taxation of non-Indians on reservations may be pre-empted if such taxation interferes with a tribal tax on the same sources. For further discussion on the power to tax, see *Indian Taxation,* Indian Legal Curriculum and Training Program, Institute for the Development of Indian Law, Washington, D.C. (to be published).

49 *Handbook of Federal Indian Law,* pp. 137-138.

50 *Handbook of Federal Indian Law,* p. 138.

51 *Kobogum v. Jackson Iron Co.,* 43 N.W. 602 (Mich. 1889).

52 *Raymond v. Raymond,* 83 F. 721 (8th Cir. 1897); *Fisher v. District Court,* 424 U.S. 382 (1976); *Wakefield v. Little Light,* 347 A. 2d 228 (Md. 1975).

53 *Powers of Indian Tribes,* 55 I.D. 14, 55 (1934).

54 *Handbook on Federal Indian Law,* pp. 143-145.

55 419 U.S. 544, 557 (1975) (emphasis added).

56 *Santa Rosa Band of Indians v. Kings County,* 532 F.2d 655 (9th Cir. 1975); *Snohomish County v. Seattle Disposal Co.,* 425 P.2d 22 (Wash. 1967), *cert. denied* 389 U.S. 1016; see also 25 C.F.R. § 1.4; *contra Agua Caliente Band of Indians v. City of Palm Springs,* 347 F.Supp. 42 (C.D. Cal. 1972), *Rincon Band of Indians v. County of San Diego,* 325 F.Supp. 371 (S.D. Cal. 1971), *vacated* 495 F.2d 1 (9th Cir. 1974), and *Norvell v. Sangre de Cristo Develop. Co.,* 372 F.Supp. 348 (D.N.M. 1974), *rev'd.* 519 F.2d 370 (10th Cir. 1975). Congress, in one instance, has also recognized the authority of Indian tribes to enact zoning, building, and sanitary regulations governing leased Indian lands. 25 U.S.C. §416h.

57 *Santa Rosa Band of Indians v. Kings County,* 532 F.2d 655, 663 (9th Cir. 1975).

58 *Handbook of Federal Indian Law,* pp. 139-141; *Powers of Indian Tribes,* 55 I.D. 14, 42-46 (1934).

59 See *Jones v. Meehan,* 175 U.S. 1 (1899).

60 Under the General Allotment Act of 1887, 25 U.S.C. § 348, allotted Indian lands descend according to the laws of the state in which the land is located rather than by tribal law. Another federal statute gives the Secretary of Interior unreviewable discretion to determine Indian heirs to allotted lands and final power to approve or disapprove Indian wills devising restricted lands. See 25 U.S.C. § § 372, 373.

61 Act of March 3, 1871, 25 U.S.C.A. § 71.

62 *Handbook of Federal Indian Law,* p. 67.

63 "[N]othing herein contained shall be construed to invalidate or impair the obligation of any treaty heretofore lawfully made and ratified with any such Indian nation or tribe." 25 U.S.C.A. § 71.

64 For further discussion of the possible uses of Public Law 93-638, the Indian Self-Determination and Educational Assistance Act, see Chapter III, p. 41 of this book.

65 Treaty with Kaskaskias, August 13, 1803, Art. II, 7 Stat. 78.

66 Treaty with the Cherokee, July 2, 1791, Art. II, 7 Stat. 39; *Eastern Band of Cherokee Indians v. U.S.,* 116 U.S. 288 (1886).

67 Treaty with the Osage, November 10, 1808, 7 Stat. 107, 109.

68 Treaty with the Cherokee, July 2, 1791, 7 Stat. 39.

69 10 Stat. 1132.

70 See *Handbook of Federal Indian Law,* p. xxvii.

71 Id.

72 One of the most recent examples of generally positive legislation which sought to diminish federal interference in the internal matters of Indian nations and strengthen Indian governments was the Indian Self-Determination and Education Assistance Act, Act of Jan. 4, 1975, 88 Stat. 2203, 25 U.S.C. § 450 *et seq.*

73 See, for example, the General Allotment Act discussed later in Chapter II.

74 U.S. Constitution, Art. I, § 8; *Handbook of Federal Indian Law,* pp. 91-93. See *Morton v. Mancari,* 417 U.S. 535, 551-552 (1974).

75 U.S. Constitution, Art. II, § 2; *Handbook of Federal Indian Law,* p. 91.

76 U.S. Constitution, Art. I, § 8; *Handbook of Federal Indian Law,* p. 93.

77 U.S. Constitution, Art. I, § 8.

78 U.S. Constitution, Art. IV, § 3.

79 U.S. Constitution, Art. IV, § 3; *Handbook of Federal Indian Law,* p. 94; *United States v. Kagama,* 118 U.S. 375, 379-380 (1886).

80 Examples of attempts by the United States to dominate the governments and policies of North, Central and South America are abundant. These include such arrogant policies as the Monroe Doctrine, "carry a big stick" diplomacy, and the policies which led to the

Spanish-American War.

81 187 U.S. 553 (1903).

82 The federal "trust responsibility" for Indians is a rather confusing concept which has often been greatly misunderstood by non-Indian and Indian alike. Depending upon how it is interpreted and carried out, it can be either a helpful or a stifling influence on the exercise of Indian sovereign rights. A thorough discussion of the origins and nature of the federal trust responsibility is contained in the book in this series, *Federal-Indian Trust Relationship.*

83 *Lone Wolf v. Hitchcock,* 187 U.S. 553 (1903); *United States v. Kagama,* 118 U.S. 375 (1886).

84 *Delaware Tribal Business Comm. v. Weeks,* 97 S.Ct. 911, 918 (1977).

85 See Ch. I, pp. 7-8.

86 Id.

87 In *Delaware Tribal Business Comm. v. Weeks,* 97 S.Ct. 911 (1977), *United States v. Antelope,* 97 S.Ct. 1395 (1977); and *Morton v. Mancari,* 417 U.S. 535 (1974), the Supreme Court recognized that federal Indian legislation was subject to the strictures of the fifth amendment's implied requirement of equal protection, but in each case upheld the constitutionality of the congressional action. Some lower courts have held acts of Congress relating to Indian affairs unconstitutional under the fifth amendment. *United States v. Cleveland,* 503 F.2d 1067 (9th Cir. 1974); *Northern Cheyenne Tribe v. Allottees,* 505 F.2d 268 (9th Cir. 1974), *rev'd.* 425 U.S. 649 (1976). It is possible that congressional power in Indian affairs may also be held to be limited by the trust responsibility doctrine. Cf. *Creek Nation v. United States,* 295 U.S. 103 (1935).

88 For a review of congressional policy shifts in Indian affairs, see A.I.P.R.C., Task Force No. 2, Task Force No. 9.

89 *Powers of Indian Tribes,* 55 I.D. 14, 28 (1934).

90 Act of July 22, 1790, 1 Stat. 137.

91 For a definition of "Indian Country," see *Handbook of Federal Indian Law,* pp. 5-8.

92 A.I.P.R.C., Task Force No. 9, p. 32. See also *Handbook of Federal Indian Law,* p. 6, ftn. 47, where it is noted that under the early Trade and Intercourse Acts a citizen or inhabitant of the U.S. was required to obtain a passport before entering Indian Country. This requirement was modified to exclude U.S. citizens under the 1834 Trade and Intercourse Act.

93 Act of July 22, 1790, 1 Stat. 137; Act of March 1, 1793, 1 Stat. 329; Act of April 18, 1796, 1 Stat. 452; Act of May 19, 1796, 1 Stat. 469; Act of March 3, 1799, 1 Stat. 743; Act of March 30, 1802, 2 Stat. 139; Act of April 21, 1806, 2 Stat. 402; Act of March 2, 1811, 2 Stat. 652; Act of June 30, 1834, 4 Stat. 729, 25 U.S.C. § 263; Act of

August 15, 1876, 19 Stat. 176, 200, 25 U.S.C.§261; Act of July 31, 1882, 22 Stat. 179, 25 U.S.C.§264; Act of March 3, 1903, 32 Stat. 982, 25 U.S.C.§262; Act of May 29, 1908, 35 Stat. 444.

94 *Handbook of Federal Indian Law,* p. 6. See also Act of June 30, 1834, 4 Stat. 729 *et seq.,* R.S.§2145-2157.

95 Act of June 30, 1834, 4 Stat. 729.

96 Act of June 30, 1834, 4 Stat. 738, 25 U.S.C.§9.

97 For an explanation of congressional intent in passing the Trade and Intercourse Act of 1834, see H.R. Rep. No. 474, 23rd Cong., 1st Sess., 5 (1834):

> *It is rather of courtesy than of right* that we undertake to punish crimes committed in that Indian territory by and against our own citizens. And this provision is retained principally on the ground that it may be unsafe to trust Indian law in the *early stages* of their government . . .(Emphasis added).

The admission by the Congress that the U.S. had no right to punish crimes in Indian country acknowledges that the United States had no jurisdictional authority there.

98 Act of June 30, 1834, 4 Stat. 729.

99 Act of May 28, 1830, 4 Stat. 411.

100 See the language of 25 U.S.C.§174.

101 See M. Price, *Law and the American Indian,* p. 69 (New York: Bobbs-Merrill, 1973).

102 See generally the book in this series entitled *Indian Treaties.*

103 Id.

104 See *Lone Wolf v. Hitchcock,* 187 U.S. 553 (1903). For an in-depth discussion of this case, see Indian Sovereignty and the U.S. Courts, pp. 31-32 below.

105 Appropriation Act of March 3, 1871, 16 Stat. 566.

106 Act of Mar. 3, 1885, c. 341, §9, 23 Stat. 385, as amended, 18 U.S.C.§§1153, 3242. For a general discussion of the Major Crimes Act and its implications, see *Handbook of Federal Indian Law,* Chapter 18; A.I.P.R.C., Commission Report, Chapter 5; and p. 20of this book.

107 Act of Mar. 3, 1885, c. 341, §9, 23 Stat. 385, as amended, 18 U.S.C.§1153, 3242.

108 109 U.S. 556 (1886).

109 *United States v. Kagama,* 118 U.S. 375 (1886).

[110] The crimes currently covered by the Major Crimes Act are: murder, manslaughter, kidnapping, rape, carnal knowledge of a minor female, assault with intent to rape, incest, assault with intent to murder, assault with a deadly weapon, assault resulting in serious bodily injury, arson, burglary, robbery, and larceny. 18 U.S.C.§1153.

[111] *United States v. Whaley,* 37 F. 145 (C.C.S.D. 1888) and *Sam v. United States,* 385 F.2d 213 (10th Cir. 1967) have upheld exclusive federal jurisdiction over the listed crimes, but see *Handbook of Federal Indian Law,* pp. 147, 363.

[112] Act of Feb. 8, 1887, c. 119, 24 Stat. 388. as amended, 25 U.S.C.§§331-334, 339, 341, 342, 348, 349, 381.

[113] See Table of Allotment Statutes, A.I.P.R.C., Task Force No. 9, Vol. 2, Appendix 2, p. 235.

[114] *Handbook of Federal Indian Law,* p. 208.

[115] 25 U.S.C.§331.

[116] 25 U.S.C.§331.

[117] 25 U.S.C.§§331, 462.

[118] 25 U.S.C.§461.

[119] See Ch. II, pp. 26-27 of this book.

[120] *Handbook of Federal Indian Law,* p. 216.

[121] *Handbook of Federal Indian Law,* pp. 429-430.

[122] Act of July 1, 1898, c. 545, 30 Stat. 571.

[123] Act of Apr. 26, 1906, c. 1876, 34 Stat. 137.

[124] In *Harjo v. Kleppe,* 420 F.Supp. 1110 (D.D.C. 1976) the court held that federal administrators acted beyond their statutory power by dealing with the principal chief of the Creek Nation rather than the Creek tribal council in the matter of distribution of money to the tribe. The court found that the Creek Nation, through its tribal council, still possessed some powers of self-government, since despite Congress' intention to ultimately terminate the tribal government of the Creeks, statutory dissolution of the Creek government had never been accomplished.

[125] Act of June 18, 1934, c. 576, 48 Stat. 984, 25 U.S.C.§§416 *et seq.*

[126] *Behind the Trail of Broken Treaties,* p. 187.

[127] A.I.P.R.C., Task Force No. 2, Appendix 8, p. 211.

[128] Rept. of Sec. of Interior, 1942, p. 245.

[129] 25 U.S.C. § 476.

[130] *Powers of Indian Tribes,* 55 I.D. 14, 65 (1934).

[131] A.I.P.R.C. Task Force No. 2, Appendix 8, p. 210.

[132] 25 U.S.C. § 461.

[133] 25 U.S.C. § § 465, 467.

[134] 25 U.S.C. § 476.

[135] 25 U.S.C. § 470.

[136] Act of Aug. 15, 1953, 67 Stat. 588.

[137] Pub. L. 90-284, Title IV, § § 401, 402, Act of Apr. 11, 1968, 82 Stat. 78, 79, 25 U.S.C. § § 1321, 1322. Retrocession of state jurisdiction accorded under Pub. L. 280 is allowed by Pub. L. 90-284, Title IV, § 403, Act of Apr. 11, 1968, 82 Stat. 79, 25 U.S.C. § 1323. See Executive Order No. 11435, dated November 21, 1968. Pub. L. 280 is also discussed in A.I.P.R.C., Commission Report, Chapter 3.

[138] A recent decision, *Confederated Bands and Tribes of the Yakima Indian Nation v. State of Washington,* No. 74-1225 (9th Cir., filed April 29, 1977), struck down Washington State's ". . .partial assumption of jurisdiction (under Pub. L. 280) based upon . . . land title classification. . ." as a violation of the Equal Protection Clause of the Fourteenth Amendment. The court did not reach the question of the constitutionality of Pub. L. 280 itself.

[139] A.I.P.R.C., Task Force No. 9, p. 21.

[140] Pub. L. 90-284, Title II, § 201, Act of Apr. 11, 1968, 82 Stat. 77, 25 U.S.C. § 1301 *et seq.* (1968).

[141] See *Talton v. Mayes,* 163 U.S. 376 (1896) where the crime of murder by one Cherokee against another within Indian territory was held to be an offense not against the United States but against the Cherokee Nation, and thus the provisions of the Fifth and Fourteenth Amendments to the U.S. Constitution did not apply to legislation by the Cherokee Nation.

See also *Native American Church v. Navajo Tribal Council,* 272 F.2d 131 (10th Cir. 1959) where it was held that the provisions of the First Amendment regarding separation of church and state did not apply to Indian nations. The court noted that "Indian tribes are not states. They have a status higher than that of states." Thus the 1st and 14th Amendments to the U.S. Constitution DID NOT APPLY TO THEM.

[142] *Crowe v. Eastern Band of Cherokee Indians,* 506 F.2d 1231 (4th Cir. 1974).

[143] *Johnson v. Lower Elwha Tribal Community,* 484 F.2d 200 (9th Cir. 1973).

144 See *Lohnes v. Cloud,* 366 F.Supp. 620 (1973).

145 In *Tom v. Sutton,* 533 F.2d 1101 (9th Cir. 1976), appellant Tom brought an action for a writ of habeas corpus under a provision of the Indian Civil Rights Act, 25 U.S.C. § 1303, alleging that he should have been afforded the assistance of appointed counsel in the proceedings before the Lummi Tribal Court.

Citing *Talton v. Mayes,* 163 U.S. 376 (1896), and *Settler v. Lameer,* 509 F.2d 231 (9th Cir. 1974), the court held that U.S. Constitutional provisions, specifically the Sixth and Fourteenth Amendments, do not require Indian courts to provide the assistance of counsel, unless paid for by the defendant, in matters before the tribal court.

The court also noted that while 25 U.S.C. § 1302(8) required that tribal courts must not deny due process of law to an accused, § 1302(6) clearly states that an accused may ". . . *at his own expense* . . . have the assistance of counsel for his defense;" (emphasis added). The court further observed, in footnote 5, that ". . . the courts have been careful to construe the terms 'due process' and 'equal protection' as used in the Indian Bill of Rights with due regard for the historical, governmental and cultural values of an Indian tribe. As a result, these terms are not always given the same meaning as they have come to represent under the United States Constitution."

This decision is an indication that, to a degree, Indian sovereignty is being honored by U.S. courts.

But see A. Ziontz, *In Defense of Tribal Sovereignty: An Analysis of Judicial Error in Construction of the Indian Civil Rights Act,* 20 S.D.L. Rev. 1 (1975).

146 H.R. Rep. No. 474, 23rd Cong., 1st Sess. 8, (1834).

147 There are many good histories of the Bureau of Indian Affairs, its personnel, and policies. For example, S. Lyman Tyler, *A History of Indian Policy* (Department of Interior, Washington, D.C., 1973), and F. Prucha, *American Indian Policy for the Formative Years* (Harvard University Press, 1962).

148 Federal Indian programs and responsibilities were expanded greatly in the 1960's so that now the following agencies are administering programs designed to benefit Indians: Department of Interior; Department of Commerce; Department of Labor; Department of Health, Education and Welfare; Department of Housing and Urban Development; Department of Agriculture; Department of Justice; and Department of Transportation. For an explanation of these programs, see A.I.P.R.C., Commission Report, Chapter 6.

For discussion of some of the negative aspects of this "fragmentation in Indian affairs," see the testimony of Helen Scheirbeck in hearings on H.J. Res. 881, S.J. Res. 133 "To Provide for the Establishment of the American Indian Policy Review Commission" before the Subcomm. on Indian Affairs, House Comm. on Interior, 93rd Cong., 2d Sess. (1974).

For a suggestion of the positive aspects of disbursing responsibilities for Indian programs, see S. Lyman Tyler, *A History of Indian Policy,* pp. 7-10.

149 *Worcester v. Georgia,* 31 U.S. 515, 553 (1832).

150 Cohen, *Erosion of Indian Rights 1950-1953: A Case Study in Bureaucracy*, 62 Yale L.J. 348 (1953).

151 See generally A.I.P.R.C., Task Force No. 2 and Task Force No. 9.

152 4 Stat. 564; 25 U.S.C.A. § 2.

153 Id.

154 4 Stat. 738; 25 U.S.C.A. § 9.

155 For example, see *Armstrong v. United States*, 306 F.2d 520 (10th Cir. 1962).

156 25 U.S.C.A. § 13.

157 A.I.P.R.C., Task Force No. 9, p. 343.

158 Id.

159 See Ch. I, pp 11-12 of this book.

160 25 U.S.C. § § 331 *et seq.*, 348.

161 25 U.S.C. § 461.

162 25 U.S.C. § § 392, 393, 396, 415 relate to administrative control over the sale or leasing of restricted Indian lands. 25 U.S.C. § 372 deals with inheritance of Indian lands. Under 25 U.S.C. § 404 the Secretary may sell allotted Indian lands if he determines the heirs are "incompetent." See also 25 U.S.C. § 295 which permits the Secretary of Interior to lease allotted Indian lands when the allottee is "incapacitated." Some of these laws do not require the consent of the Indian owners. Much of Title 25 of the U.S. Code is devoted to laws relative to Indian lands. For a discussion of these laws, most of which delegate administrative control over Indian lands, see A.I.P.R.C., Task Force No. 9, pp. 231-250.

163 See, for example, 25 U.S.C. § § 396a, 397, 398, 415.

164 25 U.S.C. § 407.

165 25 U.S.C. § § 312, 319.

166 25 U.S.C. § 311 *et seq.*

167 25 U.S.C. § 321.

168 25 U.S.C. § 323.

169 25 U.S.C. § 325.

170 25 U.S.C. § 324.

[171] Under 25 U.S.C. §476, Indian governments may prevent the sale of other disposition of tribal lands by federal administrators without their consent. 25 U.S.C. §415 provides that secretarial approval for leasing of tribal lands is no longer required for the Tulalip Tribe. See *Pyramid Lake Paiute Tribe v. Morton,* 354 F.Supp. 252 (D.D.C. 1973), *Seminole Nation v. United States,* 316 U.S. 286 (1946).

[172] See A.I.P.R.C., Task Force No. 9, pp. 236-238; A.I.P.R.C., Task Force No. 2, Ch. 1.

[173] A.I.P.R.C., Commission Report, Chapter 4 and sources cited therein.

[174] See, generally, A.I.P.R.C., Task Force No. 2 and Task Force No. 3; E. Cahn, *Our Brother's Keeper: The Indian in White America,* (World Publishing Co., 1970); F. Cohen, *Erosion of Indian Rights 1950-1953: A Case Study in Bureaucracy,* 62 Yale L.J. 348 (1953).

[175] A.I.P.R.C., Commission Report, Chapter 4, *Wardship v. Trusteeship.*

[176] Id.

[177] See the book in this series, entitled *Federal-Indian Trust Relationship.*

[178] See the discussion on p. 17.

[179] See generally, A.I.P.R.C., Task Force No. 9, Part VI, Chapter 6.

[180] See A.I.P.R.C., Task Force No. 9, pp. 303-304, for a discussion of the various types of Indian trust funds.

[181] For example, the legal concept of a trust and the trustee-beneficiary relationship must be understood. When real or personal property is held "in trust," title and/or possession of that property is held by one party (the trustee) for the benefit of another party (the beneficiary).

In Indian Affairs, the U.S. government, through the B.I.A., holds land and/or funds of individual Indians and Indian nations in trust and assumes the legal responsibility to manage those lands and funds in the best interests of the beneficiary Indians. This responsibility is called the "fiduciary duty" of the trustee. The standard for maintaining such a duty is a high one, and the trustee-U.S. government may be sued for breach of fiduciary duty by the beneficiary Indian(s) when such a high standard of care is not maintained.

[182] See *Manchester Band of Pomo Indians v. United States,* 363 F.Supp. 1238 (N.D.Cal. 1973), and *Cheyenne-Arapaho Tribes of Indians of Oklahoma, et. al v. United States,* 512 F.2d 1390 (Ct. Cl. 1975). Both cases are discussed in A.I.P.R.C., Task Force No. 9, pp. 307-310.

[183] 25 U.S.C. § § 151, 152, 155, 161, 161a, 161b, 161c, 162a.

[184] 187 U.S. 553 (1903).

[185] See generally, *Handbook of Federal Indian Law,* Ch. 5 § 10.

[186] Id., pp. 105-107. Cohen's fourth category of "tribal funds," Indian moneys, proceeds of labor (I.M.P.L.), have generally been held to be tribal trust funds (category 3).

[187] See 25 U.S.C. § 162a for the statutory requirement that trust funds be invested in ". . . any public-debt obligations which are unconditionally guaranteed as to both interest and principal by the United States: [if such investment is in] . . .the best interest of the Indians. . . ."

[188] 295 U.S. 103 (1935).

[189] The lower court decision, 78 Ct. Cl. 474, 485 (1933).

[190] See A.I.P.R.C., Task Force No. 9, pp. 310-311.

[191] See A.I.P.R.C., Task Force No. 9, pp. 312-320, reproducing a report by B.I.A. Branch of Investments dated June 30, 1975.

[192] Subcommittee on Constitutional Rights, Senate Committee on the Judiciary, S. Rep. No., 88th Cong., 2nd Sess. (1964).

[193] See generally, A.I.P.R.C., Commission Report, Task Force No. 2 and Task Force No. 9.

[194] Generally this is only true when Indian lands and resources which are "in trust" are concerned. See *Federal-Indian Trust Relationship* in this series.

[195] For further discussion of this, see A.I.P.R.C., Task Force No. 2, Chapter 1.

[196] In the case of *Harjo v. Kleppe*, 420 F.Supp. 1110 (D.D.C. 1976) federal officials virtually ignored for a period of sixty years the government of the Creek Nation, thereby suppressing it. The court enjoined the officials from failing to deal with the duly constituted governing body of the Creek Nation and held that they had acted unlawfully and *beyond any authority granted to them by Congress.* Characterizing the actions of the federal officials as an example of "bureaucratic imperialism," the court said that ". . . the influence and control of the [B.I.A.] over. . .the Creek national government between 1920 and 1970 was exercised wholly without the benefit of any specific Congressional mandate." 420 F.Supp. at 1139. Criteria for review of administrative decisions may be found in *Pyramid Lake Paiute Tribe v. Morton,* 354 F.Supp. 252 (D.D.C. 1973) and *Manchester Band of Pomo Indians v. United States,* 363 F.Supp. 1238 (N.D. Cal. 1973).

[197] See *Bryan v. Itasca County,* 96 S.Ct. 2102 (1976) and *Jones v. Meehan,* 175 U.S. 1 (1899); *Pyramid Lake Pauite Tribe v. Morton,* 354 F.Supp. 252 (D.D.C. 1973), *Manchester Band of Pomo Indians v. United States,* 363 F.Supp. 1238 (N.D. Cal. 1973). Statutory codification of these judicially-developed canons of construction has been suggested. A.I.P.R.C. Task Force No. 9, pp. 70-73.

[198] See generally Ch. II, Sections A and B, of this book.

[199] See e.g. *United States v. Kagama,* 118 U.S. 375 (1886).

[200] See e.g. *Lone Wolf v. Hitchcock,* 187 U.S. 553 (1903).

201 *Jones v. Meehan,* 175 U.S. 1 (1899); *Bryan v. Itasca County,* 96 S.Ct. 2102 (1976).

202 30 U.S. 1 (1831).

203 Article III of the U.S. Constitution gave the court power to hear cases between states, and cases between a state and a foreign state. Since the Cherokee Nation was not one of the United States, it could sue Georgia in the U.S. courts only if it were a foreign state.

204 *Cherokee Nation v. Georgia,* 30 U.S. 1, 15 (1831).

205 31 U.S. 515 (1832).

206 Even though the Supreme Court overturned Worcester's conviction, Georgia ignored the mandate and Worcester served his full term.

207 *Worcester v. Georgia,* 31 U.S. 515, 561 (1832).

208 Id. at 557.

209 Id. at 556.

210 See, e.g., *Williams v. Lee,* 358 U.S. 717 (1959); *United States v. Mazurie,* 419 U.S. 544 (1975).

211 109 U.S. 556 (1883).

212 See Ch. II, p. 20 of this book.

213 118 U.S. 375 (1886).

214 *United States v. Kagama,* 118 U.S. 375, 381-382 (1886).

215 Id. at 384.

216 187 U.S. 553 (1903).

217 *Lone Wolf v. Hitchcock,* 187 U.S. 553, 565, 568 (1903).

218 "Political" questions are questions which are committed to the executive and legislative branches of government rather than the judicial branch under the Constitution. See Ch. II, section A, p. 17 of this book.

219 231 F.2d 89 (8th Cir. 1956).

220 358 U.S. 217 (1959).

221 411 U.S. 164 (1973).

222 31 U.S. 515 (1832).

223 *McClanahan v. Arizona Tax Commission,* 411 U.S. 164, 171 (1973).

[224] Id. at 172.

[225] Id. at 168-171.

[226] 544 F.2d 1007 (9th Cir. 1976).

[227] *Oliphant v. Schlie,* 544 F.2d 1007, 1009 (9th Cir. 1976).

[228] 419 U.S. 544 (1975).

[229] 533 F.2d 1101 (9th Cir. 1976).

[230] *Tom v. Sutton,* 533 F.2d 1101, 1104, ftn. 5 (9th Cir. 1976).

[231] 18 U.S.C. § 1162, 28 U.S.C. § 1360.

[232] 532 F.2d 655 (9th Cir. 1975).

[233] *Santa Rosa Band of Indians v. Kings County,* 532 F.2d 655, 663 (9th Cir. 1975).

[234] 96 S.Ct. 2102 (1976).

[235] A.I.P.R.C., Task Force No. 2, p. 4.

[236] U.S. Bureau of Census, Department of Commerce, *Subject Report: American Indians,* June 1973.

[237] Act of Apr. 12, 1974, 88 Stat. 77, 25 U.S.C. § 1451 *et seq.*

[238] Act of January 4, 1975, 88 Stat. 2203, 25 U.S.C. § 450 *et seq.*

[239] For a discussion of the Indian Land Acquisition Loan Fund administered by the Farmers Home Administration, see A.I.P.R.C., Task Force No. 7, pp. 27-34.

[240] The Act of Apr. 11, 1968 amended Public Law 280 so that states could not assume criminal or civil jurisdiction in Indian country without Indian consent. 25 U.S.C. § 1325. It also provided for retrocession of jurisdiction back to the U.S. and the tribe. 25 U.S.C. § 1323.

[241] Act of Dec. 18, 1971, 85 Stat. 688, as amended, 43 U.S.C. § 1601 *et. seq.*

[242] One writer has stated that out of 25 major Indian cases decided by the U.S. Supreme Court in the last 15 years, 21 of those cases were "favorable" to Indian tribes. D. Israel, Native American Rights Fund. *The Reemergence of Tribal Nationalism,* Institute on Indian Land and Development (1976), p. 10-18.

[243] This term was used by the federal court in *Harjo v. Kleppe,* 420 F.Supp. 1110 (D.D.C. 1976).

[244] For a rather thorough examination of the subject, see A.I.P.R.C., Commission Report, Ch. 5.

[245] See Chapter I, p.10-11of this book. *Iron Crow v. Oglala Sioux Tribe,* 231 F.2d 89 (8th Cir. 1956); *Handbook of Federal Indian Law,* pp. 142, 266; A.I.P.R.C., Task Force No. 2, Appendix XIV, p. 307.

[246] *Handbook of Federal Indian Law,* p. 142.

[247] During the last half of the 1800's, the Five Civilized Tribes imposed a number of different taxes on non-Indians. The Choctaws enacted a $25 per year occupation tax and a property tax on non-Indian cattle. The Cherokees imposed an export tax on hay. The Creeks imposed a sales tax of 1½% and a business permit tax of $200 per year. A Creek tax of $25 per year on non-Indian lawyers was upheld in *Maxey v. Wright,* 105 F. 1003 (8th Cir. 1900). See also *Morris v. Hitchcock,* 194 U.S. 384 (1904) (Chickasaw permit tax). Eugene Roy Fidell, "Taxes, Development and American Indians: Background, Policy, and Alternatives" (unpublished paper in A.I.P.R.C. files).

[248] J.V. White, *Taxing Those They Found Here,* (Washington, D.C.: Institute for the Development on Indian Law).

[249] A.I.P.R.C., Commission Report Ch. 5.

[250] Carole Goldberg, *A Dynamic View of Tribal Jurisdiction to Tax Non-Indians,* 40 Law and Contemporary Problems 166-189 (Winter 1976).

[251] Id., at 182-187; Daniel Israel, *The Reemergence of Tribal Nationalism,* Institute on Indian Land and Development (1976), p. 37.

[252] Goldberg, *A Dynamic View of Tribal Jurisdiction to Tax Non-Indians,* 40 Law and Contemporary Problems 166-189 (Winter 1976).

[253] Development of a solid basis of taxation would, for instance, permit Indian governments to more readily offer bond issues pledging the tribe's taxing power as security.

[254] Comment, *The Case for Exclusive Tribal Power to Tax Mineral Lessees of Indian Lands,* 124 U. Pa. L. Rev. 491 (1975).

[255] Goldberg, *A Dynamic View of Tribal Jurisdiction to Tax Non-Indians,* 40 Law and Contemporary Problems 166, 175-180 (Winter 1976). Although some people argue that taxation of non-Indians by Indian governments is taxation without representation and therefore illegal, the argument is not very persuasive. See A.I.P.R.C., Commission Report, Ch. 5.

[256] Goldberg, *A Dynamic View of Tribal Jurisdiction to Tax Non-Indians,* 40 Law and Contemporary Problems 166, 173-175 (Winter 1976).

[257] Memorandum of Solicitor of Interior Department re Tribal Jurisdiction over Non-Indians in Civil Matters, Oct. 13, 1976.

[258] A.I.P.R.C., Task Force No. 2, Appendix 15, p. 315.

[259] Id. at 316.

260 *Taxing Those They Found Here,* p. 22.

261 *Pierce v. State Tax Commission,* 274 N.Y.S.2d 959 (1966), *aff'd.* 286 N.Y.S.2d 162 (1967). See *Williams v. Lee,* 358 U.S. 217 (1959) and *McClanahan v. Arizona Tax Comm'n.,* 411 U.S. 164 (1973).

262 Bills were introduced in the 93rd Congress which would have equalized, in large part, the tax treatment of Indian and non-Indian governments under the Internal Revenue Code but failed to pass. See A.I.P.R.C., Task Force No. 9, pp. 251-285.

263 A.I.P.R.C., Task Force No. 2, pp. 77-78.

264 A.I.P.R.C., Commission Report, Ch. 7.

265 See Ch. I, pp. 11-12 of this book.

266 *Santa Rosa Band of Indians v. Kings County,* 532 F.2d 655 (9th Cir. 1975) and other cases, some contra, cited in footnote 56.

267 A.I.P.R.C., Task Force No. 2, Appendix 3, pp. 145-149.

268 See Ch. II, p. 21 of this book regarding the loss of Indian lands under federal allotment laws. See also A.I.P.R.C., Task Force No. 7, pp. 22-25.

269 A.I.P.R.C., Commission Report, Ch. 7.

270 Id.

271 Id., A.I.P.R.C., Task Force No. 7, p. 27.

272 25 U.S.C. § 1466.

273 A.I.P.R.C., Commission Report, Ch. 7.

274 Id. The chapter contains sections on agriculture, timber, water, and mineral resource development on Indian reservations.

275 Id.; A.I.P.R.C., Task Force No. 7, Appendix 1.

276 A.I.P.R.C., Commission Report, Ch. 7.

277 Id.

278 Id.

279 See generally the discussion in Chapter II of this book, Indian Sovereignty and the United States Government, Section A, Sovereignty and the United States Congress.

280 Act of June 18, 1934, c. 576, 48 Stat. 984, 25 U.S.C. § 461 *et. seq.* (1970).

281 Act of Apr. 11, 1968, Pub. L. 90-284, Title II, 82 Stat. 77, 25 U.S.C. § 1301 *et. seq.* (1976 Supp.).

[282] 25 U.S.C. § 1302(1) (1976 Supp.).

[283] 25 U.S.C. § 1302(6) (1976 Supp.).

[284] Act of Apr. 12, 1974, 88 Stat. 77, 25 U.S.C. § 1451 *et. seq.* (1976 Supp.).

[285] Act of Jan. 4, 1975, 88 Stat. 2203, 25 U.S.C. § 450 *et. seq.* (1976 Supp.).

[286] A.I.P.R.C., Task Force No. 2, p. 271.

[287] See *Arizona ex rel. Merrill v. Turtle,* 413 F.2d 683, 684 (9th Cir. 1969).

[288] See generally, *Indian Tribes and Full Faith and Credit,* A.I.P.R.C., Task Force No. 2, Appendix 13, pp. 285-305.

[289] See the Introduction to this section.

[290] Act of Jan. 4, 1975, 88 Stat. 2203, 25 U.S.C. § 450 *et. seq.*

[291] 25 U.S.C. § 450(a)(2).

[292] "Handbook for Decision Makers on Title I of the Indian Self-Determination and Education Assistance Act," Bureau of Indian Affairs, Washington, D.C., Nov. 18, 1975, p.3.

[293] 25 U.S.C. § 71.

[294] S. Lyman Tyler, *A History of Indian Policy,* p. 225.

Treaty Legislation

From the very beginning, with the first European colonies, treaties were an essential part of Indian-White relations. From early on, the central government maintained the right to make treaties with the Native Americans. After independence, the federal government continued this tradition; treaties, including those dealing with Indian affairs, became according to the Constitution the prerogative of the President and the Senate. In July 1862 Congress again confirmed the treaty rights of the President, and also gave him the right to abrogate treaties with hostile Indians[1].

Several treaty negotiations between the United States government and Indians were held in the 1860's, and these adhered to the new regulations issued in the legislation concerning the transaction of Indian affairs. For example, in December 1862, the Senate approved a recommendation by Benjamin Harding to authorize the Committee on Indian Affairs to look into the possibility of making a treaty with the Klamath and Modoc Indians of Oregon and Northern California[2]. The Committee produced a positive report which was introduced to the Senate by senator James W. Nesmith in January 1863[3]. This led to the law of March 25, 1864, which authorized the President to conclude a treaty with the Klamath, Modoc, and Snake Indians in Southeastern Oregon for the purchase of the land occupied by these Indians[4].

In January 1863 the then Vice-President Hannibal Hamlin introduced to the Senate a letter from the Secretary of the Interior requesting money to be used for handling matters with the Indians in Utah and with other non-treaty Indians. He also wished to send special agents to the Northern Chippewas, to the tribes of the Upper Missouri and to other tribes, with the aim of decreasing their discon-

1. 12 Stat 568, and *Federal Indian Law*, p. 113.
2. *Journal of the Senate of the United States of America*, being the Third Session of the Thirty-Seventh Congress: begun and held at the City of Washington, December 1, 1862, in the eighty-seventh year of the independence of the United States., U.S. Serial Set 1148, Washington: Government Printing Office, 1863, p. 31.
3. Ibid. p. 91.
4. 13 Stat 37.

tent and violence. The Senate delegated the matter to the Committee on Finances and the Committee on Indian Affairs, and in the Annual Appropriation Act of March 3, 1863, $50,000 was granted to the Secretary of the Interior to be used for negotiations with non-treaty Indians.[5]

Another act, in February 1865, authorized the President "to enter into treaties with the various tribes of Indians of the Utah Territory, upon such terms as may be deemed just to said Indians and beneficial to the government of the United States." With these treaties, the Indians were to surrender to the United States "their possessory right to all agricultural and mineral lands, except such agricultural lands as by said treaties may be set apart for reservations for said Indians." The act further provided "that all such reservations shall be selected at points as remote as may be practicable from the present settlements in the Utah Territory." Another clause provided that "in agreeing with said Indians upon the amounts to be paid to them under the provisions of the treaties . . . care shall be taken to obtain from the Indians to the greatest possible extent, their consent to receive for such payments agricultural implements, stock, and other useful articles, rather than money." The sum of $25,000 was appropriated for the negotiations, which included carrying out the provisions of the act, making presents to the Indians, and defraying other necessary expenses. Among other similar actions was Congressional resolution number 47 of 1866, which reserved for the President as much as $121,785.77 to negotiate treaties with the tribes of the upper Missouri and Platte Rivers. In a later law, on July 1, 1870, the President was authorized to negotiate with the Umatilla Indians for their removal from the Umatilla Reservation in Oregon, and for the dividing of their reservation lands into allotments of 160 acres. Two thousand dollars were reserved for these negotiations.[6]

Such authorizations and regulations were not a waste. On the contrary, the 1860's proved to be perhaps the most successful decade in terms of the number of Indian treaties negotiated. Countless councils were held and 59 treaties actually ratified. The most meaningful of these treaties were negotiated by the Peace Commission with the Plains Indians: with the southern Plains Indians at Medicine Lodge Creek in Kansas, and with the northern Plains Indians at Wyoming's Fort Laramie. This latter treaty ended "Red

---

5. *Senate Journal*, op.cit., pp. 103—104, and 12 Stat 792.
6. 13 Stat 432, 14 Stat 358, and 16 Stat 384.

Cloud's war." It was three large Plains Nations — the Shoshone, Sioux, and Cheyenne — who accounted for more than twenty of the treaties made in the 1860's.[7]

Congress was able to help the treaty-making process through legislation, and especially in the 1860's it seemed to be willing and even anxious to do so. Several voices were raised against the treaty system, but its supporters claimed that it worked and they remained a majority in Congress during the decade. On the other hand, though the Senate ratified the laws that promoted treaty-making, Congress as a whole interpreted the treaties anyway it pleased. It could also use its power to break treaties. Its "right" to do so was not disputed.

Angry and annoyed with the Minnesota Sioux uprising in 1862, Congress on February 16, 1863 annulled the Sisseton, Wahpeton, Medawakanton, and Wahpakoota Treaties, which in any case it had already failed to honor. With this act, Congress simply abrogated those parts of the treaties which would in the future impose any obligations on the United States. It also stated in this same law that all the lands of the offending Minnesota Indians would be forfeited to the United States, because those Indians had in the previous year "made an unprovoked, aggressive, and most savage war upon the United States, and massacred a large number of men, women and children within the State of Minnesota, and destroyed and damaged a large amount of property." Those Indians who had helped whites during this war, were given 80 acre allotments as their reward.[8]

7. For example, in June, 1862 treaties with the Blanchard's Fork and Roche de Boeuf Ottawa and with the Kickapoos came into force (12 Stat 792, 22 Stat Stat 158). During the following year, treaties were made with, among others, the Nez Percé (e.g. 14 Stat 269, 15 Stat 469, 22 Stat 158), Creeks (e.g. 13 Stat 177, 14 Stat 272), Tabequache Utes (e.g. 13 Stat 560, 14 Stat 272—273), Eastern, Northwestern, Western and Goship Shoshones (e.g. 14 Stat 269). In October 1863, a treaty was signed with the Chippewas with an addition to it the following April (e.g. 13 Stat 178, 14 Stat 270—271). In March 1863 the Chippewas had already surrendered their Gull Lake, Mille Lac, Sandy Lake, Rabbit Lake, and Rich Lake Reservations (12 Stat 1249—1255). In 1865 treaties were made with, for example, some Kiowas, Comanches and Apaches, and Omahas. Nine separate treaties with the different Sioux tribes were signed at Fort Sully in October. The Arapahoes and Cheyennes, who had been defeated at Sand Creek, gave away large territories and agreed upon a small reservation on the Kansas-Indian Territory border. (e.g. 14 Stat 273—276, and Cong. Rec., 41st Cong., II Sess., Appendix, pp. 449.) During the same year, the Senate made an addition to the treaty signed the previous year with the Winnebagos. Also, treaties were made with, for example, the Choctaw and Chickasaw Indians, and the Bois Fort Chippewas (e.g. 14 Stat 259, 265 & 274). The Choctaw and Chickasaw treaty was negotiated in the spring of 1868 to include some additions and changes, which Congress in July authorized the Department of the Interior to approve and ratify (15 Stat 77). See also, e.g., 13 Stat 629, and 14 Stat 277 & 497—511; and John R. Wunder, "Death to Diplomacy: Indian Nations, the United States and the Resolution of 1871", a paper owned by the author thanks to Peter Iverson, p. 10.

8. 12 Stat 652 & 654.

The Peace Commission made treaties in Fort Laramie with the Sioux and Cheyenne, and ended Red Cloud's war ceding victory to the Indians. (Smithsonian Institution)

The Supreme Court collaborated with Congress in its interpretations of the Indian treaties. When the two Cherokee leaders, Elias C. Boudinot and Stand Watie refused to pay an 1868 tax on the tobacco produced on Cherokee Nation territory — they claimed that the 1866 Cherokee treaty freed them from such a tax — the Supreme Court of the United States refused to uphold them. According to the Court, the 1868 tax law had changed the stipulations of the 1866 treaty. The Supreme Court declared that a "treaty may supersede a prior act of Congress, and an an act of Congress may supersede a prior treaty." These principles, according to the Court, were applied to treaties made with foreign countries; Indian treaties were to be treated similarly.[9]

Despite the many treaties and the long tradition of treaty making, treaty-making policy was often unsatisfactory. Some of the Indian treaties were never ratified, or they were ratified only after a long

9. II Wallace, 616, 620—621, as quoted in Prucha (1975), op.cit., pp. 136.

period of time[10]. One such example is the treaty between the United States and the Eastern Band of Shoshones. The treaty itself was signed on July 2, 1863. However, the Committee on Indian Affairs did not suggest its ratification to the Senate until March 7, 1864. Changes were not confirmed until August 31, 1865, and after an Indian agreement was received for the changes, the treaty did not come officially into force until June 7, 1869.[11] The treaties with the Indians in the Oregon and Washington Territories signed early in 1855, were not ratified until 1859[12]. This was typical of other treaties as well.

The Indians, for their part, did not always understand the treaties in the same way as did the federal government. Translations or interpretations into Indian languages were often intentionally or unintentionally misleading or unclear. Sometimes only a fraction of the tribe signed the papers. Indian leaders often met their white counterparts at festive occasions, where long speeches were made (many of which the chiefs seldom understood), and at the end, both parties "touched the pen." In some tribes the chief's decisions were not binding on individual tribesmen, and it was often difficult to stop young warriors who disagreed with a treaty from going on the warpath.[13]

On several occasions, the federal government did not fulfill its treaty obligations, or it did not do so in time. Quite often it either was not willing or it lacked the power to stop states or individual citizens from breaking treaty regulations.[14] This of course led to continuous

---

10. *Federal Indian law*, op.cit., p. 144, refers also to Hoopes, Indian Affairs and Their Administration (1932) pp. 86 and 115.
11. 18 Stat 685.
12. 12 Stat 927—950.
13. See, e.g., *Federal Indian Law*, op.cit., pp. 115 & 144; William Gardner Bell, "Winning the West: the Army in the Indian Wars, 1865—1890", in *American Military History*., Office of the Chief of Military History, United States Army, U.S. Government Printing Office, Washington, D.C., 1969, pp. 306—307; Dan E. Clark, "Treaties with the Indians", in James Truslow and R.V. Coleman (ed.), *Dictionary of American History*. Volume III., Charles Scribner's Sons, New York, 1946, p. 89; and David Lavender, *American Heritage History of the Great West*, American Heritage Publishing Company, New York, 1965, p. 343.
14. *Federal Indian Law*, op.cit., p. 144, refers here also to Hoopes, Indian Affairs and Their Administration (1932), p.180 & 218—219, to Kinney, A Continent Lost — A Civilization Won (1937), pp. 44—45, 68 & 71, and to Schmeckebier, The Office of Indian Affairs, Its History, Activities, and Organization (1927), p. 31. See also "Report of the Indian Peace Commission, January 7, 1868" as quoted by senator Justin Morrill in the Senate on June 2, 1870, Cong. Rec., 41st Cong., II Sess., Appendix, p. 449; and the Report by the Super-intendent of Indian Affairs in the Washington Territory on September 1, 1870, in Report of the Commissioner of Indian Affairs 1870, p. 10.

complaints from the Indians. In the early 1860's, the Wyandots complained to senator J.H. Lane that in 1855 and 1856 they had only been paid half of the annual installments that were promised to them by their treaty. The Commissioner of Indian Affairs, William P. Dole, however, told Lane that all installments had been fully paid.[15] This was enough to satisfy Congress. In 1870, Congressman O. Ferris questioned the delay of payments due to some Potawatomi Indians[16]. Even as late as 1898, some twenty Pillager Chippewas were causing trouble in Minnesota because their treaty rights were not being honored[17].

Sometimes the Indians' complaints led to favorable results. In 1880, for example, senator M.H. Carpenter was worried about a complaint from some Stockbridge Indians that they had not been paid their annuities at all. The acting Commissioner of Indian Affairs had to admit that forty Stockbridge Indians had been stricken off the payroll "by mistake," but their names, he assured the senator, would soon be put back.[18]

Most treaties were made in order to acquire land. They were usually signed after war activities in which the Indian group in question had been defeated. The Indians were generally forced to agree to the Whites' conditions, and treaties were rarely negotiated at the Indians' behest. This being the situation, the Indians were often unwilling to accept treaty regulations and were quite happy to violate them. The lack of a concept of land ownership among the Indian nations led to the fact that the borders between different tribes were flexible. A treaty with one tribe or nation did not always remove all Indian claims to the territory. When those Indians who had not signed the treaty claimed the land to be theirs, it often led to war.[19]

---

15. Dole to Lane on April 21, 1862, BIA Letters sent, 68, p. 105. See also Senate Miscellaneous Document No.16, 37th Cong., III Sess., CIS US Serial Set, No. 1150, Fiche 3.
16. Cady to Ferris on July 6, 1870, BIA, Letters Sent, 95, p. 454.
17. Rev. J.A. Gilfillan in an address to the Mohonk Conference, which was printed and supported by the Indian Rights Association on February 6, 1899. National Archives, Records of the United States House of Representatives, Committee on Indian Affairs papers, 55A-F15.1.
18. Marble to Carpenter on November 13, 1880, BIA, Letters Sent, 166, p. 405. For additional Indian complaints, see, e.g., Senate Miscellaneous Document No.73, 38th Cong., I Sess., CIS US Serial Set, No.1177, Fiche 3; Senate Miscellaneous Document No.16, 38th Cong., I Sess., CIS US Serial Set, No.1177, Fiche 6; and National Archives, Records of the United States Senate, Committee on Indian Affairs papers, 40A-H9 & 41B-C6, and Records of the United States House of Representatives, Committee on Indian Affairs papers, 50A-F16.5, 52A-F19.18(1), & 55A-F15.1.
19. Clawson, op.cit., p. 34.

In addition to acquiring land, the treaties were also used to "civilize" the Indians. The federal government wanted to convert the Indians from their aboriginal cultural patterns to the European model of agriculture and settled farming communities. This white paternalism, with its idea of lifting "the savages" a step higher in "the universal hierarchy" of cultures, was very much present in the Indian treaties. These reforming tendencies, however, were not usually understood or accepted by the Indians.[20]

Due to the inequality of the parties involved, the treaty system had been under attack by some whites for a long time, and after the Civil War criticism rose to its peak[21]. Commissioner Ely S. Parker supported the ending of the treaty system, and this was also the aim of President Grant's Indian policy. Parker admitted that in the future, arrangements would still be needed in order to move Indians onto reservations, to organize the surrendering of their lands, and to support them in their new homes. But these arrangements should not be the results of treaties. Rather, a treaty should be made only between two independent and sovereign parties. The Indian tribes did not fulfill this criterion, since according to Parker, they were not sovereign nations. None of them, in Parker's mind, had a government organized in such a way that it could guarantee the obedience of its citizens. Indians were wards of the United States government, and Parker believed that the only claim guaranteed to them by law for the lands they ruled was but a possessory title.[22]

Treaties had, however, been made with Indians to remove their title of ownership from lands on which they lived or roamed. According to Ely S. Parker, this had created a false sense of national sovereignty for Indians. The Commissioner thought that the time had come for the federal government to stop this cruel farce, by which it misled its helpless and ignorant wards. Parker believed that the government had unintentionally done a great deal of harm to the Indians by letting them believe they were independent

---

20. Francis Paul Prucha, *The Indians in American Society From the Revolutionary War to the Present*, University of California Press, Berkeley and Los Angeles, California, 1985, pp. 16—19.

21. Prucha (1975), op.cit. p. 134.

22. House Executive Document no.1, 41st Cong., 2d sess., serial 1414, p. 448, as quoted in Prucha (1975), op.cit., pp. 134-135; and *Federal Indian Law*, op.cit., p. 236, which refers here to Report, Commissioner of Indian Affairs, 1869, p. 6. See also Robert F. Berkhofer, Jr., *The White Man's Indian. Images of the American Indian from Columbus to the Present.*, Vintage Books, February 1979 (orig. 1978), New York, N.Y., p. 170.

nations, though in fact they had only the rights of wards and dependents of the United States. With white civilization encroaching upon Indian lands, the Commissioner called for wise, liberal, and just legislation for Indians, not treaties. The treaties already in force should, however, without exception, be fulfilled in order to prevent the Indians having further cause for complaint. For this same reason Parker also supported the ratification of all those treaties which were still before the Senate at that moment.[22]

In addition to Ely S. Parker, there were other significant persons who opposed making treaties with the Indians. Even before he became President, Andrew Jackson had questioned Indian treaties as early as 1817, and in the 1820's the Secretary of War, John C. Calhoun, introduced a bill to nullify treaties already made. In 1862, Secretary of the Interior Caleb Smith (1861—1863) supported the same anti-treaty position; and President Grant supported Commissioner Parker's view mentioned above. The ending of an unrealistic treaty-making policy was also suggested both by the Peace Commission and the Board of Indian Commissioners.[23] In his 1863 report on the Minnesota Sioux uprising, Indian agent Thomas J. Galbraith had also suggested that the treatment of Indians as independent nations and the treaty system should be abandoned, and that the federal government should accept its responsibility toward Indians as its wards or children.[24] Towards the end of the 1860's, more and more members of Congress also shifted their position to support the abandoning of treaty making.

In 1868 the Commissioner of Indian Affairs, Nathaniel Taylor, negotiated treaty terms with the Kansas Osages, which gave the Indian lands to a railroad company. This action provoked general opposition in Congress, and the House of Representatives demanded that the lands should be returned to the public domain. The representatives claimed that treaty-making rights could not be used for such a purpose.[25] During a discussion in the House, in March,

23. *Federal Indian Law*, op.cit., p. 236, which also refers here to Report, Commissioner of Indian Affairs, 1862, p. 7; House Executive Document no.97, 40th Cong., 2d sess., serial 1337, pp. 15—17, as quoted in Prucha (1975), op.cit., pp. 106—109; and Annual Report of the Board of Indian Commissioners 1869, pp. 5—11, as quoted in Prucha (1975), op.cit., pp. 131—134. See also Prucha(1985), op.cit., p. 20.

24. House Executive Document No.68, 37th Cong., III Sess., pp. 38—39, CIS US Serial Set, No.1163, Fiche 2.

25. Frederick Merk, "Foreword", in David M. Ellis (ed.), *The Frontier in American Development. Essays in Honor of Paul Wallace Gates.*, Cornell University Press, Ithaca, 1969, p.XVIII, and Prucha (1975), op.cit., p.115. Both Paul Gates and Francis Paul Prucha claim that this kind of argument led largely to the abrogation of treaty making in 1871.

William Lawrence from Ohio referred to two Supreme Court decisions (Johnson v. McIntosh, 8 Wheat, 543, and Clark v. Smith, 13 Peters, 195), to support a claim that the Indians never had, or could have, any other rights to land except the right of occupancy. Therefore, he argued, the land was public land, and it could not be signed away to a third party by a treaty with the Indians.[26]

In June, Congressman Sidney Clarke from Kansas observed that the treaty with the Osage Indians was the most significant land transfer to date: eight million acres of public land were transferred to a railroad company. Clarke suggested that the Senate should be informed that if it ratified the treaty, the House would not consider it valid, and would not appropriate the money needed to put the treaty into force. Glenn W. Scofield from Pennsylvania added to the debate by wondering if Congress was expected to diminish public lands according to a false interpretation of treaty rights.[27]

Despite the many criticisms of the Indian treaties, the limiting of treaty-making rights and finally the denying of them, was not, however, so much due to the unsatisfactory nature of the policy, as it was to the power struggle between the two chambers of Congress. According to the Constitution, the Senate alone had the power to ratify treaties. The House, however, wanted to have more power in Indian affairs, or in land matters, indeed in both. Thus on July 9, 1867, the Senate had to deal with a bill from the House suggesting the repeal of all laws which allowed the President, the Secretary of the Interior, or the Commissioner of Indian Affairs to make treaties with the Indians. According to the bill, in the future money would be given to fulfill treaty stipulations only by special legislation. This bill was, however, rejected by the Senate.[28]

The power struggle between the House and the Senate in the late 1860's and early 1870's was reflected in small additions to the annual appropriation acts. With the Osage treaty fresh in its memory, the House stressed in Section 5 of the Appropriation Act of April 1869, that nothing in the said act "or in any of the provisions thereof, should be construed as to ratify or approve any treaty made with any tribes, bands, or parties of Indians since the twentieth day of

26. Cong. Globe, 40th Cong., II Sess., pp. 2065—2066.
27. Congressional Globe, 40th Cong., 2d sess., pp. 3261—3264, as quoted in Prucha(1975), op.cit., pp. 115—116.
28. Cong. Globe, 39th Cong., II Sess., p. 75.

July, eighteen hundred and sixty-seven."[29] Section 2 of the 1871 Appropriation Act likewise modified a similar law of the previous year. Section 14 of that law, "which was inadvertently omitted in the enrollment of said act," now stated that nothing in the said act should "be so construed as to ratify, approve, or disaffirm any treaty made with" Indians since July 20, 1867, or to "affirm or disaffirm any of the powers of the Executive and the Senate over the subject."[30]

In that same year (1871) the House of Representatives refused to appropriate any money for Indian affairs, unless it was given more power in controlling them. In addition, the House wanted to nullify all Indian treaties already in force. To keep the already negotiated treaties in force and the Indians calm, the Senate had to agree to a compromise. This compromise was given specific statutory status by attaching it to the act "making Appropriations for the current and the contingent Expenses of the Indian Department, and for fulfilling Treaty Stipulations with various Indian Tribes," passed on March 3, 1871. The new amendment clearly stated that from then on "no Indian nation or tribe within the territory of the United States shall be acknowledged or recognized as an independent nation, tribe, or power with whom the United States may contract by treaty."[31]

Scholars have often considered this enactment of 1871 to be the turning point along the road to total Indian subjugation. For **John R. Wunder** the resolution is a major step from "old colonialism" to "new colonialism" largely resulting from the troubles of the 1860's on the Plains. Particularly the Sioux, Cheyenne, and Shoshoni were unwilling to yield to white demands, and engaged the United States in long wars in the West. Often these wars led to treaties, which did not always satisfy the government or the public. The Great Plains was the last frontier for most Americans. The scarcity of land as

29. 16 Stat 40. This can also be seen as a criticism against the so-called Peace Policy, since the date of July 20, 1867, is exactly the founding day of the Peace Commission. Before the passing of the annual appropriation acts of 1869 and 1870, some treaties negotiated by the Commission, however, had already been ratified by the Senate, such as the treaties of Medicine Lodge Creek and Fort Laramie.

30. 16 Stat 570.

31. 16 Stat 566, *Federal Indian Law*, p. 114, and Robert M. Utley, "The Celebrated Peace Policy of General Grant", in Roger L. Nichols (ed.), *The American Indian. Past and Present.*, John Wiley & Sons, New York, 1981 (orig. 1971), p. 163. A good description of the debate in Congress can be found in Wunder, "Death to Diplomacy", op.cit., pp. 11—16.

perceived by the United States government in the 1860's meant it sought new ways by which Indian lands could be separated from their lawful inhabitants. "New forms of colonialism" were obviously required, but the legal actions necessary for them conflicted with existing norms of international law. To get around this, Congress passed an 1871 resolution locating Indians outside the future protection of international law. Because after all, "the treaty also was an instrument of law which demanded a sense of fair play" and "a recognition of national status".[32]

D'Arcy McNickle sees the law as a logical development of earlier relations; in abandoning the treaty system, the United States recognized the fact that it no longer required the Indians' friendship or assistance[33]. For the Indian, however, very little changed in practice[34]. The government continued to negotiate with the tribes, and "treaties" were made. These treaties now needed approval also from the House of Representatives. They therefore could no longer be called "treaties," and came to be called "agreements." In practice, the lowering of the status of Indian treaties to Indian agreements made no difference to the Indians[35]. A symbol of the basically technical nature of the change is that the abrogation of Indian treaties was buried inconspicuously in the middle of an appropriation act. Significant riders of this kind, were normally added as separate paragraphs or sections at the end of an act. This procedure was not, however, followed when ending the treaty making period.

Between 1872 and 1902 the United States made seventy-four Indian agreements. Most of them looked exactly like the earlier treaties. The 1874 ratified agreement with the Colorado Utes was one such and simply replaced the earlier 1868 treaty. The agreement made with the Rosebud and other Sioux tribes, or the agreement about the northern border of the Coeur d'Alene Reservation, for example, were also exact equivalents of the earlier treaties. Some of

---

32. John R. Wunder, "The Enshrinement in Law of American Colonialism: From the Resolution of 1871 to Lone Wolf v. Hitchcock (1903)", a paper prepared for the Center for Great Plains Studies, University of Nebraska, March, 1986 Symposium — "The Meaning of the Plains Indian Past for Present Plains Culture", pp. 3 and 17.

33. D'Arcy McNickle, "Indian and European: Indian-White Relations from Discovery to 1887", in *American Indians and American Life. The Annals of the American Academy of Political and Social Science*, Volume 311, Philadelphia, May 1957, p. 10.

34. For changes in the theoretical status of the Indian, see below chapter 16 on the legality of Indian legislation.

35. *Federal Indian Law*, op.cit., pp. 212—213, tries to make a distinction between an Indian treaty and an Indian agreement, but the difference in practice — especially for Indians — remains nominal. See also below chapter 16.

the agreements negotiated after March 3, 1871, were even given the status of treaties. The treaty made with the Southern Utes in 1880 is one example.[36] Most agreements dealt, as one might expect, with Indian land cessions, and from the 1880's on, more often with the allotment of reservation lands[37]. All the other features related to treaties mentioned above applied to the agreements as well.

The signing of agreements still continued after 1902. In early 1904, the House of Representatives discussed the ratification of an agreement with the Rosebud Sioux. With this agreement, negotiated two and a half years earlier, the Indians gave away some 416,000 acres.[38] During the spring of 1905, senator William Stewart of Nevada introduced a bill to ratify an agreement with the Wind River Shoshones of Wyoming. In principal, the agreement was generally accepted, but there was disagreement concerning the details of how the former Indian lands should be used. The bill, therefore, was at first rejected by the House. Congressmen from the West and New England favored the bill; it was opposed mostly by Democrats, Texans included. After a great deal of discussion, the bill was, however, finally passed in both chambers of Congress.[39]

Indian treaties and agreements can be classified both as laws reflecting a "power struggle", and laws "to benefit the Indians". The abrogation of Indian treaty making in 1871 was mostly a result of the power struggle between the two chambers of Congress, but it also involved other things. The 1871 resolution was also a Congressional melding of conservative fiscal sentiment, anti-Indian settler's attitudes, and reformer conversion to the idea that the treaty system

36. 18 Stat 36—41; Cong. Rec., 53rd Cong., II Sess., pp. 1761 & 3261; and Virgil J. Vogel (ed.), *This Country Was Ours. A Documentary History of the American Indian.*, Harper & Row, New York, 1974, p. 163, where he also refers to Cyrus Thomas, "Treaties", in F.W. Hodge (ed.), Handbook of American Indians, II, 803—14.

37. See, e.g., the agreements with the following Indian groups: the Crows of the Montana Territory in 1882 (22 Stat 42—43), the Gros Ventre, Piegan, Blackfoot, Blood, and River Crows of Montana in 1888 (25 Stat 113—133), the Shoshoni and Bannock of Idaho in 1888 (25 Stat 452—457), the Shoshoni, Bannock and Sheepeater Bands of Fort Hall and Lemhi in Idaho in 1889 (25 Stat 687—689), the Yankton Sioux of South Dakota in 1894 (28 Stat 314—319), the Washington Yakima in 1894 (28 Stat 320—321), the Coeur d'Alene in 1894 (28 Stat 322—323), the Alsea and other Siletz Reservation tribes in 1894 (28 Stat 323—326), the Nez Percé of Idaho in 1894 (28 Stat 326-332), and the California Yuma in 1894 (28 Stat 332—336). On allotment and related laws, see chapters 10 and 11 below.

38. Cong. Rec., 58th Cong., II Sess., p.1421—1429 & 1469. See also National Archives, Records of the United States House of Representatives, Committee on Indian Affairs papers, 57A-F14.2, bundles 1 and 2.

39. Cong. Rec., 58th Cong., III Sess., pp. 1688, 1940—1946, 2448, 2726—2730, 3390, 3413, 3628, and 3904.

unfairly took advantage of Indians[40]. The reforming nature of most other treaty laws should not be overlooked either. In all of these kinds of laws, Congress's paternalistic belief in "linear development" is quite evident.

In addition to the government of the United States, several individuals, societies, organizations, and companies had treaty-like relations with the Indians. Fur hunters used Indians as their subsidiary producers; farmers and ranchers often rented Indian land for fields or for pasture; and mining companies made contracts for mineral rights. All these private treaties, agreements, and contracts needed regulations and rules defined by legislation. The first such rules, drawn up at the time of American Independence, were included in the early laws of trade and intercourse, and they defined the conditions and limits of licensed trade with the Indians. In 1866, every loyal citizen of the United States was allowed to trade with the Indians, under the assumption that all trade and intercourse acts and other related laws would be obeyed. Such a trader was also required to deposit a bond to be held by the district court of his trading territory, as a guarantee that he would obey all the rules and regulations of licensed trade.[41]

The 1871 Appropriation Act which ended the making of treaties with Indians also stipulated that thereafter no contract or agreement of any kind should be made with Indians unless in writing and approved by the Commissioner of Indian Affairs and the Secretary of the Interior[42], represented in practice by an Indian agent. The following May, Congress passed a special act regulating the mode of making private contracts with Indians. It also described in more detail the regulations of the 1871 act, adding to it some further refinements.[43] In 1874, a law was passed that all private contracts should be registered with the Indian Bureau, and the Secretary of Interior would make a list of all private contracts in force[44]. This law, which created a lot of paper work, was supposed to end — or at least limit — discord over private agreements, as such discord possibly

40. See Wunder, "The Enshrinement in Law of American Colonialism", op.cit., page 4, where he refers to Wilcomb Washburn, *The Indian in America* (New York: Harper & Row, 1975), pp. 97—98; Francis Paul Prucha, *The Great Father: The United States Government and the American Indians*, 2 vols. (Lincoln: University of Nebraska Press, 1984), I:527—533.
41. 14 Stat 280.
42. 16 Stat 570.
43. 17 Stat 136—137.
44. 18 Stat 35—36.

caused troubles and even wars with the Indians.

Through fear of corruption and abuse, from time to time Congress passed laws to limit the rights of Indian Bureau personnel to make private contracts with Native Americans. Commissioner of Indian Affairs Nelson Cooley was especially anxious in the mid 1860's to develop legislation in this direction[45]. His example was followed in the 1874 Appropriation Act, which prohibited Indian agents and other federal officials from taking part in any treaty or contract with the Indians, whether these treaties and contracts were made by private citizens or the government, or whether they were still under negotiation.[46] A timber trade scandal involving Commissioner Edward Parmelee Smith was partly responsible for the passing of this act[47].

An 1882 law ordered anyone who was not a full-blooded Indian but who tried to live on Indian land and trade there without a license to forfeit all his merchandise to the government, and possibly even pay a $500 fine. No one was allowed either to act as a clerk for a trader doing business with Indians, or to trade with Indians without a permit from the Commissioner of Indian Affairs. This law did not apply, however, to the territory of the Five Civilized Tribes, or to the people living on it.[48] This area was in this regard, as often also in other regards, considered more civilized and closer to white society than other Indian tribes. Therefore Congress saw no need for any special legislation for the Five Tribes, only for the other, less civilized tribes.

In the 1880's the system of licensed trade caused debate about its effects on Indian civilization. Some members of Congress believed that licensed trading hindered Indian freedom and was a threat to Indian civilization: it benefitted only certain traders[49]. Massachusetts senator Henry L. Dawes forecast in 1886 that the time when a special license was needed to trade with Indians would soon disappear; indeed, may already have done so. Dawes criticized the licensing system, because under it no individual white trader was bound to the agreement he had made with the Indians. The reason

45. Gary L. Roberts, "Dennis Nelson Cooley 1865—66," in Robert M. Kvasnicka and Herman J. Viola (ed.), *The Commissioners of Indian Affairs, 1824—1977.*, op.cit., p.102.
46. 18 Stat 177.
47. See pp.37—49 above about the BIA personnel, particularly p.44 regarding Smith.
48. 22 Stat 179—180.
49. See Cong. Rec., 49th Cong., I Sess., pp. 5244—5247.

was, that in order for it to come into force, the agreement required the approval of the Secretary of the Interior. Senator Matthew C. Butler of South Carolina thought, on the other hand, that this same loophole could also be used by the Indians.[50] But despite these and other disagreements as to its practicality, Congress neither then nor now has evolved a better system than licensed trade.

As can be seen from the above, the legislation on private treaties again included elements of paternalistic civilizing of the Indians. These laws were, at least to a certain extent, hoped to be useful in lifting Indians up to a higher stage of civilization.

50. Cong. Rec., 49th Cong., I Sess., p. 5245.

Implications of Treaty Relationships Between the United States and Various American Indian Nations

Ward Churchill

> The Treaty today is the foundation on which the Indian people now stand. . . . We are the nation. We are a nation even before the government, before we signed any treaties. We are a nation.
>
> —Leonard Crow Dog,
> 1974 Sioux Sovereignty Hearings[1]

MUCH CONTROVERSY and confusion has prevailed in recent years concerning the implications of the 371 formal treaties entered into by the U.S. government with the various American Indian nations between 1778 and 1871.[2] This essay is intended to clarify the fundamental status of treaties and treaty-making parties under U.S. (constitutional) law and, concomitantly, within conventional international understanding.

No particular attempt beyond appropriate reference will be made to follow the investigation either into the arena of international law, or through the maze of what has come to be termed "interpretation doctrine" by the practitioners of American jurisprudence. It is hoped that such a procedure will allow for the desired clarification of basic issues without leading the reader willy-nilly back into the crucible of polemic and political posturing which has accompanied most discussions of the meaning of American Indian treaty prerogatives of late.

THE CONSTITUTION

Within the domain of U.S. law, the essentials through which the meaning of treaties, treaty-making, and treaty status may be apprehended are lodged in Articles I and VI of the Constitution. The relevant language of Article I (Section 10) reads, "No State shall enter into any Treaty, Alliance, or Confederation . . ." Article VI (2) continues: "This Constitution, and the laws of the United States which shall be made in Pursuance thereof, and *all the Treaties made, or which shall be made,* under the Authority of the United States, *shall be the supreme Law of the Land*; and the Judges in every State shall be bound thereby and any Thing in the Constitution or Laws of any State to the Contrary notwithstanding" (emphasis added).

The first passage cited clearly reserves U.S. treaty-making prerogatives to the federal sector, a firm denial of sovereign status to any subordinate component of the American republic, whether that be a state, a county, a city, a village, or individual. It is generally understood that this stipulation simultaneously precluded the federal sector from entering into treaty relationships with states, counties, cities, or other such bodies. In other words, U.S. treaty making is definitionally restricted to the level of interaction between sovereign entities. Treaties are thus inherently international arrangements.

The passage from Article VI logically follows from this position. Given that treaty law is formally restricted to a level that transcends other legal strata within the United States, it assumes a status on par with that of the Constitution itself. As internal U.S. legislation must conform to the postulations of the Constitution, so too must it conform to the terms and conditions of the various treaties to which the United States is a party.

The Constitution makes no distinction between types or "orders" of treaties, whether these be entered into with entities internal or external to U.S. territoriality. To the contrary, it has been held that treaties with Indian nations are of the same dignity as treaties with foreign nations:

It is contended that a treaty with Indian tribes, has not the same dignity or effect, as a treaty with a foreign and independent nation. This distinction is not authorized by the constitution. Since the commencement of the government, treaties have been made with the Indians, and the treaty-making power has been exercised in making them. They are treaties, within the meaning of the constitution, and, as such, are the supreme laws of the land.[3]

This position has been reinforced from various quarters over the years, not least importantly by Attorney General William Wirt in 1828:

If it be meant to say that, although capable of treating, their [the Indians'] treaties are not to be construed like the treaties of nations absolutely independent, no reason is discerned for this distinction in the circumstance that their independence is of a limited character. If they are independent to the purpose of treating, they have all the independence that is necessary to the argument. The point, then, once conceded, that the Indians are independent to the purpose of treating, their independence is, *to that purpose,* as *absolute* as that of any other nation [emphasis in the original].[4]

Wirt went on to affirm that:

Nor can it be conceded that their [the Indian nations'] independence as a nation is a limited independence. Like all other independent nations, they are governed solely by their own laws. Like other independent nations, they have the absolute power of war and peace. Like all other independent nations, their territoriality is inviolable by any other sovereignty. Questions have arisen as to their title to that territory; but these discussions have resulted in this conclusion: that, whether their title be that of sovereignty in the jurisdiction or the soil, or by title of occupancy only, it is such title as no other nation has a right to interfere with, or to take from them. . . . As a nation, they are still free and independent. They are entirely self-governed—self-directed. . . . In their treaties, in all their contracts with regard to property, they are as free, sovereign and independent as any other nation.[5]

Such articulations of the status of American Indian nations (legally defined through treaty relationships) have been concretized in terms of the hierarchy and protocols of U.S. jurisprudence:

> the treaty, after [being] executed and ratified by the proper authorities of the Government, becomes the supreme law of the land, and the courts can no more go behind it for the purpose of annulling its effect and operation, than they can behind an act of Congress.[6]

The legal status of treaties within the parameters of U.S. law seems clear enough. Of course, there is nothing in the Constitution mandating the government to enter into treaty relationships, either generally or with particular entities. As regards treaty making with American Indian nations, Congress acted to formally terminate such practices in 1871. While it has been argued that this action undercut the force and validity of treaties with Indians, the legislative language used flatly refutes such contentions: "nothing herein contained shall be construed to invalidate or impair the obligation of any treaty heretofore lawfully made and ratified with any Indian tribe."[7]

Hence, while congress exercised an entirely legitimate option in declining to pursue further treaty relationships with American Indians, it also opted not to enter into areas of potential illegitimacy by unilaterally voiding the standing treaties upon which much of the legal title to U.S. territoriality was and is contingent. This is borne out in an attorney general's opinion of the period: "Congress has never abrogated treaties promiscuously by legislation, those with the Indians, Chinese, and the French treaty of 1778, being the chief ones in point."[8]

In large part, the consistency of the various positions taken by the U.S. government vis à vis American Indian nations seems due to a firm understanding of the inherent *inter*national stature (i.e., sovereign status) of the latter. As Felix S. Cohen has observed, "That treaties with Indian tribes are of the same dignity as treaties with foreign nations is a view which has been repeatedly confirmed by the federal courts and never successfully challenged." Cohen goes on to note as corroboration that, "Until the last decade of the treaty-making period, terms familiar to modern international diplomacy were used in the Indian treaties. . . .

Many provisions show the international status of Indian tribes, through clauses relating to war, boundaries, passports, extradition and foreign relations."[9]

As has been previously demonstrated, he might well have also noted that, in dealing with Indian treaties and Indian nations in such fashion, the government was simply fulfilling the most basic constitutional requirements of entering into treaty relationships. Having chosen, for whatever reason(s), to enter into an array of treaty agreements with Indian peoples, the government held—and holds—no *legal* alternative but to view these peoples as sovereign nations, fully entitled to treatment in accordance with the strictures of international law, custom, and convention.

Sovereignty, the concept that legally undergirds virtually the entirety of United States–Indian relations (in both historical and contemporary terms), is itself a much used and usually misunderstood word. In order to further clarify the significance of the existence of treaty relationships between the United States and various American Indian nations, it is thus essential to examine the meaning of this term.

Sovereignty

According to the well-noted American Indian legal scholar, Vine Deloria, Jr., sovereignty is an ancient concept. Originally theological in its implications, it was politically appropriated during the period of the emergence of the "divine right of kings" doctrine. During the period of the conceptual formation of what was to be the American Revolution and resultant United States, the notion had become rather more politically concretized. To quote Deloria: "In the technical language of the seventeenth and eighteenth centuries, sovereignty was the absolute power of a nation to determine its own course of action with respect to other nations."[10]

This then was the basis of the thinking of the signers of the Constitution in their establishment of purely international criteria by which the U.S. government was empowered to enter into treaty relationships. The specificity of such a position in relation to the Constitution is brought out compellingly in Deloria's further observation that: "The American Revolution revived the idea of Indian sovereignty. While reciting polite phrases about the equality of man, the American revolutionaries were plainly outside the law of civilized societies in their revolt, and to gain respectability they adopted the most acceptable posture toward the Indians possible with the hope that by demonstrating their ability to act in traditional political terms they could allay the fears of other nations so as to legitimate their activities."[11]

Deloria's perspective concerning the intentions of the participants at the constitutional convention relative to the sovereignty implications of treaty making in general, and treating making with American Indians in particular, receives strong validation through various positions assumed by Chief Justice of the U.S. Supreme Court John Marshall. For example, in *Worcester v. Georgia*, Marshall held that: "It is difficult to comprehend the proposition that the inhabitants of either quarter of the globe could have rightful original claims of dominion over the inhabitants of the other, or the lands they occupied; or that discovery of either by the other should give the discoverer rights in the country discovered, which annulled the pre-existing rights of its ancient possessors."[12] In effect, this statement posits an unconditional sovereignty in behalf of American Indian nations, and accordingly implies that the *only* rights held by non-Indians to North America (and South America, for that matter) accrue through exercise of international agreements such as treaties—that is by legal arrangement(s) between the United States and appropriate native sovereign(s). Although it is not explicitly stated, it is a further implication of this passage that any ongoing legitimacy of the assertion of U.S. rights within North America is contingent upon the continued honoring (by the United States) of obligations incurred under the terms and conditions of the various treaties by which American Indian nations ceded land and otherwise allowed the United States to exercise (limited) dominion in this hemisphere.

This perhaps seems a bit much to attribute to a single quotation, regardless of its fundamental clarity. Marshall, however, articulated variations on the same theme in other contexts, thereby removing all reasonable doubt as to the link between American Indian sovereignty and legal status under U.S. law. For instance, in *Johnson v. McIntosh*, he wrote: "They [the Indians] were admitted to be the rightful occupants of the soil, with a legal as well as a just claim to retain possession of it, and to use it according to their own discretion; but their rights to complete sovereignty, and their power to dispose of the soil at their own will, to whomsoever they pleased, was denied by the original fundamental principle that discovery gave exclusive title to those who made it."[13] Here we find Marshall clearly enunciating the governing condition of U.S. treaty making with the Indian nations: sovereignty of the sort defined by Deloria, and consciously acknowledged by the treaty makers as residing within Indian peoples. Simultaneously, he points clearly to another doctrine, that of "title of discovery," which he had already denounced (in note 13, above) as both incomprehensible and as being contradictory to the spirit and intent of the U.S. Constitution and its subordinate body of law.

In other words, in Marshall's Supreme Court view, Indian sovereignty was established in *fact* prior to the formation of U.S. law. The constitution and other U.S. legalisms were therefore designed and intended to accurately reflect this reality. Elsewhere, Marshall was at pains to counter other doctrines which he perceived as being employed to contradict U.S. legality and negate the sovereign status of Indian nations. Returning to *Worcester v. Georgia*, we find him addressing the principle of "might makes right," as incorporated in the doctrine of "the rights of conquest:"

> The Indian nations had always been considered as distinct, independent, political communities, retaining their original natural rights . . . with the single exception of that imposed by irresistible power, which exclude them from intercourse with any other European potentate than the first discoverer of the coast of the particular region claimed; and this was a restriction which those European potentates imposed on themselves, as well as on the Indian. . . . the settled doctrine of the law of nations is, that a weaker nation does not

> surrender its independence—its right to self-government—by associating with a stronger, and taking its protection. A weak state, in order to provide for its safety, may place itself under the protection of one more powerful, without stripping itself of the right of government and ceasing to be a state.[14]

In contemporary terms, Marshall's contention in this regard is, of course, readily borne out through the continuing and viable sovereign existence of nations such as Luxembourg, Monaco, Lichtenstein, the various entities within Micronesia, Sri Lanka, El Salvador, and so forth. Many nations today may claim a considerably less substantial land/resource base than can some American Indian nations (consider, for example, a comparison between the recognized holdings of the Navajo nation on the one hand, and Luxembourg on the other). Again, in terms of population size, American Indian nations such as the Lakota and Navajo equal or outstrip several recognized nations in the Pacific region.

Even when such factors as landbase do not prevail, Marshall's estimate of inherent Indian sovereignty has a firm grounding in constitutional formulation. Consider, as but one example, Justice (of the Supreme Court) McLean's conclusion in *Cherokee v. Georgia*: "Their [the Indians'] condition is something like that of the Israelites, when inhabiting the deserts. Though without land they can call theirs in the sense of property, their right to personal self-government may exist though the land be occupied by another. . . . And such they do possess; it has never been questioned."[15]

McLean, in other words, insisted that sovereignty was a condition inherent to American Indian nations, other factors or conditions notwithstanding. And indeed he might well so argue. Such a condition was/is an absolute necessity for the government he represented to have entered into a legal (under the Constitution) treaty relationship with Indians in the first place. His logic was simple: either the Indian had to be sovereign or the U.S. government had conducted its affairs in treaty making on an utterly illegitimate basis from the founding fathers onward—and would continue to do so for fully a half-century after McLean's conclusion was drawn.

Sovereignty—the fully self-determining right of nations—as demanded by the U.S. Constitution of any entity with which the United States treats, is overwhelmingly acknowledged as held by American Indian nations through a proliferation of treaties entered into by the federal executive and duly ratified by Congress. Accordingly, this sovereignty has been articulated with both clarity and firmness within the seminal writings of the U.S. judiciary.

In essence, American Indian nations are entitled to the same self-determining prerogatives as are Belgium, Algeria, and China. Contradictions of this self-determining status by any power are both illegal within the parameters of U.S. law, and open for consideration within the arena of international law. Such a situation carries with it certain implications relative to U.S. practice, both historically and in the most topical sense, vis-à-vis American Indians. It is to a summary of these implications which we turn in the following, final section.

Implications

Given the special status accorded American Indian nations within the strictures of U.S. jurisprudence, a status corresponding to a concrete recognition of the inherent sovereignty of these nations, certain implications emerge which bear serious reexamination within the context of contemporary U.S. law and policy. Although such considerations are hardly confined to the list which follows, the matters listed number among the more salient.

1. *Territoriality*

It seems most fundamental that the various territories reserved by a host of American Indian peoples unto themselves by treaty during the process of ceding other territory to the United States continue to constitute separate and distinct *nations* within the contemporary U.S. geographical corpus. The territoriality of American Indian nations is thus entitled to the same integrity as that of Canada or Mexico, including the right to freedom from physical incursion by the United States or any other foreign country. Similarly, lands reserved unto the various American Indian nations by treaty stipulation, but which are currently occupied by the United States in contravention of such treaty stipulations, cannot be said to be legally possessed by the United States; such land is clearly Indian land in the sense of American Indian national territoriality. In effect, the U.S. presence is tantamount to formal invasion in such instance (the Lakota territory guaranteed under provisions of the Fort Laramie Treaty of 1868 is a prime example of this phenomenon).[16]

Mechanisms currently prevailing under U.S. law (or which, like the Indian Claims Commission, have prevailed heretofore) which serve to "legally" preclude return of contested lands that can be demonstrated to have been illegally acquired by the United States would seem, at best, to hold minimal constitutional integrity.

2. *Governance*

It is axiomatic that any sovereign and self-determining nation has the right to decide and maintain its own means of self-governance. The imposition, by the United States, of "acceptable" governmental forms upon American Indian nations through the expedient of the Indian Reorganization Act of 1934 would seem, at best, to be of dubious constitutionality. At worst, such practice smacks of very pronounced colonial methods employed by the French in Indochina, Algeria and elsewhere.

3. *Jurisdiction*

Again, any sovereign and self-determining nation is both entitled to and responsible for the enactment and enforcement of its own judicial structure. Jurisdiction was accordingly reserved by most American Indian nations unto themselves under the articles of their various treaties with the United States. The U.S. extension of its own jurisdiction over American Indian nations through such legislation as the "Seven Major Crimes Act" (1885) and the Act of March 4, 1909, therefore seem as extraconstitutional as points (1) and (2) above.[17]

As Vine Deloria, Jr., has observed, it seems likely that the United States holds no more legal basis for jurisdiction over the various American Indian nations internal to its geography than it does over Sweden or Sudan.[18]

4. *Citizenship*

Sovereign nations, it is generally understood, inherently possess the right to determine the nature and definition of the characteristics of citizenship within themselves. Hence, methods of "identifying" American Indians (such as the so-called system of blood quantum) imposed by the United States—even when these methods are sanctioned by tribal governments established under provisions of the Indian Reorganization Act—fly in the face of constitutionality and international convention or practice. Perhaps even more extreme is the Indian Citizenship Act of 1924 wherein the United States unilaterally imposed its own citizenship upon the citizens of the various American Indian nations located within the geographical corpus of the forty-eight contiguous states (and later, Alaska and Hawaii).

Definitional considerations concerning citizenship within American Indian nations, including questions centering upon naturalization (i.e., non-racially specific citizenship criteria), must be articulated by these nations themselves—without external interference—in order to conform to constitutional expectations of sovereignty, as well as those lodged within the international arena.

Finally, to the extent that American Indian nations might opt to retain aspects of "dual citizenship" (i.e., citizenship within an Indian nation *and* the United States), it must be understood that they occupy a special status as "federal citizens of the United States" unencumbered by the specificity of interstate regulation and boundaries affecting the U.S. citizenry at large.

The United States of course possess the power and sheer weight of numbers to elect to utterly disregard such implications of American Indian treaties as are elaborated within this brief essay. It is starkly evident that the Indian nations, either individually or collectively, are in no position to challenge the United States in a military sense, even as an expedient to protect their most basic rights to sovereignty and self-determination. The question then is whether the United States is prepared to make good on its solemn promises to Indian people, promises extended in writing and "in utmost good faith." Such would be the only honorable—indeed, the only *legal* course of action.

To do otherwise is to act dishonorably in the extreme, to engage in an intentional process of wanton internal and international illegality. Such a posture on the part of the United States opens an entire Pandora's box of implications in its own right. As I have observed elsewhere in this connection:

> Of course, the United States has not been alone in this behavior. Other nations have been guilty of using treaties and agreements with this sort of cynicism, as devices through which to gain tactical advantages in wars of territorial expansion. They too have been wont to define their adversaries in terms of genetic codes rather than nationalities, of imposing strange and wonderful systems of legalism, of establishing forms of governance conducive to their own interests within the occupied areas.
>
> France, England, Spain, Holland, Italy, Japan and the Soviet Union number among those guilty of such practices in modern times. But none perhaps so nearly coincides with the U.S. model as does the Third Reich of Germany. The *Anschluss* is surely a correlative example. So too, the Munich travesty, the tentative "understanding" with Poland, and the "Mutual Non-Aggression Pact" with the USSR. The "eugenic" codes by which the Nazis defined Jewish, Slavic and other groups must surely correlate to U.S. quantum policies. The Nuremburg "Laws" and other pseudo-legal doctrines by which ethnic group expropriation was duly sanctified bear more than passing conceptual resemblance to the convoluted logic through which the U.S. has expropriated Indian lands. The establishment of a series of "Quisling" governments to administer occupied Europe corresponds to the U.S. reliance upon the regimes, such as those of Dick Wilson (Pine Ridge) and Peter McDonald (Navajo) in principal, if not in particulars.[19]

Practical and conceptual linkage to Nazi theory and practice should be the last thing desired by the "land of the free and the home of the brave," the nation which was so instrumental in formulating, establishing, and executing the Nuremburg Doctrine through which both the Nazi leadership and the Nazi state were tried, convicted, and liquidated for "crimes against humanity" and "crimes against the peace."

The matter cannot, however, be had both ways. Either the United States follows through on its multitudinous commitments to Indian people—with *all* that this implies—or it must inevitably find itself in conformity to the essential Nazi posture. There is obviously a choice to be made in the matter. It is not a choice for Indian people or Indian nations to make. Rather, it is a choice imposed by historical necessity upon the United States of America. And, as the Lakota elder and spiritual leader Henry Crow Dog has stated, "The clock is marked twelve."[20]

NOTES

1. The statement by the Brulé Lakota spiritual leader was entered into the hearing transcript, as recorded in Roxanne Dunbar Ortiz, *The Great Sioux Nation. Sitting in Judgment on America* (New York and San Francisco: International Indian Treaty Council/Moon Books, 1977), p. 41.

2. For the complete text of the treaties, as well as the text of formal agreements entered into through 1883, see Charles J. Kappler, *Indian Treaties, 1778–1883* (New York: Interland Publishing Co., 1973).

3. See *Turner v. American Baptist Missionary Union*, 24 Fed. Cas. No. 14251 (C.C. Mich. 1852). For supporting arguments, see *Holden v. Joy*, 17 Wall. 211, 242–43 (1872), and *Worcester v. Georgia*, 6 Pet. 515, 559 (1832).

4. 2 Op. A.G. 110 (1828).

5. Ibid.

6. See *Fellowes v. Blacksmith*, 60 U.S. 366, 372 (1856). Also see *United States v. Forty-three Gallons of Whiskey*, 93 U.S. 188 (1876), to wit: "the Constitution declares a treaty to be the supreme law of the land; and Chief Justice Marshall, in *Foster and Elam v. Neilson*, 2 Pet. 314, has said, 'That a treaty is to be regarded, in courts of justice, as equivalent to an act of the legislature.'"

7. See *House Indian Appropriations Act, Fiscal Year 1872* (16 Stat. L.,

566; approved March 3, 1871). The appropriations act rider which ushered in the termination of U.S. treaty making with American Indian nations was presaged by section 6 of the Act of March 29, 1867 (15 Stat. 7, 9), which read: "And all laws allowing the President, the Secretary of Interior, or the commissioner of Indian affairs to enter into treaties with any Indian tribes are hereby repealed, and no expense shall hereafter be incurred in negotiating a treaty with any Indian tribe until an appropriation authorizing such expense shall be first made by law." The provision did not pass in the Senate. See also the Act of April 10, 1869, sec. 5, 16 Stat. 13, 40. Also, both the first annual report of the Board of Indian Commissioners (December 1869) and the 1869 report of the Commissioner of Indian Affairs recommended the abolition of the continuation of opening new treaty relationships with the Indian nations.

8. 13 Op. A.G 354 (1870).

9. Felix S. Cohen, *Handbook of Federal Indian Law* (Albuquerque: University of New Mexico Press, n.d.), pp. 31–34, 39. Cohen notes that his observation is based upon conclusions drawn by the judiciary in *Holden v. Joy*, op. cit., *Worcester v. Georgia*, op. cit., and *Turner v. American Baptist Missionary Union*, op. cit.

10. Vine Deloria, Jr., "Self-Determination and the Concept of Sovereignty," in *Economic Development in American Indian Reservations*, ed. Roxanne Dunbar Ortiz and Larry Emerson, p. 22 (Albuquerque: University of New Mexico American Indian Studies Center, 1979).

11. Ibid., pp. 22–23.

12. *Worcester v. Georgia*, op. cit., p. 515.

13. *Jones and Graham's Lessee v. McIntosh*, Wheat Reports, vol. 8 (1832), p. 523.

14. *Worcester v. Georgia*, op. cit., p. 517.

15. *Cherokee Nation v. Georgia*, 5 Pet. 1 (1831), p. 1.

16. See Nick Meinhardt and Diane Payne, *Reviewing U.S. Treaty Commitments to the Lakota Nation* (Rapid City, S.D.: Pine Ridge Education/Action Project, 1979). This is a revision of an earlier essay published by the authors under the same title which appeared in *American Indian Journal* (Washington, D.C.: Institute for the Development of American Indian law, 1978).

17. The first statute (23 Stat. 362, 385, 18 U.S.C. 548) designated the crimes of murder, manslaughter, rape, assault with intent to kill, arson, burglary, and larceny as being within U.S. jurisdiction even when occurring within American Indian nations. The second (sec. 328, 35

Stat. 1088, 1151) added robbery, incest, and assault with a deadly weapon. In the latter connection, also see the *Act of June 28, 1932* (47 Stat. 336, 337).

18. Vine Deloria, Jr., "The United States Has No Jurisdiction in Sioux Land," in Ortiz, *The Great Sioux Nation,* pp. 141–46.

19. Ward Churchill, "The 'Trial' of Leonard Peltier," in Jim Messerschmidt, *The Trial of Leonard Peltier* (Boston: South End Press, 1983), p. x.

20. Henry Crow Dog, "The Clock Is Marked Twelve," in Ortiz, *The Great Sioux Nation,* pp. 188–91.

THE U.S. SUPREME COURT'S EXPLICATION OF "FEDERAL PLENARY POWER:"
AN ANALYSIS OF CASE LAW AFFECTING TRIBAL SOVEREIGNTY, 1886-1914

BY DAVID E. WILKINS

The 200-year-old political relationship between American Indian tribes and the United States remains both problematic and paradoxical because of the conjuncture of geographical, historical, political, and constitutional issues and circumstances that influence tribal-federal affairs. A central feature of this dynamic dialogue is the incongruous relationship between the United States Congress's exercise of plenary power and the tribes' efforts to exercise their sovereign political rights. This essay traces the historical, legal, and political origins and transformation of this pivotal concept from 1886 to 1914, an important period in its development. Analysis of 107 federal court cases and of the plenary power concept reveals that congressional plenary power has several distinctive definitions. Depending on which definition is used by the court and whether the term is based on constitutional or extra-constitutional doctrine, determines whether the court's decision will adversely or positively affect tribal sovereignty, political rights, and resources.

One of the perennial puzzles in intergovernmental relations and constitutional law is the following question: What is the relationship between American Indian tribal governments, that exercise certain sovereign rights, and the United States government which presumes a plenary power with regard to tribes? Despite the federal government's presumption[1] of vast authority over tribes,[2] plenary power remains a problematic concept, particularly when paired with the doctrine of tribal sovereignty.

There is also considerable disagreement among scholars on whether plenary power is a necessary congressional power which protects tribes, or whether it is an abhorrent and undemocratic concept because it entails the congressional exercise of wide political authority over tribes. While the principal focus of this essay is to detail the history and evolution of plenary power as defined by the Supreme Court during a critical historical era, it is important first to provide some discussion of an equally pivotal concept: tribal sovereignty.

There is a startling array of interpretations of tribal sovereignty. For years the classic reference has been that of Felix Cohen who asserted that "from the earliest years of the Republic the Indian tribes have been recognized as 'distinct, independent, political communities,' and as such, qualified to exercise powers of self-government, not by virtue of any delegation of powers

DAVID E. WILKINS IS AN ASSISTANT PROFESSOR IN THE DEPARTMENT OF POLITICAL SCIENCE AND THE AMERICAN INDIAN STUDIES PROGRAM AT THE UNIVERSITY OF ARIZONA IN TUCSON.

from the Federal government but rather by reason of their original tribal sovereignty" (1972 ed.:122). John Marshall, in the pivotal case *Worcester v. Georgia*, 21 U.S. (6 Pet.) 515, defined tribal sovereignty as a function of collective political rights. He described tribes as "distinct peoples, divided into separate nations, independent of each other, and of the rest of the world, having institutions of their own, and governing themselves by their own laws" (pp. 542-543).

For Vine Deloria Jr. (1979), on the other hand, sovereignty has less to do with self-government and political rights and more to do with "continuing cultural and communal integrity." "Sovereignty," Deloria said, "in the final instance, can be said to consist more of continued cultural integrity than of political powers and to the degree that a nation loses its sense of cultural identity, to that degree it suffers a loss of sovereignty" (pp. 26-27).

For the purpose of this essay, we define tribal sovereignty as an understanding that every tribal person has the right and the responsibility to be an actor, not merely an object, in decisions affecting his or her community. It is the political will of the people that ensures the vitality of sovereignty.

The usage of plenary power to describe the Congress's political relations with North American tribes distinguishes America's indigenous groups as the nation's original peoples. On the other hand, the fact of its persistence entails an exceptional political status for tribal nations that find their pre-constitutional sovereign political and legal status can be radically reaffirmed or unilaterally altered, even quashed, at any time by congressional laws, judicial opinions, or administrative actions of the Bureau of Indian Affairs.

The vacillations in the way the term plenary has been defined and the manner in which it has been institutionalized indicates a critical difference between the political status of American states and tribes with respect to their relationship to the federal government. The Supreme Court has held that while "the sovereignty of the States is limited by the Constitution itself," *Garcia v. San Antonio Metro. Transit Authority*, 469 U.S. 528, 548 (1984), states do enjoy legal and constitutional protections against arbitrary federal action because of the doctrine of enumerated powers. In other words, while Congress can exercise significant power over the states, it is doubtful that it could legislate a state out of existence. Regarding tribes, however, the Congress has acted to "legislate tribes [and bands and rancherias] out of existence" (Rotenberg, 1987:92), through the termination[3] policy initiated in 1953 and continuing into the 1960s.

However, a little-known dimension which further complicates tribal-federal intergovernmental relations involves the fact that both before and even during the period 1886 to 1914 when congressional plenary power (defined as unlimited-absolute) was exercised in its most virulent and unabashed form, there were numerous occasions where Congress and the executive branch could not or would not employ the plenary power doctrine to force tribes to comply with a particular treaty, agreement, or federal statute. Frequently, tribal leaders and their constituencies simply voted down pending bilateral agreements or laws perceived as potentially injurious or unfair.[4] These laws, treaties, or agreements would then be returned to Washington for revision or tabled indefinitely if Washington could not secure tribal consent.[5]

This prompts an important question. If the Congress did indeed have unfettered plenary power over the tribes–and the Supreme Court in a 1903 decision, *Lone Wolf v. Hitchcock*, 185 U.S. 553, went so far as to say that Congress had always had this power–why did it not simply use it all the time? "Why," as Deloria asked (1989), "all the hoopla over treaties and agreements? Why, at that very moment, were a number of treaty and agreement commissions in the field on several reservations asking the tribes to make treaties and agreements with the United States?" (pp. 221-222).

In this essay we explore the following questions: What does "plenary power" mean? What conjuncture of events accounts for its eruption in the area of Indian law and policy in the 1880s? What factors led the Supreme Court to suggest a modicum of moral constraint on the Congress's exercise of power in 1914, without foreclosing the possibility that Congress could still wield unfettered political authority over tribes so long as the action is not "arbitrary" and is founded on some "reasonable basis"? Finally, how and why does the concept plenary power continue to be a viable political doctrine in a democratic country founded on the principles of limited government?

SCHOLARLY VIEWS AND EXPECTATIONS

Research on plenary power has increased considerably since the 1970s. These were the halcyon days of tribal self-determination and Indian political activism, when Vine Deloria Jr. in a number of publications (1969, 1970, 1974, 1977) urged tribal people and the scholarly community to systematically investigate the linchpin legal and political doctrines that undergirded the tribal-federal relationship.

One of the first scholars to focus some attention on the relationship between federal plenary power and tribal sovereignty was Robert Coulter. He wrote two articles in the late 1970s (1977, 1978) that briefly examined how plenary power had worked to seriously disadvantage tribes in fundamental legal ways. Coulter admitted, however, that "the origins of the plenary power doctrine and the legal foundations were unclear" (1977:8).

In the 1980s two important legal studies sought to bring clarity to the subject. They focused on the origins and the factors involved in the perpetuation of the plenary power concept. These articles, the first a note titled "Federal Plenary Power in Indian Affairs after *Weeks* and *Sioux Nation*" (1982) and the second, an excellent piece by Nell Jessup Newton called "Federal Power over Indians: Its Sources, Scope, and Limitations," (1984), went far toward explaining the legal history of the concept.

Other researchers also employed the term (Barsh and Henderson, 1980; Ball, 1987; Wilkinson, 1987; Kronowitz et al., 1987; Laurence, 1988;

Townsend, 1989; Williams Jr., 1990; Shattuck and Norgren, 1991; and Hauptman, 1992). Most of these commentators, excepting Shattuck and Norgren (political scientists) and Hauptman (historian), and those previously cited, are legal scholars. While law is certainly a fundamental discipline, political scientists–who should be concerned about a subject that encompasses institutional autonomy and interaction, constitutional allocations of authority, legitimate use of power, and federalism–have paid negligible attention to this concept and its relation to tribal sovereignty.[6]

Moreover, there has been no systematic or long-term examination of empirical data on the Supreme Court's activities during the critical era[7] in which the plenary power doctrine as applied to tribes by the Supreme Court first appeared, was then expanded to unparalleled proportions, and was finally dampened in the 1914 *Perrin* case.

This three decade period comprised the federal government's most intensive effort to assimilate American Indians. The General Allotment policy, inaugurated in 1887 (24 St. 388), whereby the Congress sought to turn American Indians into Christianized private property landowners, was the central weapon in the federal government's assimilative arsenal. There was a multi-pronged effort to detribalize indigenous peoples. The principal components in the federal government's assimilation policy[8] were:

> Land loss via surplus land sales, specific allotment acts, amendments to the allotment policy, and fraudulent activities by land speculators and some state officials;
>
> Sponsorship of efforts to Christianize tribal members;
>
> Imposition of federal criminal jurisdiction over certain crimes in Indian Country (35 St. 1088);
>
> Eradication of Indian culture as a federal goal. This was facilitated by the establishment of Courts of Indian Offense.

Most commentators agree that the plenary power era for Indian tribes and their relations to the federal government was inaugurated with the Supreme Court's decision in *U.S. v. Kagama*, 118 U.S. 375 (1886), though the term was used in previous cases outside Indian law.

Although the term "plenary" is absent from *Kagama*, other language evidences the court's support of Congress's efforts to diminish tribal sovereignty by affirming the constitutionality of the Major Crimes Act (23 St. 362, 385). The court exercised what Deloria has termed plenary interpretive power to rationalize Congress's "exercise of plenary legislative power" (1988: 261). Unable to locate a constitutional basis for its decision, the court crafted an ingenious and bizarre two-pronged explanation: Indian helplessness and land ownership. First, Justice Miller transmuted John Marshall's analogy of Indians as "wards" to their federal "guardians," (see *Cherokee Nation v. Georgia*, 30 U.S. (5 Pet.) 1, 1831), to a principle of law. Miller said: "These Indian tribes are wards of the nation. They are communities dependent on the United States" (pp. 383-84).

The court said that federal power over these "weak" peoples was "necessary to their protection, as well as to the safety of those among whom they dwell." This power, the court held, "must exist in that [United States] government, because it never has existed anywhere else." (p. 384). However, scholars have pointed out several untenable errors in the court's analysis.

First, how could Congress apply its laws to tribes that until that time had not been subject under the Constitution to congressional jurisdiction? (Rotenberg, 1987:87).

Second, if the Constitution limits the authority of the various branches to enumerated powers, why did the court cite extra-constitutional or extra-legal[9] reasons for holding a congressional statute to be constitutional? (Deloria, 1988:261).

Finally, "consent of the governed" is a treasured democratic principle. The fact that most Indians were excluded from the American political arena because they had an extra-constitutional status[10] and treaty-defined rights and were not U.S. citizens seemed irrelevant to the court (Newton, 1984: 215).

Coincidentally or not, the same day as *Kagama*, the court unanimously held in *Santa Clara v. Southern Pacific Railroad*, 118 U.S. 394 (1886) that the Fourteenth Amendment's due process clause protected corporations as "legal persons" (p. 396). In effect, one could argue that corporate property rights were extended constitutional protection, while tribal political and property rights could be quashed.

In 1914 the Supreme Court in *Perrin v. United States*, 232 U.S. 478, suggested that congressional authority was limited: "As the power is incident only to the presence of the Indians and their status as wards of the Government, it must be conceded that it does not go beyond what is reasonably essential for their protection, and that, to be effective, its exercise must not be purely arbitrary but founded upon some reasonable basis" (p. 486).

The *Perrin* court, however, remained extremely deferential[11] to Congress. In fact, Justice Van DeVanter conceded that Congress, because of its exclusive status as the branch denominated to deal with tribes, be "invested with a wide discretion, and its action, unless purely arbitrary, must be accepted and given full effect by the Court" (p. 486).

Without stating it, the *Perrin* court had invoked a different definition of "plenary power" than the one developed in *Kagama* and *Lone Wolf*. Here the court was referencing Congress's "exclusive" power to "preempt" state law and authority.

Perrin arose during a time of flux in federal Indian policy, some of which was beginning to favor a degree of tribal self-governance. It was an era of federal administrative incompetence and Bureau of Indian Affairs corruption; an era in which a growing number of federal policymakers accepted that tribal cultures could not be physically or intellectually eradicated and that the country would be better off if it preserved some aspects of indigenous cultures.

It was also an era in which some efforts were made at political reform. In fact, several bills were introduced between 1912 and 1916 that were designed to allow reservation Indians the right to nominate and even to recall the Indian agents (Deloria & Lytle, 1984: 30-36). Most importantly, the first two decades of the twentieth century represented a period in which federal Indian legislation focused less on protecting Indians from whites and more on "providing a form of trust for Indian property. Indians became an attachment to their lands rather than owners, and although the avowed policy was that of assimilation, the change in emphasis within the executive branch of the federal government meant that the vested interest of the Interior Department would always work to thwart whatever initiatives Congress might take in resolving the Indian problem" (Deloria, 1985:248).

Hence, while *Perrin* represented a victory of sorts for tribes in that the court urged the Congress not to act "arbitrarily" when dealing with Indians, administrative agencies like the Bureau of Indian Affairs remained largely unaccountable to Congress and especially to tribes. More importantly, Congress's power was not constrained in any fundamental way.

PLENARY POWER DEFINED

First cited by the Supreme Court in the seminal case, *Gibbons v. Ogden* (22 U.S. (9 Wheat.) 1, 197 (1824), plenary power often has been used in cases dealing with the extent of federal powers. It is a confusing concept "because it conceals several issues which, for purposes of constitutional analysis, must be kept clear and distinct" (Engdahl, 1976:363). Engdahl incorrectly posits, however, that "no federal power is plenary in the full sense of the term, because as to all of them at least the prohibition of the Bill of Rights apply" (Ibid.). The Bill of Rights, however, is somewhat problematic as applied to tribes because tribal governments were not created pursuant to the Constitution. While the Indian Civil Rights Act (82 St. 77-80) of 1968 applied portions of the Bill of Rights to tribal governments in regards to their activities over reservation residents, the Bill of Rights still does not protect tribes or their members from congressional actions aimed at reducing tribal sovereignty, political rights, or aboriginal Indian lands.

In addition, the concept of plenary "merge[s] several analytically distinct questions" (Engdahl, 1976: 363). This is the crux of the scholarly and public confusion about the term. First, and most important for our purposes, there is plenary meaning *exclusive*. This is the definition Congress uses most frequently in enacting Indian-specific legislation, such as the Indian Reorganization Act (48 St. 985), or when it enacts Indian preference laws that withstand reverse discrimination suits (*Morton v. Mancari*, 417 U.S. 535 (1974). This is an exclusively legislative power Congress may exercise in keeping with its policy of treating with tribes in a distinctively political manner or to provide a recognition of rights (i.e., American Indian Religious Freedom Resolution, 92 St. 469) that Indians have been deprived of because of their extra-constitutional standing. As Deloria astutely observes:

> There may indeed be some kind of establishment of religious freedom for American Indians. If so, it is because Congress has dealt with the question of the practice of Indian religions and felt it to be necessary to extend the protection of federal laws further in the case of Indians than the Constitution allows it to extend to ordinary citizens. In this instance Indians are not to be regarded as "supercitizens"; rather, the practice of Indian religion is to be regarded as under the special protection of the federal government in the same way that Indian water rights, land titles, and self-government are protected. Congress has always dealt with Indians in a special manner; that is why Congress and the federal courts cherish and nourish the doctrine of plenary powers in the field of Indian affairs" (1985: 247).

Plenary also is an exercise of federal power which may *preempt* state law. Again, Congress's commerce power is an example, as is the treaty-making process, which precludes state involvement. Constitutional disclaimers that a majority of western states had to include in their organic documents before they were admitted into statehood are also evidence of federal preemption. Typically, these disclaimers consisted of provisions in which the state declared that it would never attempt to tax Indian lands or property without both tribal and federal consent.[12]

Finally, there is plenary meaning *unlimited* or *absolute* (Newton, 1984: 196, note 3). This third definition includes two subcategories: a) power which is not limited by other textual constitutional provisions; and b) power which is unlimited regarding congressional objectives (Ibid.). There is ample evidence in Indian law and policy of plenary power being applied by the legislative branches and the federal courts to tribes and individual Indians in all three ways.[13]

When Congress is exercising plenary power as the voice of the federal government in its relations with tribes, and is acting with the consent of the tribal people involved, it is exercising legitimate authority. When Congress is acting in a plenary way to preempt state intrusion into Indian Country, absent tribal consent, it is properly exercising an enumerated constitutional power.

However, when Congress is informed by the federal courts that it has "full, entire, complete, absolute, perfect, and unqualified" (*Mashunkashey v. Mashunkashey*, 134 P.2d 976 (1943) authority over tribes and individual Indians, something is fundamentally wrong. Canfield, writing in 1881, long before individual Indians were enfranchised, observed that congressional power over tribes was absolute because tribes were distinct and independent, if "inferior" peoples, "strangers to our law, our customs, and our privileges." He went on to say that "[t]o suppose that the framers of the Constitution intended to secure to the Indians the rights and privileges which they valued

Table 1 Plenary Power Spectrum
Radical
Negative, Unlimited Devastating to Tribal Sovereignity
Anonymous, Comment, 1982
Ball, Milner, 1987
Barsh & Henderson, 1980
Cohen, Felix S., 1948, et al.
Coulter, Robert, 1977
Deloria, Vine, Jr., 1977, et al.
Kennan, George, 1902
Kreiger, Heinreich, 1933
Kronowitz, Rachel, 1987
O'Brien, Sharon, 1980
Rottenberg, Daniel, 1987
Shattuck & Norgren, 1979
Townsend, Mike, 1989
Williams, Robert, 1983, et al.
Mixed
Unlimited, Exclusive Hurts/Helps Tribal Sovereignty
Cohen, Felix S., 1942
Deloria, Vine, Jr., 1985
Newton, Nell J., 1984
Pound, Cuthbert, 1922
Orthodox
Positive, Limited, Exclusive Protects Tribal Sovereignty
Cohen, Felix S., 1940
Collins, Richard, 1989
Deloria, Vine, Jr., 1985
Laurence, Robert, 1988
Wilkinson, Charles, 1987

as Englishmen is to misconceive the spirit of their age." (pp. 26-27). But by the time *Mashunkashey* was decided, in 1942, all Indians had been enfranchised and yet they were informed by the court that absolute power was a reality confronting them.

Table 1 is a depiction of what we term the "plenary power spectrum." Two authors under the orthodox heading (Collins and Laurence) assert, without citing strong evidence, that federal plenary power "has never been construed as absolute, in the sense of beyond constitutional limits" (Collins, 1989:368, note 24).

Deloria, Cohen, and Wilkinson are also listed under this category because they, in some of their writings, have utilized the "exclusive" or "preemptive" definition of plenary to argue particular points. In addition, we have shown that there is ample case law confirming the view that federal plenary power has indeed been defined as absolute, and is beyond the usual constitutional limits precisely because tribes are extra-constitutional entities.

However, the largest group of authors, listed under the radical category, argue more persuasively that as regards tribal sovereignty, treaty interpretation, and Indian property rights, federal power in relation to tribes and individual Indians has often been exercised in an "unlimited" manner. See Table 2 for a description of these cases.

A much smaller group of commentators listed under the heading "mixed" argue, however, that plenary power is a necessary congressional power "precisely because they [Indians] are outside the protection of the Constitution." (Deloria & Lytle, 1984:233; Deloria, 1985:240).

Data and Findings

This essay separates the concept of plenary power into three categories. First, we inquired whether the concept was contained in the court case, a yes or no question. In some cases where the concept plenary was not mentioned, it was evident by the court's use of words such as "unlimited," "absolute," or "no restrictions," that plenary power was still being exercised (i.e., *Kagama* and *Lone Wolf*). This required the addition of a third component "implicit."

Most Indian law scholars and historians assert that *United States v. Kagama*, 118 U.S. 375 (1886) is the seminal case presenting the advent of the plenary power era. However, as noted earlier, the term "plenary" does not appear in the decision, though it is clear by the court's unambiguous language that it was intent on establishing the political superiority of the federal government, no matter the constitutional cost (Deloria, 1985; Rotenberg, 1987). The first appearance of the term plenary regarding tribal sovereignty was in *Stephens v. Cherokee Nation*, 174 U.S. 445, 478 (1899) in which a split court held that Congress had "plenary power of legislation." In this case the Supreme Court was using two of the three analytically distinct definitions: unlimited and exclusive.

Second, if plenary power was cited we asked two further questions: 1) How is it defined—exclusive, preemptive power precluding state law, or unlimited, absolute; and 2) What is the basis of plenary power—a constitutional provision(s) (commerce or treaty clauses), or an extra-constitutional doctrine(s) (federal property ownership, Indian wardship, the theory of Indian "dependency"), or was it unclear what basis was used?

Scholars have often combined the analytically distinctive categories of plenary power into one monolithic term. This is both confusing and inaccurate. By breaking down the concept into its three components a more dynamic and slightly less complicated pattern emerges. Table 2 contains every Supreme Court case from 1886 to 1914 that involved congressional power in relation to tribal sovereignty. It shows that a plenary power citation alone does not ensure a legal defeat for American Indians in the court although there is certainly a greater likelihood of a loss, (12-3-1 in the cases in which it was found). In the three Indian legal "victories," the court used the exclusive definition of plenary power.

When plenary power was defined as unlimited and absolute and when it was based on an extra-constitutional doctrine, tribal sovereignty and individual Indian rights were negatively affected (10-1).

DISCUSSION

An important concept in the field of Indian law and policy introduced by Ball (1987) is that of "irreconcilability."

Ball posits, "we [Americans] claim that the 'Constitution, and the laws of the United States which shall be made in pursuance thereof ... shall be the supreme law of the land.' But we also claim to recognize the sovereignty of Native American Nations, the original occupants of the land. These

Table 2 Plenary Power Cases

Case	Date	Issue(s)	Citation 1	Definition 2	Plenary Power Basis 3	Legal Outcome 4
U.S. v. Kagama	1886	Congressional power; criminal law	Implicit	Unlimited/Absolute	Extra-Constitutional	Loss
Cherokee Nation v. Georgia	1890	Congressional power; tribal sovereignty	Implicit	Exclusive, Unlimited; Preemptive	Constitutional Clause	Loss
U.S. v. Thomas	1894	Congressional power; criminal law	Implicit	Exclusive; Preemptive	Extra-consitutional	Loss
Missouri Kansas & Texas Railway Co. v. Roberts	1894	Congressional power; railroads	Implicit	Exclusive, Unlimited/Absolute; Preemptive	Extra-constitutional	Loss
Spalding v. Chandler	1896	Land Title	Implicit	Exclusive, Unlimited/Absolute; Preemptive	Constitutional Clause	Loss
Talton v. Mayes	1896	Tribal Sovereignty; 5th Amend. (Grand Jury)	Implicit	Exclusive	Constitutional Clause	Victory
Stephens v. Cherokee Nation	1899	Congressional Power	Explicit	Exclusive	Constitutional Clause	Loss
Cherokee Nation v. Hitchcock	1902	Congressional Power	Explicit	Unlimited/Absolute	Constitutional Clause	Loss
Leavenworth v. Hitchcock	1903	Congressional Power	Explicit	Unlimited/Absolute	Extra-constitutional	Loss
Matter of Heff	1905	Civil Law	Explicit	Unlimited/Absolute	Extra-constitutional	Anomalous
Wallace v. Adams	1907	Congressional Power; tribal membership	Explicit	Unlimited/Absolute	Extra-constitutional	Loss
Tiger v. Western Investment Co.	1911	Congressional Power; Allotment	Explicit	Unlimited/Absolute	Extra-constitutional	Loss
Heckman v. U.S.	1912	Allotment; Congressional Power	Explicit	Unlimited/Absolute	Extra-constitutional	Loss
Choate v. Trapp	1912	5th Amend. (just compensation); tribal sovereignty	Explicit	Exclusive; Unlimited/Absolute	Extra-constitutional	Victory
U.S. v. Mille Lac Chippewa	1913	Tribal Claims	Explicit	Unlimited/Absolute	Unclear	Loss
Perrin v. U.S.	1914	Congressional power; liquor law	Implicit	Exclusive; Preemptive	Constitutional Clause	Victory

Key

1. If the term plenary is used in the case, then it is cited as *explicit*. If the concept plenary is not evident in the case, however, and the Court instead uses terms like Congress's unlimited authority, supreme right, or paramount power, then it is given an *implicit* citation.

2. Exclusive: Congress, because of the location of tribes in the Commerce Clause and its role in ratifying Indian treaties, is the sole branch of government constitutionally authorized to deal with tribes. The Congress has sometimes delegated its authority to federal administrative officials and occasionally to states.

Preemptive: An exercise of federal power which preempts, or precludes, state law.

Unlimited/Absolute: This category includes exercises of federal power which are unencumbered by constitutional constraints.

3. This category details the basis of the plenary power term. Historically, the court has cited *constitutional* clauses (i.e., Commerce, Treaty, Property, expenditures for the general welfare, and the war-making clause) to justify congressional plenary power. Other times, the court has given extra-consitutional or extra-legal reasons for holding that Congress has plenary power over tribes (i.e., federal property ownership, Indian wardship, or tribal dependency). Finally, the court has occasionally been equivocal and has failed to articulate precisely what the U.S. government's authority over tribes is based on. This is labeled unclear.

4. As Jonathan Casper (1976) has shown, judicial decision-making is often much more than a winner-take-all/loser-go-home scenario. In fact, judicial outcomes are not always decisive and sometimes even losers contribute importantly to outcomes that later emerge. For our purposes, a victory is recorded if the Supreme Court awards the tribe most of its demands, or if the court shields the tribe from constitutional or state imposition not requested or consented to by the Indians. A loss is recorded if the court affirms in the United States a legal right to confiscate Indian land, abrogate Indian treaties (or provisions of treaties), or reflects a diminution of tribal rights even when Indians are not parties in the case. The one case listed as anomalous, *Matter of Heff*, did not involve tribal sovereignty.

claims—one to jurisdictional monopoly, the other to jurisdictional multiplicity—are irreconcilable" (p. 3).

A primary irreconcilable difference centers on the dissonance of the following concepts: 1) congressional plenary power (as absolute and unlimited), and 2) tribal sovereignty (a culturally distinct people within territorial limits with a leadership capable of making governmental arrangements).

Tribal sovereignty, like the sovereignty of nation-states, is a dynamic, not an absolutist concept. Plenary power, on the other hand, is considered static and absolutist whether it is wielded by proponents of federal supremacy over tribes or by advocates of tribal sovereignty. Nevertheless, as described earlier, plenary power has three meanings. Congress and the courts are the entities which unilaterally transmuted the bilateral relationship between tribes and the United States and they, not the tribes, are in the position of choosing which definition of plenary power to apply. Tribes lack such a definitional luxury.

To improve intergovernmental relations, a way should be found to reconcile these two terms. The United States could settle on one of the two following definitions of plenary power: a) exclusive or b) an exercise of federal power preemptive of state law (Engdahl, 1976:363). The United

States would then disavow use of the unlimited/absolute definition as being violative of enumerated powers, limited government, consent of the governed, and the rule of law.

This action would pay immediate dividends in improved tribal-federal relations, especially from the tribal perspective, because it would send a strong message to tribal groups and individual Indians that the federal government was prepared to return to a genuinely bilateral political stance regarding those tribes.

Furthermore, tribes would welcome steps by the United States to reduce its use of non-constitutionally enumerated powers over their territories and sovereign rights. More importantly, tribes have a clear understanding of the doctrine of consent, and they realize that in the past 130 years or so this treasured democratic principle has sometimes been ignored (i.e., the BIA's administrative power over tribal resources; the acquisition and alienation of tribal lands and resources; the tribes' inability to punish non-Indians and non-member Indians; and tribes being denied the right to enter into foreign agreements, see Ball, 1987).

The legislative branches of the federal government have begun to seriously consider the need to reestablish bilateral relations with tribes. Congress has established the experimental Tribal Self-Governance Demonstration Project (102 St. 2285; as amended 105 St. 1278) which is a major step toward restoring the tribal right of self-determination. Congress also is discussing re-establishing a more constitutionally grounded policy with tribes—"New Federalism." This policy would resemble the bilateral agreement period (which followed in the wake of the treaty period which ran from 1775 to 1868) between tribes and the United States which lasted from 1875 to 1914 (Senate Rep't., No. 102-216, 1989; see S. 2512 "New Federalism for American Indian Act, April 25, 1990).

On the executive side, the Clinton Administration is on record[14] as being supportive of tribal sovereignty. In his plan Clinton noted that while "Republican administrations have given nothing but lip service over the past twelve years to an affirmation of the government-to-government relationship," his administration would "give tribal governments more say in the distribution of federal funds geared toward economic growth, universal access to quality, affordable health care, and improved education."

The Clinton Plan consists of three parts:

Guaranteeing Rights

- support of tribal sovereignty and self-determination
- reaffirm the government-to-government relationship
- protect Indian religious sites and freedoms
- reforms in the Bureau of Indian Affairs
- support tribal efforts to resolve local disputes with states in accordance with federal law
- reaffirm U.S. citizenship of Indians and improve their voting access

ECONOMIC DEVELOPMENT

- –generate innovative strategies to develop self-sufficient economies
- –create public-private partnerships to give low-income tribal entrepreneurs assistance
- –implement a New Enterprise Tax Cut and create community development banks
- –expand Earned Income Tax Credit
- –repair infrastructure of reservations

HEALTH CARE

incorporate goals of the Indian Health Care Improvement Act
provide a core benefits package to improve:

- –ambulatory physician care
- –mental health services
- –develop more effective measures to combat Fetal Alcohol Syndrome and AIDS
- –keep hospital clinics open longer

It is, however, far too early to ascertain what will transpire from a policy perspective during the Clinton-Gore administration, though his selection of Bruce Babbitt as Interior Secretary and his appointment of Ada Deer as Assistant Secretary of Indian Affairs, have generally been well-received by tribes.[15]

Returning to our historical discussion, why did the Supreme Court sporadically apply the "unlimited-absolute" definition of plenary power to tribes, their members, and their resources in the 1880s? The judicial, political, and historical evidence supports what many other scholars have maintained: Broadly put, it was to legitimate the unabashed and forced congressional policy of assimilation and acculturation of tribal members into the American mainstream. As John Oberly, Commissioner of Indian Affairs, noted in his 1888 Annual Report, the Indian "must be imbued with the exalting egotism of American civilization, so that he will say 'I' instead of 'We,' and 'This is mine,' instead of 'This is ours' " (*ARCIA*, 1888).

It needs to be reiterated, however, that even the doctrine of plenary power, when defined as unlimited/absolute, was enforced only sporadically.[16] As the case law attests, in several important decisions the Supreme Court—using the exclusive and preemptive definitions of plenary power—acknowledged the government's lack of jurisdiction in Indian Country, although it never denied that the United States could exert its jurisdiction if it chose. In fact, when the courts relied upon Congress's enumerated exclusive authority to deal commercially with tribes, it employed plenary power in a more viable sense.

The idea of enumeration embodies the soul of the constitutional conflict between tribes and the federal government. In constitutional law matters not involving tribes, the court has maintained, as it did in *Kansas v. Colorado*, 206 U.S. 46 (1907), that the United States "is a government of enumerated [explicitly identified] powers" (p. 88). The court acknowledged that the Constitution "is not to be construed technically and narrowly," and went on to say that "it is still true that no independent and unmentioned power passes to the National Government or can rightfully be exercised by the Congress" (Ibid).

However, when Congress deals with tribes additional variables must be factored in: the treaty-defined, not constitutionally-defined political relationship, and the pre- and extra-constitutional status of tribes. The combined effect of these factors is illustrated by the statement that "general acts of Congress do not apply to Indians, if their application would affect the Indians adversely, unless congressional intent to include them is clear" (Cohen, 1972 ed.:173). Moreover, there is also ample historical, political, and legal precedent for the principle that "Congress has no constitutional power over Indians except what is conferred by the Commerce Clause and other clauses of the Constitution" (Ibid.:90).

As Deloria (1985:240) noted: "Indians receive the protection of the federal government precisely because they are outside the protections of the Constitution; they need and receive special consideration when the federal government interacts with them and handles their affairs. We have often called the government's power to accomplish this task 'plenary' because we supposed that it needed to be immune from arbitrary challenges which might otherwise hamper the wise administration of the affairs of Indians."

Conclusion

This essay has attempted to explain the origins and clarify the confusion surrounding a pivotal concept undergirding the tribal-federal relationship: plenary power. The evidence shows that two of the analytical definitions of plenary power—preemption and exclusivity—sometimes are used in a constitutionally permissible way that recognizes and protects tribal autonomy. This needed protection is most evident when states and private interests have sought to make jurisdictional inroads into tribal territory or over tribal rights.

However, there remains the reality that although many tribes remain extra-constitutional political bodies, their political status has sometimes been characterized by the courts as "inferior" to the "superior position" Congress is said to occupy in relation to tribes.[17] Tribes, despite a preponderance of evidence of their "foreign" political relationship to the states and the federal government, were informed beginning in the 1880s that they were to be treated as "wards of the nation," and that they were in a "condition of pupilage or dependency" (*Cherokee Nation v. Southern Kansas Railway Co.*, 135 U.S. 654 (1890). Although the *Perrin* decision appeared to place some moral constraints on congressional power over tribes, the last eighty years bear out a stark reality: there are no constitutional restrictions on what the federal government may do to tribes or the remaining vestiges of tribal sovereign rights or aboriginal lands.

This is evident in the Indian reorganization era of the 1930s which resulted in the forced abandonment and delegitimation of some traditional tribal governments.[18] It is evident in the federal government's termination and relocation policy of the 1940s-1960s.[19] It is most recently evidenced by a host of Supreme Court decisions effectively disregarding the rights of tribes and their citizens in several areas of law: non-member Indian criminal jurisdiction (*Duro v. Reina*, 110 S.Ct. 2053 (1990), double taxation (*Cotton Petroleum Corporation v. New Mexico*, 57 USLW 4445 (1989); zoning regulations of Indian land (*Brendale v. Confederated Tribes and Bands of Yakima*, 109 S. Ct. 2994 (1989); and most significantly the free exercise of religion (*Lyng v. Northwest Indian Cemetery Protective Association*, 484 U.S. 439 (1988) and *Employment Division v. Smith*, 108 L. Ed 2d 876 (1990).

Tribal nations, as pre- and extra-constitutional political-cultural-economic entities, will continue to occupy a distinctive position in the United States. Tribes have a political status that is both dynamic and extremely tenuous. Tribes face the structural disadvantage of having rights which the federal government is not constitutionally mandated to protect. Notwithstanding the Commerce Clause and the treaty relationship, tribes remain "beyond the pale of the constitutional framework ... [a]nd unless and until there is some positive move by the federal government to accept limitations on its exercise of naked political power over the tribes, Indians will remain people without a status and, more importantly, without the ability to protect themselves from the continuing exploitation visited upon them by the U.S." (Deloria, 1988: 266).

Until this disparity in tribal-federal political power is rectified it is doubtful whether a viable domestic solution is possible to tribal-federal relations.

NOTES

1. The Constitution does not explicitly grant the federal government the power to regulate Indian affairs, it merely states that Congress shall be the branch with the power to "regulate commerce with foreign nations . . . and *with* the Indian tribes." (Article 1, sec. 8, cl. 3) (emphasis added).

2. For the purposes of this study my focus will be on tribes rather than individual Indians. The Commerce Clause empowers Congress to oversee the federal government's commercial relations with Indian tribes. Individual Indians who had not yet been naturalized were extended federal citizenship in 1924 (43 St. 253). Nearly two-thirds of all Indians, however, had already been enfranchised before 1924. Indians became citizens through several routes: as a result of treaty stipulations; the General Allotment Act of 1887, as amended; or having served in World War I (see Haas, 1957:16; and Rice, 1934:86-87). The granting of U.S. citizenship did not end tribal citizenship, however. The 1924 Act read: "That the granting of such citizenship shall not in any manner impair or otherwise affect the right of any Indian to tribal or other property . . ." Hence, this created a class of Americans with dual citizenship. Furthermore, as citizens, Indians are ostensibly accorded the same constitutional safeguards as other individuals. But this is problematic as well (see Ball, 1987:11;

and Barsh and Henderson, 1980:96; and Deloria, 1977:6).

3. "Termination" was the term developed in the late 1940s and eventually sanctioned in 1953 under House Concurrent Resolution 108, whereby the U.S. government sought to unilaterally sever, end, or "terminate" the federal government's political relationship with various Indian tribes, bands, and rancherias. See Donald Fixico's *Termination and Relocation* (Albuquerque: UNM Press, 1986); and Charles F. Wilkinson and Eric R. Biggs, "The Evolution of Termination Policy" *American Indian Law Review* 5 (Summer 1977):139-184. Termination, although renounced on several occasions from 1958 forward, was not congressionally disavowed until April 28, 1988 (102 St. 130).

4. Special thanks to Professor Vine Deloria, Jr. for bringing this list of infrequently cited laws to my attention. See the following documents and their provisions for explicit examples of such tribal non-compliance:

a) Treaty with Mixed Bands of Bannacks and Shoshones [*sic*], October 14, 1863 (Kappler, Vol. V, 1941:693).

b) U.S. Statute. "An act authorizing the payment of annuities into the treasury of the Seminole tribe of Indians. April 15, 1874. 18 St. 29 (Kappler, Vol. I, 1904:150) [See the proviso which reads: "Provided, That said agreement shall provide that the sum of five thousand dollars shall be annually appropriated out of said annuity to the school fund of said tribe: And provided further, That the consent of said tribe to such expenditures and payment shall be first obtained." An attached note at the bottom of the document stated the following: "Note.–Indians withhold assent."]

c) Agreement with the Crows. May 14, 1880. (Kappler, Vol. II, 1904:1063).

d) U.S. Statute. "An Act to graduate the price and dispose of the residue of the Osage Indian trust and diminished-reserve lands . . ." March 3, 1881. 21 St. 509. [See the attached proviso which reads: "Provided, however, That no proceeding shall be taken under this act until at least two-thirds of the adult males of said Osage Indian tribes shall assent to the foregoing provisions."]

e) U.S. Statute. "An Act to accept and ratify the agreement (a)["The agreement of May 14, 1880 (Letter C above) . . . was not ratified by the Crow Indians and this agreement was substituted therefore.] submitted by the Crow Indians of Montana for the sale of a portion of their reservation in said Territory . . ." April 11, 1882. 22 St. 42. (Kappler, Vol. I, 1904:195).

f) U.S. Statute. "An Act to divide a portion of the reservation of the Sioux Nation of Indians in Dakota into separate reservations and to secure the relinquishment of the Indian title to the remainder." April 30, 1888. 25 St. 94 [See section 24, which stated: "That this act shall take effect only upon the acceptance thereof and consent thereto by the different bands of the Sioux Nation of Indians, . . . and upon failure of such proof [vote by adult Indians] and proclamation (issued by the President) this act becomes of no effect, and null and void."

g) U.S. Statute. An Act to ratify and confirm an agreement with the Muscogee or Creek tribe of Indians, and for other purposes." March 1, 1901. 31 St. 861. [See the preamble which states in relevant parts: "That the agreement negotiated between the Commission to the Five Civilized tribes and the Muscogee or Creek tribe . . . as herein amended, is hereby accepted, ratified, and confirmed, and the same shall be of full force and effect when ratified by the Creek National Council. . ."]

5. Of course, history is replete with a multitude of examples where federal officials ignored the doctrine of tribal consent and proceeded to act unilaterally.

6. Political scientists are, however, finally beginning to study some areas of the tribal-federal relationship, though they have not focused systematically on the case law during this particular era. See the writings of Fetzer (1981), McCool (1985), McCulloch (1988), Holland (1989), Gross (1989), O'Brien (1989), and Shattuck and Norgren (1991).

7. This article is extracted from my dissertation, The Legal Consciousness of the United States Supreme Court: A Critical Examination of Indian Supreme Court Decisions Regarding Congressional Plenary Power and Tribal Sovereignty–1870-1921 (Chapel Hill: University of North Carolina: 1990). That larger study looked at 107 federal court cases (ninety Supreme Court decisions: a list of the cases is available from the author) which arose during what many consider the darkest chapter in federal-tribal relations.

8. See Loring B. Priest *Uncle Sam's Stepchildren: The Reformation of United States Indian Policy, 1865-1887.* (New Brunswick: Rutgers University Press, 1942); Henry E. Fritz, *The Movement for Indian Assimilation, 1860-1890.* Philadelphia: University of Pennsylvania Press, 1963; the diverse historical works of Francis Paul Prucha, including *Americanizing the American Indians: Writings by the 'Friends of the Indian' 1880-1900.* Cambridge: Harvard University Press, 1973; and Janet A. McDonnell, *The Dispossession of the American Indian, 1887-1934.* Bloomington: Indiana University Press, 1991.

9. By extra-constitutional and extra-legal we mean factors that are not derived from constitutional sources. These may include non-constitutional doctrines or legal constructs like the alleged "wardship" and/or "dependent" status of Indians; the use of the "doctrine of discovery" to justify exertions of federal power over Indians and their resources; the presumption of plenary power not related to Indian commerce; the alleged "incorporation" of Indians into the American polity; or the racial constitution of a reservation or Indian community, to name but a few. See Philip Lee Fetzer, "Jurisdictional Decisions in Indian Law: The Importance of Extra-legal Factors in Judicial Decision-Making," *American Indian Law Review*, 9 (1981): 253-272; and see Nancy Carol Carter, "Race and Power Politics as Aspects of Federal Guardianship Over American Indians: Land-Related Cases, 1887-1924," *American Indian Law Review*, 4 (1976): 197-248, for two good examples of writings which focus on some of these extra-legal factors and their implications for tribal sovereignty.

10. Tribes have both a pre- and extra-constitutional status because of their original sovereignty. Tribal nations are sovereign since they were not created pursuant to the federal Constitution or by state action. As the Supreme Court said in *Talton v. Mayes*, (163 U.S. 376 (1896)), tribal rights of self-government were not delegated by Congress and were thus not powers arising from or created by the federal constitution. Tribal sovereignty, therefore, "is neither derived from nor protected by the Constitution" (dissenting opinion of Justice Stevens in *Merrion v. Jicarilla Apache Tribe*, 455 U.S. 130, 170 (1982). Thus, the U.S. Bill of Rights does not apply to the acts of tribal governments. The continuing legality of Indian treaties and the fact that Congress and the tribes have never jointly participated in any action that would lead to an amendment to the U.S. Constitution which would effectively incorporate tribes into the American political system is all the proof necessary evidencing this ongoing extra-constitutional tribal political status.

11. William H. Riker and Barry R. Weingast in an article, "Constitutional Regulation of Legislative Choice: The Political Consequences of Judicial Deference to Legislatures," 74 *Virginia Law Review* (February 1988):373-401, persuasively argue using modern social choice theory, that although the Court assumes that legislative and electoral majorities are effective in protecting the economic rights of citizens, particularly of minority groups, there actually is little data to support this view. They find that "majority rule provides no inherent protection for the rights of minorities" and that "the Court's deference to legislatures in the area of economic rights is puzzling, and is inconsistent with its scrutiny of other rights." (p. 374-375). In conclusion, Riker and Weingast explicitly state that "judicial deference to legislatures, as past actions of legislatures clearly reveal, leads to policies that compromise the rights of minorities" (p. 399). Judicial deference, particularly in the way the Supreme Court has utilized the political question doctrine to avoid examining issues in Indian law it deems more suitable for the legislative branches, has been especially problematic for tribal groups which inhabit a unique political and legal space as extra-constitutional entities. Judicial deference, therefore, continues to be one of the most troublesome areas in the tribal-federal relationship. And so long as tribes remain lodged in the Commerce Clause of the Constitution there is little chance that the Court will exercise the degree of judicial scrutiny of congressional actions that tribal nations would like to see.

12. Article 26 of Washington State's Constitution provides a clear example of a disclaimer clause: "That the people inhabiting this state do agree and declare that they forever disclaim all right and title to the unappropriated public lands lying within the boundaries of this State. . . ."

13. See Table 2 for a list of historical cases citing the doctrine of plenary power in all three ways. As recently as 1989 in *Cotton Petroleum Corporation v. New Mexico*, 109 S. Ct. 1698, a case involving the question of whether New Mexico could apply severance taxes to a company located within the Jicarilla Indian reservation and already paying tribal taxes, the Court, utilizing the exclusive definition said that "the central function of the Indian Commerce Clause is to provide Congress with plenary power to legislate in the field of Indian affairs."

And, in *Duro v. Reina*, 110 S. Ct. 2053 (1990), which dealt with whether Indian tribes had criminal jurisdiction over non-member Indians, Justice Brennan (joined by Marshall), who dissented from the majority's ruling that tribal governments lack the power to try non-member Indians, noted that "the Court's 'consent theory' is inconsistent with the underlying premise of Indian law, namely, that Congress has plenary control over Indian affairs." "Congress," Brennan said, "presumably could pass a statute affirmatively granting Indian tribes the right to prosecute anyone who committed a crime on the reservation." (p. 2071). Brennan in this statement seems to be utilizing both the exclusive and preemptive definitions of plenary power. The *Duro* decision was legislatively overturned by Congress October 28, 1191 (105 St. 646). This law "reinstated" the power of tribes to exercise criminal jurisdiction over all Indians within their jurisdiction, whether enrolled or not.

14. Author has copy of "The Clinton Plan for Native Americans."

15. See "Clinton Names Deer to Head B.I.A." in *News From Indian Country*, vol. 7, no.

10 (Late May, 1993):1.

16. See note 4 which contains several examples supporting the fact of the Congress's sporadic enforcement of plenary power.

17. See *Merrion v. Jicarilla Apache Tribe*, 455 U.S. 130, 155, n.21 (1982) which held that Congress' paramount authority over tribes is derived "by virtue of [Congress's] superior position over the tribes."

18. See Kenneth R. Philp, ed., *Indian Self-Rule*. (Salt Lake City, UT: Howe Brothers, 1986).

19. See endnote 4.

REFERENCES

Adams, Hank.
1988 "Tribal Sovereignty: Roots, Expectations, and Limits." In *Indian Self-Rule* edited by Kenneth R. Philp. Salt Lake, UT: Howe Brothers.

Anonymous
1982 "Federal Plenary Power in Indian Affairs After *Weeks* and *Sioux Nation*." *University of Pennsylvania Law Review* 131:235-272.

Ball, Milner S.
1987 "Constitution, Court, Indian Tribes." *American Bar Foundation Research Journal* 1:1-139.

Barsh, Russell L. and James Y. Henderson
1980 *The Road: Indian Tribes and Political Liberty*. Berkeley: University of California Press.

Black's Law Dictionary
1979 5th ed. St. Paul, MN: West Publishing Company.

Canby, William C., Jr.
1981 *American Indian Law in a Nutshell*. St. Paul, MN: West Publishing Company.

Canfield, George F.
1881 "The Legal Position of the Indian," *The American Law Review* January: 21-37.

Chaudhuri, Joyotpaul
1985 "American Indian Policy: An Overview." in *American Indian Policy in the Twentieth Century*. edited by Vine Deloria Jr. Norman: University of Oklahoma Press.

Cohen, Felix S.
1972 Reprint ed. *Handbook of Federal Indian Law*. Albuquerque, NM: University of New Mexico Press.
1982 Revised ed. *Handbook of Federal Indian Law*. Edited by Rennard Strickland, et al. Charlottesville, VA: Michie, Bobbs-Merrill.

Collins, Richard B.
1989 "Indian Consent to American Government." *Arizona Law Review* 31:365-387.

Coulter, Robert T.
1977. "The Denial of Legal Remedies to Indian Nations Under United States Law." *American Indian Journal* 3:5-11.
1978 "Lack of Redress," *Civil Rights Digest* 10:30-37.

Deloria, Vine, Jr.
1969 *Custer Died For Your Sins*. New York: Avon Books.
1970 *We Talk, You Listen*. New York: MacMillan.
1974 *Behind the Trail of Broken Treaties*. New York: Delacourte Press.
1977 *A Better Day for Indians*. New York: Field Foundation.

Deloria, Vine, Jr. and Clifford M. Lytle
1984 *American Indians, American Justice.* Austin: University of Texas Press.
1985 "The Distinctive Status of Indian Rights." In *The Plains Indians of the Twentieth Century.* edited by Peter Iverson. Norman: University of Oklahoma Press.
1988 "Beyond the Pale: American Indians and the Constitution." In *A Less than Perfect Union* edited by Jules Lobel. New York: Monthly Review Press.
1989 "Laws Founded in Justice and Humanity; Reflections on the Content and Character of Federal Indian Law." *Arizona Law Review* 31:203-223.

Engdahl, David E.
1976 "State and Federal Power over Federal Property." *Arizona Law Review* 18:283-384.

Fetzer, Philip Lee
1981 "Jurisdictional Decisions in Indian Law: The Importance of Extralegal Factors in Judicial Decision-Making." *American Indian Law Review* 9:253-272.

Gross, Emma R.
1989 *Contemporary Federal Policy Toward American Indians.* Westport, CN: Greenwood Publishing Company.

Haas, Theodore H.
1957 "The Legal Aspects of Indian Affairs from 1887 to 1957." *The Annals of the American Academy of Political and Social Science* 311:12-22.

Hauptman, Laurence M.
n.d. "Congress, Plenary Power, and the American Indian, 1870 to 1992." In *Exiled in the Land of the Free: Democracy, Indian Nations, and the U.S. Constitution* edited by Oren Lyons and John Mohawks. Santa Fe, NM: Clear Light Publishers.

Holland, Lauren
1989 "The Use of Litigation In Indian Natural Resource Disputes," *Journal of Energy Law & Policy.* 10:33-55.

Kappler, Charles J. comp.
1904-1941 *Indian Affairs: Laws and Treaties.* Five volumes (1904, 1904, 1913, 1929, 1941). Washington: Government Printing Office.

Kronowitz, Rachel San, et al.
1987 "Toward Consent and Cooperation: Reconsidering the Political Status of Indian Nations." *Harvard Civil Rights—Civil Liberties Law Review* 22:507-622.

Laurence, Robert
1988 "Learning to Live with the Plenary Power of Congress Over the Indian Nations." *Arizona Law Review* 30:413-437.

McCool, Daniel C.
1985 "Indian Voting." In *American Indian Policy in the Twentieth Century* edited by Vine Deloria Jr.. Norman: University of Oklahoma Press.

McCulloch, Anne Merline
1988 "Domestic Dependent Nations: Analytic Perspectives of Native Americans by Political Scientists." Paper delivered at Annual Meeting of the American Political Science Association, September 1-4, Washington, D.C.

Murchison, Kenneth S.
1973 Reprint ed. *Digest of Decisions Relating to Indian Affairs,* Vol. 1. Millwood, NY: Kraus Reprint Company.

Newton, Nell Jessup
1984 "Federal Power Over Indians: Its Sources, Scope, and Limitations." *University of Pennsylvania Law Review* 132:195-288.

O'Brien, Sharon
1989 *American Indian Tribal Governments.* Norman: University of Oklahoma Press.

Pevar, Stephen L.
1983 *The Rights of Indians and Tribes.* New York: Bantam Books.

Price, Monroe E.
1973 *Law and the American Indian.* New York: Bobbs-Merrill Company.

Rice, W.G., Jr.
1934 "The Position of the American Indian in the Law of the United States." *Journal of Comparative Legislation and International Law* 16:78-95.

Rotenberg, Daniel L.
1987 "American States and Indian Tribes: Power Conflicts in the Supreme Court." *Dickinson Law Review* 92:81-103.

Shattuck, Petra T. and Jill Norgren
1991 *Partial Justice: Federal Indian Law in a Liberal Constitutional System.* New York: Berg Publishers.

Townsend, Mike
1989 "Congressional Abrogation of Indian Treaties: Reevaluation and Reform." *The Yale Law Journal* 98:793-812.

United States Department of the Interior
1888 *Annual Report of the Commissioner of Indian Affairs.* Washington: Government Printing Office.

United States Senate
1989 *Final Report. A Report of the Special Committee on Investigations of the Select Committee on Indian Affairs.* S. Rept. 101-216, 101st Congress, 1st session.

Wilkins, David E.
1990 The Legal Consciousness of the United States Supreme Court: A Critical Examination of Indian Supreme Court Decisions Regarding Congressional Plenary Power and Tribal Sovereignty—1870-1921. Ph.D. Dissertation. Chapel Hill, NC: University of North Carolina.

Wilkinson, Charles F.
1987 *American Indians, Time, and the Law: Native Societies in a Modern Constitutional Democracy.* New Haven: Yale University Press.

Williams, Robert, Jr.
1990 *The American Indian in Western Legal Thought: The Discourses of Conquest.* New York: Oxford University Press.

SELF-DETERMINATION AND THE CONCEPT OF SOVEREIGNTY

Vine Deloria, jr.

Sovereignty is an ancient idea, once used to describe both the power and arbitrary nature of the deity by peoples in the Near East. Although originally a theological term it was appropriated by European political thinkers in the centuries following the Reformation to characterize the person of the King as head of the state. The complicated political intrigues of medieval Europe had produced the strange doctrine that rulers of the temporal realm were chosen by God and divinely ordained to rule their nations. Political power was thus located in the person of the sovereign who was limited only by his relationship with God.

As European nations encountered peoples of other continents their first presumption was that these peoples shared the view that political power must be located in a specific person and they attributed immense absolute powers to those spokesmen of other nations who dealt with them. Thus leaders of Indian communities, before they were called "chiefs" were commonly called "kings" and were believed to represent the nationhood of the people they represented.

In the technical language of the seventeenth and eighteenth centuries, sovereignty was the absolute power of a nation to determine its own course of action with respect to other nations. Quite often this power was interpreted as the independent power of making war although even Europeans would admit that for smaller nations, sovereignty was restricted to the power to regulate one's own internal functions in the field of domestic relations. Few nations were powerful enough to insist upon total independence from other nations and legal fictions replaced a frank discussion of the actual state of affairs. Treaties between equal "sovereigns" often disguised the fact of interdependence of European nations.

With the eighteenth century colonial wars for possession of North America, Indian communities were acknowledged to have a European version of sovereignty as long as they held sufficient territory and military strength to be an important factor in determining the outcome of the colonial conflicts. As the respective European nations retired from the field and England became predominant on the continent the idea of Indian sovereignty became less popular. The Iroquois, for example, under their famous Haldimand agreement with England, became joint conquerors of Canada during the French and Indian War (Seven Years War) which concluded in 1763. But with the French excluded from political activities in North America and England and Spain comfortably dividing the continent and separated geographically, there was no need to dwell upon the elevation of the League of the Iroquois to international status. While such political theorists as John Locke and Charles Montesquieu referred to the Iroquois as an instance of nonwestern people establishing a government with sufficiently precise institutions to be accorded national status among the other countries, in practical terms the English preferred not to mention Indian nations and the idea of political sovereignty in the same context.

The American Revolution revived the idea of Indian sovereignty. While reciting polite phrases about the equality of man, the American revolutionaries were plainly outside the law of civilized societies in their revolt, and to gain respectability they adopted the most acceptable posture toward the Indians possible with the hope that by demonstrating their ability to act in traditional political terms they could allay the fears of other nations so as to legitimize their activities. Thus in order to neutralize the Indians on their northern and western frontiers the Americans signed several treaties during the course of the Revolution which greatly expanded the acknowledged powers and status of these Indian peoples.

Two of the first series of treaties with the Indians, the Delaware and Cherokee treaties, made provisions for the appointment by the Indians of a delegate to the Continental Congress when they wished to be represented in the councils of the new American nation. These articles were later neglected but they serve as an indication of the political status which the Americans perceived the Indians to possess. The first period of political relationships between Indians and the United States can be said to begin with the Revolutionary War and continue through the War of 1812 until the conflict with the British was resolved and the Americans were assured of their own political independence. During this time Indian treaties carefully distinguished the respective political rights of the two contracting parties and passports, provisions for civil and criminal jurisdiction and extradition indicated the belief that Indian governments were fully capable of dealing with both internal and external affairs. With the withdrawal of Great Britain from activites in the Ohio and Mississippi valleys following the War of 1812, the respective Indian communities who had been allies with the United States and Great Britain were required to sign peace treaties acknowledging as superior sovereign that larger nation within whose territorial claims they found themselves at the conclusion of the war.

The United States claimed political sovereignty over the interior of North America almost by default. Neither Britain nor Spain could afford to carry on extensive military activites in North America and were content to allow the Americans to push their way into the midcontinent area without much molestation or conflict. But the United States, arguing that its claim to lands in the Interior was a valid one that should be respected by European nations, adopted the posture that it had inherited from Britain the superior title to lands based on the doctrine of discovery which had been used a century earlier to establish European state claims to various parts of the nonwestern world. Discovery was a difficult doctrine to defend. John Marshall, describing it in *Worcestor v. Georgia,* remarked:

> It is difficult to comprehend the proposition that the inhabitants of either quarter of the globe could have rightful original claims of dominion over the inhabitants of the other, or over the lands they occupied; or that discovery of either by the other should give the discoverer rights in the country discovered, which annulled the pre-existing rights of its ancient possessors.[1]

But the need to classify and identify the actual status of the Indian governments continued to be a pressing problem if the United States were to successfully expand westward.

Marshall linked the status of Indian lands and governments together to insist that as lands were sold or taken, the extent of sovereignty also declined in importance. In *Johnson v. McIntosh,* he wrote:

> They were admitted to be the rightful occupants of the soil, with a legal as well as just claim to retain possession of it, and to use it according to their own discretion; but their rights to complete sovereignty, and their power to dispose of the soil at their own will, to whomsoever they pleased, was denied by the original fundamental principle that discovery gave exclusive title to those who made it.[2]

Marshall's reconciliation of political sovereignty and land ownership did not last a decade after he first articulated it.

In two Cherokee cases the question arose concerning the precise status of Indian governments: If the Cherokees were a "foreign" nation, they had access to the Supreme Court in an original action; if not, then they were barred from the United States courts and their remedies. These cases tied jurisdictional questions involving lower American political entities such as counties and states with Indian governmental sovereignty which had traditionally been a subject of international interest thus developing a most confusing and conflicting theoretical basis for dealing with Indians by the United States. In *Cherokee Nation v. Georgia,* Justice McLean, concurring with Marshall's majority opinion, developed a much more comprehensive analogy to then-existing doctrines of political rights when he said of the Cherokees:

> Their condition is something like that of the Israelites, when inhabiting the deserts. Though without land that they can call theirs in the sense of property, their right of personal self-government may exist though the land occupied be in fact that of another. The right to expel them may exist in that order, but the alternative of departing and retaining the right of self-government may exist in them. And such they certainly do possess; it has never been questioned, nor any attempt made at subjecting them as a people, or restraining their personal liberty except as to their land and trade.[3]

Here Justice McLean attempts to sever political status from land ownership in effect making the Cherokees what one would describe as an "expectant" or "incipient" nation in the eyes of the United States.

In *Worcester v. Georgia,* the companion case which was heard the year following Cherokee Nation, both Marshall and McLean made another attempt to define the status of Indian tribes with some clarity. Marshall suggested a peculiar status for the Cherokees, writing:

> The Indian nations had always been considered as distinct, independent, political communities, retaining their original natural rights . . . with the single exception of that imposed by irresistible power, which excluded them from intercourse with any other European potentate than the first discoverer of the coast of the particular region claimed; and this was a restriction which those European potentates imposed on themselves, as well as on the Indians . . . the settled doctrine of the law of nations is, that a weaker power does not surrender its independence—its right to self-government—by associating with a stronger, and taking its protection. A weak state, in order to provide for its safety, may place itself under the protection of one more powerful, without stripping itself of the right of government and ceasing to be a state.[4]

Marshall described Indian peoples as "domestic dependent nations."

Once possessing this status as domestic dependent nation, an Indian people could only lose it by voluntarily surrendering the remaining attributes of sovereignty or by becoming so shattered by the passage of events as to be incapable of exercising any social or political powers whatsoever. Justice McLean suggested the latter alternative when he wrote:

> If a tribe of Indians shall become so degraded or reduced in numbers, as to lose the power of self-government, the protection of the local law, of necessity, must be exteneded over them. The point at which this exercise of power by a state would be proper, need not now be considered: If indeed it be a judicial question . . . so long as treaties and laws remain in full force, and apply to Indian nations, exercising the right of self-government, within the limits of a state, the judicial

> power can exercise no discretion in refusing to give effect to those laws, when questions arise under them, unless they shall be deemed unconstitutional.[5]

The anomaly of federal Indian law is that the two Cherokee cases represent the best efforts of the United States legal authority to arrive at a satisfactory definition of the status of an Indian government with respect to state and federal governments. All subsequent decisions revolve about the definitions given in these two cases and variances occur in direct proportion to the relative knowledge of the federal government with respect to the conditions of the Indians involved in any specific despute.

As this century began the historical pendulum was swinging toward a more profound definition of Indian sovereignty and the original content of sovereignty as a reservoir of political powers was revived with respect to Indian governments. In *Talton v. Mayes* the Supreme Court carefully distinguished those political powers which had been inhibited by Congress and those which flowed from the natural rights of a "distinct people" which could not be curtailed by legislative action:

> But the existence of the right in Congress to regulate the manner in which the local powers of the Cherokee nation shall be exercised does not render such local powers federal powers arising from and created by the constitution of the United States . . . It follows that as the powers of local self-government enjoyed by the Cherokee nation existed prior to the constitution, they are not operated upon by the fifth amendment, which, as we have said, had for its sole object to control the powers conferred by the Constitution on our national government.[6]

With *Buster and Jones v. Wright*, the idea of a residual sovereignty inherent in Indian governments became a positive factor in protecting the communal decisions and values of Indian communities:

> The authority of the Creek nation to prescribe the terms upon which non-citizens may transact business within its borders did not have its origin in an Act of Congress, treaty or agreement of the United States. It was one of the inherent and essential attributes of its original sovereignty. It was a natural right of that people, indispensible to its autonomy as a distinct tribe or nation, and it must remain an attribute of its government until by the agreement of the nation itself or by the superior power of the republic it is taken from it . . . The fact remains nevertheless that every original attribute of the government of the Creek nation still exists intact which has not been destroyed or limited by Act of Congress or by the contracts of the Creek tribe itself . . .[7]

While court decisions have generally supported this doctrine during this century, different administrations have seen attempts to erode or replace the idea of inherent sovereignty.

During the Eisenhower administrations, Congress "terminated" federal supervision over several Indian peoples. But this "termination" was made subject to the most excruciating examination by the Supreme Court which concluded in the case of the Menominees that no intention existed in the minds of Congress to violate any treaty which the government had with them. Nearly all efforts to restrict inherent sovereignty, if contemplated by the legislative branches of state and federal governments, have generally failed to survive the precision demanded by the courts which would assure them constitutionality.

In the course of these developments, it has become increasingly clear that the idea of Indian sovereignty is not simply a legal concept. Numerous references to sovereignty cite the notion of a distinct people, separate from others, as the chief characteristic of Indian sovereignty indicating that so long as the cultural identity of Indians remains intact no specific political act undertaken by the United States government can permanently extinguish Indian peoples as sovereign entities. Although sovereignty originated as a means of locating the seat of political power in European nations, it has assumed the aspect of continuing cultural and communal integrity when transferred to the North American setting.

Sovereignty has become a difficult political issue in recent years because of its exclusive use as a legal concept. The Supreme Court has shied away from articulating an expanded theory of Indian sovereignty in recent years although it has used peripheral doctrines to bolster sovereign and self-governing powers of Indian governments. The Supreme Court, referring to Indian sovereignty in the McClanahan case, tried to avoid the issue:

> The trend has been away from the idea of inherent Indian sovereignty as a bar to state jurisdiction and toward reliance on federal pre-emption . . . The modern cases thus tend to avoid reliance on platonic notions of Indian sovereignty and to look instead to the applicable treaties and statutes which define the limits of state power.[8]

The reasoning is deceptive here. Obviously, the "applicable treaties and statutes" are precisely those which describe and articulate the sovereignty of the respective Indian nations in relation to the United States. So little is gained with this definition except additional time in which the passage of events can present a better opportunity to comment on the topic.

The conflict over Indian sovereignty today originates in part because of the misconception held by the non-Indians with respect to social institutions and nationality and the adoption of that misconception by Indian political leaders, in some cases, as a means of communicating with and influencing the larger social and political institutions. North Americans have a tendency to look at the sources of power rather than the proper exercise of it. Thus concern is focused on whether or not a certain institution has the right to do certain things rather than the wisdom of what it does. American politicians are discarded when they have lost their sources of power (usually financial), not when they have done wrong. Social and moral responsibility does not revolve about right and wrong but whether, in fact, an institution or person should be involved with the subject matter under consideration.

This tendency to focus on the origin of things rather than their essential characteristics has led American society into a desperate situation in which it cannot solve the simplest problems but only seems to aggravate conditions with each attempt to bring about order. The decline of American prestige abroad and the drastic reduction of faith in the American system as indicated by the "credibility gap" which public institutions now suffer is further testimony to this ingrained fallacy and misidentification of the source for the substance of things. When we focus specifically on the field of Indian affairs it is not difficult to see that the major concern of the Bureau of Indian Affairs with respect to the Indian peoples is whether they can exercise certain powers, not the wisdom of the course under consideration.

In the 1970's American Indians have made their appearance on the world stage. This movement began with the widespread publicity which the occupation of Wounded Knee received and continued on with the efforts of delegations of traditional Indians to achieve recognition in the eyes of various United Nations committees and commissions. The presentation at the Palais des Nations (UN) in Geneva, Switzerland, in the fall of 1977 brought home to many Indians the realization that certain types of political and cultural activities had a place on the world stage and could not be restricted to the domestic affairs of the United States. Insightful American thinkers are also beginning to realize the radical change which this perception is making in the eyes of other nations regarding the

American postion in the world. The discussions which some resource-rich Indian governments have had with OPEC nations are certain to have additional repercussions.

What is particularly important in the movement of Indians onto the world stage is that the cultural traditions have proven the most fruitful manner of communicating national and political existence to other nations. This aspect of communal existence is precisely on point in historical perspective since the recognition of political sovereignty was originally a projection by Europeans of their own institutional structures into the activities of another cultural tradition. The majority of Supreme Court decisions which treat with sovereignty refer to the Indians as a "distinct people" and this characteristic seems to dominate the immediate perceptions which courts have concerning the continued existence of attributes of sovereignty. Sovereignty, in the final instance, can be said to consist more of continued cultural integrity than of political powers and to the degree that a nation loses its sense of cultural identity, to that degree it suffers a loss of sovereignty.

When we view sovereignty in this broadly expanded light, new possiblities for constructive action arise. Cultural integrity involves a commitment to a central and easily understood purpose that motivates a group of people, enables them to form efficient, albeit informal social institutions, and provides for them a clear identity which cannot be eroded by the passage of events. Sovereignty then revolves about the manner in which traditions are developed, sustained, and transformed to confront new conditions. It involves most of all a strong sense of community discipline and a degree of self-containment and pride that transcends all objective codes, rules, and regulations. Unless individuals have a commitment to a larger whole they cannot function efficiently and unless a nation is composed of committed individuals it cannot function with the efficiency that sovereignty is meant to describe.

A self-disciplined community that holds itself together and acts with a unified vision possesses sufficient sovereignty to confront and resolve any difficulty. Much of the erosion of Indian sovereignty is not through the passage of laws of Congress taking away powers of self-government, but rather the alienation of Indian citizens who refuse to be bound by Indian community decisions and values. Unless a political entity can act with the overwhelming majority of its constituents supporting it, it cannot function for long. The Viet Nam experience had demonstrated this truth to the United States though few politicians seem to have learned this important lesson.

An urgent need exists to return to traditional ways of participating in social and cultural functions of the community. This need is presently articulated under the general theme of self-determination and is expressed politically in support of Indian sovereignty. But complex institutions and institutional habits which have been imposed over the course of this century cannot be eliminated in an instance even with the most profound exercise of the commuity will and determination. A gradual transition back to a more normal and spontaneous expression of community values and traditions must be encouraged so that individual and community growth becomes a natural rather than an artificial or repressive development. The first step in this process of restoration and reconstruction is transferring educational and social welfare functions to complete Indian community control. Indian governments must be allowed to structure these activities according to traditional precepts rather than being required to follow rules, regulations, and eligibility standards established for American society.

The standard arguments against total local control of these important social and cultural functions usually revolve about the ability of the local community to finance its own activities. But this argument is based upon the assumption that human experiences are contingent upon one's ability to pay without the corresponding admission that a situation artificially produced will continue to produce problems until it is returned to its normal condition. If we base peoples' opportunity to solve problems upon their ability to finance their opportunities we simply aggravate conditions in which no solutions can be found and ultimately produce a situation in which all of society begins to falter.

If there was an assurance, with no substantial doubt, that the present direction of social programming would produce predictable results, then this argument would have some validity. But the present configuration of social problems, in Indian communities as well as other poor communities in the larger society, would argue against current theories and concepts and in favor of more traditional methods. Since the continuance of Indian cultural traditions is well within the concept of sovereignty and at the same time falls within the mainstream of human development processes, both cultural and political solutions can be devised through this strategy.

Insofar as Indian goals and customs may not correspond to present understanding of national education, economics, and social welfare concepts, a word of caution must be given. The present developments in American society in the creation of institutional solutions are all divisive steps which do not bring together ideas but perpetuate isolation of individuals and institutions. The direction proposed is a means of allowing human energies and understandings to converge and come together to form a more sensible picture of human life. If the same process could be initiated in the larger society the problems would begin to resolve themselves as growth processes would bring presently isolated programs and ideas into relationship with each other.

"Sovereignty" is a useful word to describe the process of growth and awareness that characterizes a group of people working toward and achieving maturity. If it is restricted to a legal-political context, then it becomes a limiting concept which serves to prevent solutions. The legal-political context is structured in an adversary situation which precludes both understanding and satisfactory resolution of difficulties and should be considered as a last resort, not as a first instance in which human problems and relationships are to be seen.

NOTES

1. *Worcestor v. Georgia,* United States Reports (Vol. 315, 1832) p. 515.
2. *Johnson and Graham's Lessee v. McIntosh,* Wheat Reports (Vol. 8, 1823) p. 523.
3. *Cherokee Nation v. State of Georgia,* United States Reports (Vol. 30, 1831) p. 1.
4. *Worcester v. Georgia,* p. 517.
5. *Ibid,* p. 518.
6. *Talton v. Mayes,* United States Reports (Vol. 16, 1904) p. 376.
7. *Buster and Jones v. Wright,* Federal Reports (Vol. 135, 1905) p. 947; Appeal, United States Reports (Vol. 203, 1906) p. 599.
8. *McClanahan v. State Tax Commissioner,* Arizona Appelate Reports (Vol. 14, 1971) p. 452.

The Origins of Self-Determination Ideology and Constitutional Sovereignty

What policy specialists mean by "self-determination" is crucial for understanding Indian policy development in the 1970s. There were, however, several perspectives on self-determination that influenced their approach to Indian legislation (see Figure 3.1). Despite the variety of interpretations involved, policymakers nevertheless agreed that self-determination meant self-government for Indian tribes (66.7 percent) and economic development (69.7 percent) (see Table 3.1).

However, these tabulations do not show that the two definitions of self-determination are related, although on different sides of the same coin. Thus, for policymakers involved with Indian affairs during the 1970s, self-determination was the belief that Indian tribes and communities could become economically and politically autonomous by applying their powers of self-government to the pursuit of economic development and self-sufficiency. The policy community's consensus on this view of self-determination thus enabled quick and responsive action on Indian issues, especially after 1975. This was not the case before 1975 because the consensus was still being hammered out between President Nixon and Congress.

The view that self-determination meant economic development through self-government, however, was not everyone's. Thus, many

Figure 3.1
Perspectives on Self-Determination

	Political Sovereignty	Legal Sovereignty	Self-Determination	Self-Governance
Main Ideas	Independent/ Nation Status	Honor Treaty Terms/Trust Relationship	Participation in Decision-Making Process/ Contracting	Tribal Self-Government/ Limited Jurisdiction
Proponents	Social Movement Organizations/ AIPRC	Indian Legal Movement/ Washington Representatives	President Nixon/ Congress	NTCA/ Indian Tribes
Strategy	Collective Actions/ Militancy	Legal/Judicial Decisions	Legislative	Strengthen Tribal Government/ Administrative Relationships

Table 3.1
Policy Specialists' Definitions of Self-Determination Ideology

Definition	Percent of Respondents Citing Definition[a] (N = 66)	Number of Times Mentioned in an Interview[b]	
		1 & 2	3 or More
Self-determination as economic development; self-sufficiency	69.7	44	28
Self-determination as self-government; powers of tribal self-government	66.7	44	53

[a]Percentages refer only to those respondents who cited the definition indicated. For example, forty-six respondents, or 69.7 percent of the total, cited economic development as a definition of self-determination; twenty respondents did not give economic development as a definition for self-determination.

[b]The number of times a definition was cited in the interviews is given here as a measure of the importance with which it was regarded by the respondents who mentioned it as a reason for the 1970s policy shift.

pro-Indian policy advocates held views that defined self-determination as legal or political sovereignty, or some combination of both. The legal sovereignty perspective emphasizes honoring the treaties, preserving the land base, and enforcing the trust relationship. Political sovereignty focuses on obtaining independence or separate nation status for the tribes.

All of these ideas about self-determination—as self-governance, or as legal or political sovereignty—had been around for some time, at least since the first treaties were signed. Thus, a central ideological innovation of the seventies was to contribute a new, minority, perspective that has come to define sovereignty in terms of the Constitution. This belief was first promulgated by the American Indian Policy

Review Committee (AIPRC). Its main tenet holds that the tribes are like the states and local governments in that they, too, have sovereign rights under the Constitution of the United States.[1] Although this view created significant controversy in 1977 when it was made public, and is still poorly understood, the notion of constitutional sovereignty has become increasingly influential both in legislating and in litigating Indian affairs.

The willingness of the AIPRC, and other minority advocates of the constitutional view, to go along with the prevailing definition of self-determination as economic development was probably related to strategic considerations. If so, it may have reflected a pragmatic awareness that policy would be easier to legislate if the more moderate, and not the more radical, perspective was espoused. The analysis of Representative Lloyd Meeds' rejection of the AIPRC's position presented in this chapter suggests this was indeed the case. Moreover, the constitutional perspective that emerged from the policy debate of the seventies can be traced to four origins: President Nixon's 1970 Message to the Congress, post–1975 congressional legislation, the American Indian Review Committee's *Final Report*, and to ongoing jurisdictional issues between the tribes and the states.

PRESIDENT NIXON AND CONGRESS DEFINE SELF-DETERMINATION

Policy specialists are generally in accord that the federal government's contemporary definition of self-determination dates from President Richard Nixon's Message to the Congress, on July 8, 1970. Coming as it did at the height of a climate of opinion favorable to the advancement of minority interests, self-determination ideology reflects a strong value for Indian participation in, and control over, the policies and programs that affect Indian life. Thus, the "romantic revolt" of the 1960s meant "identifying the powerlessness of the poor as the principal source of their inability to cope with their surroundings and break out of a 'culture of poverty' " (Beer, 1978, p. 26). The federal government's response was to try to empower minorities through the social programs of the War on Poverty and the philosophy of "maximum feasible participation."

It is within this context that policymakers defined a post–1975 perspective on self-determination. Thus, their emphasis was on creating opportunities for the Indians to participate in decision-making processes involving outcomes affecting their lives. Those few respondents who saw the president's message as an extension of the self-government philosophy of the 1934 IRA legislation are correct only in that the earlier legislation made it possible for Congress to begin to consider

Indians as entitled to the right of self-government. President Nixon's statement, however, went well beyond this recognition to suggest how the federal government might encourage real political autonomy for Indian communities, without severing the trust relationship.

In his opening remarks to Congress, and consistently throughout his message, the president made it clear that future federal policy should not continue to be paternalistic but "build upon the capacities and insights of the Indian people" (p. 101-A).[2] In order for this to occur, he argued, Congress must repudiate its terminationist and assimilationist biases. Moreover, the trust relationship should no longer be unilaterally defined but developed in consultation with the Indian people; "we must make it clear that Indians can become independent of federal control without being cut off from federal concern and federal support." Thus, termination policy, which had seriously undermined the trustee relationship, must be rejected because the premises upon which it rests are wrong. Here, Nixon argued that the trust relationship is a special relationship between Indians and the federal government and, as we have seen, one that is constitutionally and morally binding. The trust relationship will continue to mean that government owes the Indian in keeping with treaty and other formal obligations—but that from now on the relationship will be guided by egalitarian and sovereign, rather than paternalistic, principles.

Second, Nixon pointed out that the consequences of termination have been "clearly harmful"—that "their economic and social condition has often been worse after termination than it was before" (p. 101-A). Third, the president was aware that termination had created a great deal of "apprehension" among Indian groups and that, therefore, "any step that might result in greater social, economic, or political autonomy is regarded with suspicion by many Indians who fear it will only bring them closer to the day when the federal government will disavow its responsibility and cut them adrift" (p. 101-A). Accordingly, he stated, that:

> Because termination is morally and legally unacceptable, because it produces bad practical results, and because the mere threat of termination tends to discourage greater self-sufficiency among Indian groups, I am asking the Congress to pass a new Concurrent Resolution which would expressly renounce, repudiate and repeal the termination policy as expressed in House Concurrent Resolution 108 of the 83rd Congress. . . . self-determination among the Indian people can and must be encouraged without the threat of eventual termination. In my view, in fact, that is the only way that self-determination can be effectively fostered. This then, must be the goal of any new national policy toward the Indian people: to strengthen the Indians' sense of autonomy without threatening his sense of community. (p. 102-A)

Even though President Reagan reaffirmed Nixon's position, in 1983, President Nixon's unprecedented disavowal of the termination policy significantly stands alone as the clearest, least compromised, rejection of this policy to date. Perhaps more than any other sentiment or proposal his statement contains, it served to persuade both Indian and Indian advocate alike that a new era had dawned for Indian policy.

In order to fully understand this point, we must remember that Indian preoccupation with the trust responsibility is central to any definition of Indian policy interests. The idea that government is constitutionally as well as morally obligated to protect the rights and well-being of the tribes is essential to the definition of the trust relationship as well as to the Indian claim of sovereignty. In the Indian conception, therefore, the trust relationship exists because treaties were once negotiated with them in recognition of their sovereign status as nations. Thus, to relinquish the trust relationship or to have it unilaterally abrogated by Congress, is equivalent to giving up or losing sovereignty.[3] This, as has become clearer since 1970, is precisely what Indians are willing to fight to prevent from happening.

As it turns out, in fact, Indian advocates—for example, Donna Harris, then wife of Democratic Senator Fred Harris (also an advocate in Congress) and an Indian leader in her own right, and, non-Indian advocates—like Senator Ted Kennedy, or academics like Edgar Cahn and Alvin Josephy, both of whom had written extensively on the subject of federal Indian policy abuse—were notably influential in developing the president's position on Indian self-determination, as were bureaucrats in the Department of Interior and the White House. During the 1970s, advocates were able to gain unprecedented access to Congress and the White House and so to bring their considerable political acumen to bear on questions of Indian policy and self-determination.

In the meantime, there is another sense in which the president's message to Congress was essential for the development of a consensus on self-determination. Nixon accompanied his statement with a list of concrete legislative and bureaucratic reforms that, if enacted, would further the goal of Indian self-determination. In fact, all but the Indian Trust Counsel Authority proposal were eventually passed by Congress. Those proposals on which action favorable to Indian interests was taken were: (a) that Blue Lake be restored to the Taos Pueblo; (b) that tribes be allowed to establish control over their educational programs; (c) that tribes be permitted to administer their own (Johnson O'Malley) educational funds; (d) that Congress enact financing legislation to guarantee loans to the Indians for economic development purposes; (e) that an Assistant Secretary for Indian Affairs be created in the Department of Interior; (f) to increase funds for Indian health; and (g) to support urban Indian centers. In justifying these proposals Nixon provided further clarification of what he meant by self-determination:

> In the past, we have often assumed that because the government is obligated to provide certain services for Indians it therefore must administer those services.... there is no necessary reason for this assumption. Federal support programs for non-Indian communities—hospitals and schools are two ready examples—are ordinarily administered by local authorities. There is no reason why Indian communities should be deprived of the privilege of self-determination merely because they receive monetary support from the federal government. Nor should they lose federal money because they reject federal control. (p. 102-A)

Nixon's reasoning here is key to understanding not only the minority position on self-determination—that Indian communities should be treated like local governments—but also because it may explain Congress' delay in taking action on his proposals. In view of the president's strong rejection of termination policy and his support of greater powers of self-government for the tribes, his use of the hospitals and schools example is revealing and, as far as Congress might have been concerned, too extreme. The president, that is, appears to be saying that Indians are like other local authorities, by which he means state and local governments. Thus, Congress' resistance to enacting the president's proposals—it was five years before the Indian Self-Determination and Education Act was passed—was in keeping with the terminationist and assimilationist orientation that Indians would be better off free from the trust relationship that had evolved after World War II. To suddenly, after twenty years of believing that Indians were being assimilated, be asked to view Indian tribes as potentially sovereign entities, in the same way as states and local governments, was probably asking too much of Congress in 1970.

On the other hand, policy specialists appear to think that political factors, primarily in the nature of the rivalry that existed between a Democratic Congress and a Republican president, were partially responsible for the delay. They also argue that major legislative proposals are often years in the making before policymakers can be educated to the need for enacting them or before a combination of certain people and events are in place to make them happen. Although both of these reasons are cogent, especially in that major changes took place in Indian Committee chairmanships in the mid-seventies, it is difficult to explain Congress' delay in acting without referring to the ideological radicalness of Nixon's self-determination philosophy and therefore to the need to find a more moderate view before consensus could be achieved.

Given these constraints, when the Congress' endorsement of self-determination ideology finally did occur, in the Self-Determination and Education Act of 1975, it manifested itself in an operative, technical sense, not at all in keeping with the president's more radical sentiments. Congress' self-determination principle, known as *contracting*, is in keeping, however, with the notion that self-determination means economic development through self-governance. In contracting, tribes are able to decide for themselves when and how they will administer federal programs on Indian reservations. This principle enables dealing directly with federal agencies for the delivery of services to Indian communities. Implementation data on how contracting has worked are not yet available but they will probably show that most tribes are ill-equipped to take advantage of this option. Policy specialists are aware that most Indian communities lack the human, financial, and physical plant resources necessary to manage their own programs. Some Indians also feel that to act too quickly with respect to contracting may be to court termination.

Apprehension that economic and political self-sufficiency may lead to termination is always present in Indian country and is enjoying something of a comeback, given the backlash that has occurred in response to Indian treaty victories and because of federal budgetary cutbacks. With respect to Indian child welfare policies and programs, however, Indian tribes and communities have been exercising sovereign rights.

SELF-DETERMINATION AND INDIAN CHILD WELFARE

Of all the legislation enacted by Congress during the 1970s, the Indian Child Welfare Act (ICWA) of 1978 provides perhaps the purest and most comprehensive example of self-determination ideology at work.[4] The purpose of the legislation was to create new standards for the placement and adoption of Indian children in order to prevent the unwarranted removal of Indian children from their tribal environments and thereby to protect Indian cultural and tribal identity and integrity. Significantly, the act is a radical departure from historical practices in that it gives the Indian tribes, and not state governments, exclusive jurisdiction in child custody proceedings. It is this approach to questions of Indian child welfare that is in line with the view that the tribes have sovereign rights.

The ICWA requires the tribes to decide placement and adoption policies. Thus, preference must first go to a member of the child's extended family, then, to other members of the child's tribe, and finally, to another Indian family. Other provisions enable the states and tribes to work out their own arrangements on these matters and specify that grants should be made available to the tribes for implementing child welfare programs—for licensing operating facilities, staff training, and day-care schools, for example.

An examination of the Senate hearings that were held on this legislation in 1974 and 1977, as well as respondent opinions on the subject of the act, indicates that there was very little real opposition to the legislation. Having already become sensitized to Indian demands for self-determination, Congress was largely receptive to the request for greater tribal jurisdiction in matters of child welfare policy. We should note, however, that this policy is of the social welfare type and therefore less likely to be controversial than policies that legislate land and natural resources type issues, and involve non-Indian interests. If in this sense we therefore control for the type of policy, we find that the case for the ICWA was made largely on its merits. It is one of those rare instances where social science data and the statistics on the number of Indian children placed outside of tribal settings or Indian homes persuade policymakers and potential opponents alike that something must be done to protect Indian interests.

Toward this end, studies conducted by the Association on American Indian Affairs, the American Academy of Child Psychiatry, the American Indian Policy Review Commission, the National Tribal Chairmen's Association (a Department of Health, Education and Welfare contract for the study), and the North American Indian Women's Association (a Bureau of Indian Affairs [BIA] contract for the study) were singularly influential in making the case for Indian control. The statistics they contain—showing disproportionate rates for the placement of Indian children in non-Indian settings—are extensively cited in the hearings.

In addition to providing proof that discrimination and prejudice have been the rule in placement and adoption practices, the hearings reflect widespread emotional commitment to the ideal that Indian children are a tribal resource—its primary means of insuring continued survival and cultural integrity. Senator Abourezk, who chaired the hearings, for example, pointed out that there was "no reason or justification for believing that... Indian parents are unfit to raise their children, nor ... to believe that the Indian community itself cannot, within its own confines, deal with the problems of child neglect when they arise" (Hearings, Senate Subcommittee, 1977, p. 1).

The combination of statistical fact and emotional appeal resulted in a blanket indictment of government and private agency placement and adoption programs and personnel. It is an indictment with which few at the hearings were prepared to disagree, even the legislation's strongest opposition, the Church of Jesus Christ of Latter-day Saints (LDS or Mormon).[5]

No one, however, was more instrumental in making the case for Indian self-determination in child welfare policy than William Byler and Bertram Hirsch of the Association of American Indian Affairs. The association is a pro-Indian advocacy organization that has been in existence since the 1920s, and in this case, had been documenting abuses in Indian child welfare matters since 1967. Byler's report, an "Indian Child Welfare Statistical Survey" (July 1976), and Hirsch's subsequent work on the legislation itself, constitute remarkable examples of the influence that this "friend of the Indian" organization, and its two representatives, had on the development of legislation that was so obviously in keeping with Indian policy preferences. We return to the subject of non-Indian organizational and entrepreneurial influence in a later chapter.

This discussion of the ICWA illustrates how self-determination ideology influenced Indian policy development after 1975. It also suggests that, in addition to reflecting an operative consensus, the self-determination legislation contained the seeds of an alternative view, that Indian tribes are entitled to sovereign rights, like those held by the states. This position is best exemplified in the American Indian Policy Review Commission's *Final Report* to Congress in 1977.

THE AMERICAN INDIAN POLICY REVIEW COMMISSION TACKLES THE STATUS QUESTION

Although the commission endorsed the consensus on self-determination defined as economic development and self-government for the Indian tribes, its major contribution was to present the view that self-determination should mean considering the tribes a third unit of government within the federal system of states and the national government. Although not as radical a notion as the historical idea that tribes are separate nations, the view that tribes should be thought of as having the same sovereignty as states and local governments was met with a great deal of opposition. Despite this initial resistance to it, however, the idea that the tribes should be defined as constitutional sovereigns has caught on. President Reagan's Indian policy, for example, stipulates a "government-to-government" relationship with the tribes.

Still, the idea that tribes are constitutionally sovereign remains embryonic. It has yet to be defined legally, or to achieve consensus. Nevertheless, it may have already come to reflect the sentiments of an increasingly larger number of Indian advocates and communities. Because Indian policy development is importantly preoccupied with the question of political status, the origins of the idea of constitutional sovereignty are examined more closely.

An act creating the AIPRC was passed in 1975. The commission was to consist of three Senators, three Representatives, and five Indians. It was chaired by Senator James Abourezk (D-South Dakota) and the vice chairman was Representative Lloyd Meeds (D-Washington). In addition, Ernest Stevens, of the Oneida tribe, served as executive director of the commission and Kirke Kickingbird, of the Kiowa Tribe, as general counsel. The only other upper echelon staff member was Max Richtman, a non-Indian. By statute also, the eleven task forces, of three members each, were required to have a majority of Indian staff. Actually, however, thirty-one of the thirty-three task force members were Indian. Moreover, all of the commission's members at the time were widely regarded as Indian advocates.

The commission's purpose was to conduct a comprehensive study of the conduct of Indian affairs and it was to expire six months after the submission of its final report to Congress, or no later than June 30, 1977. Pursuant to its mandate, the commission conducted extensive hearings, in Washington and regionally, on a variety of subjects relevant to Indian affairs: the trust relationship, tribal government, federal administration, jurisdiction, education, health, alcohol and drug abuse, reservation development, urban Indians, Indian law, and political status. It published eleven task force reports and several special studies, for example, on Alaska natives and the BIA. Although it published 206 recommendations dealing with these topics, the commission's work is largely remembered for its controversial views on the nature of Indian status and for Congressman Meeds' public rejection of them.

Proponents of the AIPRC's conclusions agree with its view that "Indian tribes are governments . . . the federal policy must accept the position that the supervisory authority it asserts must be limited and flexible" (AIPRC, *Final Report*, 1977, pp. 100–101, pp. 103–107). Accordingly, federal policy should be aimed at

> aiding the tribes in achievement of fully functioning governments exercising primary governmental authority within the boundaries of the respective reservations. This authority would include the power to adjudicate civil and criminal matters, to regulate land use, to regulate natural resources such as fish and game and water rights, to issue business licenses, to impose taxes, and to do any and all of those things which local governments within the United States are presently doing. (AIPRC, *Final Report*, 1977, p. 143)

In addition to these views, the commission concluded that the growth and development of tribal government into fully functioning governments necessarily meant exercising some tribal jurisdiction over non-Indian people and property, especially those within reservation boundaries (AIPRC, *Final Report*, 1977). In defense of its position, the commission pointed out that:

> Tribal governments are emerging from an essentially dormant period forcibly imposed upon them by federal policies directed toward their ultimate destruction. The tribes are beginning to assert those governmental powers necessary to take their proper place in the role of governments within the United States. The powers they are seeking to assert are no more and no less than those of any local sovereign of these United States. The objectives they seek to attain are peace and tranquility within the reservation boundaries and economic independence which will permit them to operate free of the federal purse strings without fear of termination. (AIPRC, *Final Report*, 1977, p. 153)

The commission is clearly defining the tribes as equal to the states and other forms of local government. The response of other Indian groups, although not of non-Indian organizations, was generally favorable to this new definition of Indian status. Thus, in an otherwise qualified letter of support from the conservative National Tribal Chairman's Association, there is explicit endorsement of the commission's definition of Indian status. This letter stated that:

> the Indian people will never surrender their desire to control their relationships both among themselves and with non-Indian governments, organizations, and persons.... Indian tribes possess the moral right to endure and shall do so as self-determining people.... It must not be forgotten that before the age of European discovery Indian tribes enjoyed complete mastery of the continent, governing their land and people as fully sovereign, self-determining policies. ...Thus, the Constitution expressly recognizes Indian tribes and identifies them as political entities separate from the states and foreign nations—to be dealt with as tribes (Article I, Section 8, Clause 3). (Chino and Townsend, 1977, pp. 570–572)

For the association, as for the commission, "The long-term objective of Federal-Indian policy 'should' be the development of tribal governments into fully operational governments exercising the same powers and shouldering the same responsibilities as other local governments" (AIPRC, *Final Report*, 1977, pp. 13, 143).

Meeds' lengthy dissent forcefully rejected these views and thus exemplifies resistance to the idea that Indian tribes may be seen as constitutionally sovereign. Meeds first accused the commission of "one-sided advocacy"; of seeking to "convert a romantic political notion into a legal doctrine" (AIPRC, *Final Report*, 1977, pp. 571, 391). In fact, as another memorandum to the commission pointed out, the commission was never intended to be objective:

Congressman Meeds... should know better than anyone else that there was not the slightest pretense of staffing the Task Forces with neutral people. Everyone was an Indian leader or well-known advocate of Indian causes. They were, in truth, expected to be Indian and tribal advocates... what was expected was the gathering of facts and arguments to express and document the tribal and Indian views. (Dellwo, 1977, p. 301)

Meeds went on to reject the proposition that tribes are like the states:

American Indian tribes are not a third set of governments in the American federal system. They are not sovereigns.... To the extent American Indian tribes are permitted to exist as political units at all, it is by virtue of the laws of the United States and not by any inherent right to government, either of themselves or of others. (AIPRC, *Final Report*, 1977, p. 573)

In one sentence, for which there is item-by-item rebuttal from a number of sources (AIPRC, *Final Report*, 1977), Meeds summed up the opposition's position on the AIPRC's version of Indian status. "The doctrine of inherent tribal sovereignty adopted by the majority report," he argued, "ignores the historical reality that American Indian tribes lost their sovereignty through discovery, conquest, cession, treaties, statutes, and history" (AIPRC, *Final Report*, 1977, p. 574).

Meeds also went to the heart of the matter by indicating that there is more at stake, in his view, than legal or philosophical arguments. He obviously believed that the commission's view of sovereignty, should it ever prevail, will do irreparable harm to non-Indians: "Doing justice to the Indians does not require doing injustices to non-Indians" (AIPRC, *Final Report*, 1977, p. 612, see also p. 579), and, "if Congress should ever think it wise to give Indian people experience in government by letting them practice on non-Indians, I predict we would be swiftly set straight by the vast majority of our constituents" (AIPRC, *Final Report*, 1977, p. 391).

Apparently, Meeds was strongly advised by his colleagues in Congress not to make public his disagreement with the commission's views. Nevertheless, by doing so, he affirmed the opinion of many policy specialists that Indian policy decisions will remain inconclusive so long as the question of Indian status remains unsettled. In Meeds' views, moreover, settling the question of sovereignty can be accomplished by Congress. The commission's position, on the other hand, implies that Congress should not legislate in regard to these matters—that sovereignty and the trust relationship are evolving doctrines best left to the courts and to "intergovernmental agreements" between the tribes and the states (AIPRC, *Final Report*, 1977, pp. 5, 143, 624).

As this discussion indicates, the commission's position, and Meeds' response to it, were rooted in very different interpretations of Indian sovereignty. The federal government, represented by Meeds' views, believed it has absolute authority in Indian matters and that, therefore, the tribes cannot have rights in the same sense that the Constitution reserves sovereign rights to the states. The commission, however, believed that the constitution already contained or, logically, by extension, might be amended to grant states' rights to Indian tribes.

Actually, the commission's interest in redefining the Indian's political status was entirely consistent, in view of the ambiguity with which Indian status has historically been defined. Thus, the idea that Indian tribes are "domestic dependent nations," from which government derives its authority over Indian affairs, has not been definitively interpreted, despite Supreme Court decisions that have, over time, extended the government's authority. It is this very absence of clarity with respect to the status of Indian tribes that makes the commission's position credible. In other words, as long as the federal-state-tribal relationship remains open to interpretation, then it will be possible to generate serious discussion, as the commission has, about the future nature of political relationships. In the words of one policy specialist:

> Sovereignty was not an issue in the sixties but it was in the seventies. The Commission brought it front and center.... Sovereignty is the last thing the Congress wants to hear about for the next 200 years, but it's there.... In the meantime, the tribes are getting ready with brilliant lawyers, graduates from the best law schools...and they start winning cases on sovereignty in the courts. They are pushing it right up to the point where some Supreme Court Justice is going to have to say, "This is what Marshall meant...." When it's all over, who knows what will happen? There's frustration at the Court for not going all the way. But, how much, short of writing a new Constitution, can you go? Because that's what sovereignty would mean: "We the people of the United States and the Indian Nations."

One important source of ambiguity with respect to defining political status has been jurisdiction. In particular, the Indian political agenda continues to pose a serious challenge to state authority over tribal affairs.

STATE AND TRIBAL RELATIONS: HOW ARE THE TRIBES LIKE THE STATES?

State and tribal relations are typically questions over criminal and civil jurisdiction and the extent to which the tribes may be said to have power over the governance of their own affairs vis-à-vis states' rights. Current issues over which tribes and the states are in conflict include: criminal jurisdiction, water rights, land use and development, and gaming policies. Other issues involve the power to tax, license, and zone as well as to regulate hunting and fishing and other treaty rights (Hall, 1979; Medcalf, 1978; Pevar, 1983).[6] These are rights associated with sovereign status, so Indian rights may be expected to conflict with those of the state governments, who usually claim the same jurisdictional powers the tribes want.

Generally, the tribes have exclusive jurisdiction unless a treaty or a federal statute stipulates otherwise, and not because their rights are stated in the Constitution (Institute for the Development of Indian Law, 1983). However, despite instances where the states have been able to extend their power to tax or extend criminal and civil jurisdiction over the tribes, as through allotment policies, via PL 280, or in energy resource development, the states have been singularly unsuccessful in promoting their own interests over those of the tribes. For example, every state attempt to regulate activities involving only reservation Indians has failed either the preemption or infringement test that is required before a state can exert jurisdiction without congressional authority (Pevar, 1983).

The constitutional mandate on Indian affairs has thus meant that the federal government's trust responsibility extends to protecting Indian communities from intrusion by the states even when—as in the case of bifurcated briefs, land claims, water rights, or mismanagement by the BIA—the government has had to make the case against itself in order to protect Indian rights (Hall, 1979). In the 1970s, for example, two practices—*bifurcated* and *split* briefs—were instituted to enable Indian legal issues to be handled either directly by the Supreme Court, without going through the Department of Justice, as in the first example, or which required solicitors from the Department of Interior to present one set of arguments in behalf of the Indian position and another in behalf of the government's, as in the case of split briefs.

Despite these constraints, PL 280, enacted in 1953, seriously undermined tribal authority by allowing the states to extend jurisdiction to the tribes. PL 280 was limited by the Indian Civil Rights Act of 1968, but it has been viewed by many as "perhaps the most widely denounced federal Indian legislation in recent years" (Kickingbird, et al., 1983, p. 12). Similarly, the 1978 Supreme Court decision in *Oliphant v. Suquamish* has been widely viewed as a major setback for Indian criminal jurisdictional authority.

The Oliphant decision denied tribal courts' jurisdiction in cases where a non-Indian has committed a crime in Indian Country. Critics of the decision are afraid that the decision thus creates a new doctrine—that of "inherent limitations" on sovereignty—which may lead to even more negative consequences for the tribes, namely, by limiting the vision of constitutional sovereignty (Institute for the Development of Indian Law, 1983).

Even with these setbacks, however, the Institute for the Development of Indian Law has concluded that U.S. law "endorses Indian sovereignty and tribal self-government and generally supports the exercise of tribal jurisdiction in Indian territory" (Institute for the Development of Indian Law, 1983, pp. 7–8, 13–14). Such success, however, has not been accomplished without rigorous vigilance by Indian constituencies and often at great personal and financial cost. Indian hunting and fishing rights in Washington, and currently in Minnesota, for example, have been gained despite sometimes life-threatening opposition from non-Indians (Josephy, 1984). Moreover, as far as many are concerned, Indian successes on an issue-by-issue basis still do not resolve the all-important question of political status.

Similarly, in the example of Indian water rights, the extension of the trust principle to Indian-state relations has had the effect of helping the tribes resist encroachment of their water rights by the states. Particularly in the western United States, and in view of water needs related to technological and energy resource development, water is a precious commodity over which Indian and non-Indian interests are in direct conflict.

Although Indian water rights are protected by the treaties and upheld in the "Winters Doctrine" (*Winters v. U.S.*, 1908), the states have consistently tried to assert their own "prior appropriation" doctrine over Indian rights. Recently, these efforts have led to a push to quantify water rights that, if successful, would be detrimental to the interests of the tribes because quantification would require the tribes to use their water under conditions over which they would have less control.

Thus, although water rights cases may be heard in state as well as federal courts, pursuant to the 1952 McCarren Amendment, Indians have chosen to litigate in federal court, with some success. The northern Paiute victory with respect to Nevada's Pyramid Lake, Truckee River, dispute is an example (Josephy, 1984). Furthermore, Indian success in federal court has helped to sustain their opposition to national quantification policies that would mandate a legislative solution over questions about who gets how much water. So far, Indian opposition has held up enactment of such legislation, first proposed in 1981. Moreover, since 1982, Indian groups have attempted to bring together a coalition to protect Indian water interests.

Gaming policies, bingo games and other types of gambling on Indian reservations, are another area in which the tribes have successfully opposed the infringement of state jurisdiction over tribal affairs and kept alive the question of their sovereignty. Ever since reservations introduced bingo as a way to accomplish economic development, states have opposed the right of the tribes to regulate gambling operations. Nevertheless, Indian persistence on this issue has led to favorable court decisions as in *California et al. v. Cabazon Band of Mission Indians et al.* (February 1988). Currently, several bills that would designate which activities may be regulated by the tribes and which by the state, and to establish a National Indian Gaming Commission are before Congress.

These examples illustrate how issues of political status have been exemplified in state-tribal relationships. As illustrated elsewhere in this study, Indian activism, buttressed by the federal mandate to protect and enhance Indian interests, has helped to keep sovereignty questions at the forefront of the Indian affairs agenda. It remains to be seen if a consensus on constitutional sovereignty will establish itself, thus extending the view of self-determination that has prevailed in the Indian policy arena since the early 1970s.

In the meantime, and although policy specialists are very much aware of the nuances in meaning that accompany the debate on sovereignty, there is no agreement about how the question of constitutional sovereignty will be resolved. The Reagan administration's Indian policy, however, does spell out the contradictions that need to be resolved:

> When European colonial powers began to explore and colonize this land, they entered into treaties with sovereign Indian nations. Our new nation continued to make treaties and to deal with Indian tribes on a government-to-government basis. Throughout our history, despite periods of conflict and shifting national policies in Indian affairs, the government-to-government relationship between the United States and the Indian tribes has endured. The Constitution, treaties, laws, and court decisions have consistently recognized a unique political relationship between Indian tribes and the United States which this Administration pledges to uphold . . . by removing obstacles to self-government and by creating a more favorable environment for development of healthy reservation economies. (Friends Committee on National Legislation, 1984, p. 4; Press Release, 1983)

Close examination of this text reveals an inconsistency between the rhetoric claiming a government-to-government relationship and the emphasis on economic development and self-government that, we have seen, expresses the old view of self-determination and not the emerging consensus on constitutional sovereignty for Indian tribes. Furthermore, President Reagan's inability at the Moscow summit on arms control to remember his own words on tribal sovereignty suggests that, so far, the government's new policy has been rhetorical.[7]

The main thrust of the Reagan administration's Indian policy, the work of the Commission on Reservation Economies, has been to affirm the view of self-determination as economic development and self-government, not as a third form of government. Future debates on Indian sovereignty will continue to grapple with these definitional issues.

NOTES

1. For instance, the AIPRC's *Final Report* lists forty recommendations in support of greater powers of self-government for Indian tribes and forty-four in support of economic development policies. Together, these recommendations account for 43 percent of the total; obviously, both self-government and economic development policies are basic components of the self-determination philosophy, but not the definition the AIPRC chose to emphasize.

2. These quotations, and those that follow, are from President Nixon's Message to the Congress, *Congressional Quarterly Almanac* (1970), pp. 101A–105A.

3. That the Indian policy community equates sovereignty with self-government and the trust relationship can be seen in the AIPRC's *Final Report*, pp. 100–103, 622.

4. This discussion of the legislation is taken from the hearings before the Senate Subcommittee on Indian Affairs, 1974 and 1977; House Report 95–1386 (July 24, 1978); and Senate Report 95–597 (November 1, 1977).

5. The Mormon church (LDS) was prominently represented in the hearings, because its adoption programs were frequently cited as a primary example of the historical trend to remove Indian children from tribal to non-Indian home environments. Citations to the AIPRC in this chapter are from the *Final Report*, 1977.

6. Jurisdictional power is, for example, the power to license, tax, or zone as well as the assertion of treaty rights in regard to hunting, fishing, leasing, and economic development in general.

7. President Reagan's remarks to Soviet students drew criticism from American Indian leaders. Reagan, for example, said the American people made a mistake when they gave Indians reservations rather than integrating them into society. He went on to betray his ignorance that American Indians have been U.S. citizens since 1924 by commenting that "we should not have humored them in . . . wanting to stay in that kind of primitive lifestyle . . . we should have said: – 'No, come join us. Be citizens along with the rest of us.' " The president also mistakenly referred to Indians as "very wealthy because some of those reservations were overlaying great pools of oil. And you can get very rich pumping oil" (*New York Times*, 1988, p. 7, A13).

THE CHALLENGE OF INDIGENOUS SELF-DETERMINATION†

Russel Lawrence Barsh*

Those who ought to know better nourish our crazy dreams of resurrection and redemption; those safely beyond the borders of our madness underwrite our lunacies.[1]

Last year world leaders met in Rio de Janeiro to agree on the terms of a global compact on the environment.[2] The final document of the "Earth Summit" is potentially far-reaching and as ponderous as it is complex. It breaks new ground on a number of fronts, including the conservation of the world's forests, and the establishment of a United Nations Commission on Sustainable Development.[3] It also recognizes for the first time that the world's indigenous peoples "have a vital role in environmental management and development because of their knowledge and traditional practices,"[4] and directs every national government and United Nations agency to develop a procedure for involving indigenous peoples in all relevant decisionmaking.[5]

† In Volume 25 of the *University of Michigan Journal of Law Reform*, Dean Suagee, in *Self-Determination for Indigenous Peoples at the Dawn of the Solar Age*, described the new opportunities for self-determination of indigenous peoples that are opening up under international law. *See* 25 U. MICH. J. L. REF. 671 (1992). In this Article, Russel Barsh presents a less optimistic view of the short-term prospects for American Indian tribes. This view is based on an assessment of social and political trends within the Indian community, as opposed to Mr. Suagee's critique of international law.

* Professor of Native American Studies, University of Lethbridge; United Nations Representative, Mikmaq Grand Council and Four Directions Council (Eskasoni, Nova Scotia). J.D. 1974, Harvard Law School. This essay is based on remarks made March 20, 1992, at the Native American Law Day program organized by the Native American Law Students Association at the University of Michigan Law School. It represents a synthesis of many of my earlier works, which are cited throughout the text. Unreferenced observations and opinions are based on my personal experiences in tribal politics and United Nations negotiations and are my responsibility alone.

1. SHIVA NAIPAUL, BLACK AND WHITE 16–17 (1980).
2. *See* 1 *Report of the United Nations Conference on Environment and Development*, U.N. Doc. A/Conf. 151/26/Rev. 1 (1992).
3. *See id.* ch. 38, at 459–460.
4. *Id.* "Rio Declaration," Principle 22, at 7.
5. *Id.* ch. 26, at 385–88.

The Earth Summit at Rio was the first global negotiation in which indigenous peoples participated directly. They did so with the aim of advocating land rights and greater self-determination in the fields of natural-resource management and development.[6] They justified these claims by arguing that indigenous peoples are superior stewards of the land and that strengthening indigenous peoples' traditional economies would contribute to solving global ecological and economic problems.[7] This approach succeeded all too well. Jaded diplomats and environmental ministers seized on the hopeful possibility that indigenous economics actually might work better than discredited socialism and overextended capitalism, and they invited indigenous peoples to accept a leadership role, nationally and globally. A few weeks after Rio, Latin American presidents announced the establishment of a regional development fund to be managed jointly by indigenous peoples and governments.[8]

Can indigenous peoples deliver on their commitments at Rio? What role, in particular, can be played by American Indian tribes, who were conspicuously underrepresented in the preparatory negotiations for the Earth Summit and other

---

6. *See, e.g.*, Francois Coutu, *Les autochtones veulent leur organisme de l'ONU*, 3 CROSSCURRENTS 4 (1992); Declaration of the Indigenous People in Paris 1991 (Indigenous Network trans.) (unpublished manuscript, prepared for the Paris United Nations Conference on Environment and Development, Non-Governmental Organizations, on file with the *University of Michigan Journal of Law Reform*); Final Proposal of the Indigenous Peoples Representatives Attending PrepCom IV (Mar. 1992) (unpublished manuscript, concerning U.N. Doc. A/Conf. 151/PC/100/Add.13, on file with the *University of Michigan Journal of Law Reform*) (endorsed by 16 organizations); National Maori Congress, Inter-generational Responsibility: Position Paper for United Nations Conference on Environment and Development (1992) (unpublished manuscript, on file with the *University of Michigan Journal of Law Reform*); World Council of Indigenous Peoples, Declaración de Panajachel: A los Pueblos del Mundo (Feb. 20, 1992) (unpublished manuscript, on file with the *University of Michigan Journal of Law Reform*).

7. *See* Russel L. Barsh, *Indigenous Peoples, Racism and the Environment*, 49 MEANJIN 723, 725, 728 (1990); Russel L. Barsh, *Indigenous Peoples' Role in Achieving Sustainability*, 1992 GREEN GLOBE Y.B. (Fridtjof Nansen Inst.) 25, 31–33.

8. AGREEMENT ESTABLISHING THE FUND FOR THE DEVELOPMENT OF THE INDIGENOUS PEOPLES OF LATIN AMERICA AND THE CARIBBEAN, (1992) (available from the Fund for the Development of the Indigenous Peoples of Latin America and the Caribbean, Inter-American Development Bank Office, Wash., D.C.), *see also Letter Dated 30 July 1992 from the Permanent Representative of Spain to the United Nations, Addressed to the Secretary-General*, at 13, U.N. Doc. A/47/356 (1992).

recent international meetings?[9] The answers to these questions are suggested by a critical assessment of what American Indian tribal governments have achieved after sixty years of "self-government" and twenty years of "self-determination."[10] We begin with a threshold problem: the characteristic isolationism of American Indian leadership in the twentieth century.

I. AGAINST ISOLATIONISM

American Indians were not always isolationists. There are Mikmaq stories about the first Europeans who stumbled ashore on what today is called Nova Scotia. After their long ocean voyage and miserable diet of dried bread and peas, they were a pretty sorry sight, and American Indians took pity on them. Not only did they feed these visitors, but they began to wonder what kind of terrible country they must have come from, to be willing to cross the ocean to escape from it. Emissaries were sent to Europe to meet European princes, study the situation, and report back to their communities.[11]

North American Indians had visited Europe in the 1500s, even before the Jamestown and Plymouth settlements were

9. The author participated in the negotiations in which the indigenous peoples of Canada, New Zealand, the Nordic countries, and the Circumpolar and Amazonian regions were represented by national organizations or coalitions. From the United States' territory only the Six Nations (Haudenosaunee) were actively involved in the meeting.

10. These terms refer to the Indian Reorganization Act of 1934, 25 U.S.C. §§ 461–479 (1988), and the "self-determination" policy inaugurated by President Nixon in 1970. *See generally* AMERICAN INDIAN POLICY IN THE TWENTIETH CENTURY (Vine Deloria, Jr. ed., 1985); ROBERT L. BEE, THE POLITICS OF AMERICAN INDIAN POLICY (1982); FELIX S. COHEN'S HANDBOOK OF FEDERAL INDIAN LAW (Rennard Strickland ed., 1982). For a recent presidential policy statement on this subject, see Statement Reaffirming the Government-to-Government Relationship Between the Federal Government and Indian Tribal Governments, Pub. Papers 662, 662 (June 14, 1991), which describes relations between the Federal Government and tribal governments as "a vibrant partnership in which over 500 tribal governments stand shoulder to shoulder with the other governmental units that form our Republic."

11. Marie Battiste, *A History of the Grand Council to 1800*, *in* 1 MIKMAQ STATE PAPERS (FOREIGN AFFAIRS) 1977–1984, at 1, 3–4 (Russel L. Barsh, Sakej Henderson, and Bernie Francis eds., 1984).

established.[12] There are no firsthand written records of their observations, but it is probably safe to assume that they were not positively impressed by the dirt, disease, overcrowding, violence, and poverty that they witnessed in Paris and London. They returned to their families in America with stories of a terrible imbalance in the world, which they feared could destroy all life.[13]

Their compassion for the earliest European explorers and settlers was not confined to the care of individuals whom they found stranded, starving, or lost on their shores. It was also a wider concern for balance and justice in the world. Their traditions taught them that all living things and every human family share responsibility for maintaining this fragile planet, that a plague in Lisbon was as much their concern as the sickness which was beginning to blow through their own villages. Everything in the world was connected. Hence, the struggle to restore harmony was necessarily a global one.

American Indians still believed in these principles in 1918, when nearly a third of all Indian men served in the armed forces, half of whom were volunteers.[14] Indians saw the European war as a contest over respect for treaties and the self-determination of nations. It was natural, then, for Levi General, or Deskaheh, the Speaker of the Six Nations, later to seek an audience with the League of Nations.[15] It also was natural for American Indians to be involved in the evolving international labor movement in the 1910s and 1920s, when

12. *See* CAROLYN T. FOREMAN, INDIANS ABROAD 1493–1938, at 3–21 (1943) (noting that a great many Indians reached Europe as victims of kidnappings for research or for the slave trade); *cf.* RICHMOND P. BOND, QUEEN ANNE'S AMERICAN KINGS (1974) (recounting the positive treatment of a few Indian visitors to Europe in the 1700s); DAVID H. CORKRAN, THE CREEK FRONTIER 1540–1783, at 85–89 (1967) (same).

13. Although Indian visitors reportedly were awed by the sheer size of European cities and the opulence of the royal courts, it was clear to the missionary Pierre Biard, writing in 1616, that they preferred "their own kind of happiness to ours." 3 THE JESUIT RELATIONS AND ALLIED DOCUMENTS 135 (Reuben G. Thwaites ed. & John C. Covert trans., Cleveland, Burrows Brothers Co. 1897). A Mikmaq likewise told Christien LeClercq in 1690 that "'there is no Indian who does not consider himself infinitely more happy and more powerful than the French.'" CHRISTIEN LECLERCQ, NEW RELATION OF GASPESIA 106 (William F. Ganong trans., 1910).

14. *See* Russel L. Barsh, *American Indians in the Great War*, 38 ETHNOHISTORY 276, 277 (1991).

15. LAURENCE M. HAUPTMAN, THE IROQUOIS AND THE NEW DEAL 16 (1981). Although Deskaneh was unsuccessful in his plea for recognition by the League, some member states defended his claim and Canada felt obliged to make a formal response. APPEAL OF THE "SIX NATIONS" TO THE LEAGUE, 5 LEAGUE OF NATIONS O.J. 829 (1924).

the movement was still committed to world socialism.[16] After the long darkness of colonialism and threatened extermination, Indians were reemerging, in the 1920s, as a social force and universalist voice.

A. From Integration to Nationalism

Somewhere along the path to this reemergence, however, American Indian consciousness turned inwards. While Indians in the United States have the highest per capita income and education levels of indigenous peoples anywhere in the world, they have the lowest level of involvement in both the world indigenous struggle and the global campaign for the environment.[17] Those Indian leaders who continue to assume global responsibility, such as Haudenosaunee chief Oren Lyons and Hopi messenger Thomas Benyaca, Sr., represent relatively small, traditionalist communities which are viewed as marginal by most elected tribal councils and mainstream Indian associations. A "tribal summit" on United Nations

16. The "Wobblies," members of the Industrial Workers of the World, supported the Mexican revolution and the Mexican Liberal Party (PLM) founded by that country's first Indian president, Benito Juarez. They went so far as to land a military force of Wobblies—including several Indians—in Baja California in 1911. JAMES A. SANDOS, REBELLION IN THE BORDERLANDS: ANARCHISM AND THE PLAN OF SAN DIEGO, 1904–1923, at 27 (1992). Indian rights also formed a major plank in the 1915 Plan of San Diego, prepared by pro-Revolution elements in the Southwest. *Id.* at 80–82. For the text of the plan, see OSCAR J. MARTINEZ, FRAGMENTS OF THE MEXICAN REVOLUTION: PERSONAL ACCOUNTS FROM THE BORDER 145–48 (1983). Yaqui Indians, who routinely obtained their guns and ammunition in Arizona, played a major role in Villa's army. LINDA B. HALL & DON M. COERVER, REVOLUTION ON THE BORDER: THE UNITED STATES AND MEXICO, 1910–1920, at 41–42, 143–44 (1988). On the other hand, Pershing used Apache scouts in his 1917 punitive expedition against Villa and the Yaquis. *Id.* at 36, 58.

17. Indian income figures from the 1990 census are not yet available. In 1980, Indian income levels were roughly 80% of white income levels. Unless this ratio has fallen to 50% or less, U.S. Indians today are enjoying incomes greater than the per capita GDPs of any of the non-OPEC developing countries. *See* UNITED NATIONS DEVELOPMENT PROGRAMME, HUMAN DEVELOPMENT REPORT 1992, at 160–61, 197. *See generally* Leonard A. Carlson & Caroline Swartz, *The Earnings of Women and Ethnic Minorities, 1959–1979*, 41 INDUS. & LAB. REL. REV. 530 (1988); C. Matthew Snipp & Gary D. Sandefur, *Earnings of American Indians and Alaskan Natives: The Effects of Residence and Migration*, 66 SOC. FORCES 994 (1988) (examining the effect on income of residence in, and migration to, metropolitan areas). This is not to belittle the relative and absolute poverty on U.S. reservations. *See* Judith Valente, *A Century Later, Sioux Still Struggle, and Still Are Losing*, WALL ST. J., Mar. 25, 1991, at A1.

strategy, convened in Denver last June at the suggestion of several Canadian aboriginal organizations, only attracted representatives of four United States tribal governments.[18]

This is not merely a question of isolation from the struggles and peoples of other continents, but from the peoples of this continent as well. When Europeans arrived, North American Indian tribes were in a process of integration, and great tribal confederacies continued to bridge the Canadian border as late as the 1800s. The Great Council Fire combined the Iroquois, Wabanaki, Anishinawbe, and Wyandot leagues,[19] while the Blackfoot Confederacy and Great Sioux Nation spanned the border in the west.[20] It took a number of punitive expeditions, ending only in 1918, to divide the Indians of the Southwest from their kinsfolk in Mexico.[21] Today, the Mexican and Canadian borders are cultural and political barriers. Moreover, there is no longer an effective *national* coalition of American Indians.[22]

Isolationism is a peculiarly American problem. In Latin America, Indians are forming national political parties and building regional coalitions spanning the Andes. Although frictions occur, these represent ideological and leadership

---

18. The meeting was organized by the Council of Energy Resource Tribes (CERT), the only major United States tribal organization with Canadian members. *See* UNITED NATIONS, ECONOMIC AND SOCIAL COUNSEL, SUB-COMMISSION ON PREVENTION OF DISCRIMINATION AND PROTECTION OF MINORITIES, STANDARD SETTING ACTIVITIES: EVOLUTION OF STANDARDS CONCERNING THE RIGHTS OF INDIGENOUS POPULATIONS, REPORT OF THE TRIBAL SUMMIT ON THE DRAFT DECLARATION OF THE RIGHTS OF INDIGENOUS PEOPLES, DENVER, JUNE 1992, U.N. Doc. E/CN.4/Sub.2/AC.4/1992/3/Add.1 (1992). One of Canada's aboriginal leaders, George Manuel, was organizing the World Council of indigenous peoples at the same time that Vine Deloria, one of the best-known U.S. Indian writers and activists, was arguing unsuccessfully for an Indian political appeal to other nations. *See* VINE DELORIA, JR., BEHIND THE TRAIL OF BROKEN TREATIES: AN INDIAN DECLARATION OF INDEPENDENCE (1974); GEORGE MANUEL & MICHAEL POSLUNS, THE FOURTH WORLD: AN INDIAN REALITY (1974).

19. *See* THE HISTORY AND CULTURE OF IROQUOIS DIPLOMACY (Francis Jennings et al. eds., 1985) (detailing the pre-19th-century structure and function of the confederacy); FRANCIS JENNINGS, THE AMBIGUOUS IROQUOIS EMPIRE (1984) (same).

20. *See* JOHN C. EWERS, THE BLACKFEET: RAIDERS ON THE NORTHWESTERN PLAINS (1958); HANA SAMEK, THE BLACKFOOT CONFEDERACY 1880–1920: A COMPARATIVE STUDY OF CANADIAN AND U.S. INDIAN POLICY (1987); C. FRANK TURNER, ACROSS THE MEDICINE LINE (1973).

21. *See generally* HALL & COERVER, *supra* note 16, at 42.

22. Canada's Assembly of First Nations is recognized by the press and government as a national political force, comparable to a major opposition political party. Statements by the National Chief of the Assembly routinely receive national press coverage. By comparison, the National Congress of American Indians (NCAI) is almost invisible. Most of the tribes divided by the border have evolved separate tribal governments and programs, even if linguistic and social links remain.

disputes, rather than a lack of commitment to regional solidarity. At least one of these emerging organizations, composed of Indian parliamentarians, includes Canadians but not Americans. Global summits of indigenous leaders have recently been convened in Mexico City, Lima, Quito, and Rio de Janeiro. In the Pacific, likewise, there has been a growing regional mobilization that involves both indigenous peoples and small island States. The Sami people of Norway, Sweden, Finland, and Russia have established a single representative organization, the Nordic Sami Council. Alaskan Eskimos, together with their counterparts in Greenland, Russia, and Canada, are part of the Inuit Circumpolar Conference but this only highlights the relative isolation of indigenous Americans south of Fairbanks.

A critical case in point is Guatemala, where a succession of regimes backed by the United States have conducted a vicious war of extermination against a Mayan Indian majority for nearly thirty years.[23] Guatemalan Indians have flocked to the United States as refugees, but have received no official support or recognition from American Indian tribal governments. How can American Indian tribal leaders pretend to have achieved any measure of "sovereignty," when plainly they are either powerless or unwilling to respond to the murder of so many Indians, just a few hundred miles south of the Rio Grande? Indeed, if tribes have a "government-to-government relationship" with Washington, as they routinely boast, do they not share blame for United States-financed genocide in Central America? American Indian tribal leaders have taken a direct stand in support of their Latin Indian cousins only once, and that was to condemn the Sandinista government's policies in Nicaragua—a convenient convergence with United States foreign policy which joined the National Tribal Chairmen's Association and the American Indian Movement together for the first and last time.[24]

---

23. *See* SUSANNE JONAS, THE BATTLE FOR GUATEMALA: REBELS, DEATH SQUADS, AND U.S. POWER (1991); *see also* Pierre L. van den Berghe, *The Ixil Triangle: Vietnam in Guatemala*, *in* STATE VIOLENCE AND ETHNICITY 253, 253–54, 277–78 (Pierre L. van den Berghe ed., 1990).

24. This is not to defend the Sandinistas; their original plans for the Indians of the Atlantic Coast were heavy-handed and paternalistic, and perhaps a little naive. It is only to suggest that American Indian tribes are incapable of defining an independent, indigenous foreign policy.

This political isolationism underscores the extreme vulnerability of American tribal institutions to federal government retaliation. Most tribes continue to be heavily dependent on discretionary federal aid.[25] Paradoxically, this dependence increased in the 1980s as federal Indian spending dwindled because tribes meanwhile had built a costly administrative infrastructure that they needed to maintain. As a consequence of this growing fiscal squeeze, tribal leaders grew increasingly competitive in their demands for federal aid, and in desperation agreed to more conditions.[26] Such intensified pork-slicing obviates any measure of national Indian unity on basic policy issues, domestic or foreign. At the same time federal officials, who never had hesitated to interfere in tribal decisions,[27] found themselves possessed of even greater leverage. It is no wonder, then, that tribal leaders hesitate to embarrass the United States abroad, while damning it privately at home.

I recently saw a staff memorandum prepared for the elected chairman of one of the largest tribes in the United States, urging participation in a United Nations program to help North and South American Indian communities work together on environmental protection. He returned it marked, "We have our own problems—NO!" His tribe is widely perceived as strongly traditional and enjoys a multimillion-dollar annual operating budget. What does this say about the roots of American Indian isolationism?

---

25. *See* Russel L. Barsh & Katherine Diaz-Knauf, *The Structure of Federal Aid for Indian Programs in the Decade of Prosperity, 1970–1980*, 8 AM. INDIAN Q. 1 (1984); George P. Castille, *Federal Indian Policy and the Sustained Enclave: An Anthropological Perspective*, 33 HUM. ORGANIZATION 219 (1974).

26. *See* Russel L. Barsh, *Indian Policy at the Beginning of the 1990s: The Trivialization of Struggle*, *in* AMERICAN INDIAN POLICY: SELF-GOVERNANCE AND ECONOMIC DEVELOPMENT (Fremont J. Lyden & Lyman H. Legters eds., forthcoming); *see also* C. Patrick Morris, *Termination by Accountants: The Reagan Indian Policy*, *in* NATIVE AMERICANS AND PUBLIC POLICY 63 (Fremont J. Lyden & Lyman H. Legters eds., 1992).

27. *See, e.g.*, *Occupation of Wounded Knee: Hearings Before the Subcomm. of Indian Affairs of the Senate Comm. of Interior and Insular Affairs*, 93d Cong., 1st Sess. (1973) [hereinafter *Occupation of Wounded Knee*]; JAMES J. LOPACH ET AL., TRIBAL GOVERNMENT TODAY: POLITICS ON MONTANA INDIAN RESERVATIONS 44, 50, 90, 126–29, 183 (1990); Felix S. Cohen, *The Erosion of Indian Rights, 1950–1953: A Case Study in Bureaucracy*, 62 YALE L.J. 348 (1953).

B. *Cultural Abuse and Self-Rejection*

If there is a fundamental cause of American Indian isolationism, it is 500 years of abuse. Colonialism and oppression operate at a personal, psychological, and cultural level, as well as in the realms of political and economic structures. The children of dysfunctional, abusive parents grow up in a capricious world of arbitrary punishment, humiliation, and powerlessness. They suffer from insecurity, low self-esteem, and a loss of trust in others.[28] Colonialism is the abuse of an entire civilization for generations. It creates a culture of mistrust, defensiveness, and "self-rejection."[29] The effect is greatest on women, who already are suffering from patriarchal domination in some cultures, and in others, are subjected to patriarchal domination for the first time by the colonizers.[30] This can produce a politics of resignation, reactiveness, and continuing dependence on outsiders for leadership.[31]

Arguably the worst abuse of indigenous peoples worldwide has taken place in the United States, which not only pursued an aggressive and intrusive policy of cultural assimilation for more than a century, but also has preserved a particularly self-confident cultural arrogance to this day, denying Indians

---

28. *See generally* RACHEL CALAM & CRISTINA FRANCHI, CHILD ABUSE AND ITS CONSEQUENCES 6–8 (1987); ALICE MILLER, BANISHED KNOWLEDGE: FACING CHILDHOOD INJURIES (1990).

29. *See* ALBERT MEMMI, DOMINATED MAN: NOTES TOWARDS A PORTRAIT 16–20, 107 (1968). In his famous study of the psychiatric casualties of French colonialism in Algeria, Frantz Fanon observed: "Because it is a systematic negation of the other person and a furious determination to deny the other person all attributes of humanity, colonialism forces the people it dominates to ask themselves the question constantly: 'In reality, who am I?'" FRANTZ FANON, THE WRETCHED OF THE EARTH 203 (Constance Farrington trans., 1966).

30. *See* TRINH T. MINH-HA, WOMAN, NATIVE OTHER, 79–80 (1989). Women played distinct and critical roles in most original American Indian cultures. *See* PAULA G. ALLEN, THE SACRED HOOP: RECOVERING THE FEMININE IN AMERICAN INDIAN TRADITIONS (1986).

31. *See* OSCAR LEWIS, LA VIDA: A PUERTO RICAN FAMILY IN THE CULTURE OF POVERTY—SAN JUAN AND NEW YORK (1966). *But see* Charles A. Valentine, *The "Culture of Poverty": Its Scientific Significance and Its Implications for Action*, *in* THE CULTURE OF POVERTY: A CRITIQUE 193 (Eleanor B. Leacock ed., 1971) (criticizing Lewis's data and theory). There is no disputing, however, that poverty and powerlessness can, through the power of self-fulfilling prophecy, grow into a vicious circle of self-rejection and failure.

the recognition that they need to begin healing themselves.[32] The negative effects of cultural abuse are proportional to the thoroughness with which the colonizer intervenes in the daily lives of ordinary people. Intense warfare can be less damaging than the captivity and daily "disciplining" of an entire population, which characterized reservation life at the end of the last century.[33] Under these conditions, the only avenue of escape permitted is to embrace the habits and values of the oppressor, leaving people with a cruel choice between being victimized as "inferior" Indians or as second-class whites. In either case, much more was lost than cultural knowledge. Also lost was confidence in the possibility of genuine self-determination.

Global action is an act of faith and self-confidence. Prolonged exposure to the perspectives of others casts a long, critical shadow on one's own beliefs and actions. It shatters assumptions about what is, what ought to be, and what may be possible. People confident in their identity and values have nothing to fear from this, and much to gain. People stricken with self-rejection and doubt, on the other hand, prefer to remain safely within familiar orbits, avoiding what they fear will be the definitive confirmation of their inferiority. Isolated within the borders of the United States, American Indian leaders can perpetuate the illusions of "sovereignty" and self-determination among themselves, without risk of challenge by indigenous peoples who come from other, less damaging experiences. It is no wonder, then, that they avoid participating in international political activities, and it is equally clear why the next generation of American Indians must begin their political education far away from North America. Without a comparative perspective, today's anaesthetic illusions can persist indefinitely.

---

32. *Cf.* ANN H. BEUF, RED CHILDREN IN WHITE AMERICA (1977) (explaining the development of negative self-images in Native American children). Australia, however, with its systematic removal of aboriginal children from their communities, marketing of aboriginal children as domestic servants, and "breeding-out" policies, is also a strong competitor for first place. *See generally* BARBARA CUMMINGS, TAKE THIS CHILD . . . FROM KAHLIN COMPOUND TO THE RETTA DIXON CHILDREN'S HOME (1990); J.J. FLETCHER, CLEAN, CLAD AND COURTEOUS: A HISTORY OF ABORIGINAL EDUCATION IN NEW SOUTH WALES (1989); ANNA HAEBICK, FOR THEIR OWN GOOD: ABORIGINES AND GOVERNMENT IN THE SOUTHWEST OF WESTERN AUSTRALIA, 1900–1940 (1989).

33. *See, e.g.*, WILLIAM T. HAGAN, INDIAN POLICE AND JUDGES: EXPERIMENTS IN ACCULTURATION AND CONTROL (1966); FREDERICK E. HOXIE, A FINAL PROMISE: THE CAMPAIGN TO ASSIMILATE THE INDIANS, 1880–1920 (1984); D.S. OTIS, THE DAWES ACT AND THE ALLOTMENT OF INDIAN LANDS (Francis P. Prucha ed., 1973).

C. *Isolationism as a Culture*

Indian isolationism is a symptom of Americanization, and American Indians are more assimilated than they would like to believe. This is evident at many levels, from personal values to political culture. It is apparent symbolically in the prominent place given to the U.S. flag at tribal meetings and pow-wows, for instance. National flags are not seen at indigenous meetings in other countries; aboriginal Australians meet under the red, yellow, and black Land Rights Flag, just as Mikmaq display the Mikmaq Grand Council's red sun-moon-and-cross flag, rather than the red maple leaf of Canada. National flag worship is inconsistent with the rhetoric of independent tribal sovereignty.

At the level of personal values, the materialism that makes bingo[34] a more important policy issue than environmental health or substance abuse[35] for contemporary tribal governments also is reflected in their sense that other countries have nothing to offer except trade dollars. Americans return from abroad thankful for the high standards of material comfort that they enjoy at home, and this is true even of Indians, who continue to be among the very poorest Americans.[36] Little matter that this American material superiority was achieved at the expense of Indians' own land[37] and has been maintained by dominating the economies of other countries and destroying the land of other indigenous

---

34. For examples of tribal enthusiasm for gambling, see David Holmstrom, *Bingo! Indian Tribes Find Way to Make Money*, CHRISTIAN SCI. MONITOR, Sept. 4, 1991, at 8; Wayne King, *Atlantic City Shivers at Indians' Casinos to Come*, N.Y. TIMES, May 28, 1991 at B4; Pauline Yoshihashi, *Indian Tribes Put Their Bets on Casinos*, WALL ST. J., Aug. 5, 1991, at B1. Gambling has become a bitter election issue on New York reservations. *See e.g.*, *Sovereignty and Casino Beckon to a Tribe*, N.Y. TIMES, Oct. 29, 1992, at B8.

35. On the growing reservation problems of substance abuse and violence, see Michael Dorris, THE BROKEN CORD (1991); MICHAEL S. MONCHER et al., *Substance Abuse Among Native-American Youth*, 58 J. CONSULTING & CLINICAL PSYCHOL. 408; Thomas J. Young, *Poverty, Suicide, and Homicide among Native Americans*, 67 PSYCHOL. REP. 1153 (1990) [hereinafter Young, *Poverty, Suicide, and Homicide*]; Thomas J. Young, *Suicide and Homicide among Native Americans: Anomie or Social Learning*? 68 PSYCHOL. REP. 1137 (1991) [hereinafter Young, *Suicide and Homicide*].

36. *See supra* note 17.

37. Russel L. Barsh, *Indian Resources and the National Economy: Business Cycles and Policy Cycles*, *in* NATIVE AMERICANS AND PUBLIC POLICY, *supra* note 26, at 193.

peoples.[38] As they prosper, albeit only comparatively, American Indians share the benefits of the United States' economic expansion; hence, they also should share some of the blame and take responsibility for change. Instead, it seems that Indians today *like* being "number one" in the world as part of the United States, and that they rely on the military power that once oppressed them to protect them from others.[39]

On the political plane, American Indians seem to have assimilated the American perception that global affairs are basically irrelevant, because all real power is found in Washington and all truly important decisions are made there. The egocentricism of American textbooks and journalism certainly has laid the foundation for this parochial view. Americans learn very little even about their closest neighbors, Canada and Mexico, and most Indians have been taught from the same books and have watched the same television programming for a generation. Years of domination by federal bureaucrats and sending tribal officials off to plead for money on Capitol Hill, no doubt have helped reinforce the nationalist prejudices Indians share with other Americans.

Indeed, American Indians seem to think of themselves as superior to other indigenous peoples, not in terms of traditional culture, but because they believe they have made so much progress gaining political and economic power within

---

38. Two recent United Nations documents detail the impact of United States and international developments on indigenous peoples. See UNITED NATIONS, ECONOMIC AND SOCIAL COUNSEL, SUB-COMMISSION ON PREVENTION OF DISCRIMINATION AND PROTECTION OF MINORITIES, DISCRIMINATION AGAINST INDIGENOUS PEOPLES: TRANSNATIONAL INVESTMENTS AND OPERATION ON THE LANDS OF INDIGENOUS PEOPLES, REPORT OF THE UNITED NATIONS CENTRE ON TRANSNATIONAL CORPORATIONS PURSUANT TO SUB-COMMISSION RESOLUTION 1990/26, U.N. Doc. E/CN.4/Sub.2/1992/54 (1992) [hereinafter DISCRIMINATION AGAINST INDIGENOUS PEOPLES 1992]; UNITED NATIONS, ECONOMIC AND SOCIAL COUNCIL, SUB-COMMISSION ON PREVENTION OF DISCRIMINATION AND PROTECTION OF MINORITIES, DISCRIMINATION AGAINST INDIGENOUS PEOPLES: TRANSNATIONAL INVESTMENTS AND OPERATIONS ON THE LANDS OF INDIGENOUS PEOPLES, REPORT OF THE UNITED NATIONS CENTRE ON TRANSNATIONAL CORPORATIONS PURSUANT TO SUB-COMMISSION RESOLUTION 1990/26, U.N. Doc. E/CN.4/Sub.2/1991/49 (1991) [hereinafter DISCRIMINATION AGAINST INDIGENOUS PEOPLES 1991]; *cf.* JOHN H. MAKIN, THE GLOBAL DEBT CRISIS: AMERICA'S GROWING INVOLVEMENT 57–71 (1984) (examining American dependence on raw materials).

39. It should be noted that Europeans are fascinated with Indians and annually go to great lengths to attract Indian performers and speakers. *See* INDIANS AND EUROPE (Christian F. Feest ed., 1987) (offering a variety of views on this phenomenon). Some American Indians find this attention and flattery redemptive and thus Europe continues to be a favored travel destination, as opposed to Latin America or Southeast Asia, where there is great poverty—and where there are other indigenous peoples.

the United States.[40] They offer themselves, their contemporary tribal institutions, and current United States Indian policy and law as a global standard of comparison and evaluation, with little self-criticism. No effort is made to search for better models abroad; it is assumed that none can be found. Of course, this is not true of all American Indians. A handful annually travel to the United Nations to condemn the United States' treatment of its own people, but they generally are individual dissidents, academics, or traditional religious elders.[41] U.S. diplomats dismiss them by pointing out that only malcontents bother to make these pilgrimages; the elected tribal chairpersons and mainstream organizations such as the National Congress of American Indians and Native American Rights Fund, stay home.[42]

D. The Price of Isolationism

Isolationism deprives American Indians of international political support, which they need to compensate for their numerical inferiority and the extraordinary power and arrogance of the non-Indian majority. It also leaves U.S. institutions relatively free to exploit indigenous people elsewhere. American industry plays a major role in development projects affecting indigenous lands in other regions, particularly in Latin America.[43] The United States government, meanwhile, staunchly resists the United Nations'

40. *See generally* Russel L. Barsh, *Political Diversification of the International Indigenous Movement*, 5 EUR. REV. NATIVE AM. STUD. 7 (1991) (discussing the different strategic approaches of indigenous peoples).

41. No summary statistics of participation in United Nations meetings are published, but a sense of geographic distribution can be gleaned from the annual reports of the Working Group on Indigenous Populations, most recently *Report of the Working Group on Indigenous Populations*, at 3–4, U.N. Doc. E/CN.4/Sub.2/1992/33 (1992).

42. One U.S. case, the Navajo-Hopi relocation dispute, which was raised by community leaders from the affected areas, has been on the U.N. human rights agenda for several years. UNITED NATIONS, ECONOMIC AND SOCIAL COUNCIL, COMMISSION ON HUMAN RIGHTS, REPORT OF THE SUB-COMMISSION ON PREVENTION OF DISCRIMINATION AND PROTECTION OF MINORITIES ON ITS FORTY-FOURTH SESSION at 87–88, U.N. Doc. E/CN.4/1993/2 (1992). The tribal councils have avoided direct involvement in the United Nations process, however, and the State Department has actively discouraged it.

43. *See* DISCRIMINATION AGAINST INDIGENOUS PEOPLES 1992, *supra* note 38; DISCRIMINATION AGAINST INDIGENOUS PEOPLES 1991, *supra* note 38.

efforts to recognize indigenous peoples' collective rights as distinct societies, contending that such recognition would be "fundamentally inconsistent" with international law.[44] The United States repeatedly has opposed funding for United Nations programs aimed at indigenous communities, threatening to vote against establishing 1993 as the International Year of the World's Indigenous People if it involved any spending; opposing the launching of a United Nations study of indigenous treaties on the grounds that it was anti-American; and at one point hinting that it would try to have the United Nations' ten-year-old Working Group on Indigenous Populations dissolved because it had the poor taste to discuss Navajo relocation.[45] Other governments have tried to slow the United Nations' work in this field, among them Canada and Brazil, but their indigenous peoples are well-organized nationally and respond quickly and effectively to any threat in the national press and legislature.[46]

More is at stake than the protection of indigenous rights. Since the disintegration of the Soviet Union in 1989, the United States, unimpeded by other superpowers, has been able to dominate international politics as never before. This may be only temporary. Europe eventually will get beyond its current preoccupation with regional integration, and Japan may emerge more self-consciously as a political and ideological rival, particularly in Asia.[47] As the American deficit soars,

44. U.S. Delegation Statement at the Tenth Session of the Working Group on Indigenous Populations 6–7 (July 23–31, 1992) (speech draft, on file with the *University of Michigan Journal of Law Reform*).

45. I was personally involved in these discussions. Because of the financial and military power of the United States, its opinions carry a disproportionate weight in negotiations and need only be expressed at an informal level to be effective.

46. In the case of the treaty study, for example, Canadian resistance was exposed at a press conference of national Indian leaders, leading to the questioning of the responsible minister in parliament and, in less than two days, a reversal of position.

47. Japan already is by far the largest investor and aid-donor in East and Southeast Asia, and a close runner-up to the United States and Europeans in other regions. Japanese diplomats, meanwhile, have taken a surprisingly progressive stance on a number of humanitarian, aid, and environmental issues at the United Nations and have positioned Japanese nationals in two key U.N.-system directorships—the World Health Organization (WHO) and the U.N. High Commission for Refugees. *See* Lawrence K. Altman, *Head of U.N. Health Agency Is Embroiled in Battle for Re-election*, N.Y. TIMES, Aug. 10, 1992, at A3. WHO Director General Hiroshi Nakajima was reelected in a bitter campaign that reportedly was financed heavily by his government; Sadako Ogata remains as U.N. High Commissioner for Refugees.

U.S. borrowing no longer can be fully absorbed by European and Japanese lenders. The weakness of the American economy has been noted even by the International Monetary Fund, a steadfastly conservative institution that the United States long controlled.[48] In the meantime, a great deal of lasting damage may be done. A case in point is the Earth Summit last June, where the United States distinguished itself as the only industrialized country to oppose *combatting poverty* as a strategy for achieving "sustainability."[49] American diplomats also blocked consensus on a plan to enable all countries to tackle their environmental problems with comparable resources, on the grounds that it cost money and required the free sharing of "green" technology.[50]

Some American Indian tribal leaders flew to Rio to be part of the American entourage but did nothing to influence President Bush. Although world leaders had kind words for indigenous peoples and adopted an important declaration recognizing indigenous rights, their hopes for indigenous peoples' guidance and support were seriously misplaced—at least as far as American Indians were concerned.

American Indian tribal leaders could play a pivotal international role as the voice of conscience, reason, and generosity within the United States itself, not only with respect to the fate of other indigenous peoples, but the fate of the planet, too. Instead, they continue to be preoccupied with domestic issues, competing with one another for larger shares of federal program dollars and bigger bingo halls. Global consciousness, which was central to aboriginal religion and philosophy, has collapsed into competitive capitalism.

---

48. *See* Steven Greenhouse, *I.M.F. Head Scolds U.S. and Bonn for Deficits*, N.Y. TIMES, Sept. 23, 1992, at D6. For background on the impact of U.S. deficits on developing countries, see UNITED NATIONS, ECONOMIC AND SOCIAL COUNCIL, REPORT OF THE COMMITTEE FOR DEVELOPMENT PLANNING ON ITS TWENTY-SEVENTH SESSION, U.N. Doc. E/1991/32 (1991); Charles F. Meissner, *Debt: Reform Without Governments*, 56 FOREIGN POL'Y 81 (1984).

49. The author was present at the negotiating session in which U.S. representatives broke the consensus on this issue. *See generally* Laura Paull, *'Finger-pointing' in the Charter Debate*, CROSSCURRENTS at 5, Mar. 12, 1992; *US Seeks to Axe Global Consumption Sections*, CROSSCURRENTS at 8, Mar. 16, 1992.

50. *See* Steven Greenhouse, *Ecology, the Economy and Bush*, N.Y. TIMES, June 14, 1992, § 4, at 1; *The Road from Rio*, N.Y. TIMES, June 15, 1992, at A18; Keith Schneider, *Bush Aide Assails U.S. Preparations for Earth Summit*, N.Y. TIMES, Aug. 1, 1992, at A1.

II. DECOLONIZATION WITHOUT COMMITMENT

Apart from their potential role as American citizens and voters in restraining the immature political excesses of non-Indian Americans abroad, do American Indians have a substantive contribution to make to the liberation and development of other indigenous peoples? Answering this question leads unavoidably to another. Have American Indians any special wisdom or successful experience to share in rebuilding other indigenous societies racked by racism and colonialism? The answer to that question depends on whether American Indians genuinely have succeeded in liberating or decolonizing themselves.

Anticolonial struggles are preoccupied with wresting power from the colonizer. Little serious thought is given to the problem of what to do with power once it is obtained. A vacuum lies at the end of nearly every revolution which quickly fills with borrowed slogans and ideas. There is some truth in Ambrose Bierce's observation, nearly a century ago, that revolution is "an abrupt change in the form of misgovernment."[51] Indigenous peoples everywhere like to believe that the critical difference, in their case, is culture. Traditional cultures, which are diametrically opposed to the competitive individualism and insatiable appetite of industrialized societies, supposedly will insulate leaders from the corrupting influences of power and the "demonstration effect" of Western prosperity. But Africa's leaders made the same arguments a generation ago when they launched the idea of "African socialism," the beautiful dream behind which a number of oppressive dictatorships have safely lurked.[52]

Will the world's indigenous peoples escape Bierce's futile loop? The United States is a critical test case. American Indian tribes are wealthier and have enjoyed greater powers of internal self-government far longer than indigenous peoples anywhere else. The rhetoric of sovereignty, antimaterialism, and traditionalism is stronger here than anywhere else. But

---

51. AMBROSE BIERCE, THE DEVIL'S DICTIONARY 161 (1957).

52. *See generally* KWAME A. APPIAH, IN MY FATHER'S HOUSE: AFRICA IN THE PHILOSOPHY OF CULTURE (1992) (rendering a more philosophical view of African Socialism); AHMED MOHIDDIN, AFRICAN SOCIALISM IN TWO COUNTRIES (1981) (providing a critical assessment of African Socialism); JULIUS K. NYERERE, UJAMAA—ESSAYS ON SOCIALISM (1968) (presenting a classical exposition on African Socialism).

is this rhetoric meaningful, or is it merely rhetoric? To what extent have American Indian tribal governments achieved the ideals of community responsibility and ecological stewardship so often expressed in public debates? Are they truly decolonized at all? The answers to these questions explain American Indian tribes' marked isolationism in world affairs, and pose a serious challenge for future generations of indigenous leaders in all countries.

A. *Symbolic Development*

What has been achieved after fifty years of nominal self-government under the Indian Reorganization Act[53] and twenty-five years of federal financing of tribal programs and development?[54] Are reservations more democratic or ecologically sound than other North American communities? Are tribal schools, courts, and social programs better, or just different? Do they really differ at all, other than being staffed by Indians?

The number of books in print extolling traditional Indian values and beliefs grows exponentially,[55] but Indian tribal governments do not seem to put any of these beliefs into practice. It is also difficult to find published studies of the effectiveness of contemporary tribal institutions in relation to traditional values. Analysts simply seem to assume that anything run by Indians *is* more effective, and culturally appropriate, than the same institutions run by whites.[56]

---

53. 25 U.S.C. §§ 461–479 (1988).

54. For data on the distribution of federal aid at its peak, see Barsh & Diaz-Knauf, *supra* note 25, at 21.

55. *See, e.g.*, DAVID MAYBURY-LEWIS, MILLENNIUM: TRIBAL WISDOM AND THE MODERN WORLD (1992); DAVID SUZUKI & PETER KNUDTSON, WISDOM OF THE ELDERS: HONORING SACRED NATIVE VISIONS OF NATURE (1992). Although genuinely traditional knowledge still holds great scientific and ethical value, enthusiasts should take caution from DANIEL FRANCIS, THE IMAGINARY INDIAN: THE IMAGE OF THE INDIAN IN CANADIAN CULTURE 109–43 (1992), which depicts "celebrity Indians" and "plastic shamans."

56. Differences in cultural values are highlighted in *Native Americans and Public Policy*, particularly in the essays by Trosper and by Lyden, which argue that tribal governments *could* accommodate Indian values by making them explicit in their planning documents and econometric models. *See* Fremont J. Lyden, *Value Orientations in Public Decision Making*, *in* NATIVE AMERICANS AND PUBLIC POLICY, *supra* note 26, at 295; Ronald L. Trosper, *Multicriterion Decision Making in a Tribal Context*, *in* NATIVE AMERICANS AND PUBLIC POLICY, *supra* note 26, at 223. As to the

Indian policy literature is preoccupied with the *quantity* of Indian control, rather than the *quality* of its exercise.[57] This lack of self-criticism shifts all blame to the residual elements of colonialism and relieves tribal leaders of responsibility for the conditions in which Indians continue to live.[58]

Indian and non-Indian institutions have converged far more than tribal leaders or scholars want to admit. Reservation economies are centralized, industrialized, and bureaucratic. They measure success in terms of industrial through-put: budgets, payrolls, office space, and prison cells. Gross domestic product has replaced unity, family integrity, personal dignity, and mutual respect as a standard of good government. Tribal officials proudly show visitors their police cars, jails, mines, and factories. They do not discuss the growing frequency of child abuse or elder neglect, or ask the Indians in those jails whether they believe they live in a just society. The majority of tribal governments steadfastly refuse to collect and publish social statistics on which objective assessments of changing welfare could be based. They publish financial reports, like the business corporations they emulate.

These are all examples of what John Kenneth Galbraith once aptly described as "symbolic modernization."[59] The official visitor to any Third World capital will get the same kind of tour: office blocks, factories, armies, and airports. These are symbols of success, in Western terms, but they do not necessarily reflect self-determination or development. On the contrary, they demonstrate the increasing power of "indigenous" governments to oppress their own people, and they tend to mask growing gaps between rich and poor and among ethnic groups in society—which, incidentally, create the need for those armies and jails. A society that can parade

---

extent to which this kind of accommodation is actually pursued, however, they are silent. Moreover, adjusting the weighting of target outputs as a planning tool falls far short of adopting a culturally appropriate planning *process*. It is something Western-trained technocrats can do without changing the basic parameters of their jobs.

57. *See, e.g.*, MARJANE AMBLER, BREAKING THE IRON BONDS: INDIAN CONTROL OF ENERGY DEVELOPMENT (1990); Lynne Duke, *Indians Appeal to U.S. to Preserve Tribal Rule*, WASH. POST, Apr. 22, 1991, at A4 (illustrating the focus tribal leaders place on self-governance).

58. LOPACH ET AL., *supra* note 27, at 186.

59. Galbraith defined symbolic modernization in part as "a form of monument building by which politicians have undertaken to commemorate their existence (and perhaps ultimately their inadequacy) at the public expense." JOHN K. GALBRAITH, ECONOMIC DEVELOPMENT 5 (1964).

an army or build office towers is not a fairer, freer, or happier one as a result. Nor is it "progress" to have the ability, and the need, to control people. From a traditional Indian viewpoint, the accumulation and use of power is evidence of social breakdown and decay, not progress, and the number of battered children, inmates, and suicides is a better measure of social welfare than public budgets and payrolls.

Financing the symbolic accumulation of elite payrolls and public buildings takes more than aid flows. Emerging governments, whether in Africa or the Americas, must help pay their own way. Because their appetite far exceeds their fledgling industrial capacity, they must raise funds by borrowing and by exporting raw materials. This leads to a cycle of growing indebtedness and resource liquidation that is environmentally destructive and gradually forecloses every other development option.[60] In the case of American Indian tribes, the driving force was less debt than a reduction in aid flows, beginning in the late 1970s. Cutbacks were not across-the-board, but targeted resource-rich reservations on the theory that they could afford to pay for a larger share of program costs.[61] Many tribal governments had to choose between shutdowns and accelerated natural resource extraction.[62] The net effect has been to reduce the environmental assets of reservations without replacing them with industrial assets.

Some observers are prescribing even *greater* authoritarianism, and more technocratic decisionmaking, to remedy the reservations' sluggish economies and endemic corruption.[63] It is implied that having adopted a capitalist path, tribal governments have no choice but to engage in *good*

---

60. The relationship between debt, poverty, and ecological destruction has been underscored by the leaders of developing countries. *See, e.g.*, UNITED NATIONS, ECONOMIC AND SOCIAL COUNCIL, CARACAS DECLARATION OF THE MINISTERS OF FOREIGN AFFAIRS OF THE GROUP OF 77, DEVELOPMENT AND INTERNATIONAL ECONOMIC CO-OPERATION ¶ 34, U.N. Doc. A/44/361 (1989); UNITED NATIONS, ECONOMIC COMMISSION FOR AFRICA, AFRICAN ALTERNATIVE FRAMEWORK TO STRUCTURAL ADJUSTMENT PROGRAMMES FOR SOCIO-ECONOMIC RECOVERY AND TRANSFORMATION ¶ 38, U.N. Doc. A/44/315 (1989); *cf.* ROBERT DEVLIN, DEBT AND CRISIS IN LATIN AMERICA: THE SUPPLY SIDE OF THE STORY 254–58 (1989) (discussing economic reform as a development option).

61. *See* Morris, *supra* note 26, at 75.

62. For a description of historical trends in reservation-resource outputs, see Russel L. Barsh, *Indian Resources and the National Economy: Business Cycles and Policy Cycles*, *in* NATIVE AMERICANS AND PUBLIC POLICY, *supra* note 26, at 207–13.

63. *Cf.* LOPACH ET AL., *supra* note 27, at 121–29 (detailing one reservation's problems with its decision making).

capitalism, even if this conflicts with the personal autonomy, kinship loyalties, and political values embedded in tribal traditions. "Modern tribalism," in this view, is equated with the collective self-interest of shareholders in a joint-stock company. It is pure materialism with all countervailing, inefficient cultural elements deleted. This, too, is symbolic development. An Indian tribe that is run like a Fortune 500 company appears successful to visitors, and the foreign press may praise its leaders,[64] but to its own citizens it still may be an insufferable tyranny. American economists promoted the same authoritarian prescription in the Third World a generation ago.[65] While it worked in some parts of Southeast Asia, such as Singapore and South Korea, it was a disaster nearly everywhere else.[66] More democratic and less culturally disruptive development paths have worked about equally as well as the corporatist solution.[67]

American Indian tribal leaders and their academic supporters are locked in a conspiracy of denial. They fear that should white Americans discover that there is nothing qualitatively different, or substantially better, about Indian self-government, they will abolish it. There is plentiful historical evidence to support this proposition.[68] Thus, tribal leaders pretend that their governments are culturally distinct when they are not. Simultaneously, they insist that the right to self-government does not depend on whether or not it

---

64. *See, e.g.*, Carmella M. Padilla, *Picuris Indians Acquire a Subsidized Stake in Hotel*, WALL ST. J., Sept. 13, 1991, at B2; Yoshihashi, *supra* note 34.

65. *See* Russel L. Barsh, *Democratization and Development*, 14 HUM. RTS. Q. 120, 125–26 (1992).

66. *See* DIRK BERG-SCHLOSSER & RAINER SIEGLER, POLITICAL STABILITY AND DEVELOPMENT: A COMPARATIVE ANALYSIS OF KENYA, TANZANIA, AND UGANDA (1990); Ralf Dahrendorf, *Transitions: Politics, Economics, and Liberty*, 13 WASH. Q. 133, 138–39 (1990). This approach has been laid to rest officially by the non-aligned countries. *See The Challenge to the South: An Overview and Summary of the South Commission Report*, 45th Sess., Agenda Item 79, at 8–9, 12, U.N. Doc. A/45/810 (1990).

67. For a critique of this model, see Vernon W. Ruttan, *What Happened to Political Development?*, 39 ECON. DEV. & CULTURAL CHANGE 265 (1991).

68. The "termination" of tribal governments in the 1950s was justified on the grounds that convergence had rendered them superfluous: Indians were ready to be absorbed into white communities and governed by white governments. RUSSEL L. BARSH & JAMES Y. HENDERSON, THE ROAD: INDIAN TRIBES AND POLITICAL LIBERTY 123, 127 (1980). Ironically, the Supreme Court is convinced that tribal courts are culturally distinct and argued that this required limiting their jurisdiction over non-Indians. *See* Oliphant v. Suquamish Indian Tribe, 435 U.S. 191 (1978); Russel L. Barsh & James Y. Henderson, *The Betrayal:* Oliphant v. Suquamish Indian Tribe *and the Hunting of the Snark*, 63 MINN. L. REV. 609 (1979).

works, either in Indian or Western terms. This strategy may prolong tribal autonomy in the short run. If the contradiction between cultural ideals, rhetoric, and practice persists for another generation, however, American Indian governments may self-destruct without any help from outsiders. In the long run, tribal governments will survive only by becoming culturally and spiritually superior governments.

B. Tradition and Materialism

What makes a political system "tribal?" By definition, it is one that is based on *kinship*. Political rights and responsibilities arise from genealogy and are highly differentiated. Kinship assigns fixed roles to individuals, as if they were species in an ecosystem. At the same time, each individual plays multiple roles in relation to others: as a father to one, uncle to another, cousin to still another. Thus, a tribal political system is a web of reciprocal relationships without a separately institutionalized "state."[69] Leaders are recognized speakers for segments of the web (families, genders, generations), representing countervailing responsibilities. By contrast, European "liberal" political systems treat individuals as if they all were identical in their relationships with the state. Responsibilities are to the state; rights are limitations on the power of the state. Good government is equated with regulating the state, rather than strengthening families.[70]

Traditional tribal political systems were quite ingenious when it came to devising checks and balances against natural concentrations of power. A multitude of institutions were locked, through ritual, in an endless cycle of neutralizations. These neutralizations were based not on function or ideology, like the concept of "separation of powers" and the party systems of liberal European politics, but on more fundamental and inevitable divisions in biology: gender, family, and (through clans and religious societies) species and spirits. Collective action was possible only if women and men agreed;

69. *See generally* MORTON H. FRIED, THE NOTION OF TRIBE (1975) (arguing that the term "tribe" has been widely abused by scholars).

70. *See* Russel L. Barsh, *The Nature and Spirit of North American Political Systems*, 10 AM. INDIAN Q. 181 (1986).

if families agreed; if the deer, wolves, and ravens agreed; and if the dead and the unborn agreed. There was no notion of "majority," since the objective was not to find the most popular decision, but the decision that maintained the social and ecological order. Changes are very slow but very stable in such a system.[71]

Reciprocity and redistribution provided the stitching which held this social fabric together. Wealth was produced in order to distribute it among kinsmen, gaining prestige and respect for its producers. Savings were reinvested in kinship, rather than in the production of greater quantities of goods, and this provided a kind of universal social security. Giving ensured receiving. It spread the risk of seasonal and local variations in the productivity of resources, and balanced family management of resources with much wider collective access to their use and enjoyment.[72] Early European explorers were struck by the Indians' relative freedom from greed and possessiveness. In Europe, Pierre Biard observed, "our desire tyrannizes over us and banishes peace from our actions."[73] Aboriginal ethics began to break down, however, when Europeans interfered with aboriginal ecosystems, and forced mass migrations.[74] Increasingly dependent on external economic relationships, Indians neglected their responsibilities to their human and animal kinsmen. Survival took priority over kinship and identity. This psychology of scarcity and insecurity still dominates contemporary tribal governments. There is more accumulation and less investment in people. Redistribution is limited to smaller circles and shorter-term goals. What has changed is that now the power of tribal governments has been harnessed for these purposes.

Collapsing the multifarious checks and balances of tribal systems into a chairman-and-council model has the effect of liberating gender, family, interspecific, and intergenerational

---

71. For a general theory, see *id.* This discussion obviously does not apply to the authoritarian regimes that periodically emerged in aboriginal North America, some of which became aggressive and destructive empires.

72. *See* RESOURCE MANAGERS: NORTH AMERICAN AND AUSTRALIAN HUNTER-GATHERERS 69–91 (Nancy M. Williams & Eugene S. Hunn eds., 1982); WAYNE SUTTLES, COAST SALISH ESSAYS 15–25 (1987).

73. 3 THE JESUIT RELATIONS AND ALLIED DOCUMENTS, *supra* note 13, at 85. Biard's compatriot LeClercq confirmed a generation later, "In a word, they rely upon liking nothing, and upon not becoming attached to the goods of the earth, in order not to be grieved or sad when they lose them." LECLERCQ, *supra* note 13, at 243.

74. *See generally* INDIANS, ANIMALS, AND THE FUR TRADE (Shepard Krech III ed., 1981) (examining Indian participation in the fur trade and the effects this had on their society).

antagonisms. Suddenly, it is possible for a temporary tactical coalition of men to dispossess women, for a handful of families to monopolize public funds for a few years, for one generation to prosper at the expense of future ones or the loss of the land. Social order is sacrificed for speed and growth, with very exciting, short-term material results. By the time people realize that these advantages can evaporate in a few generations, they have lost the mutual trust and respect necessary to restore a balance. They have launched an irreversible social war against themselves.

Tribal electoral politics today is dominated by a rotating spoils system.[75] Coalitions of strongmen and their families take turns on the council, where they pass out jobs, subsidized housing, and grants until opposing families demand their turn at the table. There are few long-term policies because the electorate has grown cynical, and has little confidence that tribal leaders can improve the quantity or quality of their economy sustainably. The goals of political action are largely distributive, rather than aimed at structural improvement. This feeds itself relentlessly. Reformers must promise pork to get elected. They serve an average of only two years in office, and may be recalled even sooner if they fail to reward their supporters. Moreover, federal officials can easily terminate the careers of any genuine reformers by reducing discretionary aid flows after their election.

In terms familiar to liberal political theory, traditional tribal systems were designed, in their structures and rituals, to include all relevant parties in decisions—even animals and the unborn. European parliamentary systems *exclude* all relevant parties *except* adult living citizens, and condition *effective* participation on having the leisure, literacy, and financial resources to make politics a profession. Those present and voting are free to steal from the unrepresented.[76]

Although they are products of this underrepresentative political model, American Indian tribal leaders persist in deploying the rhetoric of Indian values as a badge of

75. *See, e.g.*, *Federal Acknowledgement Administrative Procedures Act of 1989: Hearing on S. 611 Before the Senate Select Comm. on Indian Affairs*, 101st Cong., 1st Sess. (1989); *Occupation of Wounded Knee*, *supra* note 27; LOPACH ET AL., *supra* note 27, at 48, 57, 64–67, 88, 103, 181.

76. Lawyers like to believe that constitutional law provides a check against at least the worst excesses of electoral majorities. There is little evidence, however, that law is adequate, even in the United States, to protect women, minorities, children, or the environment. Ultimately, law is not a satisfactory substitute for representation in decision making—though it may suffice to prevent revolutions.

legitimacy. Contradictions abound between stated beliefs and practice. Compare, for instance, the oft-heard slogans on the importance of children and elders with the worsening statistics on reservation child abuse, family violence, and neglect of the aged.[77] Likewise, compare popular romanticism about Indian earth stewardship with the number of strip mines and landfills on reservations.[78] Consider the significance of the recent emergence of Indian feminism, which asserts a basis in traditional gender relationships.[79] Who has been Westernized here, Indian women who claim to have been dispossessed politically, or Indian men who accuse Western culture of turning women against them?

The most poignant illustration of cultural contradiction today is the battle over "federal acknowledgment" of Indian tribes. The entire premise of this federal policy should make Indians suspicious: that an Indian tribe is genuine, and accordingly entitled to self-government, only if a panel of

---

77. *See, e.g.*, *Indian Protective Services and Family Violence Act: Hearing on S.2340 Before the Senate Select Comm. on Indian Affairs*, 101st Cong., 2d Sess. (1990); DORRIS, *supra* note 35; Moncher, *supra* note 35; Young, *Poverty, Suicide, and Homicide*, *supra* note 35; Young, *Suicide and Homicide*, *supra* note 35.

78. *See, e.g.*, WARD CHURCHILL, STRUGGLE FOR THE LAND: INDIGENOUS RESISTANCE TO GENOCIDE, ECOCIDE AND EXPROPRIATION IN CONTEMPORARY NORTH AMERICA (1933); ALVIN M. JOSEPHY, JR., NOW THAT THE BUFFALO'S GONE: A STUDY OF TODAY'S AMERICAN INDIANS 221–24, 233–35 (1982); NATIVE AMERICANS AND ENERGY DEVELOPMENT II (Joseph G. Jorgensen ed., 1984). *See generally* Ward Churchill & Winona LaDuke, *Native America: The Politics of Radioactive Colonialism*, 13 J. ETHNIC STUD. 107 (1985) (describing resource extraction and its effects on tribes); Lynn A. Robbins, *Navajo Energy Politics*, 16 SOC. SCI. J. 93 (1979); Marjane Ambler, *The Lands the Feds Forgot*, SIERRA, May–June 1989, at 44 (detailing Congressional efforts to grant tribes the same authority as states to regulate the environment); John Harmon, *Environmental Plight of Reservations Spurs Indians, EPA to Seek Solutions*, ATLANTA CONST., May 20, 1992, at A3 (reporting on a meeting of tribal leaders with the EPA to address toxic waste and other hazards on Indian lands); Paul Schneider, *Other People's Trash*, 93 AUDUBON, July–Aug. 1991, at 108 (on tribal resistance to landfills); Roger Worthington, *Tribes Resist Tempting Landfill Offers*, CHI. TRIB., Sept. 22, 1991, § 1, at 4 (noting recent tribal opposition to leasing reservations for waste disposal).

79. For surveys of recent Indian feminist writing, see A GATHERING OF SPIRIT (Beth Brant ed., 1988); SPIDER WOMAN'S GRANDDAUGHTERS: TRADITIONAL TALES AND CONTEMPORARY WRITING BY NATIVE AMERICAN WOMEN (Paula G. Allen ed., 1989); *see also* LORETTA FOWLER, ARAPAHOE POLITICS, 1851–1978: SYMBOLS IN CRISES OF AUTHORITY 271–73, 281 (1982) (describing the traditional role of Araphoe women); Carla Christofferson, *Tribal Courts' Failure to Protect Native American Women: A Reevaluation of the Indian Civil Rights Act*, 101 YALE L.J. 169 (1991) (detailing discrimination against Native American women); Diane Rothenberg, *The Mothers of the Nation: Seneca Resistance to Quaker Intervention*, *in* WOMEN AND COLONIZATION: ANTHROPOLOGICAL PERSPECTIVES 67–70, 78–83 (Mona Etienne & Eleanor Leacock eds., 1980) (describing the change in the role of Native American women brought about by colonization).

federal anthropologists and historians certify that it is sufficiently Indian.[80] The power to define what constitutes "Indian culture" would be the ultimate achievement of arrogant colonialism, if Indian tribes accepted it. The sad truth is that many tribes welcome this program and even have gone to Congress and the courts to defend it, because they see it as a way of rationing limited resources such as federal aid and fishing rights.[81] Often there are relatives on both sides of these disputes;[82] hence, tribal leaders are advocating the disinheritance of their own kin. It is a triumph of materialism over family, kinship, tribe, and tradition.

On a wider scale, the centralization of reservation economies and their continued dependence on scarce outside resources has intensified disputes over tribal membership.[83] These conflicts not only have cross-cut kinship lines, but have embraced increasingly strident racist language which equates blood quantum with cultural integrity. Originally, race was strictly a European category. It was a classification scheme used to demonstrate European superiority—one that pretended to be simple, obvious, and objective. Comparing cultural characteristics was much more tedious and philosophically perilous than comparing skin tones.[84] What

---

80. *See* Rachael Paschal, *The Imprimatur of Recognition: American Indian Tribes and the Federal Acknowledgment Process*, 66 WASH. L. REV. 209, 216–17 (1991); William A. Starna, *"Public Ethnohistory" and Native-American Communities: History or Administrative Genocide?*, 53 RADICAL HIST. REV. 126 (1992); *cf.* JACK CAMPISI, THE MASHPEE INDIANS: TRIBE ON TRIAL (1991) (relating one tribe's efforts to obtain federal recognition).

81. *See, e.g.*, Greene v. Lujan, 911 F.2d 738 (9th Cir. 1990) (text in Westlaw) (dismissing intervenor's interlocutory appeal for lack of jurisdiction) (appeal from judgement on the merits (order of October 18, 1992) is pending); *Federal Acknowledgment Administrative Procedures Act of 1989: Hearings on S.611 Before the Select Comm. on Indian Affairs*, 101st Cong., 1st Sess. (1989). The author was the counsel of record for the Samish Indian Tribe in *Greene*.

82. In the dispute over recognition of the Samish, considered only in its procedural aspects by *Greene*, 911 F.2d 738, there were cousins on the tribal councils of the Samish Tribe and the Tulalip Tribes, which opposed the Samish; and a sibling of the Samish tribal chairwoman on the council of the Lummi Tribe, which also opposed the Samish, albeit politically rather than in court.

83. *See* FOWLER, *supra* note 79, at 221–23, 234; LOPACH ET AL., *supra* note 27, at 85–86, 103, 147, 160–61.

84. For background on the use of racial arguments to justify dispossession and exploitation, see FRANCIS JENNINGS, THE INVASION OF AMERICA: INDIANS, COLONIALISM, AND THE CANT OF CONQUEST (1975); Russel L. Barsh, *Are Anthropologists Hazardous to Indians' Health?*, 15 J. ETHNIC STUD. 1, 3 (1987). *See generally* WILLIAM STANTON, THE LEOPARD'S SPOTS: SCIENTIFIC ATTITUDES TOWARD RACE IN AMERICA 1815–59 (1960) (discussing various scientific views on the origin of race in the 19th century).

does it mean when Indians—the oppressed—adopt the same standard of comparison among themselves? In part, the cultural determinants of tribal identities have grown so confused and attenuated that it is far easier to talk about race than about culture. Tribal governments have seized upon race as a criterion for building coalitions and rationing scarce resources—just like oppressive regimes everywhere.

Why has this come about? If it is true that the structures of political institutions reflect their underlying functions, it is important to explore the historical origins of today's system of tribal governments, for evidence of their purpose. What were they designed to achieve, and whom were they intended to serve?

Historically, tribal councils and courts were organized by Indian agents to help them manage the Indians on reservations. They were the instruments of colonial administration. Although they did not always do what they were told, and sometimes even were disbanded or punished for their disobedience, nineteenth century councils and courts were designed to control Indians and promote assimilation, not to serve them.[85] While the adoption of the 1934 Indian Reorganization Act[86] was heralded in the nation's capitol as the end of paternalism, this official fanfare did not prevent the Bureau of Indian Affairs (BIA) from designing "reorganized" councils along the same basic structural lines as their predecessors. Reorganization simply achieved greater standardization. The BIA retains residual control through discretionary funding and its veto power over constitutional amendments (and to varying degrees, tribal legislation). Arguably, tribal governments have grown stronger and somewhat more independent since 1934, but decision-making processes have changed little. Rooted in problems of social control rather than the promotion of families, justice, or equity, tribal governments are ideal vehicles for self-serving elites and "strongmen."

The bottom line is power without legitimacy. Tribal governments can collect taxes, lease land, build housing projects, and jail Indians, but they cannot mobilize Indian people or give voice to their cultural and spiritual aspirations. Instead, they intensify conflict, disregard civil rights, and even

---

85. *See* HAGAN, *supra* note 33; HOXIE, *supra* note 33.
86. 25 U.S.C. §§ 461–479 (1988).

resort to political violence to suppress dissent.[87] Tribal governments view all possible political competition with suspicion or hostility: formal political parties, trade unions, social and religious organizations, private businesses. All criticism is met with admonitions of the need for unthinking loyalty to "the tribe," or charges that the critics are undermining "tribal sovereignty." Who is "the tribe" if not its citizens—who after all, are, mostly relatives? The separation of "the tribe" from the people in contemporary American Indian political rhetoric is a disturbing development, which hails the emergence of "the state" as an entity with rights and privileges quite distinct from living, breathing human beings. Indians have grown very Westernized, indeed, if they accept the existence of such an imaginary Leviathan within communities of a few thousand people! In fact, what has emerged is the *one-party* state, which condemns dissent as foreign-inspired subversion and limits politics to personality disputes among a clique of strongmen.[88]

Contemporary tribal leaders accordingly seek external rather than internal legitimacy. In the words of one tribal member, "The tribes . . . must act how we expect to be treated."[89] Thus, tribal councils, courts, and laws must be recognizable to outsiders and compatible with white Americans' conceptions of good government. Heavily dependent on corporate investors, public aid, and the political goodwill of federal bureaucrats, "[t]he tribes discovered that they could deal successfully in these relationships only if they adopted organizational values and processes that outsiders

---

87. *See, e.g.*, *Occupation of Wounded Knee*, *supra* note 27; Robert C. Jeffrey, Jr., *The Indian Civil Rights Act and the Martinez Decision: A Reconsideration*, 35 S.D. L. REV. 355, 355–57, 364 (1990); Sandy Tolan, *Showdown at Window Rock*, N.Y. TIMES, Nov. 26, 1989, § 6 (magazine) at 29. *See generally* LOPACH ET AL., *supra* note 27, at 138–43, 184–88 (examining the problems with tribal government and discussing means to resolve these problems).

88. This presents striking parallels with post- or neocolonial Africa and its preoccupation with national political unity. *See* RHODA E. HOWARD, HUMAN RIGHTS IN COMMONWEALTH AFRICA 119–44 (1986); *cf.* ALI A. MAZRUI, THE AFRICAN CONDITION: A POLITICAL DIAGNOSIS 90–112 (1980) (arguing that modern African states are becoming more pluralistic and more open societies). Howard argues that the persistence of communal solidarity at the family and tribal levels is a compelling justification for strong countervailing human rights mechanisms to prevent groups from abusing their individual members or (through the state) one another. Rhoda E. Howard, *Group Versus Individual Identity in the African Debate on Human Rights*, *in* HUMAN RIGHTS IN AFRICA: CROSS-CULTURAL PERSPECTIVES 159, 162, 178–83 (Abdullahi A. An-Na'im & Francis M. Deng eds., 1990).

89. LOPACH ET AL., *supra* note 27, at 54.

respected."[90] Under these conditions, tribal governments are growing indistinguishable from white governments while tribal leaders appeal to cultural unity to discredit dissenters.

All this belies the basic legal insecurity of tribal governments, which lack the constitutional footing and Congressional representation necessary to combat encroachments upon their autonomy. Tribal sovereignty was historically a judicial construction, to which Congress has added and subtracted.[91] To borrow a Canadian Indian metaphor, tribal sovereignty is like a box of powers and immunities, which the courts and Congress occasionally empty or refill as the spirit moves them. Because Supreme Court justices have far longer tenures than do members of Congress, the Court and Congress tend to behave countercyclically in this regard. When Congress tried emptying the box during the 1950s "termination" era, the Court began refilling it. In the 1970s, Congress was back filling the box, while the Court was conscientiously emptying it again. This ceaseless legal seesaw exhausts tribal resources in court battles and dilutes Congressional advocacy, while frustrating any long-term reservation policy planning.

Why, then, don't American Indian tribal leaders try to put an end to it? It is for the same reason that they fail to restore reservation democracy to traditional principles. They are part of this problem, preoccupied with tedious, daily struggles with federal regulations, jurisdictional disputes, and budgetary negotiations, as if these marginal adjustments can achieve substantial improvements in reservation life. Uncertainty over tribal authority is an excuse both for expensive tribal political activity and for tribal failure to improve human conditions. A campaign to clarify tribal authority might succeed and leave tribal leaders in undisputed control of their domestic agendas with no one but themselves to blame for the results.

---

90. *Id.* at 167.

91. *Cf.* BARSH & HENDERSON, *supra* note 68, at 209–10 (noting the changing role of Congress in overseeing tribes); LOPACH ET AL., *supra* note 27, at 33–34 (addressing the increased role of the federal government in Indian affairs); Russel L. Barsh, *Is There Any Indian 'Law' Left? A Review of the Supreme Court's 1982 Term*, 59 WASH. L. REV. 863 (1984) (contending that the Supreme Court's treatment of Indian affairs does not amount to "law" because it lacks generality and constancy).

C. Culture and Disillusionment

If structure follows function, it is true also that culture tends to follow structure. The social, economic, and political institutions of a highly regulated society create a learning environment. From day to day, they reward and punish certain kinds of behavior, encouraging what is rewarded and suppressing what is punished. People who succeed and "get ahead" become role models, and their conduct is emulated even if it is less than exemplary in moral terms. What lessons are taught, particularly to Indian youth, by the structure and behavior of today's tribal governments?

Contemporary tribal electoral politics is aggressive, competitive, and materialistic. Candidates prevail by distributing money, goods, or jobs before and after the election. Once elected, they may "do little, provide no supervision, travel all of the time, and exploit the tribe for private gain."[92] Their political survival depends on securing federal aid and resource rentals that can be distributed as jobs or per capita payments. As a consequence, "[a]gency paternalism is replaced by tribal paternalism."[93] To make matters worse, this kind of politics attracts people who cannot succeed at anything else (or, alternatively, who are elected by suspicious voters because they are "'too dumb to steal'").[94]

The longevity and apparent success of this kind of tribal leader has a demonstration effect on Indian youth. Reservation life teaches them to equate selfishness with popularity and power, and forces them to choose between materialism and personal insignificance. It is practically impossible to combat cynicism and resignation in the face of such daily evidence of the futility of holding fast to traditional Indian ideals. Indeed, tribal leaders discredit Indian values by routinely using them merely as a convenient camouflage for pursuing selfish ends.[95]

---

92. LOPACH ET AL., *supra* note 27, at 48.

93. Harry W. Basehart & Tom T. Sasaki, *Changing Political Organization in the Jicarillo Apache Reservation Community*, 23 HUM. ORGANIZATION 283, 288 (1964).

94. LOPACH ET AL., *supra* note 27, at 126, 140.

95. German scholars have told me that Hitler, for admittedly more vicious objectives, succeeded in discrediting pre-Christian Germanic tribal traditions by exploiting them in constructing the ideology and symbolism of his Nazi state. For

The Northwest Indian fishing rights controversy illustrates these processes.[96] Until tribal jurisdiction over off-reservation Indian fishing was confirmed by the Supreme Court in the 1970s,[97] the BIA had little interest in financing marine industries, and tribal councils had little police power or financial power over Indian fishers. A string of legal victories reversed this. Suddenly, federal agencies and private financial institutions were anxious to subsidize marine development, and tribal councils found themselves in possession of aid, bank credit, and considerable regulatory power. Many councils used this to reward themselves, resulting in Indian ownership of fishing gear and the significant concentration of Indian fishing income over the past decade. This has deprived a great many Indian families of their chief source of livelihood and was done all in the name of the collective good. Thus, a resource originally divided among all has become an oligopoly, and the excuse used for this was "tribal tradition."[98] The logic is Orwellian, and the message sent to Indian youth is that tradition is defined by power, not by wisdom.

Indian communities respond to government elitism in various ways. Indian voter turnouts are very poor. On many reservations a majority of tribal members never participate in elections, either as a protest against what they consider to be an illegitimate process, or because they simply do not believe it matters who nominally is in charge.[99] Even if only a small

---

example, the Swastika was a symbol of the perpetual motion of life and the universe. *See* MARIJA GIMBUTAS, THE LANGUAGE OF THE GODDESS 298 (1989).

96. This discussion is summarized from Russel L. Barsh, *Backfire from Boldt: The Judicial Transformation of Coast Salish Proprietary Fisheries into a Commons*, 4 W. LEGAL HIST. 85 (1991).

97. *See* Washington v. Washington State Commercial Passenger Fishing Vessel Ass'n, 443 U.S. 658 (1979).

98. *See* Daniel L. Boxberger, *The Lummi Indians and the Canadian/American Pacific Salmon Treaty*, 12 AM. INDIAN Q. 299 (1988) (shifting some of the blame to the U.S. government for failing to protect tribal fishers from high-seas interception). *See generally* Russel L. Barsh, *The Economics of a Traditional Coastal Indian Salmon Fishery*, 41 HUM. ORGANIZATION 170 (1982) (discussing the economics of fishing in a community still practicing traditional forms of management and allocation).

99. *Cf.* Thomas Holm, *Indian Concepts of Authority and the Crisis in Tribal Government*, SOC. SCI. J., July 1982, at 59 (discussing the illegitimacy of tribal politics). *But see* LOPACH ET AL., *supra* note 27, at 126 (discussing the high voter turnout on one reservation, possibly due to concerns about corruption); Robert L. Bee, *The Predicament of the Native American Leader: A Second Look*, 49 HUM. ORGANIZATION 56 (1990) (arguing that the increasing volatility in tribal electoral politics in the 1980s is a sign of democratization).

proportion of each community is interested in competing for elite power, this political system is reproduced and can perpetuate itself because the federal government finances it and defends it against dissidents. Washington supplies the spoils that successful candidates distribute to their supporters, and recognizes as lawful no regimes other than its own creatures. Popular support, then, is of secondary importance, if any at all. This is the most depressing fact of life on Indian reservations: the *inevitability* of the existing scheme of tribal government. When combined with the psychological legacy of cultural abuse, mistrust, and self-rejection, it should be no wonder that disillusionment, depression, and suicide have reached an epidemic scale.

At least when white Americans were in direct and visible control of reservations there was a feeling of Indian solidarity: us against them. Now it is *us against us*, families against themselves. It is no wonder that self-destructiveness has increased dramatically during the era of "self-determination."

D. Redefining "Development"

American Indian tribes need a better definition of "development" and a better way to measure progress. Defining success as the total production of goods and services ("gross product"), like the rest of Western society, tribal governments today plan and spend in ways that maximize measured financial throughput rather than human happiness. Indeed they assume (just like everyone else) that throughput and happiness are the same, which only emphasizes the convergence of values between Indian America and European America. This is not a question just of measurement, but also of "development paths." We must agree upon the trajectory tribal development should take before determining how best to measure progress along that path. The conventional approach gives priority to product-capital[100] and mechanical technology. Another option would be to focus on families,

100. The term "product-capital" is used here to distinguish productive assets which are the products of human artifice, including money, buildings, and equipment, from assets which exist naturally in ecosystems, whether renewable or nonrenewable.

healthy childhoods, and individual creativity. What are Indian tribes trying to "grow" through development—things or people?

The choice of development paths also involves fundamental issues of a *procedural* nature. Is the *political* means of reproducing society broad-based, popular, and legitimate? Is it democratic, in the sense of active participation and genuine choices, not merely in the formality of periodic balloting? Tribal governments have become technocracies. Like their non-Indian neighbors, they are dominated by experts, and by a process of "consultation." This means that citizens have the right to make public complaints and have their complaints duly noted for the record. Ordinarily, they are not involved directly in decisions, but participate only in electing and chastising decision makers, or the people who hire the decision makers. Unfortunately, a noninvolved citizenry is generally a poorly informed one. It becomes mistrustful, reactive, and worst of all, guided by superficial slogans and symbolism. A genuine democracy may no longer be possible for Euro-Americans, at least at the national level, as a consequence of sheer scale. This is no reason to abandon it at the tribal level, however. Among many Indian tribes, there has been a resurgence of demand for real democracy, reflected in actions as varied as the formation of women's groups, the aggressive use of recall elections, and violence against incumbent administrations.[101]

What are the alternatives, then, for steering and monitoring the development process? One approach, championed in recent years by the United Nations Development Programme (UNDP), is "human development."[102] The long-term goal is maximizing human "choices," including productive capacity and personal life-options. Productive capacity is defined in terms of health, lifespan, education, and income, all of which can be measured relatively easily in most countries.[103] Of

---

101. *See, e.g.*, LOPACH ET AL., *supra* note 27, at 126, 136–39, 143; Holm, *supra* note 99, at 59; Bee, *supra* note 99, at 57–62; Tolan, *supra* note 87.

102. *See* UNITED NATIONS DEVELOPMENT PROGRAMME, HUMAN DEVELOPMENT REPORT 1992 (1992); *Human Development Report, Regional Consultations on the Human Development Report, Report of the Administrator*, Governing Council of the U.N. Development Programme, Special Sess., Provisional Agenda Item 6, U.N. Doc. DP/1992/13 (1992). The World Bank also endorses this approach. *See The Development of Human Resources in Developing Countries*, 28 DEV. ISSUES 33 (1991).

103. See UNITED NATIONS DEVELOPMENT PROGRAMME, *supra* note 102, at 91–96 (1992) for details on the calculation of UNDP's Human Development Index.

course, there is no objective way to standardize the scales for highly qualitative conditions, such as "health," so that they can be compared cross-culturally. Even greater problems confront those who attempt to devise standardized scales for freedom of choice. UNDP's efforts to use checklists derived from United Nations human-rights legislation have been criticized widely on political and methodological grounds.[104] While frequencies of torture or politically inspired murder are reasonably objective measures (assuming that there are reliable sources of raw data), there is no valid universal standard for measuring subjective ideals such as a "fair trial." People may agree on the definition of a "fair trial" at some general level, but disagree, across cultures, about whether a particular trial was "fair."

Despite these analytical difficulties, the human development idea seems far more compatible with traditional Indian conceptions of human dignity and development than do gross-product models. This makes it all the more disturbing that contemporary tribal governments avoid models and measures based on human conditions. Such models already exist and readily could be adapted to specific tribal cultural contexts. Indian tribes even might make an important contribution to improving on them. What they fear, however, is exposing the contradictions between stated commitments to social justice and poor social conditions, poor records on human rights, and public disapproval of tribal policies.

Another important alternative development model is "environmental accounting," which has gained popularity since the 1992 Earth Summit. The underlying idea is simple: environmental quality is treated as a productive capital asset, which changes in book value as a consequence of (for example) pollution, exploitation, and rehabilitation.[105] Although all economic activity involves trade-offs between production and long-term environmental productivity, these trade-offs are rarely explicit. Gross-product models omit them; indeed, toxic chemicals are an "asset" in the gross-products model as long

104. *See* Russel L. Barsh, *Measuring Human Rights: Problems of Methodology and Purpose*, 15 HUM. RTS. Q. 87, 104 (1993) (summarizing criticisms of the UNDP checklist).

105. *See* U.N. TRANSNATIONAL CORPS. AND MANAGEMENT DIV., ENVIRONMENTAL ACCOUNTING: CURRENT ISSUES, ABSTRACTS AND BIBLIOGRAPHY, at 18–19, U.N. Doc. ST/CTC/SER. B/9, U.N. Sales No. E.92.II.A.23 (1992).

as they continue to be useable or marketable.[106] Environmental accounting shifts the analysis from current production and consumption to the *sustainability* of production, or, in terms familiar to tribal teachings, to the "seventh generation" yet to come. If this is compatible with traditional values, why is it nearly absent in contemporary tribal government planning?

Tools exist for basing development strategy on human dignity and ecological values. What is missing is genuine commitment to these goals. Like their neighbors, tribal governments appear to give priority to current consumption, and then make marginal adjustments, as needed, to respond to the most pressing concerns for social equity and ecological protection. This scheme is not sustainable, however, for any society.

Ecological problems are an inevitable consequence of materialism, even in societies that avoid symbolic development. Industrialization, at least in its early stages, breeds large inequalities in employment and income. Instead of resolving these inequalities through taxation and redistribution, which may slow growth, governments typically try to achieve social justice through *more* growth—that is, a policy of *more for everyone*. While politically appealing, this approach accelerates the utilization of the environment, unsustainably. Once rich and poor emerge from socioeconomic transformations, growth becomes a political imperative. The rich want to keep what they have, and the poor aspire to be like the rich. Rich and poor can agree only on producing everything faster, engendering an accelerating cycle of accumulating goods, unhappiness, and demands for equality. When the foundation of social life shifts from relatives (including animals) to things, there is an inevitable trajectory towards accumulating material goods at the expense of environmental sustainability.

Here is where most contemporary prescriptions for the environment go wrong. They are based on slowing down the destruction of the earth by restricting the most damaging forms of consumption. The idea is to curb the worst excesses, such as reducing toxic waste to "safe" levels or disposing of toxic materials in a "safe" manner. The only genuine, lasting

---

106. *See* CHOOSING A SUSTAINABLE FUTURE: THE REPORT OF THE NATIONAL COMMISSION ON THE ENVIRONMENT 30–32 (1993).

solution must come from changing the aims and organization of our societies—changing our culture—rather than hemming in the worst manifestations of our present way of life. This means addressing the *incentives* for material consumption, or what people strive to achieve in their lives. Is their aim to accumulate love and respect, as among aboriginal Americans, or is their aim to accumulate goods? Indian tribes, building upon their traditional strengths and values, could have been the vanguard of this transformation.

Unfortunately, tribal governments already have largely adopted a conventional approach to environmental management, in their actions if not in their words. They measure progress in terms of cash flow[107] and respond to environmental threats by placing regulatory outer limits on the amount of damage done.[108] They are adopting European mechanisms to control a European problem which now has become an Indian problem. Thus, the debate between kinship and materialism is no longer between Indian people and their European colonizers; it is within the Indian community itself.

III. RESTORING COMMITMENT

More than a century ago, the Pequot preacher and abolitionist William Apess denounced the racism and hypocrisy of white Christians from his pulpit in Boston.[109] American Indians today need some fiery preaching against hypocrisy in tribal government.

An old saw in Indian country provides, "It's hard to be an Indian." This saying is not about discrimination, racism, or poverty. Rather, it is a reminder that Indian values are hard. They demand great commitment and self-discipline. It is time, to borrow again from Ambrose Bierce, to give this old saw

107. For a defense of this conventional approach see ROBERT H. WHITE, TRIBAL ASSETS: THE REBIRTH OF TRIBAL AMERICA 276–77 (1990).

108. By regulatory limits, I mean, for example, placing ceilings on the quantity of toxic materials that can be discharged into soil or water, or setting aside ecologically sensitive sites as reserves. These are forms of "growth management." They accept a calculated amount of irreversible ecological sacrifice in exchange for increasing present-day production and consumption. Preserving future generations' options requires the elimination, not reduction, of irreversible harm.

109. *See* ON OUR OWN GROUND: THE COMPLETE WRITINGS OF WILLIAM APESS, A PEQUOT (Barry O'Connell ed., 1992).

some new teeth.[110] Culture is not genetic and does not come without effort. If it is to achieve a sustainable future for Indian communities and make a contribution to global survival, Indian politics must be renewed on a clear philosophical basis by people who are prepared to live according to their stated beliefs.

There no longer seems to be much difference in the Westernization of the Third World and of the indigenous world. Indigenous societies are usually more isolated geographically, so the process of convergence is understandably slower. But they are catching up. While world leaders lament the loss of biological diversity, which holds the key to the renewal and survival of ecosystems, our planet rapidly is losing its cultural diversity, which holds the key to the renewal and survival of human societies. Scientists and scholars search for an alternative in their theories while real alternative cultures disappear.

It will be a real struggle to reassert an indigenous perspective on social justice, democracy, and environmental security. The hardest part of the struggle will be converting words to action, going beyond the familiar, empty rhetoric of sovereignty and cultural superiority. The struggle will be hardest here in the United States, where the gaps between rhetoric and reality have grown greater than anywhere on earth. This is the best place to begin, however, because this is the illusory "demonstration" that is studied by the rest of the world, including the indigenous peoples of other regions.

Are American Indians ready to accept this global responsibility? The current generation of tribal leadership appears unwilling to try. It is firmly committed by its actions to the materialist path, and it is neutralized by its dependence on a continuing financial relationship with the national government and developers. The next generation of American Indians may be another matter. Disillusioned and critical, they may yet find a voice of their own that is both modern and truly indigenous, and they may have the courage to practice the ideals that their parents merely sloganize. Let us hope so. There is no alternative for Indian survival or for global survival.

---

110. *See* BIERCE, *supra* note 51, at 171.

Indian Tribal Taxation: A Cornerstone of Sovereignty

Ann McCullogh

IN 1970, President Nixon, in accord with his perspective on the "New Federalism," stated his support for increased local, self-governance by Indian tribes through: "a proposal providing for Indians to assume control of Federal programs established for their benefit; a proposal whereby Federal employees who accompanied programs transferred to the tribes could retain their civil service benefits; and a proposal to amend the Johnson-O'Malley Act by adding Indian tribes to the list of parties with whom the Secretary of the Interior can contract out the education of Indians."[1]

This message and the emphasis placed by the Nixon administration on Indian issues resulted in the 1975 Indian Self-Determination and Education Assistance Act that made it possible for Indian tribes to be treated for the first time as governments in contracting with federal agencies.[2] After a century of wardship, tribes were again enjoying the full-fledged powers, benefits, and responsibilities of governmental entities. This naturally meant that the tribes would not only take on the responsibility of providing services to their members but would also finance those services through the common channels, that is, grants, loans, and *taxes*. Within three years the Navajo Nation established its tribal tax code.[3] A number of tribes later followed the lead of the Navajo and established tax commissions and tax codes.[4]

The significance of these events was that within little over a decade, the federal relationship between the national government, state governments, and Indian tribes underwent a huge change. Tribal tax codes reflect the magnitude of that change. They, perhaps more than any other factor, illustrate the evolving issue of Indian sovereignty within our federal system. It is my thesis that the establishment of tribal tax codes legitimizes Indian tribes as sovereign governments and provides the mechanism for achieving self-sufficiency and self-government. This essay analyzes the fundamental bases upon which tribal tax codes are built, the limitations placed on tribal taxes, and the types of taxes being levied.

I

In the history case of *McCulloch v. Maryland* (4 Wheat, 316 [1819]), Chief Justice John Marshall uttered the famous phrase of taxation and federalism: "The power to tax is the power to destroy." Significantly, it was a taxation case that defined the relationship between the sovereign states and an equally sovereign national government, rather than the more emotional questions of slavery or tariffs that buffeted the country at that time.

Two fundamental concepts underlie the right of a government to levy taxes. The first involves the sovereignty of the government. A government must have the legitimate authority to take property from its citizens. The second relates to justification for taxing. For taxing schemes to be supported there should be some rational relationship between the paying of taxes and the rights and benefits received from the government. Taxes that seem capricious and arbitrary cannot retain popular compliance for long.

According to Bernard Schwartz's commentary on property rights within the Constitution, the power to tax is an inherent power of government and is normally vested in the government in unqualified terms.[5] In referring to the extent of this power, he cites the New York Supreme Court: "There is no express restriction upon this power in our . . . Constitution and no implied restriction, except by the primary guaranties relating to life, liberty, property and due process of law."[6] Even these constitutional limitations are very broad. For instance, a government may tax a product so heavily that it may destroy that area of business,[7] or it may select out a particular category of persons or things to tax without taxing the whole class of objects.[8] Only when the tax is so "palpably unreasonable that it violates due process" will the courts be willing to overturn it; yet even in this area, the Supreme Court has severely limited any challenge. In *Magnano Co. v. Hamilton* (292 U.S. 40 [1934]), the Court expressed the view that due process in tax matters only applies if the state is doing something forbidden.

Thus the power of a government to tax is virtually unrestricted. But for Indian tribes, the legitimacy of a tribal tax rests with the claim of tribes to being *sovereign* governmental entities. To understand the position of tribes within the federal system, it is helpful to use the analogy of state and local governments. According to Dillon's Rule,[9] states are sovereign bodies under the Constitution, but local governments are simply "creatures of the state." As such the power of taxation is inherent to state government, but not to local government. The latter may only levy those taxes that are expressly delegated to them by state statute. To determine the extent of taxing powers afforded to Indian tribes, one must first determine whether they are sovereign governments, analogous to state government, or whether they hold a position reminiscent of local government. In other words, are Indian tribes sovereign nations or federal instrumentalities?

In the body of the Constitution, there are only two references to Indians: Article I, Section 2, defines apportionment of the House of Representatives according to population, "excluding Indians not taxed," and Article I, Section 8, contains the Indian commerce clause. In both references, Indians who have not left their tribes and become "civilized" by adopting the ways of the white man and by paying taxes, are considered to be within the netherland between foreign nations and the several states.

In assessing the original intent of the Framers, one can only infer the considered status of the Indians by a few brief references in Madison's *Notes*.[10] According to the *Notes*, on August 18, 1787, Madison proposed to the Committee of Detail that among the powers to be added to the Congress would be the power "to regulate affairs with the Indians as well within as without the limits of the United States."[11] Certainly this original phrasing seems to indicate that Indian tribes resembled foreign nations more than they did states, as Congress was to treat all Indians (regardless of tribal affiliation) in like manner whether they resided within the boundaries of the United States or without. Marshall elaborated on this position in *Worcester v. Georgia* (315 U.S. 515 [1832]):

> The Indian nations had always been considered as distinct, independent political communities, retaining their original natural rights, as the undisputed possessors of the soil, from time immemorial, with the single exception of that imposed by irresistible power, which excluded them from intercourse with any other European potentate than the first discoverer of the coast of the particular region claimed. . . . The constitution, by declaring treaties already made, as well as those to be made, to be the supreme law of the land, has adopted and sanctioned the previous treaties with the Indian nations, and consequently admits their rank among those powers who are capable of making treaties.

The sole exception (at that time) to the powers retained by the tribes were the powers of war and foreign affairs.

Marshall's view was seriously compromised by Supreme Court decisions in the latter half of the nineteenth and early twentieth century when Indians were termed to be "wards" of the government. The change from viewing Indians as nations to regarding them as individuals was largely a result of the end of the Indian wars. Many of the treaties with the warring tribes were signed in the late 1860s,[12] and shortly thereafter (in 1871), Congress, in a rider to an appropriations bill, announced that it had plenary power over Indian matters. This action, along with several court cases,[13] had the effect of subjecting the tribes totally to the whims of Congress. It was not until 1959, in *Williams v. Lee* (358 U.S. 217), that the Court began to revert back to the Marshall doctrine. In this case the Court opined that states could not interfere in tribal matters where it would "infringe" on the right of Indians to govern themselves. Finally, in *United States v. Wheeler*

(435 U.S. 313 [1978]), the Court again asserted that "Indian tribes still possess those aspects of sovereignty not withdrawn by treaty or statute, or by implication as a necessary result of their dependent status."[14] The crucial question, given *Wheeler,* becomes whether the power to tax is an inherent aspect of sovereignty and whether that power has been withdrawn.

During the period when Indians were considered mainly wards of the government, tribes and tribal government were to a certain extent overlooked or dismissed. It was generally perceived by non-Indians that what government existed on the reservations, consisted mainly of the paternalism of the Bureau of Indian Affairs. Indians were viewed as individual wards who needed the protection and teaching of the white man in order to become assimilated. For instance, the allotment acts of the time were phrased in tems of competency.[15] When an individual Indian was deemed competent to handle his or her own affairs, the trust status on the land was to be withdrawn. Therefore, to view Indian governments as sovereign was impossible within a mind set that did not see Indians as having governments. It was only with the passage of the Wheeler-Howard Act (Indian Reorganization Act, IRA) in 1934 that tribal governments were again recognized as legitimate bodies.

Vine Deloria and Clifford Lytle recently recounted the events surrounding the passage of the Indian Reorganization Act. They point out in their commentary that although the senators deleted language from the original bill (written by then-BIA commissioner, John Collier) which would have given the tribes the basic powers of a government—to negotiate contracts, to levy taxes, to establish a local court system, to condemn property, etc.—Collier was able to get those powers reinstated by making an "end-run" around Congress. After the IRA was enacted, Secretary of the Interior Harold Ickes asked Interior Solicitor Nathan Margold, a confidant of Collier's, to render a solicitor's opinion on the meaning of the new act. Margold declared that "those powers which are lawfully vested in an Indian tribe are not, in general, delegated powers granted by express acts of Congress, but rather inherent powers of a limited sovereignty which has never been extinguished."[16] Under the rubric of *inherent* powers, the following powers were identified as belonging to tribal government:

> Right to adopt a form of government; to create various offices and prescribe their duties; to prescribe the procedures and forms through which the will of the tribe was to be expressed; to define conditions of membership; to provide or withhold suffrage; to regulate domestic relations; to prescribe rules of inheritance; to levy fees, dues, and taxes; to remove or exclude nonmembers; to regulate the use of property; to administer justice; and to describe the duties of federal employees insofar as such powers were delegated by the Interior Department.[17]

In the end, many of these powers were later given credence by legislation, the Governmental and Tax Status Act, and by *Washington v. Confederated Tribes of the Colville Reservation* (447 U.S. 134 [1980]). Quoting from Margold, Justice White stated in the *Colville* case: "The power to tax transactions occurring on trust lands and significantly involving a tribe or its members is a fundamental attribute of sovereignty which the tribes retain unless divested of it by federal law or necessary implication of their dependent status."[18]

The validation of inherent taxing powers in this case is particularly significant given its holding which invalidated a tribal policy of exempting customers from paying state sales tax on cigarettes bought on the reservation. The Court argued that the tribes had no inherent interest in the product (cigarettes) and hence they were really simply marketing a tax exemption. It held that where the tribes were selling items to their members, or where they were selling reservation-produced goods and services, then the sales tax exemption would be proper since the State of Washington would have no jurisdiction in those areas. However, where the item was produced off-reservation and consumed by non-Indians, off-reservation, then the Court found that the states did have some jurisdiction for taxing, as the tribes were only "marketing a tax exemption."[19]

The Colville tribes, in order to forestall this holding, had implemented a tribal cigarette tax. Using the above logic, the

Court refused to recognize a tribal preemption of the state excise tax even though when both taxes were added on to the selling price, the cost became uneconomical for the consumer. However, despite the general negative tone of this ruling, the Supreme Court did recognize almost without debate a broad right of Indian tribes to tax.

Ultimately, general recognition of tribal tax authority and its relation to other taxing entities within the federal system came with the Indian Tribal Governmental Tax Status Act of 1982. This act provided that Indian tribal governments would be considered as "states" relative to the federal tax code, with the same exemptions and benefits that states now enjoy. The only major difference was that Indian tribes were not given the tax exemption for industrial development bonds.[20] In an effort to overcome this restriction, hearings were held in Congress in the autumn of 1987 on a bill which would have allowed tribal governments to be considered "economic enterprise zones," and to be able to issue tax-exempt industrial development bonds. Though the bill did not pass at that time, continuing work is still being done in this area, in hopes of passing a revised form of the bill or a similar measure.[21]

The special significance of the Governmental Tax Status Act was not simply that it gave Indian tribes exemption from federal taxation, but that it did so in a very broad manner. In fact the benefits gained by the tribes were in some ways broader than those enjoyed by the states. In the early days following the *McCulloch* ruling, intergovernmental tax exemptions applied to everything and everybody associated with a government. The resulting lack of general taxing power led to the adoption of the common law distinction between "governmental" activities and "proprietary" activities.[22] Though the distinction is hazy, the definitions can be meaningfully understood within a capitalistic paradigm. Since that paradigm does not always apply on Indian reservations due to the communal nature of the tribes, such a distinction is difficult to make when applied to tribal enterprises. Therefore, under the 1982 act, Congress applied the exemption to any essential governmental function of an Indian tribal government that is eligible for funding under the Snyder Act or under the Indian Self-Determination Act.[23]

Given this background, it seems clear that there is an inherent right of tribes to tax, that that right has not been withdrawn by Congress, and that it was merely reaffirmed by *Washington v. Colville* and by the Governmental Tax Status Act.

II

Once it is established that tribes do have the right to levy taxes, the next question becomes, what are the limitations on that right? The three relevant limitations on tribal taxation are boundary jurisdiction, interstate commerce, and representation.

The standard limit for all governments is that of geographical boundaries. The Supreme Court has ruled that states may only tax those persons and things that are situated within their boundaries.[24] This includes businesses that are incorporated within one state but do business in another. In those cases, only the value added within the state can be taxed. Similarly, the Court has ruled that tribes have jurisdiction over their lands and boundaries.[25] The sticking point concerns residents. Under a variety of cases and federal statues, tribal jurisdiction has often been limited to tribal members.[26] The extent of this rule, however, is not entirely clear, since many of these early cases and acts related mainly to questions of criminal jurisdiction. For instance, the Major Crimes Act specifically restricts tribes from execising jurisdiction in certain areas. Commentary on these restrictions points to the fact that the Supreme Court is concerned over due process rights of its citizens.[27] Since tribal governments are not subject to all of the constitutional provisions, it has been presumed by judges and legislators that non-Indians may face a deprivation of their rights if subject to tribal courts.

At the same time, except where preempted by Public Law 280,[28] tribes have been able to regulate their reservation and tribal activities. Much of the regulation traditionally has related to trust lands, such as leases and royalties, on tribal lands. Until recently, activities by business and industry on reservation lands were handled mainly by private contracts or by federal law rather than by tribal ordinances. The decision to tax industries (particularly those involved in the extraction of natural resources) rather than simply requiring royalty payments, resulted in a new perspective on the economic relationship. Previously it was one of parties to a contract; with the advent of tax codes it became one of government/subject. The prior arrangement was one of equals; the latter arrangement placed the corporation (which may be larger, richer, and more sophisticated than the tribe) in a subordinate position to the legitimate governing authority.

The result of these restrictions is that tribal jurisdiction tends to be related to subject matter rather than to geography, that is, tribes may tax lands and people as long as they can demonstrate that they have the jurisdiction—not the state.[29]

The second limitation on tribal taxes is that of interstate commerce. In *Gibbons v. Ogden* (9 Wheat. 1 [1824]) the Supreme Court established the right of the federal government to regulate interstate commerce. That regulation has often come into conflict with state taxing policies. In an effort to delineate the overlapping jurisdictions, the Court in *Complete Auto Transit, Inc. v. Brady* (430 U.S. 274 [1977]) set out four rules or tests governing the taxation of interstate commerce. They are: (1) the tax can only be applied to an activity which has a substantial nexus with the taxing state; (2) the tax must be fairly apportioned; (3) the tax cannot discriminate; (4) the tax must be fairly related to the services provided by the taxing government.

When applied to tribal taxing schemes these tests have the following effects. In the first place, the activity taxed must have some connection to the tribe or the reservation. Without such a connection, taxation would be a violation of the interstate commerce clause and a violation of the federal government's preemption of this area. It is unclear whether simply transporting goods across reservation boundaries creates the required nexus. For instance, truckers are assessed a ton/mile tax by state governments which goes into dedicated highway funds. The rational nexus in this case is the highways. Generally tribes could not show that nexus unless they are building and maintaining the highways within the reservation boundaries—a rare occurrence because interstate highways, federal highways, and state roads generally have rights-of-way across reservation lands and are maintained by the respective governments. But this does bring up the case of public utility rights-of-way.

There are numerous electrical lines, pipelines, and railroads crossing the country's reservations. In most instances, the tribes simply collect royalties from these public utilities for the privilege of crossing reservation land. (Railroads are an exception; they own their roadbeds outright.) The states, however, collect the property tax on the power lines, pipelines, and mainline tracks according to an apportionment formula which includes such factors as the size of the line, the number of linear miles within a county and or state, and the value of the capital equipment involved. In order for tribal governments to find the required nexus to tax public utilities, they must show that they have delivered some service to or incurred some cost from the right-of-way. A sufficient case for the nexus might be based on safety and health concerns. In *Colville Confederated Tribes v. Walton* (647 F.2d 42 [1981]), the court noted:

> A tribe's inherent power to regulate generally the conduct of non-members on land no longer owned by or held in trust for a tribe was impliedly withdrawn but the tribe retains inherent power to exercise civil authority over conduct of non-Indians on fee lands within its reservations when that *conduct threatens or has some direct effect on the health and welfare of the tribe* [emphasis added].

However, the tribes have tended not to pursue rights-of-way as a potential revenue source (other than royalties), in favor of concentrating on those revenue bases that are more politically certain.

The second test requires that the tax must be fairly apportioned so as not to interfere with interstate commerce. An underlying principle of this test is that if all governments taxed a business in the same manner, the total taxation would not be more than the total of the unitary business's income. This means that one state or taxing entity cannot levy such a burdensome tax that if all did it would bankrupt the business. The test also tends to distinguish between vertically integrated companies, such as oil companies, in which all income is considered for purposes of apportionment, and conglomerates, in which only that income from a particular subsidiary that does business within the state or reservation is taxed.[30]

The third test applies the Equal Protection Clause of the Fourteenth Amendment to the taxing of interstate goods and services. Accordingly, taxes must treat not only individuals equally but also businesses. The Supreme Court summed up its view concerning this matter in *Bacchus Imports, Ltd. v. Dias* (104 S.Ct. 3049 [1984]): "discrimination between in-state and out-of-state goods is as offensive to the Commerce Clause as discrimination between in-state and out-of-state taxpayers."

In a related concept, the court has ruled that states may not levy a tax that only falls on non-residents, not on residents.[31] By this rule, it must be assumed that discrimination in taxing non-Indians versus Indians is also prohibited. Though on its face such a statement would seem self-evident, for tribal governments the intent may be to do just that—not because of discrimination against non-Indians but rather because reservation economies tend to be poverty-stricken and an extra tax burden would be disastrous to many struggling families and businesses. The solution to this dilemma is to levy taxes that discriminate according to income level or sales receipts.

The final test relates to a connection between services and the person or company being taxed. Generally states and local governments are not hard pressed to demonstrate some connection between their taxing powers and services rendered; therefore, this test is often simply assumed when the taxing entity is a state. However, where tribes and reservations are concerned it may become a controversial provision. Two recent cases have provided some leeway for tribal tax codes. In the case involving Montana's severance tax,[32] the Supreme Court refused to accept the argument that the fair relationship prong of the *Complete Auto Transit* test required a factual inquiry into the costs and benefits of state services provided to the taxpayer. Ruling on a tribal severance tax, a lower court sustained the concept that the "general advantages of a civilized society" and the privilege of depleting the resources were sufficient justification for the tax (*Southland Royalty Co. v. Navajo Tribe*, 715 F.2d 486 [CA 10, 1983]).

Since this test relates to benefits received from the taxing authority, a discussion of the two major principles of taxation, benefits received and ability to pay, is germane at this point. Under the first principle, taxes should be related to the benefit received in return for the tax. For instance, gasoline taxes, highway tolls, postage stamps, and park fees are all examples of taxes and fees that are tied to some form of benefit. However, taxation as a broad concept can also be understood according to this principle. Generally taxes are perceived as legitimate if one can enjoy some of the benefits through the goods and services that those taxes create. Public schools, highways, clean air, defense spending, and so on, are all benefits that the average person can expect to receive from his or her taxes. In these latter cases, generally there is not a direct linkage between the amount of good received and the amount of taxes paid, as with the user fees, but the benefits are still visible. As was noted above, the challenge for the tribes is to demonstrate the nexus between those being taxed and the benefits received.

The other principle, ability to pay, rests upon the premise that those who are wealthier can afford (and do not mind) paying relatively more than their poorer neighbors. This principle assumes the proposition of decreasing marginal utility: the more one makes in income, the less the marginal utility attached to each additional dollar. Progressive income taxes are based on this principle. Those at higher income levels not only pay more absolutely, but also pay more relatively. The concept of ability to pay also includes an equity argument, in that any tax based on this principle, ultimately involves redistribution of income and or wealth.

Justifying the redistribution of wealth and income requires a commitment to the value of equality, not simply in opportunity, but also in condition. Poverty is ethically unacceptable for some people. For others, redistribution of income is a form of insurance against crime. And for still others, redistribution is simply an equitable solution to a relationship that has historically been one of exploitation.[33] As mentioned earlier, tribal taxation is basically an enterprise in taxing non-Indians and off-reservation businesses that have historically exploited the natural resources of reservation economies, rather than taxing tribal members and reservation residents whose economic plight is well documented.[34]

The third and final limitation on tribal taxes is the idea of taxation by a representative body. The American Revolutionary War was precipitated by tax legislation and a lack of representation in Parliament. In fact, the basic rights of Englishmen were often obtained by political strife precipitated by the structure of the tax burdens and benefits.[35] It was the American colonists, however, who coined the phrase "no taxation without representation." The idea was based on the Lockean concept of government by consent, that the basis for governmental power and legitimacy rested with the consent of those over whom the government was to exercise power. If a government were imposed upon a people or if it failed to protect the people and their natural rights of life, liberty, and *property*, then that government was not legitimate and should be resisted.[36] The American interpretation of this concept was ably expressed by John Dickinson:

> Let these truths be indelibly impressed on our minds—that we cannot be happy, without being free—that we cannot be free, without being secure in our property—that we cannot be secure in our property, if, without our consent, others may, as by right, take it away—that taxes imposed on us by parliament, do thus take it away—that duties laid for the sole purpose of raising money, are taxes—that attempts to lay such duties should be instantly and firmly opposed—that this opposition can never be effectual, unless it is the united effort of these provinces—that therefore benevolence of temper towards each other, and unanimity of councils, are essential to the welfare of the whole.[37]

Due to our English and Revolutionary War history, the concept of taxation by representation has become so thoroughly ingrained in our political senses that the question of taxation without representation is no longer debated. However, when tribal taxes are concerned the question becomes of vital importance. The tribes that levy the taxes are made up of enrolled members whose enrollment is based, in part, upon a specified amount of tribal blood. Since Congress restricted tribes from adopting outsiders,[38] this means that the taxes levied by Indian tribes often fall upon persons who are not and *cannot* become members of the tribes—hence taxation without representation.

It has been argued that the lack of representation of nontribal taxpayers is analogous to aliens or foreign companies that pay taxes to the United States or to the several states.[39] In the case of businesses and corporations doing business on the reservation or exploiting the natural resources, the argument is well founded. It is the nature of modern business to engage in economic activities outside its home area and to pay taxes to the prevailing government. Beyond that, the corporation, although enjoying the fiction of being "a person" under the law, is simply an artificial civil construction.[40] This must be contrasted with human beings who, under the philosophy upon which the Constitution was founded, enjoy certain natural rights of life, liberty, and property. That protection is insured by the political equality of the members of the community. Within reservation boundaries, political equality does not exist in the same measure as in the rest of the United States. Aliens within the state of California may pay taxes to that government, but they may also enjoy the right of becoming citizens through a due process procedure. To all non-Indians on reservation land, that option does not exist. Therefore, the analogy between aliens paying state taxes and non-Indians paying tribal taxes does not hold.

The courts have been reluctant to discuss the question of taxation based on representation. This holds for federal, state, and local cases as well as tribal cases. When hearing state tax cases, the closest the Supreme Court has come to referring to representation is in the test of boundaries. The assumption seems to be that boundaries insure geographical representation. The fact that geography does not necessarily mean representation does not seem to bother the Court. Furthermore, as has already been discussed, boundaries of reservations are very fluid where jurisdiction questions are concerned; yet, in a series of cases, the Court has asserted the right of tribes to tax nonmembers.[41] Unfortunately, the legality of an action does not necessarily make it politically palatable. The lack of perceived representation has created an atmosphere of uneasiness among non-Indians, now that tribes are beginning to enforce tax codes.

There is no simple solution to this dilemma. If tribes are prevented from taxing anyone but tribal members, then the power of taxation would become merely a legal nicety without any real usefulness. On the other hand, if tribes can tax the nonmember (non-Indian) residents of the reservation without any *political* recourse for those individuals then a fundamental regime value will be cast aside. Still, it is the right of tribes to determine their membership, and it is this pre-Columbian right that in many ways has preserved the Indian culture. To treat Indians like other racial minorities, on an individual basis rather than as tribes, would deny tribal sovereignty. Therefore, for Indian tribes to maintain their sovereignty they must be able to wield the powers of a sovereign government, including that of defining membership and taxing those within their jurisdictions.

Although not immediately practical, the long term solution for those tribes that occupy reservations is to remove all non-Indians as permanent residents from the reservation. To some extent this is being done by tribal councils who are buying up non-Indian land as it becomes available on the reservations and returning that land to trust status. Once the reservation land is all in Indian hands again, then nonmembers and non-Indians living and working on the reservation would have a status more analogous to the temporary nonresident.[42]

III

As can be deduced by the previous discussion, taxation by Indian tribes is not as simple a matter as it is for state or even local governments. As noted above, the tribes are limited in their jurisdiction to the geographic boundaries of the reservation, to areas that have not been preempted by the states within the limits of PL 280, to those areas that *are* preempted by federal jurisdiction, and in some cases only to tribal members. If all that sounds confusing, it is. Rather than being able to levy taxes on persons and property within the boundaries, each tax must be carefully scrutinized to determine its applicability to the special features of a reservation, or to its particular characteristics as it affects tribal jurisdiction. The following is a brief analysis of a selected number of tribal taxes to demonstrate to the reader the difficulty of creating a tribal tax code.

Property taxes, long the mainstay of local governments, are generally not feasible as tribal taxes. The major reason for their inapplicability is that much of the land on reservations is trust land, that is, land held in trust by the federal government and therefore not subject to sale. Trust land may be tribal lands (lands held in common by the tribe), allotted/heirship lands (lands that were originally allotted under the Dawes Act and that have been divided over the years as they were passed down through the generations), and fee simple lands owned by the tribal members. Since these lands cannot be sold, determining their property value as a basis for taxing them would be an exercise in creative speculation.

Because of the difficulties inherent in the property tax, the most popular of the tribal taxes is the possessory interest tax. This is a tax on leaseholders, based on the value of their leases. The Navajo tribe was the first to levy a possessory interest tax, and its tax code has become a model for other tribes. The possessory interest tax has become the reservation property tax, since it is based on the way land is valued on reservations (i.e., leases), and it is levied on those who derive the most economic benefit from the reservation. It is also flexible enough to apply to farm lands, rights-of-way, and mining interests just like the property tax.

Ahmed Kooros and Theodore Reynolds Smith have proposed an alternative method by which the value of reservation land could be determined. Their method would include the calculation of opportunity costs, that is, the cost of foregone alternatives.[43] Under this method, the land's worth would be calculated by how much it would cost the lessee to get the same land off-reservation or, in cases of rights-of-way, the cost of going around the reservation. If this method were to be used, one could figure the effect of the tax on demand through the substitution effect, as well as the income effect.[44] It would also recognize the value of non-Indians being able to use and or cross the lands of the Native Americans. Unfortunately, the market is not always structured in such a form to make possible the determination of such opportunity costs. Therefore, this alternative, though theoretically more correct than the property tax, may in practice suffer from the same fate as the property tax: there is no valid form of measurement.

In addition to the trust lands, there are lands on the reservations where property values can be easily determined. These are lands held in fee simple title by non-Indians or nontribal members. Normally once a piece of land goes out of trust, the county picks up that land on its property tax roles, because at the present time the county (state) usually has jurisdiction over nontribal members' property, wealth, and income. However, it may be possible, under the benefits received principle, for a tribe to argue that it has a right to preempt those property taxes based on a comparison of services rendered to reservation residents by both the tribe and the county. If a tribe can demonstrate that it has provided the majority of services on the reservation, or that federal law has preempted this jurisdictional area, or that state law infringes on the ability of Indian tribes to make their own laws, then the tribe may sue for preemption of the tax. However, given the *Colville* case there is some question as to whether a tribe could *fully* preempt state taxes on non-Indians.[45]

The most likely taxes for the tribes to preempt are the taxes on mining. Given that mines intensively use the property upon which they are situated and that the property, in many cases, is rendered useless for a number of generations after the mining is completed, most states levy several taxes on the property. Included among these are property taxes, mine license fees, and severance taxes. The property tax is generally based on the value of minerals or metals produced and on the personal property associated with the mine. It has a regulatory effect on the use of the property depending upon the form of appraisals and the depreciation formulas used. Some formulas make it more advantageous to mine as much ore as fast as possible. Other formulas promote a more managed approach to mining. Whereas the property tax generally goes into the coffers of local government, the mine license fee is a tax the state levies on the right of a mining company to do business within the state. Preempting either or both of these taxes would depend on the mining concern. Because most mining companies are not wholly situated on reservation property, it may be difficult for the tribes to argue that they are providing the major benefits of a society to the company, in order to preempt the mine license tax. However, a tribe could levy a license tax on the right to do business on the reservation. (As already noted in *Colville*, double taxation by the tribe and the state is not unconstitutional.) That could be done in addition to any state tax, given the basic justification of the Indian traders' license, and the ruling in *Morris v. Hitchcock* giving Indians control over their borders.[46] The property tax is a likely candidate for preemption of state (county) revenues. Tribes can argue in most instances that because the profits are created on the reservation, the counties are basically being given a free ride.

The third form of mining tax, the severance tax, has been a successful tax for a number of tribes. In a recent Tenth Circuit case, *Crow v. Montana* (819 F2d 895 [1987]), the court held that coal mined on the Crow reservation was exempt from state taxation based on (1) federal preemption under the 1938 Mineral Leasing Act[47]; and (2) interference with tribal self-government. Montana appealed the case to the Supreme Court but *certiorari* was denied and the lower court's decision affirmed. A similar case concerning oil and gas production on the Wind River Reservation arose in 1988. This case involved a tax ordinance passed in 1987 by the Shoshone and Arapahoe tribes that laid claim to Wyoming's severance and property taxes generated on the reservation.[48] Reacting to the tribes' action, Senator Malcolm Wallop noted that "if the tribes actually get all those taxes and have the money coming in to pay for their own services, the federal government will certainly have to reevaluate and perhaps reinterpret the treaties regarding services that are now being supplied."[49]

Wallop's comment reflects a pervasive attitude among many non-Indian lawmakers, as well as the public at large. From the Indian's perspective, the reservations created by the nineteenth-century treaties were just that, "reserved." They were part of a large land deal, and the Indians agreed to stay on a portion of the land "reserved" to them. In return for the rest of the land "ceded" to the U.S. government, they were to receive not only a lump sum payment of money or goods, but also were to be provided education and health services for some undetermined future period.[50] On the other hand, the non-Indian perspective often does not recognize the relationship as a contract but rather sees transfer payments to reservations, Indian tribes, and individual Indians, as a form of charity. Given the two radically different viewpoints, the new issue of tribal taxes poses an immediate conflict.

From the Indian perspective, much of the federal aid is simply a function of treaty rights. Therefore, any new revenue sources such as taxes would simply be added to that base. It is analogous to the millionaire (a bit far-fetched, given reservation economies), who still draws social security. His income and wealth are a result of his work and inheritance; the social security payment in an "entitlement." Indian health service could thus be viewed as a "treaty entitlement," and taxes as a product of sovereignty. Nevertheless, the redistributive effects of taxation are enough to send political shivers through many a lawmaker's system. In 1987, after the Blackfeet Nation implemented a tribal tax code and sent out tax notices without prior notification to the taxed parties, Senator Melcher of Montana, along with Senator Simpson of Wyoming and Senator Bauchus of Montana, introduced a bill into Congress which would have imposed a two-year moratorium on further tribal tax codes.[51] Though the bill died in committee, it caused much trepidation in Indian country and demonstrated that there is still an uneasiness felt by many non-Indians toward politics on the reservations. That tension was again felt in December 1987 when a Senate amendment sponsored by Senator James McClure of Idaho was added to a farm credit bill that would have made any reservation land upon which a loan had been defaulted subject to "state, county, municipal, or other local taxes, even after those lands have been taken into trust."[52] After a quickly organized and intense lobbying effort by the Indian tribes, that clause was deleted in the conference committee. However, it can be expected that Congress will continue to propose legislation to limit the taxing authority of tribes.

CONCLUSION

In 1879, the Senate Judiciary Committee, reporting on powers of Indian tribes noted:

> We have considered [Indian tribes] as invested with the right of self-government and jurisdiction over the persons and property within the limits of the territory they occupy, except so far as that jurisdiction has been restrained and abridged by treaty or act of Congress. Subject to the supervisory control of the Federal Government, they may enact the requisite legislation to maintain peace and good order, improve their condition, establish school systems, and aid their people in their efforts to acquire the arts of civilized life.[53]

The words of the Senate Committee are still applicable today. The inherent power of a sovereign government, the power to tax, is still held by Indian tribes. The fact that the Supreme Court has placed no more restrictions on tribal tax codes than it does on state tax codes is indicative of the status Indian tribes hold within the federal system. Tribes have the authority to levy taxes on members and nonmembers alike within the constraints of the Due Process and Commerce (Interstate and Indian) clauses. The only major constraint against the tribes today is the political environment, and as the tribes gain one legal victory after another, accommodations are starting to be made by non-Indian politicians. Still the Indian wars have not ended. Both sides recognize that the establishment of tribal tax codes portends a restructuring of federalism in the long run and a redistribution of tax revenues in the short run. Yet the outcome is providentially determined. The power of taxation gives the tribes the power to govern and lays a solid foundation from which to exercise the sovereignty Justice Marshall envisioned when he termed them "Domestic Dependent Nations."

NOTES

1. Vine Deloria and Clifford Lytle, *The Nations Within: The Past and Future of American Indian Sovereignty* (New York: Pantheon Books, 1984), p. 222.

2. 25 U.S.C. 4502–450n.

3. The Navajo Tribal Tax Code was passed by the tribal council in 1978, but Kerr-McGee quickly filed suit and the District Court permanently enjoined the tribe from collecting the tax until the case was settled. In 1985, the Supreme Court ruled in favor of the Navajo Nation, *Kerr-McGee Corporation v. Navajo Tribe* 471 U.S. 195 (1985).

4. The list of tribes now levying some form of taxes on their reservations is growing almost daily. In this essay, the tax codes of the Navajo, the Blackfeet, the Crow, the Shoshone and Arapahoe, the Confederated Tribes of the Colville Reservation, and the Jicarilla Apache are all referred to. The Council on Energy Resource Tribes (CERT) has several publications on the tax activity of tribes and probably has the most up-to-date list of the present status of tribal tax codes.

5. Bernard Schwartz, *A Commentary on the Constitution of the United States: Part II, The Rights of Property* (New York: Macmillan Company, 1965), p. 307.

6. *People ex rel. Hatch v. Reardon*, 184 N.Y. 431, 444 (1906), affirmed 204 U.S. 152 (1907).

7. *City of Pittsburg v. Alco Parking Corp.*, 417 U.S. 369 (1974); *Stewart Dry Goods Co. v. Lewis*, 294 U.S. 550 (1935); *Veazie Bank v. Fenno*, 8 Wall. 533 (1869); and *Loan Association v. Topeka*, 20 Wall. 655 (1875).

8. *Gautier v. Ditmar*, 204 N.Y. 20 (1912); *Matter of McPherson*, 104 N.Y. 306 (1887); and *License Tax Cases*, 5 Wall. 462 (1867).

9. Justice John S. Dillon first expressed the views toward local government that have become accepted legal opinion today: "Municipal corporations owe their origin to, and derive their powers and rights wholly from, the [state] legislature. It breathes into them, the breath of life, without which they cannot exist. As it creates, so it may destroy." *City of Clinton v. Cedar Rapids and Missouri R.R. Co.*, 24 Iowa 475 (1868). The opinion of Justice Dillon was upheld by the Supreme Court in *Barnes v. District of Columbia*, 91 U.S. 540 (1875).

10. James Madison, *Notes of Debates in the Federal Convention of 1787* (New York: W.W. Norton, 1987).

11. Ibid., p. 477.

12. In 1868, for instance, the treaties with the Sioux, the Shoshone, and the Navajo were all signed. The basic format was the same for these treaties, with only some particularized wording relating to the boundaries of the reservations and a few other specific promises.

13. *U.S. v. Kagama*, 118 U.S. 375 (1886); *Lone Wolf v. Hitchcock*, 187 U.S. 553 (1903).

14. 435 U.S. 313, 323.

15. Burke Act, 1906. See: American Indian Policy Review Committee, *Final Report*, vol. 1, (Washington D.C.: U.S. Government Printing Office, 1977), p. 67.

16. U.S. Department of Interior, *Opinions of the Solicitor: Indian Affairs* (Washington: U.S. Government Printing Office, 1946), p. 410, as quoted in Deloria and Lytle, *Nations Within*, p. 158.

17. Deloria and Lytle, *Nations Within*, p. 159.

18. 447 U.S. 134, 152.

19. 447 U.S. 134, 155.

20. 26 U.S.C. 103 (a) (b).

21. Charles Pace, "Always More Powder: The Role of Federal Incentives in Promoting Indian Commerce and Encouraging Economic Development," paper delivered at the Western Political Science Association Convention, San Francisco, California, March 10–12, 1988. "Sho-Bans: Access to Financial Markets Critical," *Sho-Ban News*, November 19, 1987, p. 7.

22. Harold M. Groves and Robert L. Bish, *Financing Government* 7th ed. (New York: Holt, Rinehart & Winston, 1972), pp. 333–334.

23. Robert L. Pirtle, Mason D. Morisset, and James J. Purcell, *Taxation and Indian Affairs*, 4th ed. (Seattle: Ziontz, Pirtle, Morisset,

Chestnut & Anderson, 1986), p. 110. The Snyder Act of 1921 (42 Stat 208) gave the secretary of interior general authority to expend federal monies for Indian "benefit, care and assistance." The Johnson-O'Malley Act (48 Stat. 596) expanded the Snyder Act for educational assistance. The Self-Determination and Educational Assistance Act of 1975 (25 USC 4502-450n) authorized federal agencies to contract with and make grants directly to Indian tribal governments. Vine Deloria and Clifford Lytle, *American Indians, American Justice* (Austin: University of Texas Press, 1984), pp. 103.

24. *Adams County v. Northern Pacific Ry Co.*, 115 F.2d 768, 782 (9th Cir., 1940); *Marshall-Wells Co. v. Commissioner*, 20 N.W. 2d 92, 94 (Minn, 1945); *Austin v. New Hampshire*, 420 U.S. 656 (1975).

25. *Morris v. Hitchcock*, 194 U.S. 384 (1904).

26. *U.S. v. McBratney*, 104 U.S. 621 (1881); *U.S. v. Pelican*, 232 U.S. 442 (1914).

27. Deloria and Lytle, *American Indians, American Justice*, p. 11.

28. Public Law 280 was passed by the Eighty-third Congress. It transferred civil and criminal jurisdiction over reservation Indians to five states. California, Minnesota (except the Red Lake Chippewa Reservation), Nebraska, Oregon (except the Warm Springs Reservation), and Wisconsin (except the Menominee Reservation). It also allowed other states to amend their constitutions so that they could assume jurisdiction. Ibid., pp. 175–77.

29. See *U.S. v. Mazurie*, 419 U.S. 544 (1975); *Babbit Ford Ind. v. Navajo Indian Tribe*, 710 F2d 587 (1983); *Cardin v. De La Cruz*, 617 f.2d 363 (9 Cir. 1982); and *Confederated Salish and Kootenai Tribes v. Namen*, 665 F.2d 951 (1982).

30. M. David Gelfand and Peter W. Salish, Jr., *State and Local Taxation and Finance*, Nutshell Series, (St. Paul: West, 1986), pp. 17–21.

31. *Austin v. New Hampshire*, 420 U.S. 656 (1975).

32. The tax could be as high as 30 percent of the price of mineral extracted. Gelfand and Salish, *State and Local Taxation*, p. 71.

33. Edgar K. Browning and Jacquelene M. Browning, *Public Finance and the Price System* (New York: Macmillan, 1979), pp. 185–90.

34. For an excellent review see: Chuck Cook, Mike Masterson, and Mark N. Trahant, "Fraud in Indian Country," *Arizona Republic*, October 4–11, 1987.

35. In particular see: the Magna Carta, 1215, and the English Bill of Rights, 1689. The British House of Commons from its earliest days (est. 1265) demanded the right of taxation. Louis S. Snyder, *The Making of Modern Man* (Princeton: Van Nostrand, 1967), pp. 212–13.

36. John Locke, *Second Treatise on Government*, sec. 142 (New York: New American Library, 1965), p. 409.

37. John Dickinson, *Twelfth Letter*, quoted in *American Political Thought*, rev. ed., ed. Alan Pendleton Grimes (Lanham: University Press of America, 1983), p. 81.

38. Generally the requirement is one-quarter Indian (tribal) blood. Felix Cohen notes that the degree of blood necessary to be recognized an Indian has varied from one-half at the time of the adoption of the Indian Reorganization Act in 1934 to an act in 1924 (43 Stat. 366) concerning the Cherokee which recognized Indians of less than one-sixteenth blood. Felix Cohen, *Handbook of Federal Indian Law* (Albuquerque: University of New Mexico Press, 1971), pp. 4–5.

39. Barsch and Henderson assert that Congress limited tribal adoptions to individuals of Indian blood in order to limit the financial responsibility of the United States. Russel Lawrence Barsh and James Youngblood Henderson, *The Road: Indian Tribes and Political Liberty* (Berkeley and Los Angeles: University of California Press, 1980), pp 244–45.

40. *San Mateo Co. v. Southern Pacific RR*, 116 U.S. 138 (1883).

41. In a case concerning a tribe's right to zone land that was not in trust and owned by non-Indians, the circuit court said: "The interest of the Tribes in preserving and protecting their homeland from exploitation justifies the zoning code. The fact that the code applies to and affects non-Indians who cannot participate in tribal government is immaterial." *Knight v. Shoshone and Arapahoe Indian Tribes*, 670 F.2d 900 (1982).

42. Beyond the controversy between Indians and Non-Indians there is a controversy over the right of jurisdiction over Indians who do not happen to be on their own reservations—temporarily or permanently. According to the *Colville* decision, tax exemptions only apply to tribal members on their own reservations. Thus as Indians travel from one reservation to another they lose the protection of tribal law and become subject to state law, even though they may be residing on reservation land and trust property. Since enrollment requirements of tribes are very specific, this could result in some members of a family being tax exempt, while others are taxable.

43. Ahmed Kooros and Theodore Reynolds Smith, "The Opportunity Cost Doctrine: An Application to the Value of Tribal Land," *The Appraisal Journal* (April 1983), pp. 294–98.

44. Bernard P. Herber, *Modern Public Finance*, 4th ed. (Homewood, Ill.: Richard D. Irwin, 1979), pp. 89–90.

45. It should be noted that in a partially concurring and partially dissenting opinion by justices Brennan and Marshall in the *Colville* case, they argued that by refusing to let the Colville tribe credit their tribal cigarette tax against the state tax, the Court was allowing the state of Washington to "infringe" on the ability of the tribe to govern itself through raising revenues.

46. There is within the Trade and Intercourse Act of 1790 a provision for the federal government to levy an Indian traders' license (25 CFR 140). The intent of this legislation was to prevent unscrupulous individuals from taking advantage of the unsophisticated Indians. Thus this early regulation could be viewed as the first "Indian tax," in that its intention was to regulate economic activity with the tribes. While this "tax" is seldom levied today, some tribes are beginning to eye it as a way of seizing control of their reservation borders. If the tribes can levy a fee for doing business on the reservation (the fee is presently $5), then they can begin to demonstrate jurisdiction over economic activity within reservation boundaries.

47. 25 U.S.C. 396a–396g.

48. *Sho-Ban News*, January 28, 1988, p. 5.

49. *Sho-Ban News*, January 28, 1988, p. 11.

50. Typically each adult Indian was allotted a specified number of acres (80) that were to be taken out of the common store and recorded in his or her name. In addition: "[the] United States agrees to deliver at the agency-house on the reservation herein provided for, on the first day of September of each year, for thirty years, the following articles, to wit: For each male person over fourteen years of age, a suit of good substantial woollen clothing, consisting of coat, hat, pantaloons, flannel shirt, and a pair of woollen socks; for each female over twelve years of age, a flannel skirt, or the goods necessary to make it, a pair of woollen hose, twelve yards of calico; and twelve yards of cotton domestics. . . . The United States hereby agrees to furnish annually to the Indians the physician, teachers, carpenter, miller, engineer, farmer, and blacksmith, as herein contemplated, and the such appropriations shall be made from time to time, on the estimates of the Secretary of the Interior, as will be sufficient to employ such persons." From the Treaty with the Eastern Band Shoshoni and Bànnock, Fort Bridger, 1868.

51. S. 1039, 100th Congress, 1st Session, March 30, 1987.

52. *Congressional Record*, December 18, 1987.

53. S. Rep. No. 698, 45th Cong. 3d Sess. 1–2 (1879). Quoted in *Merrion v. Jicarilla Apache*, 455 U.S. 130, 140 (1981).

Policy Studies Journal, Vol. 16, No. 4, Summer, 1988

FEDERAL INDIAN IDENTIFICATION POLICY: A USURPATION OF INDIGENOUS SOVEREIGNTY IN NORTH AMERICA

M. Annette Jaimes
University of Colorado at Boulder

American Indian peoples whose territory lies within the borders of the United States hold compelling legal and moral rights to be treated as fully sovereign nations. It is axiomatic that any such national entity is inherently entitled to determine for itself the criteria by which its citizenry, or "membership," is to be recognized by other sovereign nations. This is a tenet so widely understood and imbedded in international law, custom, and convention, that it needs no particular elaboration here.

Contrary to virtually universal practice, the U.S. has opted to preempt unilaterally the rights of many North American indigenous nations to engage in this most fundamental level of internal decision-making. Instead, in pursuit of the interests of their own state rather than those of the nations which are thereby affected, federal policy-makers have increasingly imposed "Indian identification standards" of their own devising. Typically centering upon a notion of "blood quantum"--not especially different in its conception from the eugenics code once adopted by Nazi Germany in its effort to achieve "racial purity," or currently utilized by South Africa to segregate blacks and "coloreds"--this aspect of U.S. policy has increasingly wrought havoc with the American Indian sense of nationhood (and often the individual sense of self) over the past century.

FEDERAL OBLIGATIONS

The 371 formally ratified treaties entered into by the U.S. with various Indian nations represent the basic real estate documents by which the federal government now claims legal title to most of its landbase. In exchange for the lands ceded by the Indians in perpetuity, the U.S. committed itself to the permanent provision of a range of services to Indian populations (i.e., the citizens of the Indian nations with which the treaty agreements were reached), which would assist them in adjusting their economies and ways-of-life to their newly constricted territories. For example, in a 1794 treaty with the Oneidas (also affecting the Tuscaroras and Stockbridge Indians), the U.S. guaranteed provision of instruction "in the arts of the miller and sawyer," as well as regular annuities paid in goods and cash, in exchange for a portion of what is now the State of New York (Kappler, 1973:3-5). Similarly, the 1804 *Treaty with the Delaware* extended assurances of technical instruction in agriculture and the mechanical arts, as well as annuities (Kappler, 1973:7-9). As E.C. Adams frames it:

> Treaties with the Indians varied widely, stipulating cash annuities to be paid over a specified period of time or perpetually; ration and clothing, farming implements and domestic animals, and instruction in agriculture along with other educational opportunities . . . [And eventually] the school supplemented the Federal program of practical teaching (1946:30-31).

The reciprocal nature of such agreements received considerable reinforcement when it was determined, early in the 19th century, that "the enlightenment and civilization of the Indian" might yield--quite aside from any need on the part of the U.S. to honor its international obligations--a certain utility in terms of subordinating North America's indigenous peoples to Euroamerican domination. Secretary of War John C. Calhoun articulated this quite clearly in 1818:

> By a proper combination of force and persuasion, of punishment and rewards, they [the Indians] ought to be brought within the pales of law and civilization. Left to themselves, they will never reach that desirable condition. Before the slow operation of reason and experience can convince them of its superior advantages, they must be overwhelmed by the mighty torrent of our population. Such small bodies, with savage customs and character, cannot, and ought not, to be allowed to exist in an independent society. Our laws and manners ought to supercede their present savage manners and customs . . . their [treaty] annuities would constitute an ample school fund; and education, comprehending as well as the common arts of life, reading, writing, and arithmetic, ought not to be left discretionary with the parents. . . . When sufficiently advanced in civilization, they would be permitted to participate in such civil and political rights as the respective States (*American State Papers*, 1972:183-184).

The utter cynicism involved in Calhoun's position--that of intentionally using the treaty instruments by which the U.S. conveyed recognition of Indian sovereignty as the vehicle for destroying that same sovereignty--speaks for itself. The more important point for this study, however, is that a confluence of U.S. strategic interests had congealed around the notion of extending federal obligations to Indians by 1820. The tactic was therefore continued throughout the entire period of U.S. internal territorial conquest and consolidation.[1] By 1900, the federal obligations to Indian nations were therefore quite extensive.

FINANCIAL FACTORS

As Vine Deloria, Jr., has observed:

> The original relationship between the United States government and the American Indian tribes was one of treaties. Beginning with the establishment of the federal policy toward Indians in the Northwest Ordinance of 1787, which pledged that the utmost good faith would be exercised toward the Indian tribes, and continuing through many treaties and statutes, the relationship has gradually evolved into a strange and stifling union in which the United States has become responsible for all of the programs and policies affecting Indian communities (Deloria, 1976:2).

What this meant in practice was that the government was being required to underwrite the cost of a proliferating bureaucratic apparatus overseeing "service delivery" to Indians, a process initiated on April 16, 1818, with the passage of an act (*U.S. Statutes at Large,* 13:461) requiring the placement of a federal agent with each Indian nation, to serve as liaison and to "administer the discharge of Governmental obligations thereto." As the number of Indian groups with which the U.S. held relations had increased, so too had the number of "civilizing" programs and services undertaken, ostensibly in their behalf. This was all well and good during the time span when it was seen as a politico-military requirement, but by the turn of the century this need had passed. The situation was compounded by the fact that the era of Indian population decline engendered by war and disease had also come to an end; the population eligible for per capita benefits, which had been reduced to a quarter-million by the 1890s, could be expected to rebound steadily in the 20th century. With its landbase secured, the U.S. was casting about for a satisfactory mechanism to avoid paying the ongoing costs associated with its acquisition.

The most obvious route to this end, of course, lay in simply and overtly refusing to comply with the terms of the treaties, thus abrogating them.[2] The problems in this regard were, however, both twofold and extreme. First, the deliberate invalidation of the U.S. treaties with the Indians would tend simultaneously to invalidate the legitimacy which the country attributed to its occupancy of much of North America. Second, such a move would immediately negate the useful and carefully nurtured image the U.S. had cultivated of itself as a country of progressive laws rather than raw force. The federal government had to *appear* to continue to meet its commitments, while at the same time avoiding them, or at least containing them at some acceptable level. A devious approach to the issue was needed.

This was found in the so-called "blood quantum" or "degree of Indian blood" standard of American Indian identification which had been adopted by Congress in 1887, as part of the General Allotment Act (25 U.S.C.A. §331, popularly known as the "Dawes Act," after its sponsor, Massachusetts Senator Henry Dawes). The function of this piece of legislation was to expedite the process of Indian civilization by unilaterally dissolving their collectively held reservation land holdings. Reservation lands were reallocated in accordance with the "superior" (i.e., Euroamerican) concept of property: *individually* deeded land parcels, usually of 160 acres each. Each Indian, identified as being documentably of *one-half or more Indian blood,* was entitled to receive title in fee of such a parcel; all others were simply disenfranchised altogether. Reserved Indian land which remained unallotted after all "blooded" Indian had received their individual parcels was to be declared "surplus," and opened up for non-Indian use and occupancy.

Needless to say, there were nowhere near enough Indians meeting the act's genetic requirements to absorb by individual parcel the quantity of acreage involved in the formerly reserved land areas. Consequently, between 1887 and 1934, the aggregate Indian landbase within the U.S. was "legally" reduced from about 138 million acres to about 48 million (Collier, 1934:16-18). Moreover, the allotment process itself had been manipulated in such a way that the worst reservation acreage tended to be parcelled out to Indians, while the best was opened to non-Indian homesteading and corporate use. Nearly 20 million of the acres remaining in Indian hands by the latter year were arid or semi-arid, and thus marginal or useless for agricultural purposes (Deloria and Lytle, 1983:10).

By the early 1900s, then, the eugenics mechanism of blood quantum had already proven itself such a boon in the federal management of its Indian affairs that it was generally adapted as the "eligibility factor" triggering entitlement to *any* federal service from the issuance of commodity rations to health care, annuity payment and educational benefits. If the federal government could not repeal its obligations to Indians, it could at least act to limit their number, thereby diminishing the costs associated with underwriting their entitlements on a per capita basis. Concomitantly, it must have seemed logical that if the overall number of Indians could be kept small, the administrative expenses involved in their service program might also be held to a minimum. Much of the original impetus towards the federal preemption of the sovereign Indian prerogative of defining "who's Indian," and the standardization of the racist degree-of-blood method of Indian identification, derived from the budgetary considerations of a federal government anxious to avoid paying its bills.

OTHER ECONOMIC FACTORS

As the example of the General Allotment Act clearly demonstrates, economic determinants other than the mere outflow of cash from the federal treasury figure into the federal utilization of blood quantum. The huge windfall of land expropriated by the U.S. as a result of the act was only the tip of the iceberg. For instance, in constricting the acknowledged size of Indian populations, the government could technically meet its obligations to reserve "first rights" to water usage for Indians while simultaneously siphoning off artificial "surpluses"to non-Indian agricultural, ranching, municipal and industrial use in the arid west (Hundley, 1979). The same principle pertains to the assignment of fishing quotas in the Pacific Northwest, a matter directly related to the development of a lucrative non-Indian fishing industry there (American Friends Service Committee, 1970).

By the 1920s, it was also becoming increasingly apparent that much of the agriculturally worthless terrain left to Indians after allotment lay astride rich deposits of natural resources such as coal, copper, oil and natural gas. (Later in the century, it was revealed that some 60 percent of all "domestic" uranium reserves also lay beneath reservation lands.) It was therefore becoming imperative, from the viewpoint of federal and corporate economic planners, to gain unhindered access to these assets. Given that it would have been just as problematic simply to seize the resources as it would have been to abrogate the treaties, another expedient was required. This assumed the form of legislation unilaterally extending the responsibilities of citizenship (though not all the rights; Indians are still regulated by about 5,000 more laws than other citizens) over all American Indians within the U.S.

> Approximately two-thirds of the Indian population had citizenship conferred upon them under the 1877 Allotment Act, as a condition of the allotment of their holdings . . . [In 1924] an act of Congress [8 U.S.C.A. §1401(a)(2)] declared

> all Indians to be citizens of the U.S. and of the states in which they resided . . . (League of Women Voters, 1977:24).

The Indian Citizenship Act greatly confused the identification and loyalties even of many of the blooded and federally certified Indians insofar as it was held to hold legal force, and to carry legal obligations, *whether or not* any given Indian or group of Indians wished to be a U.S. citizen. As for the host of non-certified, mixed-blood people residing in the U.S., their status was finally "clarified"; they had been definitionally absorbed into the American mainstream at the stroke of the Congressional pen. And, despite the fact that the act technically left certified Indians occupying the status of citizenship in their own indigenous nation as well as in the U.S.--a "dual form" of citizenship, so awkward as to be sublime--the juridical door had been opened by which the weight of advantage would begin to accrue more to the U.S. than to Indians. Resource negotiations would henceforth be conducted between "American citizens" rather than between representatives of separate nations, a context in which federal and corporate arguments "to the greater good" could be predicted to prevail.

In 1934, the effects of the citizenship act were augmented by the passage of the Indian Reorganization Act (25 U.S.C.A. §461; also known as the "Wheeler-Howard Act," after its Senate and House sponsors). The expressed purpose of this law was to usurp finally and completely the traditional mechanisms of American Indian governance (e.g., the traditional chiefs, council of elders, etc.), replacing them with a system of federally approved and regulated "tribal councils." These councils, in turn, were consciously structured more along the lines of corporate boards than of governmental entities. As Section 17 of the IRA, which spells out the council functions, puts the matter:

> [An IRA charter] may convey to the incorporated tribe the power to purchase, take by gift, or bequest, or otherwise, own, hold, manage, operate, and dispose of property of every description, real and personal, including the power to purchase restricted Indian lands and to issue in exchange for corporate property, and such further powers as may be incidental to the conduct of corporate business, not inconsistent with the law.

Indeed, since the exercise of such typical governmental attributes as jurisdiction over criminal law had already been stripped away from the council by legislation such as the 1885 Major Crime Act (18 U.S.C.A. §1153), there has been very little for the IRA form of Indian government to do *but* sign off on leasing and other business arrangements with external interests. The situation was and remains compounded by the fact that grassroots Indian resistance to the act's "acceptance" on many reservations was overcome by federal manipulation of local referenda (Deloria and Vine, 1984, especially Chapter 11). This has left the IRA governments in the position of owing Washington rather than their supposed constituents for whatever legitimacy they may possess. All in all, it was and is a situation made to order for the rubber-stamping of plans integral to U.S. economic development, at the direct expense of Indian nations and individual Indian people.

This is readily born out by the fact that as of 1984, American Indians received on the average less than 20 percent of the market royalty rates (i.e., the rates paid to non-Indians) for the extraction of minerals from their land. As Winona LaDuke observes:

> By official census counts, there are only about 1 1/2 million Indians in the United States. By conservative estimates a quarter of all the low sulphur coal in the U.S. lies under our reservation land. About 15% of all the oil and natural gas lies there, as well as two-thirds of the uranium. 100 percent of all U.S. uranium production since 1955 has been on Indian land. And we have a lot of copper, timber, water rights and other resources, too. By any reasonable estimation, with this small number of people and vast amount of resources, we should be the richest group in the United States.
>
> But we are the poorest. Indians have the lowest per capita income of any population group in the U.S. We have the highest rate of unemployment and lowest level of educational attainment. We have the highest rates of malnutrition, plague disease, death by exposure and infant mortality. On the other hand, we have the shortest life span. Now, I think this says it all. Indian wealth is going *somewhere,* and that somewhere is definitely *not* to Indians. I don't know your definition of colonialism, but this certainly fits into mine (LaDuke, 1984).

In sum, the financial advantages incurred by the U.S. in its appropriation of the definition of Indian identity have been neatly joined to even more powerful economic motivators during this century. The previously noted reluctance of the federal government to pay its bills cannot be uncoupled from its desire to profit from the resources of others.

CONTEMPORARY POLITICAL FACTORS

The utilization of treaties as instruments by which to begin the subordination of American Indian nations to U.S. hegemony, as well as subsequent legislation such as the Major Crime Act, the General Allotment Act, the Indian Citizenship Act, the Indian Reorganization Act, and the Termination Act all carry remarkably clear political overtones. This is the language of the colonizer and the colonized, to borrow a phrase from Albert Memmi (1967), and in each case the federal manipulation of the question of American Indian identity has played its role. These examples, however, may rightly be perceived as being both historical and as parts of the "grand scheme" of U.S. internal colonialism (or "Manifest Destiny," as it was once called).

Today, the function of the Indian identity question appears to reside at the less rarified level of maintaining the status quo. In the first instance, it goes to the matter of keeping the aggregate Indian population at less than one percent of the overall U.S. population, and thus devoid of any potential electoral power. In the second instance, and perhaps of equal importance, it goes to the classic "divide and conquer" strategy of keeping Indians at odds with one another, even within their own communities. As Tim Giago, conservative editor of the *Lakota Times,* asks:

> Don't we have enough problems trying to unite without . . . additional headaches? Why must people be categorized as full-bloods, mixed bloods, etc.? Many years ago, the Bureau of Indian Affairs decided to establish blood quanta for the purpose of [tribal] enrollment. At that time, blood quantum was set at one-fourth degree for enrollment. Unfortunately, through the years, this caused many people on the reservation to be categorized and labeled. . . . [The] situation [is] created solely by the BIA, with the able assistance of the Department of Interior (Giago, 1984:337).

What has occurred is that the limitation of federal resources allocated to meeting U.S. obligations to American Indians has become so severe that Indians themselves have increasingly begun to enforce the race codes excluding the genetically marginalized from both identification as Indian citizens and consequent entitlements. In theory, such a posture leaves greater per capita shares for all remaining "bona fide" Indians. But, as American Indian Movement activist Russell Means has pointed out:

> The situation is absurd. Our treaties say nothing about your having to be such-and-such a degree of blood in order to be covered. No, when the federal government made its guarantees to our nations in exchange for our land, it committed to provide certain services to us as *we* defined ourselves. As nations, and as *people*. This seems to have been forgotten. Now we have Indian people who spend most of their time trying to prevent other Indian people from being recognized as such, just so that a few more crumbs--crumbs from the federal table--may be available to them, personally. I don't have to tell you that this isn't the Indian way of doing things. The Indian way would be to get together and demand what is coming to each and everyone of us, instead of trying to cancel each other out. We are acting like colonized peoples, like subject peoples (Means, 1985).

The nature of the dispute has followed the classic formulation of Frantz Fanon, wherein the colonizer contrives issues which pit the colonized against one another, fighting viciously for some presumed status within the colonial structure, never having time or audacity enough to confront their oppressors (Fanon, 1966). In the words of Stella Pretty Sounding Flute, a member of the Crow Creek bank of Lakota, "My grandmother used to say that Indian blood was getting all mixed up, and some day there would be a terrible mess. . . . [Now] no matter which way we turn, the white man has taken over" (Martz, 1986a).

The problem, of course, has been conscientiously exacerbated by the government, through its policies of leasing individual reservation land parcels to non-Indians, increasingly "checkerboarding" tribal holding since 1900. Immediate economic consequences aside, this has virtually insured that a sufficient number of non-Indians would be resident in reservations that intermarriage would steadily result. During the 1950s, the federal relocation program--in which reservation-based Indians were subsidized to move to cities, where they might be expected to be subsumed within vastly larger non-Indian populations--accelerated the process of "biological hybridization." Taken in combination with the ongoing federal insistence that "Indian-ness" could be measured *only* by degree of blood, these policies tend to speak for themselves.

Even in 1972, when, through the Indian Education Act (86 Stat. 334), the government seemed finally to be abandoning blood quantum, there was a hidden agenda. As Lorelei DeCora (Means), a former Indian education program coordinator, puts it:

> The question was really one of control, whether Indians would ever be allowed to control the identification of their own group members or citizens. First there was this strict blood quantum thing, and it was enforced for a hundred years, over the strong objections of a lot of Indians. Then, when things were sufficiently screwed up because of that, the feds suddenly reverse themselves completely, saying its all a matter of *self*-identification. Almost anybody who wants to can just walk in and announce that he or she is Indian--no familiarity with tribal history, or Indian affairs, community recognition, or anything else really required--and, under the law, there's not a lot that Indians can do about it. The whole thing is suddenly just *laissez faire*, really out of control. At that point, you really *did* have a lot of people showing up claiming that one of their ancestors, seven steps removed, had been some sort of "Cherokee princess." And we were obliged to accept that, and provide services. Hell, if all of that was real, there are more Cherokees in the world than there are Chinese (DeCora, 1986).

Predictably, Indians of all perspectives on the identity question reacted strongly against such gratuitous dilution of themselves. The result was a broad rejection of what was perceived as "the federal attempt to convert us from being the citizens of our own sovereign nations, into benign members of some sort of all-purpose U.S. minority group, without sovereign rights" (Means, 1975). For its part, the government, without so much as a pause to consider the connotations of the word "sovereign" in this connection, elected to view such statements as an *Indian* demand for resumption of the universal application of the blood quantum standard. Consequently, the Reagan administration has, during the 1980s, set out to gut the Indian Education Act (Jones, 1984:3-4), and to enforce degree of blood requirements for federal services, such as those of the Indian Health Service (Martz, 1986a).

At this juncture, things have become such a welter of confusion that:

> The Federal government, State governments and the Census Bureau all have different criteria for defining "Indians" for statistical purposes, and even Federal criteria are not consistent among Federal agencies. For example, a State desiring financial aid to assist Indian education receives the aid only for the number of people with one-quarter or more

> Indian blood. For preference in hiring, enrollment records from a Federally recognized tribe are required. Under regulations for law and order, anyone of "Indian descent" is counted as an Indian. If the Federal criteria are inconsistent, State guidelines are [at this point] even more chaotic. In the course of preparing this report, the Commission contacted several States with large Indian populations to determine their criteria. Two States accept the individual's own determination. Four accept individuals as Indian if they were "recognized in the community" as Native Americans. Five use residence on a reservation as criteria. One requires one-quarter blood, and still another uses the Census Bureau definition that Indians are who they say they are (American Indian Policy Review Commission, 1977).

This, without doubt, is a situation made to order for conflict, among Indians more than anyone else. Somehow, it is exceedingly difficult to imagine that the government would wish to see things turn out any other way.

IMPLICATIONS

The eventual outcome of federal blood quantum policies can be described as little other than genocidal in their final implications. As Patricia Nelson Limerick recently summarized the process:

> Set the blood quantum at one-quarter, hold to it as a rigid definition of Indians, let intermarriage proceed as it had for centuries, and eventually Indians will be defined out of existence. When that happens, the federal government will be freed of its persistent "Indian problem" (Limerick, 1987:338).

Already, this conclusion receives considerable validation in the experience of the Indians of California, such as the Juaneno. Pursuant to the "Pit River Consolidated Land Settlement" of the 1970s, in which the government purported to "compensate" many small California bands for lands expropriated during the course of non-Indian "settlement" in that state (at less than 50 cents per acre), the Juaneno and a number of other "Mission Indians" were simply declared to be "extinct." This policy was pursued despite the fact that substantial numbers of such Indians were known to exist, and that the government was at the time issuing settlement checks to them. The tribal rolls were simply ordered closed to *any* new additions, despite the fact that many of the people involved were still bearing children, and their population might well have been expanding. It was even suggested in some instances that children born after an arbitrary cut-off date should be identified as "Hispanic" or "Mexican" in order that they benefit from federal and state services to minority groups.[3]

When attempting to come to grips with the issues raised by such federal policies, the recently "dissolved" California groups, as well as a number of previously unrecognized ones such as the Cape Wampanoags (long described as extinct), confronted a Catch-22. This rested in the federal criteria for recognition of Indian existence in the present day:

1. An Indian is a member of any federally-recognized Indian Tribe. To be federally-recognized, an Indian Tribe must be comprised of Indians.

2. To gain federal recognition, an Indian Tribe must have a land base. To secure a land base, an Indian Tribe must be federally recognized (Native American Consultants, 1980).

As a Shoshone activist, Josephine C. Mills, put it in 1964, "There is no longer any need to shoot down Indians in order to take away their rights and land [or to wipe them out] . . . legislation is sufficient to do the trick legally" (Armstrong, 1975:175). The notion of genocidal implications in all this receives firm reinforcement from the federal propensity, during the second half of this century, to utilize residual Indian landbases as dumping grounds for many of the more virulently toxic by-products of its advanced technology and industry (Churchill and LaDuke, 1985:107). By the early 70s, this practice had become so pronounced that the Four Corners and Black Hills Regions, two of the more heavily populated locales (by Indians) in the country, had been semi-officially designated as prospective "National Sacrifice Areas" in the interests of projected U.S. energy development (Churchill, 1986:13). This, in turn, provoked Russell Means to observe that such a move would turn the Lakota, Navajo, Laguna and other native nations into "national sacrifice peoples" (Means, 1983:25).

AMERICAN INDIAN RESPONSE

Of late, there have been encouraging signs that American Indians of many perspectives and political persuasions have begun to arrive at common conclusions regarding the use to which the federal government has been putting their identity, and the compelling need for Indians finally to reassert complete control over this vital aspect of their lives. For instance, early in the 1980s, Dr. Frank Ryan, a liberal and rather establishmentarian Indian who has served as the director of the federal Office of Indian Education, began to reach some rather hard conclusions about the policies of his employers. Describing the federal blood quantum criteria for benefits eligibility in the educational arena as "a racist policy," Ryan went on to term it nothing more than "a shorthand method for denying Indian children admission to federal schools [and other programs]" (Ryan, 1979:3). He concluded that, "The power to determine tribal membership has always been an essential attribute of inherent tribal sovereignty," and called for abolition of federal guidelines on the question of Indian identity without *any* lessening of federal obligations to the individuals and group affected (Ryan, 1979:41-44).

The question of the [re]adoption of blood quantum standards by the Indian Health Service, proposed during the 80s by the Reagan Administration, has served as even more of a catalyst. The National Congress of American Indians (NCAI), never a bastion of radicalism, took up the issue at its 43rd Annual Convention, in October 1986. The NCAI produced a sharply worded statement rejecting federal identification policy:

> [T]he federal government, in an effort to erode tribal sovereignty and reduce the number of Indians to the point where they are politically, economically and culturally insignificant, [is being censured by] many of the more than 500 Indian leaders [attending the convention] (Martz, 1986b).

The statement went on to condemn:

> . . . a proposal by the Indian Health Service to establish blood quotas for Indians, thus allowing the federal government to determine who is Indian and who is not, for the purpose of health care. Tribal leaders argue that *only* the individual tribes, *not* the federal government, should have this right, and many are concerned that this debate will overlap [as it has, long since] into Indian education and its regulation as well [emphasis added] (Martz, 1986a).

Charles E. Dawes, Second Chief of the Ottawa Indian Tribe of Oklahoma, took the convention position much further at about the same time:

> What could not be completed over a three hundred year span [by force of arms] may now be completed in our life-span by administrative law. . . . What I am referring to is

> the continued and expanded use of blood quantum to determine eligibility of Indian people for government entitlement programs . . . [in] such areas as education, health care, management and economic assistance . . . [obligations] that the United States government imposed upon itself in treaties with sovereign Indian nations. . . . We as tribal leader made a serious mistake in accepting [genetic] limits in educational programs, and we must not make the same mistake again in health programs. On the contrary, we must fight any attempt to limit any program by blood quantum every time there is a mention of such a possibility . . . we simply cannot give up on this issue--ever. . . . Our commitment as tribal leaders must be to eliminate any possibility of *genocide* for our people by administrative law. We must dedicate our efforts to insuring that our Native American people[s] will be clearly identified without reference to blood quantum . . . and that our sovereign Indian Nations will be recognized as promised [emphasis added] (Dawes, 1986:7-8).

On the Pine Ridge Reservation in South Dakota, the Oglala Lakota have become leaders in totally abandoning blood quantum as a criterion for tribal enrollment, opting instead to consider factors such as residency on the reservation, affinity to and knowledge of, as well as service to the Oglala people (Martz, 1986a) This follows the development of a recent "tradition" of Oglala militancy in which tribal members played a leading role in challenging federal conceptions of Indian identity during the 1972 Trail of Broken Treaties takeover of BIA headquarters in Washington, and seven non-Indian members of the Vietnam Veterans Against the War were naturalized as citizens of the "Independent Oglala Nation" during the 1973 seige of Wounded Knee (Akwesasne Notes, 1973:78; Burnette and Koster, 1974:238). In 1986, at a meeting of the United Sioux Tribes in Pierre, South Dakota, Oglala representatives lobbied the leaders of other Lakota reservations to broaden their own enrollment criteria beyond federal norms, despite recognition that, "in the past fifty years, since the Indian Reorganization Act of 1934, tribal leaders have been reluctant to recognize blood from individuals from other tribes [or any one else]" (Martz, 1986b).

In Alaska, the Haida have produced a new draft constitution which offers a full expression of indigenous sovereignty, at least insofar as the identity of sovereignty and citizenry is concerned. The Haida draft begins with those who are not acknowledged as members of the Haida nation and posits that all those who marry Haidas will also be considered eligible for naturalized citizenship (just as in any other nation). The children of such unions would also be Haida citizens from birth, regardless of their degree of Indian blood, and children adopted by Haidas would also be considered citizens (*Haida Constitution,* 1982). On Pine Ridge, a similar "naturalization" plank had surfaced in the 1982 TREATY Platform upon which Russell Means attempted to run for the Oglala Lakota tribal presidency before being disqualified at the insistence of the BIA (*Treaty,* 1982:3).

An obvious problem which might be associated with this trend is that even though Indian nations begin to recognize their citizens by their own standards rather than those of the federal government, the government may well refuse to recognize the entitlement of unblooded tribal members to the same services and benefits as any other. In fact, there is every indication that this is the federal intent. Such a disparity of "status" stands to heighten tensions among Indians, destroying their fragile rebirth of unity and solidarity before it gets off the ground. Federal policy in this regard is, however, also being challenged.

Most immediately, this concerns the case of Dianne Zarr, an enrolled member of the Sherwood Valley Pomo Band of Indians, who is of less than one-quarter degree of Indian blood. On September 11, 1980, Ms. Zarr filed an application for higher educational grant benefits, and was shortly rejected as not meeting quantum requirements. Zarr went through all appropriate appeal procedures before filing a suit on July 15, 1983 in federal court, seeking to compel award of her benefits. This was denied by the district court on April 2, 1985. Zarr appealed and, on September 26, 1985, the lower court was reversed on the basis of the "Snyder Act" (25 U.S.C. S297), which precludes discrimination based solely on racial criteria.[4] Zarr received her grant, setting a very useful precedent for the future.

Still, realizing that the gains offered by U.S. courts will necessarily be limited, a number of Indian organizations have recently begun to seek to bring international pressure to bear on the federal government. The Indian Law Resource Center, National Indian Youth Council and, for a time, the International Indian Treaty Council and World Council of Indigenous peoples have repeatedly taken Native American Indian issues before the United Nations Working Group on Indigenous Populations (a component of the U.N. Commission on Human Rights) in Geneva, Switzerland,since 1977. Another forum which has been utilized for this purpose has been the Fourth Russell International Tribunal on the Rights of the Indians of the Americas, held in Rotterdam, Netherlands, in 1980. Additionally, delegation from various Indian nations and organizations have visited, often under auspices of the host governments, in more than 30 countries during the past decade.[5]

CONCLUSION

The history of the U.S. imposition of its standards of identification upon American Indians is particularly ugly. Its cost to Indians has involved millions of acres of land, the water by which to make much of this land agriculturally useful, control over vast mineral resources which might have afforded them a comfortable standard of living, and the ability to form themselves into viable and meaningful political blocks at any level. Worse, it has played a prominent role in bringing about their generalized psychic disempowerment; if one is not allowed even to determine for oneself, or within one's peer group, the answer to the all-important question "who am I?," what possible personal power can one feel he possesses? The negative impacts, both physically and psychologically, of this process upon succeeding generations of Native Americans in the U.S. are simply incalculable.

The blood quantum mechanism most typically used by the federal government to assign identification to individuals over the years is as racist in its form as any conceivable policy. It has brought about the systematic marginalization and eventual exclusion of many more Indians from their own cultural-national designation than it has retained. This is all the more apparent when one considers that, while one-quarter degree of blood has been the norm used in defining Indian-ness, the quantum has varied from time to time and place to place; one-half blood was the standard utilized in the case of the Mississippi Choctaws and adopted in the Wheeler-Howard Act, one-sixty-fourth was utilized in establishing the Santee Rolls in Nebraska. It is hardly unnatural, under the circumstances, that federal policy has set off a ridiculous game of one-upsmanship in Indian Country: "I'm more Indian than you" and "You aren't Indian enough to say (or do, or think) that" have become common assertions during the second half of the 20th century.

The restriction of federal entitlement funds to cover only the relatively few Indians who meet quantum requirements, essentially a cost-cutting policy at its inception, has served to exacerbate tensions over the identity issue among Indians. It has established a scenario in which it has been perceived as profitable for one Indian to cancel the identity of his/her neighbor as a means of receiving his/her entitlement. Thus, a bitter divisiveness has been built into Indian communities and national policies, sufficient to preclude their achieving the internal unity necessary to offer any serious challenge to the status quo. At every turn, U.S. practice *vis-à-vis* American Indians is indicative of an advanced and extremely successful system of colonialism.

The outcome of the particular process examined in this paper can only be that Indians, both as peoples and as individuals, will eventually be defined out of existence. Arithmetically, it is calculable that by some point in the next century, the simple act of suddenly enforcing the quarter-blood standards across the board would result in the aggregate Indian population *appearing* to be near zero. This, in turn, would allow the federal government to "justifiably" close the books on Indians, write off all remaining obligations to such people, and declare them extinct (as has already been done with the Juaneno and other groups). In this sense, federal control and manipulation of the criteria of Indian identity carries obvious implications, not only of colonialism, but of genocide.

Fortunately, increasing numbers of Indians are waking up to the fact that this is the case. The recent analysis and positions assumed by such politically diverse Indian nations, organizations, and individuals as Frank Ryan and Russell Means, the National Congress of American Indians and the Indian Law Resource Center, the Haida and the Oglala, are a very favorable sign. The willingness of the latter two nations simply to defy federal standards and adopt identification and enrollment policies in line with their own interests and traditions is particularly important. Recent U.S. court decisions, such as that in the Zarr case, and growing international attention and concern over the circumstances of Native Americans are also hopeful indicators that things may at long last be changing for the better.

We are currently at something of a crossroads. If American Indians are able to continue the positive trend in which they reassert their sovereign prerogative to control the criteria of their own membership, we may reasonably assume that they will be able to move onward into a true process of decolonization and reestablishment of themselves as functioning national entities. The alternative, of course, is that they will fail, continue to be duped into bickering over the question of "who's Indian" in light of federal guidelines, and thus facilitate not only their own continued subordination, expropriation and colonization, but ultimately also their own statistical extermination.

NOTES

1. The bulk of the obligations in question were established prior to Congress' 1871 suspension of treaty-making with "the tribes" (Title 25, Section 71, U.S. Code). Additional obligations were undertaken by the federal government thereafter by "agreement," and as part of its on going agenda of completing the socio-political subordination of Indians, with an eye toward their eventual "assimilation" into the dominant culture and polity.

2. This strategy was actually tried in the wake of the passage of House Concurrent Resolution 108 (67 Stat. B132, otherwise referred to as the "Termination Act") in June of 1953. Predictably, the federal dissolution of American Indian nations such as the Klamath and Menominee so tarnished the U.S. image that implementation of the policy was shortly suspended (albeit the law remains on the books).

3. The author is an enrolled Juaneno, as is her eldest son. Her younger son, born after the closing of the Juaneno rolls, is not federally recognized as an Indian, despite the fact that his genealogy, cultural background, etc., is identical to that of his brother. The "suggestions" mentioned in the text were made to the author by a federal employee in 1979. It is estimated that, by the middle of the coming century, no one recognized as being a Juaneno will still be living.

4. *Zarr v. Barlow, et al.*, No. 85-2170, U.S. Ninth Circuit Court of Appeals, District Court for the Northern District of California, Judge John P. Vukasin presiding.

5. These have included Austria, Cuba, Nicaragua, Poland, East Germany, Hungary, Rumania, Switzerland, Algeria, Grenada, El Salvador, Columbia, Tunisia, Libya, Syria, Jordan, Iran, the Maori of New Zealand, New Aotara (Australia), Belize, Mexico, Costa Rica, Guinea, Kenya, Micronesia, the U.S.S.R., Finland, Norway, Sweden, Canada, Great Britain, Netherlands, France, Belgium, Japan, West Germany, Bulgaria, Yugoslavia, and Papua (New Guinea). The list here is undoubtedly incomplete.

REFERENCES

Adams, E.C. 1946. *American Indian Education: Government Schools and Economic Progress* (New York: King's Crown Press).

Akwesasne Notes. 1973. *BIA, I'm Not Your Indian Any More* (Mohawk Nation).

American Friends Service Committee. 1970. *Uncommon Controversy: Fishing Rights of the Muckleshoot, Puyallup, and Nisqually Indians* (Seattle, WA: University of Washington Press).

American Indian Policy Review Commission. 1977. *Final Report,* Vol. 1 (submitted to Congress on May 17, 1977) (Washington, DC: U.S. Government Printing Office).

American State Papers: Indian Affairs, Vol. 2. 1972. Wilmington, DE.

Armstrong, Virginia I. 1975. *I Have Spoken: American History Through the Voices of Indians* (New York: Pocket Books).

Burnette, Robert, and John Koster. 1974. *The Road to Wounded Knee* (New York: Bantam Books).

Churchill, Ward. 1986. "American Indian Lands: The Native Ethic Amid Resource Development." *Environment* 28(6):13.

Churchill, Ward, and Winona LaDuke. 1985. "Native America: The Political Economy of Radioactive Colonization." *Journal of Ethnic Studies* 13(3):107.

Collier, John. 1934. *Memorandum, Hearings on HR 7902 before the House Committee on Indian Affairs*, 73rd Congress, 2d Session. U.S. Department of the Interior, Washington, DC.

Dawes, Charles E. 1986. "Tribal Leaders See Danger in Use of Blood Quantum as Eligibility Standard." *The Uset Calumet* (Nashville, TN), February/March.

DeCora (Means), Lorelei. 1986. Statement on radio station KILI, Porcupine, SD, October 12, 1986.

Deloria, Jr., Vine. 1976. "The Place of Indians in Contemporary Education." *American Indian Journal* 2(21):2. Institute for the Development of Indian Law, Washington, DC.

Deloria, Jr., Vine, and Clifford M. Lytle. 1983. *American Indians, American Justice* (Austin, TX: University of Texas Press).

Deloria, Jr., Vine, and Clifford M. Lytle. 1984. *The Nations Within: The Past and Future of American Indian Sovereignty* (New York: Pantheon Books).

Fanon, Frantz. 1966. *The Wretched of the Earth* (New York: Grove Press).

Giago, Tim. 1984. "Blood Quantum is a Degree of Discrimination." *Notes From Indian Country,* Vol. 1 (Pierre, SD: State Publishing Co.).

Haida Constitution. Circa 1982. Draft. Xerox copy provided to the author by Ms. Pam Colorado.

Hundley, Jr., Norris C. 1979. "The Dark and Bloody Ground of Indian Water Rights." In Roxanne Dunbar Ortiz, ed., *Economic Development in Indian Reservations* (Albuquerque, NM: University of New Mexico Press).

Jones, R. 1984. *American Indian Policy: Selected Major Issues in the 98th Congress.* Issue Brief No. 1B83083, Library of Congress, Government Division, Washington, DC (updated version, 2/6/84).

Kappler, Charles J., ed. 1973. *Indian Treaties, 1778-1883* (New York: Interland Publishing Co.).

LaDuke, Winona. 1984. Presentation at International Women's Week activities, held at the University of Colorado at Boulder on March 13, 1984; tape on file.

League of Women Voters. 1977. *Indian Country* (Washington, DC: League of Women Voters). Publication No. 605.

Limerick, Patricia Nelson. 1987. *The Legacy of Conquest: The Unbroken Past of the American West* (New York: W.W. Norton & Co.).

Martz, Ron. 1986a. "Indians Decry Verification Plan for Federally-funded Health Care." Cox News Service, Pierre, SD, October 7, 1986.

Martz, Ron. 1986b. "Indians Maintain U.S. Trying to Erode Tribal Sovereignty: Cultural Insignificance Said to be Goal." Cox News Service, Pierre, SD, October 26, 1986.

Means, Russell. 1983. "The Same Old Song." P. 25 in Ward Churchill, ed., *Marxism and Native Americans* (Boston: South End Press).

Means, Russell. 1985. Speech at the Law School of the University of Colorado at Boulder, April 19, 1985; tape on file.

Means, Ted. 1975. Statement before the South Dakota Indian Education Association, Pierre, SD, November 16, 1975.

Memmi, Albert. 1967. *The Colonizer and the Colonized* (Boston: Beacon Press).

Native American Consultants, Inc. 1980. *Indian Definition Study*. Contracted pursuant to PL 95-561, Title IV, Section 1147. Submitted to the Office of the Assistant Secretary of Education, U.S. Department of Education, Washington, DC, January 1980.

Ryan, Frank A. 1979. *A Working Paper Prepared for the National Advisory Committee on Indian Education*. Paper No. 071279, Harvard American Indian Education Program, Harvard University Graduate School of Education, Cambridge, MA, July 18, 1979.

TREATY: The Campaign of Russell Means for the Presidency of the Oglala Sioux Tribe (Porcupine, SD) (1982).

Zarr v. Barlow, et al., No. 85-2170, U.S. Ninth Circuit Court of Appeals, District Court for the Northern District of California, Judge John P. Vukasin presiding.

Crazy Snake and the Creek Struggle for Sovereignty: The Native American Legal Culture and American Law

by SIDNEY L. HARRING*

The continued strength of Native American culture in the 1980s has a clear relationship to the renewed attention that sovereignty has received as the key unifying concept in both "Indian law" (and here I mean both federal Indian law and tribal law) and in tribal politics.[1] The precise nature of this relationship is complex, for in tribal society culture, law, and politics are an indivisible part of the whole life of a people. The fact of this indivisibility should not stop us from trying to better understand each constituent part. Law has long been studied as a means of understanding tribal culture. A core value in tribal law, at least since white society entered into an imperialistic and colonial relationship with tribal society, has been sovereignty. Sovereignty, in turn, in a tribal world surrounded by an aggressive and imperialistic white culture, is critical in the protection of all forms of tribal culture and society.

The rise of a tribal law with a deep emphasis on sovereignty parallels the imposition of white laws, values, and institutional forms on tribal society. As white institutions forced themselves with ever increasing strength against the tribes the traditional legal orders of tribal peoples changed. Tribal law became more centralized, moving from operating primarily at the band and clan level to the level of the tribe or tribal nation,

* Professor of Law, City University of New York, Law School at Queens College. The research for this article was funded by a Rockefeller Foundation Senior Fellowship at the McNickle Center for the History of the American Indian at the Newberry Library, Chicago, Illinois, and by a Professional Staff Congress/City University of New York Faculty Research Grant.

1. "Indian law" refers to all laws, specific to the status of Native Americans. It encompasses at least three distinct legal traditions, with three corresponding bodies of law. (1) the traditional laws, and legal institutions of native people; (2) the enacted tribal laws of the nearly two hundred tribes with autonomous legal systems; (3) American state and federal law defining the legal rights of native Americans. The "Indian law" most commonly referred to by legal scholars is the last, particularly federal Indian law. This is based on a part of one chapter of a forthcoming book, *Crow Dog's Case: Indian Law and American Law in the Nineteenth Century* which shows how the tribes struggled to protect their law and sovereignty in order to accommodate changing American law, and in that process structured American law.

serving to create and institutionalize a political structure with sufficient power and imagination to develop effective strategies for the protection of tribal society. It also came to provide new ways of effecting some measure of social control and of structuring rapid social change. Finally, law in white society had a high symbolic value, even on the frontier.[2] Hence, tribal law provided an equally valued framework for negotiation with white society. Similarly, American law itself came to have meaning in tribal society as tribal political leaders used it in complex negotiations with the Americans.[3]

I. NATIVE AMERICAN LEGAL CULTURE

The end result of this process, begun in the nineteenth century, is that Native American societies have a unique legal culture very distinct from white American legal culture and centered on the protection of tribal sovereignty. The idea of law and of legality in the ordering of life is more deeply entrenched in native law than it is in American law generally because of the critical role that law has played in protecting tribal sovereignty. Law and legal tradition, both native and American, have been more deeply felt because of the unique legal status of Native Americans, and the key role of law in defining that status.[4] Moreover, the place of legal culture in tribal life is not only deeply intertwined with the idea of tribal sovereignty, but also with the political, economic, and social means of fighting for it. In this

---

2. There is a substantial literature in legal history on how the frontier shaped American law, an issue directly related to Frederick Jackson Turner's seminal work, *The Frontier in American History*. (New York, 1920). There are dozens of legal histories taking up this theme. The best is undoubtedly James Willard Hurst, *Law and Economic Growth: The Legal History of the Lumber Industry in Wisconsin, 1836-1920*. (Cambridge: Harvard University Press, 1964).

3. The single most important example of the tribes seizing on the form of American law as a way to retain tribal sovereignty is that of the Cherokee Nation, both in the South and in Oklahoma. On the early Cherokee adaptation see William McLoughlin, *Cherokees and Missionaries, 1789-1839*. (New Haven: Yale University Press, 1984); and *Cherokee Renascence in the New Republic Princeton: Princeton University Press, 1986. For a history including the critical period of the Cherokee Nation in the Indian Territory see Rennard Strickland.* Fire and Spirits: Cherokee Law From Clan to Court. (Norman: University of Oklahoma Press, 1975).

4. Obviously, this is a hypothesis, for it is impossible to empirically prove. For a general discussion of the sociological literature on law and legal culture, see Roger Cotterrell, *The Sociology of Law: An Introduction*. (London: Butterworth's, 1984), especially part 1, "The Social Basis of Law".

Here it might be useful to include a personal statement of how I first saw this relationship. On a Newberry Fellows tour of eight Native American communities in Southern California and Arizona in 1986, I was travelling with anthropologists, archeologists, historians, and a scholar of American Indian literature. The native people we met invariably wanted to know about our work, and, as a lawyer, I was always embarrassed when legal questions always came to dominate the discussions which followed. The fellows talked about this, and came to understand that questions of law had a special meaning in native society, quite unlike the meaning law had in the dominant American society.

context the long record of illegality of American law in relationship to the tribes has had the opposite effect on tribal law: It places renewed emphasis on traditional native principles of law and justice in sharp juxtaposition to the brutal, racist, instrumental, and corrupt character of American law. Thus, even to the extent that such laws as the Dawes and Curtis Acts represented great assaults on tribal sovereignty, they had, at least in part, the impact of encouraging traditional tribal mechanisms of protecting tribal sovereignty.[5]

While the legal culture of each tribe is distinct, the Creek history of Crazy Snake, his people's rejection of imposed white law and institutions, their retreat to Hickory Ground, their restoration of the "old law" on the Creek people, and his simple demand of American authorities: "Give us back our law," illustrates this process, one that was repeated in smaller, less spectacular (and probably less successful) ways in tribal communities all over America. While Crazy Snake's movement may have lasted for ten years on a very large scale (and doubtlessly never died) it is unique only in its size and strength. Every reservation had such nationalist movements. Crow Dog, for example, after his famous legal victory over the Bureau of Indian Affairs and a Dakota Territorial court, lived a long life on a far corner of the Rosebud Reservation, a proud and defiant member of a faction derisively called "kickers" by the Indian Agent because of their rejection of allotment, the Christian religion, and the agent's political and legal authority. It was the second decade of the twentieth century before the Agent dared create a tribal court—the kickers were too powerful, too angry, and completely unaccepting of Imposed American law.[6] Thus, it is important not to see Crazy Snake and the Creek struggle as an isolated example possible only for one very traditional people.

II. CREEK LEGAL HISTORY

Each native people has a unique legal history, the product of the meeting of that tribe's law and legal culture with American law and legal institutions which, in turn, was imposed in different ways on different tribes requiring different forms of tribal resistance to protect their sovereignty. A good deal more is known about the Creeks than we know about

5. The history of American law in its dealings with native people is the subject of a number of important works. For the time and people at hand Angie Debo's *And Still the Waters Run: The Betrayal of the Five Civilized Tribes*, (Norman: University of Oklahoma Press, 1984) is the seminal work, proving that the termination of the tribes in Oklahoma was a great crime as well as a tragedy. There is also a substantial legal literature on this history, for federal Indian law is among the most historical of all sub-fields of law. See, for example, Rob Williams, "The Algebra of Federal Indian Law: The Hard Trail of Decolonizing and Americanizing the White Man's Jurisprudence", 1986 *Wisconsin Law Review* 219.

6. Sidney L. Harring, "Crow Dog's Case: A Chapter in the History of Tribal Sovereignty," 14 *American Indian Law Review* 191 (1990).

most native people because of the fine work of historians Michael Green and Angie Debo.[7] The history of native people has been written in many different ways with any number of focuses, but both Green and Debo have Creek law and legal change a prominent place in their respective (although very different) analyses of Creek society and its relationship with the United States in the 19th century, Green for the initial period of Creek resistance in the South, Debo for the rebuilding of Creek society in the Indian Territory.

Green carefully describes the internal struggles within Creek society in early 19th century Alabama in an effort to find the most effective ways to protect Creek lands and sovereignty and to resist the violent and increasing demands of whites for land. Factional struggles were always complex in Creek society for the Muskogee people were a loose alliance of a number of different peoples with each village retaining a high level of not only political autonomy but also some measure of cultural autonomy as well. Faced with an accomodationist strategy to sell most Creek land as one way to preserve the rest of the tribal land, the Upper Creeks, meeting in council in 1824, proclaimed a "law of Polecat Springs", the first Creek law proclaimed by such a council.[8] This law forbad the selling of tribal land on pain of death. A force of up to 400 warriors later went to the plantation of Alexander McIntosh, an accomodationist Lower Creek chief, set fire to the house, permitted all guests to leave except those in violation of the law, and shot to death McIntosh and one other chief carrying out the penalty of the law.[9]

Green recognized the great significance of the "law of Polecat Springs." Not only did it become the foundation of a unique Creek legal culture a unifying force in Creek law for not only the rest of the century, but continuing to the present day. This legal event marked the beginning of a national Creek political organization, an evolution to a more formal organization on a larger scale. This was a great change from the traditionally local and autonomous Creek political and legal organization designed to meet the increasing pressure of more powerful American institutions, American law and legal institutions directly shaped tribal law and legal institutions.

7. Michael Green, *The Politics of Indian Removal: Creek Government and Society in Crisis*. (Lincoln: University of Nebraska Press, 1982), and Angie Debo, *The Road to Disappearance: A History of the Creek Indians*, (Norman: University of Oklahoma Press, 1941).

8. Michael Green, op cit, chapter four, "Creek Law and the Treaty of Indian Springs, 1818-1825." Prior to these meetings of the Creeks in national council to make laws, traditional Creek law was made and enforced at the town level. The laws made by the Creek council during this period are contained in Antonio J. Waring, ed., *Laws of the Creek Nation*, University of Georgia Libraries Miscellania Publications, No. 1, 1960. For an account of the original Creek law, see John Swanton, *Social Organization and Social Usages of the Creek Confederacy*, (Washington: 42nd Annual Report of the Bureau of American Ethnology, 1924-25).

9. This event is reported in Green, op cit, at 96. Green further reports that President John Quincy Adams, while saddened by the deaths of Creek chiefs friendly to American interests, nevertheless believed the executions "legal" and did not treat the killings as a crime inviting American punishment or retaliation. (at 100).

American pressure to buy land produced Creek laws to block that sale and Creek political and legal institutions to enforce that law. While the Creek council that made and enforced the law of Polecat Springs had clear roots in traditional Creek society, it was not the traditional council but a new form of council shaped by Creek contact with American institutions as well as with neighboring Cherokee Institutions.[10]

This changing, but still traditional and sovereign, Creek society was removed to the Indian Territory and there created the Creek Nation, a part of a unique American experiment in tribal sovereignty there. Enough is still not known about the five Indian nations that were created there but a further understanding of the nature of the institutional processes that evolved, including the legal, is a critical part of understanding native forms of adaptation to American society. Much of the historical emphasis on these governments focuses on how "civilized", meaning Americanized, they were: popularly elected chiefs, bicameral legislatures, universal male suffrage, secret ballots, two-tiered court systems, courthouses, high sheriffs, lighthorsemen, and schools. But a closer look reveals that a good many of the forms that the Americans imposed on the tribes were adopted but much less of the substance. Tribal values and tribal sovereignty lived within institutions that looked "American." There can be no question that this was one part of a conscious Creek strategy to protect tribal traditions and sovereignty.[11]

This is the central theme of Angie Debo's, *Road to Disappearance*, a now classic history of the Creek in the Indian Territory. This study is also a great work in legal history for it shows clearly that the *Road to Disappearance* was paved, not with good intentions, but with the law, both American and Creek, in every form—case after case, dispute after dispute, killing after killing, problem after problem, and resolution after resolution. Perhaps amazingly, but only from the standpoint of white society, Creek society adapted to event after event, including at least three civil wars in thirty years, that might have ripped any other society apart. This was all survived by a tribal society of 8,000 people wholly surrounded by a rapidly expanding American society of more than forty million, ripped apart by its own civil war. Angie Debo shows very clearly the centrality of a changing Creek law and Creek political and legal institutions in maintaining this complex social order in the face of Imperialism and revolutionary social change.

10. Green, op cit, at 77-81. Also Michael Green, "The Treason of William McIntosh: Creek Law and Government in the Removal Crisis of the 1820s". Paper presented at the Annual Meetings of the American Society for Legal History, New Orleans, October 1985.

11. There is a voluminous literature on the Five Civilized Tribes, including histories of each. In addition to Angie Debo's work cited above, see her *Rise and Fall of the Choctaw Republic*, (Norman: University of Oklahoma Press, 1934); and Morris Wardell's *A Political History of the Cherokee Nation, 1838-1907*, (Norman: University of Oklahoma Press, 1938) for studies of institutional development in the Indian Nations.

In the Creek, as well as in each of the other Indian Nations, the Cherokee, Choctaw, Chickasaw, and Seminole, there were two parallel sets of tribal laws. There can be no question that a traditional law, invisible to whites, functioned alongside the formal legal institutions of the Indian nations, a set of legal institutions adopted by the elected National Councils and based on American law. There are broad indications of this parallel structure time after time. For example, in the Green Peach War of 1881-82, the most serious of all Creek civil wars, with several hundreds of mounted, heavily armed men on each side, there were only a handful of killings. When the killers were brought up before the formal legal institutions of the Creek Nation a few were sentenced to death but then pardoned. It must be evident that only strong traditional laws controlling killings within the tribe could have kept the casualties so low, and structured the pardoning of the killers convicted under a national law that, while not traditional, was subject to the control of national political processes that were responsive to traditional laws and values.[12]

The two-tiered Creek court system outwardly resembled that of many American jurisdictions. But only civil cases could be appealed from the district courts to the Creek Supreme Court. Criminal cases were only appealable to the Principle Chief, who had a full pardon power unrestricted by the formal law of the Creek Nation but obviously structured by traditional law. Within a veneer of the formality of a legal system that overtly resembled American law, traditional law was not only protected, but deliberately left an important arena of function, mediating between the formal requirements of the new legal system and traditional Creek notions of law and justice.[13]

A further example of the maintenance of the core of traditional law within the written code of the Creek Nation is revealed in the trial of routine criminal cases. Even the simplest case often took three or four days to process. Court would be called early one morning, and a roll taken of a long list of jurors and witnesses, all summoned by lighthorsemen and paid $2 a day in a society with a per capita cash income of perhaps $25 to $50 a year. Inevitably some of the parties were still missing and court sessions were postponed until afternoon then until the next day. Judicial districts with populations of no more than 600 have routine trials with thirty or forty people present in various official capacities and all paid. The proceedings were slow and carefully deliberative. There can be no question that men and women met for long days—effectively but informally "in council" even though a formal, elected bicameral legislature legally had the function of national council. After three or four days one or two men would be tried,

12. Debo, *Road to Disappearance*, chapter 8, "The Green Peach War".

13. The observations of the nature of the Creek courts contained here, and in the following paragraphs, are based on an ongoing study of the records of the Creek courts. These records are on microfilm on CRN rolls 17, 18, and 19, with the originals held in the Five Civilized Tribes Archives in the Oklahoma State Historical Society.

most often for stealing livestock. Most defendants were acquitted but occasionally one was convicted and whipped on the spot and the meeting would disperse. Twenty to thirty people would be paid from $2 to $8 each, financing (and probably feeding) the whole event.[14]

The exact history of each of the American legal forms that were adopted by the Creek doubtlessly contains within it a history of how the Creeks reshaped it to protect Creek sovereignty and create an environment in which traditional Creek life could be maintained. One example where this is perhaps the most difficult is in the area of the civil law, largely the law of the Creek Nation for dealing with new property relations that had no parallel in traditional Creek law. While virtually all forms of holding property changed juridically after the formation of the Creek Nation, one new law that affected every Creek family was the law of succession. Traditional Creek society had very complex mechanisms for the disposing of a dead persons property spread throughout a clan structure. After the 1870s Creek law copied American law in largely leaving all property within the nuclear family to spouses and children. Because there was no traditional law governing these transactions almost all the civil work of the six Creek district courts consisted of dividing these small estates. The law provided a traditional mechanism for this division if it could not provide a traditional law. Each estate, Creek law provided, had to be "counted" by three disinterested persons. In the record books of the Creek district courts are found the simple reports of these "counted" estates, down to each pig and chicken, each pot and pan, each table and tablecloth, the meager property of every Creek family. The formal power of the Creek courts, even at the relatively accessible district level, was balanced with the informal input of traditional leaders here simply "counting" the property in an estate and reporting it back to the court for allocation.[15]

Since there was no place in such a legal order for the more complex legal problems that Americans brought into the Creek Nation, the Creek Nation created a unique role for its Supreme Court. This court primarily functioned as the civil trial court for all complex matters and was staffed by three judges, more skilled in the formal national law than the district court judges. Complex civil cases could be effectively adjudicated with competent decisions rendered in the form of written opinions. This two tiered system of justice while copied in form after the United States, did not copy the substance. While two-tiered in appearance, it did not actually function as a system of lower courts under an appellate Supreme Court. Rather, the Supreme Court was primarily a trial court for complex cases, and, in fact,

14. This description is not of any particular case, but describes the general processing of criminal cases. It might be noted that, for many cases, the record of expenditures is longer than the record of the disposition of the case.

15. The records of the Creek civil courts were kept in logbooks, parallel to the records of the criminal courts. The property in each estate is carefully recorded in these record books. For many of the six district courts, virtually the only civil cases are these meager estates.

there was effectively no appellate court, although a few district court civil cases were appealed. The Creek national court system was more on the model of a system of two parallel court structures, traditional at the district court level, and primarily used by local Creeks and formal at the Supreme Court level and primarily used by large property holders.[16]

Creek courts were not only very accessible to the general population because they primarily functioned at the district level and employed a large proportion of the population in various official capacities, but the selection of judges reveals a lack of professionalization and clear political responsibility to those affected by the law. In the last thirty years of the Creek Nation 147 men served as judges. They occupied only nine judicial positions, six district judges and three Supreme Court judges, indicating an average term of under two years. None had any legal training and most were not literate in English. Given the Creek Nation's small population, this indicates that perhaps 7% of all adult males served as judges during this period, establishing that the formal legal role of judge was kept open and accessible to the entire politically active population.[16a]

More study of the institutions of the Indian nations will reveal a great deal about the forms the tribes used to resist white encroachment on tribal sovereignty. But this whole legal history moves on to an unhappy ending. The territorial sovereignty of these Indian Nations was unilaterally terminated by an Act of Congress, the Curtis Act, on July 1, 1898. Although the tribal governments were left intact, they were deprived of virtually all governing functions. The story of this termination is well known, a classic example of the illegality of American law, "legal" under the plenary power doctrine.[17] The lands of the Indian Nations had been purchased in fee simple from the United States with money paid the tribes for their lands in

16. The cases heard in the Creek Supreme Court are completely different cases than the cases heard in the district courts. For example, while the district courts are full of cases involving pigs and chickens, the Supreme court is full of cases involving cattle and horses. Supreme court cases involved a full range of disputes over property and contracts, not unlike parallel courts in American society. The formal relationship between the Supreme Court and the District courts, as well as the civil and criminal law of the Creek Nation, is published in *Acts and Resolutions of the National Council of the Creek Nation*. Muskogee: Phoenix Printing Company, 1900. This is the last and most complete edition of a volume published several times in the 1880s and 1890s.

16a. A complete list of Creek judges is found in the "Creek verticle files" in the Oklahoma State Historical Society Archives, Oklahoma City, under the subject "courts." A few names appear twice and several men appear under slightly different names. In my enumeration I counted each man individually unless he had clearly previously been counted. In spite of the short terms on average, some judges had long tenures. Coweta Micco of Coweta District served for nearly twenty years. Micco was also the undisputed traditional leader of Coweta District. This suggests that many traditional Creek preferred to work at the level of the district courts instead of in national politics. Thus, even the offices of the national Creek government were divided on different levels with traditionals left in charge of local offices.

17. The "plenary power doctrine", first laid down by the United States Supreme Court in *U.S. v. Kagama* 118 U.S. 375 (1886) holds that Congress has virtually unlimited power to unilaterally enact legislation affecting the Indian tribes.

the East and were the property of the tribes. The sovereignty of these nations was more than a residual sovereignty running from the beginning of time as a free people. It was also a sovereignty recognized hundreds of times by the United States government by both treaties and all forms of relations with the Creek Nation, Cherokee Nation, and the other nations, all recognized in precisely those terms in act after act.[18]

For more than ten years the United States carried on a charade of legality in negotiating for the voluntary termination of these lands but all of the nations refused. The Curtis Act did more than terminate the territorial sovereignty of the Nations. It sought to destroy their political sovereignty as well, providing that the elected councils not exercise any powers and prohibiting their courts from hearing cases and issuing judgments. For the Creeks, this meant that the Creek National Council remained but only for the purpose of carrying out a few very limited functions necessary for the final federal termination of the tribe. For example, a major function of the tribal government was to make a tribal roll of all persons eligible for allotment of tribal lands. Thus, in its "final days" the functioning of the Creek National government was in violation of its own law, the law of Polecat Springs, and a hollow shell of its former existence serving a federal function intended to deprive the Creek of their lands.[19]

Every American now knows that the reason for that termination was imperialism, the white desire for valuable tribal lands. Ironically, at the time a major justification, put forward for more than twenty years, was to protect both Indians and whites from the corrupt and unjust legal processes of the Indian Nations. This has the double irony of traditional peoples, effectively adapting and using American legal forms, only to have that itself become evidence that they were "uncivilized."[20]

III. CRAZY SNAKE'S REBELLION

Crazy Snake, or Chitto Harjo, was one of a number of traditional Creek leaders who opposed allotment. We simply do not know what Crazy Snake did immediately after the Creek termination in the summer of 1898.

---

18. The original Creek Treaty of August 7, 1856, 11 Stat. 699, in Article XV provided:

> So far as may be compatible with the Constitution of the United States, . . . the Creek and Seminoles shall be secured in the unrestricted right of self-government and full jurisdiction over persons and property, within their respective limits.

Federal relations with the tribes recognized that treaty, incorporated its language into later treaties, and referred to the tribes as "Nations" in numerous laws, government reports, and official actions.

19. Angie Debo, *The Road to Disappearance*, chapter 11, "The End of the Tribe".

20. The U.S. Congress made extensive use of attacks on the legal systems of the Five Civilized Tribes primarily appearing in the local papers of white communities near the Indian Territory. For examples of this material see, U.S. Senate, Document no. 164, Feb. 27, 1897 (Serial Set, v. 3471), "Memorial of the Members of the Bar of Muskogee and the Northern District of the Indian Territory, . . ." and J.H. Moore, *The Political Condition of the Indians and the Resources of the Indian Territory*. (St. Louis: Southwestern Book Co, 1874).

The evidence suggests that, like Crow Dog and the "kickers" on the Rosebud, he never did anything other than honor traditional law and preserve a traditional life in a remote region of the reservation. American authorities ignored Crazy Snake and his people—and also probably lacked the authority to intervene. Moreover, the use of force against the Creek would have exposed the American myth of "voluntary" termination. But Crazy Snake and his movement grew and grew, setting the stage for confrontation. These Creeks did not recognize the federal alienation of Creek lands because they saw the sale of this land as in violation of Creek law. Within less than two years of termination a traditional Creek government met on Hickory Ground, south of Henryetta in the heart of their nation. Traditional government, not being created by the laws of the United States, could not be limited by the laws of the United States nor could it be compelled to perform federal functions in alienating Creek lands. It is not clear precisely what Crazy Snake had in mind in relation to the existing Creek National Council. A reasonable deduction, however, given the history in Creek politics of the repeated succession of opposites in the domination of the National Council, was that Crazy Snake's followers intended to contest the next national election (in 1903), an election that would put in power the Creek National Council that would exist in 1906 when the existing Creek government had agreed to permanently disband the National Council as required by an agreement supplemental to the Curtis Act, ratified by the National Council in 1901. Once in power it seems likely that the "Snakes", as they came to be called, would have renounced all collaborationist acts of the existing National Council and refused to either disband or relinquish tribal authority.[21]

A great deal more is known legally about Crazy Snake's rebellion than we know about its traditional meaning. The United States Attorney in Muskogee in March 1901 secured the indictments of 253 named Creeks for "conspiracy to deprive unknown persons of their personal liberty" and "detaining them without lawful authority." In the most massive indictment of American Indians in United States history, a federal grand jury accused these Creeks of "willfully and feloniously forming a certain government . . . purporting to be the legal and lawful government of the Muskogee tribe of

21. There is no full historical analysis of Crazy Snake and his movement. Angie Debo, for example, devotes only a single paragraph to it in *Road to Disappearance* (at 376). This account is primarily based on newspaper accounts, located through the newspaper subject index in the newspaper room of the Oklahoma State Historical Society. For an introduction see, Eleanor Patricia Atwood, "The Crazy Snake Rebellions: A Study in the Breakdown of Tribal Government". Vassar Journal of Undergraduate Studies, XV, May 1942, 44-60. For a sampling of the event as reported in the local press, see Indian Journal, Muskogee, Oklahoma, February 1, 1901, at 4, cols. 1, 2, 3; Vinita, Oklahoma, Chieftan, February 28, 1901, p. 1.

Indians, and elected a chief, second chief, a twelve member cabinet to advise the chiefs, members of the House of Warriors and the House of Kings, as well as a judicial branch and lighthorsemen."[22]

As if all these charges—of conspiring to create a traditional Creek government—were not sufficient, a number of the same people were indicted for assault and battery. The assault and battery indictment stemmed from a series of actions that this traditional government had engaged in to extend its power far out into the Creek Nation. A number of the lighthorsemen had arrested and whipped Creeks for the violation of the "old law," the law of Polecat Springs. While it had obviously taken some time for the Creeks to reorganize their entire government at Hickory Ground it was this direct action in applying that law that brought down the wrath of federal law.[23]

The primary object of this traditional Creek government was to block allotment and restore traditional law. Many of the whippings stemmed from the violation of this law posted all over the Creek Nation:

> Hickorytown, Oct. 11th, 1900
>
> From this on the citizen or Creek citizen in the Creek Nation as far as the Creek line extend and also there shall be no laborers employed. This law created according to treaty. [A]ny person violating this law shall be fined the sum of $100. . . . , and shall be payed [sic] to the Nation also shall receive fifty lashes on his bare back. Any person who was employed shall be removed by the principal chief. . . . Also any person . . . should interfere such notice shall be fined the sum of $50.

The Snakes believed they had authority under the treaties to proclaim this law. They based this authority on a letter that they had received from the Acting Secretary of the Interior promising to "honor all Indian treaties". This, to the minds of traditional Creeks, was an admission that the liquidation of their national government by the Curtis Act was illegal.[24]

We must see in this exchange a clear sense of legality in the minds of these Creek leaders. They engaged, by mail, in an exchange with the Bureau of Indian Affairs and the Department of the Interior, in a discussion about their sovereign right to their "old law". They based this on their specific right to that law, contained in each of the Creek treaties that created the Creek Nation. Therefore, the secretary's acknowledgment of that treaty created the complete legal basis to recreate the traditional Creek government. Only through the hindsight of hundreds of years of broken treaties can it now be understood how an official of the United States government

22. "Indictment: United States of America v. Chitto Harjo [and 242 named others], March 2, 1901. The indictment is held as "U.S. Court in Indian Territory—Muskogee. Criminal case 5581-5584." in Record Group 21. It is impossible to tell exactly how many men were indicted because the clerks misspelled and half-spelled so many of the names. Several people appear to have been indicted twice. This would indicate that the document was hastily put together without much care.

23. Indian Journal, February 1, 1901 at 4, cols 1, 2, 3.

24. "Indictment" op cit, page 4.

could promise to honor a treaty and not expect that statement to have any legal impact on the Creek people. But the Snakes took him at his word.

To this day we do not know the full extent of the Snake government's operations. While the press was full of exaggeration (for example, calling it Crazy Snake's rebellion, when it was a simple reassertion of traditional law), newspapers reported four large parties of Snakes, posting notices and enforcing their law in different parts of the Creek nation. No one knows how many law violators were whipped. None of them gave any evidence in any formal legal proceedings. At a time when the Creek population probably did not number much over 8,000, meaning perhaps 2,000 adult males at most, 12% of the adult males were charged, by name, in the federal indictment. There can be no question that the actual number involved was greater and the number of supporters of that old government greater still. It does not stretch the evidence far to suggest that it commanded the support of the majority of Creek men. Beyond any doubt this reveals the depth of traditional support in the Creek Nation and shows that Creek sovereignty was not terminated by the Curtis Act.

The reorganization of traditional government and its resumption of many of its functions is not the only evidence of the strength of this sovereignty. It can be seen in the events that followed as well. Few modern political movements survive the federal indictments of 253 members but Crazy Snake's movement did. All of the indicted plead guilty in a plea bargain arrangement that earned all of them pardons although they were all held in prison for a short time. While the plea bargain may have been a mistake because the government would undoubtedly not have been able to prove most of the charges, it did gain the freedom of all. Perhaps more important it spared traditional Creek political life from the intrusion of white lawyers, courts, trials, juries and exaggerated newspaper reports. In their admission of guilt (prepared by their lawyers), we gain a clear sense of the simplicity of their intention:

> We state that as citizens of the Creek Nation we have been opposed to the abolition of our courts by any act of congress and to any change in our tribal form of government, and that, in October 1900, we met together and agreed to form a government of our own . . .
>
> That it was our intention and purpose to pass laws and to execute the same upon all citizens without regard to any act of Congress in force in the Creek Nation.
>
> That said government was formed for the purpose of causing the arrest, imprisonment, and punishment of all persons, citizens of the Creek Nation, who should take any allotment of lands or rent any lands to non-citizens of this Creek Nation, or employ any White noncitizens in any capacity whatsoever.[25]

But these guilty pleas did not put an end to the Snake government. Rather, it seems to have gone underground ceasing only the highly visible enforcement of its laws by lighthorsemen. Chitto Harjo returned to his

25. "Indictment" op cit, page 6.

simple log cabin and remained a visible Creek leader through a second rebellion in 1907. Although not much is known about Chitto Harjo what is known reveals a good deal about traditional Creek life. He lived in poverty, existing on subsistence farming, an orchard, and hunting largely outside of a cash economy. In his late fifties, he had never been an important leader in Creek national politics but had served in the House of Kings, the upper house in the bicameral Creek Nation legislature. His emergence as a traditional leader after the Curtis Act suggests that there had always been two parallel power structures in the Creek Nation, one traditional and one formal. Harjo made an eloquent speech in Creek (he did not know English) before a Congressional Committee visiting Tulsa in 1906. His speech demanded simple justice and a return to traditional government.[26]

This government was functioning at Hickory Ground in 1907 probably never having ceased operation. Allotment and white encroachment had impoverished traditional Creek. Complicating our understanding of the 1907 rebellion was the presence of a large number of black Creeks as well as non-Creek blacks. Traditional Creeks had a longstanding alliance with black Creeks in national politics. By now, federal authority in the Creek Nation had been replaced by state authority and state authority was even less sympathetic to Creek sovereignty than the federal government. The presence of a Creek Nation within Oklahoma was a political embarassment to the authorities of the new state, as well as a potential challenge to state economic interests. Moreover, racism directed at both Creeks and blacks was rampant. The state militia attacked Hickory Ground using the excuse that people there were raiding local smokehouses for hams (thus the name the "smoked meat rebellion"). Several blacks were killed in the attack. Local deputies blaming Crazy Snake for the events at Hickory Ground went to his cabin to arrest him. At least nine other traditional Creeks were assembled there to escort him to Hickory Ground and gunfire broke out, killing two deputies. Crazy Snake was badly wounded but escaped living out the remaining three years of his life a wanted man hidden in the hills by traditional Choctaw.[27]

26. Crazy Snake's speech to this committee is found in John Bartlett Meserve, "The Plea of Crazy Snake," XI Chronicles of Oklahoma, 910-911 (1933). There is only sketchy biographical material on Chitto Harjo. This discussion is based on materials found in the F.S. Barde papers in the Oklahoma State Historical Society Archives. Barde was a newspaperman with some sensitivity to the Creek cause who covered the 1908 Snake uprising. This single file, all undated and unpaginated, contains both extensive contemporary press clippings, as well as copies of untitled, undated typewritten manuscripts that Barde apparently wrote as drafts of newspaper articles.

27. The 1908 Snake uprising is the subject of two articles: Daniel Littlefield and Lonnie Underhill, "The Crazy Snake Uprising of 1909: A Red, Black, or White Affair?" 20 Arizona and the West (1978), and Mel Bolster, "The Smoked Meat Rebellion," XXXI Chronicles of Oklahoma, (1953), 37-55. The State of Oklahoma treated the event as a full scale war, the state's first: see "One General, One War", Daily Oklahoman, April 1, 1951.

To this day, it is clear that the traditional councils simply moved from Hickory Ground and continued their government wherever they could meet. When anthropologist Morris Opler studied Creek political organization in 1937, he reported the traditional town governments strong and vital. Traditional Creek law moved back from the national level (where it had initially gone only in the early 19th century is response to American power) to the more traditional town level.[28] Thus, we can see the irony in the use of the legalistic term "perporting" to organize a government, and "perporting" to make law in the Crazy Snake indictments. We might better say that the United States "perported to abolish Creek sovereignty."

Through the hindsight of late 19th century federal Indian law, we can see that the impact of Crazy Snake's traditional movement was even greater than it appeared at the time. In August of 1907 the Creek National Council, still extant, although deprived of almost all of its powers, met and called for the usual four year election for tribal officers, held under the Creek constitution of 1867. This council meeting itself shows the persistence of Creek resistance, even among council members actively negotiating allotment. The council was supposed to cease existing in 1906 under an agreement between the council and the BIA. In fact the writer Hamlin Garlin wrote a moving description of the last meeting of the Creek National Council.[29] While Garlin was wrong the BIA was planning to abolish by fiat what it could not abolish in fact.

The Bureau of Indian Affairs as well as the Principle Chief, Pleasant Porter, who had presided over the allotment of Creek lands, believed that continuing the existing government would be more satisfactory to the United States than holding an election and "strengthening the Snake movement." In the midst of this confusion, Porter died suddenly. President Theodore Roosevelt, relying on Section 6 of the Five Civilized Tribes Act

---

28. Marvin Opler, "The Creek Town and the Problem of Creek Indian Political Reorganization," in Edward Spicer, *Human Problems and Technological Change*, (1953). Frank Speck, "The Creek Indians of Taskigi Town," (2 Memoirs of the American Anthropological Association, 1931) independently confirms Opler's work.

29. Lonnie Underhill, "Hamlin Garland and the Final Council of the Creek Nation," Journal of the West 511 (1976). Garlin was a member of Theodore Roosevelt's "kitchen cabinet" who advised the President on Indian affairs. The "last meeting" of the Creek National Council that he describes took place on October 10, 1904.

> While there [in Muskogee] I learned that the Creeks were having their last meeting in the council house at Okmulgee, and I at once seized the opportunity of witnessing these historic proceedings. . . . For several hours I watched these dusky warriors conferring in their bare and grimy chambers, sensing in their voices the sadness of a vanishing race whose history was fading into myth. (at 511)

Although Garland's description is a quite moving example of the "disappearing Indian" genre of writing, there can be no question that the Creek National Council met for some years after the above date. Neither Garland's description, nor the above article gives any indication of why Garland believed it to be the final meeting. Some of the language seems to indicate that after this meeting the Creeks moved out of the Council House, but it was not formally leased to the City of Okmulgee (for use as a jail) until 1907. (at 520).

of 1905 providing that the President of the United States could appoint a chief if a chief refused to perform his duties under the Act, immediately appointed a Creek Principle Chief defying the National Council and blocking a tribal election that the government was afraid the Snakes might win.[30]

These facts are among those relied on in *Harjo v. Kleppe* a 1976 United States District Court opinion holding that the Creek National Council had never been lawfully stripped of its power and was still the legal governing council of the Creeks. The court found that the Curtis Act's removal of most of the powers of the Creek Government and National Council related to territorial sovereignty only over the former Creek Nation but did not extend to any diminishing of the political power of the National Council.[31] The Snakes, of course, by not recognizing the Curtis Act contested their loss of territorial sovereignty as well as political sovereignty. By forcing President Roosevelt to name the next chief illegally by-passing the remaining political sovereignty of the national council the Snakes revealed the depth of the traditional legal culture of the Creeks, a culture that could not partition the different elements of Creek sovereignty.

IV. CONCLUSION

There can be no question that sovereignty and tribal autonomy are the main themes of the legal history of the Creek people. To the extent that a current "new sovereignty" paradigm is at the root of analysis of federal Indian law, it is important to recognize that Indian law in the United States is a law with two distinct sets of roots that are interrelated. Federal Indian law, which is most often what is referred to when we refer to "Indian law" is the history of expanding federal authority over the tribes. While sovereignty has a clear and important history here, beginning before the Cherokee cases, it is not the dominant theme. The tribes also have a law that has a long legal history with sovereignty at its core.

This is not an "Indian law" that is somehow quaint and interesting only to anthropologists and ethnologists attempting to describe tribal dispute resolution methods before white contact. Rather, this is an Indian law that reflects the evolution of traditional tribal law through a succession of periods of the increasing imposition of American law. Often this traditional law takes on the form of American law but it maintains a traditional value system at its core.

30. *Harjo v. Kleppe* 420 Fed. Supp. 1110 (1976) at 1131-32.

31. op cit. This case contains a long history of U.S./Creek relations at 1118-1142. A total of 24 pages of this 32 page opinion is devoted to a straightforward history of this relationship, and ultimately, the argument that wins the case is a historical argument—at no point in history was the National Council deprived of its authority in tribal matters. Another argument defining the current national status of the Creeks by showing this historical continuity is John H. Moore, "The Mvskoke National Question in Oklahoma", 52 Science and Society 163 (1988).

The struggle of Crazy Snake and his people for sovereignty over their land, for the restoration of the "old law," the law of Polecat Springs, shows how Creek law evolved parallel to American law over a hundred year period. Creek society underwent major social change during this period and repeatedly modified both their substantive laws and their legal institutions. But through all this the Creek people embodied the "law of Polecat Springs" in the heart of their legal culture. It was a law that permitted great flexibility and change yet which also carried certain requirements that could not be yielded. Territorial sovereignty was not negotiable nor was the sale of land. This law and legal culture was evident to the Snakes and they adhered to it until the power of their movement was felt in the White House. Nor did their culture change merely because they were defeated: indicted, imprisoned, ultimately shot and dispersed. They changed the form of Creek law and legal culture reverting to their traditional town form of government until they could rebuild a Creek national government with a good measure of tribal sovereignty.

In *Harjo v. Kleppe* we see how the Snakes struggle for sovereignty impacted on both American law and on Creek law. Even though the violently assimilationist "big stick" Indian policy prevailed in the ten year struggle with the Snakes the existence of that struggle forever prevents any legal fiction in federal Indian law that the Creeks consented. Their law and their legal position of that event stands not only in the legal culture of the Creek people, but has been recognized by federal law and may yet be reincorporated into federal Indian law. We cannot predict the outcome of the future Creek cases, but we can predict that there will be more Creek cases in the American courts. These cases will go on—forever or until the United States and the Creeks come to an agreement that recognizes Creek sovereignty in a way acceptable to the tribe. In turn, what is acceptable, exists not as an abstract and unknowable principle but in the traditional law and evolving legal culture of the Creek people.

Peterson Zah

A Progressive Outlook and a Traditional Style

George M. Lubick

In 1969, the Navajo Council's Advisory Committee recommended that the tribe hereafter use the term Navajo Nation *as a reminder to its members and non-Indians alike that both "the Navajo People and Navajo Lands are, in fact, separate and distinct." History supported such a view, the council proclaimed, because long before the United States came into being the Diné existed as a distinct ethnic, cultural, and political group; once the "New Men" arrived in the Southwest, Navajo sovereignty was further buttressed by treaties wherein Congress and the Supreme Court recognized the inherent Navajo right of self-government.*

Navajo nationalism, embodied in the emergence of the tribal council in this century, grew and changed in response to external pressures, particularly to the desires to exploit Navajo resources and to internal conflicts, such as those between the more traditional Navajos like Chee Dodge and the "progressives" represented by J. C. Morgan and his Returned Students Association. As for the internal conflicts, regardless of the lines of opposition, Navajos have generally manifested the desire to acquire greater control over their social, political, and economic lives. As Peter Iverson has written in "The Emerging Navajo Nation," the election of Peter MacDonald in 1970 as tribal chairman mirrored the mood of Navajo nationalism. From the time of his first inaugural through his reelection to an unprecedented third term as chairman in 1978, MacDonald

gave notice that his administration would seek greater sovereignty. The Diné would protect what was rightfully theirs and claim what was rightfully due to them. MacDonald also stressed self-sufficiency so that Navajos would no longer depend upon the skills of others to develop their economy and meet their society's needs.

The 1970s, however, were years of turmoil. Not only were there political scandals in Navajo tribal government, but the Navajo-Hopi land dispute raised the most troublesome questions about Navajo national sovereignty. The dispute had its origin in the withdrawal from "settlement and sale" of 2,508,800 acres from the public domain by executive order of December 16, 1882. The land was "set apart for the use and occupancy of Moqui [Hopis] *and such other Indians as the Secretary of the Interior may see fit to settle thereon." At the time of its withdrawal many Navajos resided on this land. Later, some of the reserve became assigned exclusively to the Hopis, and the remainder, about 1.8 million acres, became known as the Joint-Use Area.*

In the late 1970s, thousands of Navajos whose families had resided on this land for generations were threatened with immediate eviction, while others accepted "relocation." One such family from the Joint-Use Area was that of Peterson Zah (born 1937). While recognizing the exclusive rights of the Hopis to their reservation, the necessity of tribal resource development, the expansion of health and educational services, and cooperation with local, state, and national governments, Zah, unlike Peter MacDonald, ceaselessly voiced concerns for the traditional, least acculturated members of the tribe, and for the necessity of preserving that traditionalism which for untold generations had reminded the Diné to walk in beauty. His election as tribal chairman in 1982 represented an attempt by Navajos to adapt to the exigencies of modern society, and at the same time, to maintain their tribal heritage—a tendency that is shared by an increasing number of tribes in the 1980s.

The 1970s were years of intense activity throughout the Navajo Reservation. At the beginning of the decade, Navajos turned back Raymond Nakai's bid for a third term as tribal chairman and elected instead the articulate, well-educated Peter MacDonald. By the end of the decade, MacDonald's name would be synonymous with modern Indian leadership. His twelve-year tenure in the chairman's office was characterized by programs designed to achieve the elusive goals of Navajo self-determination and self-sufficiency. To reduce the tribe's dependence on outside sources, his administration fostered programs to stimulate employment, to develop tribal enterprises, and to teach Navajos new skills. Keenly interested in the preservation of the tribe's cultural heritage, MacDonald sought to extend control over education through the creation of a Navajo Division of Education, an agency that began operating early in his first term.

Development of the tribe's mineral resources received MacDonald's special attention; and under his leadership, the tribe negotiated leases with such corporate giants as El Paso Natural Gas and Exxon, in a concerted effort to obtain equitable royalties from the exploitation of Navajo uranium and coal and to provide employment for Navajos. In 1975, MacDonald was among the founders of the Council of Energy Resource Tribes. Funded by corporate and federal grants, CERT used its expertise to help Native Americans develop their mineral resources for their own benefit.

MacDonald's development policies were, of necessity, long-range programs, but, in the meantime, tribal government could count on federal money to finance a variety of social services on the reservation. Particularly during MacDonald's first administration, Washington provided the Navajo reservation with generous funding.

MacDonald's energy policies generated opposition in some quarters, and critics of his administration openly protested during his second term as chairman. But his adversaries remained ineffectual, and MacDonald won reelection to a third term in 1978 by a comparatively wide margin. His goals did not change perceptibly over the years, and in his third inaugural address in January 1979, he returned to themes enunciated eight years earlier. "We must claim what is ours—actively and aggressively," he told the inauguration audience. Further, he emphasized the need to strengthen tribal unity and then exhorted Navajos to "dream great dreams" and dare to put them into action.[1]

By the early 1980s MacDonald had reached the peak of his power and influence. His reputation extended well beyond the reservation boundaries, and he was recognized as one of the country's most powerful Indian leaders. At the same time, the Navajo Nation was enjoying an unaccustomed degree of economic success. Despite high unemployment on the reservation and drastic cuts in federal programs by Ronald Reagan's administration, the tribe recorded "probably the best financial year in its history" in 1981. Revenues exceeded expenditures by more than 27 million dollars—the result of the deregulation of petroleum which led eventually to increased royalties for the tribe.[2]

MacDonald also had stimulated the cause of self-determination among Navajos. His tribal counsel, George Vlassis, credits him with establishing the Navajos as an important political force in Washington, D.C. His major contribution, Vlassis contends, was to show Washington that "there was no way anybody could just buy him lunch and send him home." MacDonald shares a similar assessment of his place in modern Navajo history and regards as one of his greatest accomplishments his efforts to gain for Navajos the respect and dignity they deserve.[3]

In less than two years, however, MacDonald's seemingly unassailable political hold on the reservation had been breached. In his 1982 campaign for a fourth term as chairman, he encountered the soft-spoken head of DNA–Peoples' Legal Services, Peterson Zah, an opponent fully as articulate as the incumbent and equally charismatic. DNA *(Dinébeiina Nahiilna Be Agaditahe)*, the federally funded legal services organization on the reservation, had been immensely popular since its inception in 1967, and as head of the program since 1972 Zah had developed an extensive constituency among rural and traditionalist Navajos. Equally important, he proved to be a forceful, energetic campaigner, presenting MacDonald with his most serious political challenge since 1970. Zah's supporters never doubted his ability to defeat MacDonald, but few people anticipated the extent of his victory on November 2, 1982. As late returns trickled in from remote chapter houses, they confirmed that Zah had defeated "the most powerful Indian leader in America" by nearly five thousand votes.[4]

Zah, then forty-five years old, represented a unique blend of the traditional and progressive in modern Navajo culture. Journalists who covered the 1982 campaign typically noticed only the obvious, modern side of Zah and focused on his university education, his successful administration of the legal services program, and his promises to reform and reorganize Navajo government. Yet Zah's ideas and goals were shaped by the much more subtle forces of Navajo tradition—the beliefs and values that grew out of his background in the remote, traditional community of Low Mountain in the central part of the reservation.

During Zah's boyhood and youth, Low Mountain had little contact with the outside world and was sometimes neglected by the Navajo tribal government as well. The area had been the center of opposition to government programs, and during the stock reduction programs of the 1930s it was considered antagonistic, if not hostile, toward non-Indians. Its residents practiced some dry farming but were primarily stock raisers. Zah's father had not completed his education, and his mother received no schooling. She was an accomplished weaver, however, and her blankets were sometimes the only source of income for the family. The family's home was located in the Navajo-Hopi Joint-Use Area, where Zah's family had lived amicably with the neighboring Hopis, occasionally trading a sheep for Hopi grain and other produce.[5]

Roads were virtually nonexistent around Low Mountain, and the few owners of cars and trucks found their vehicles to be expensive and unreliable forms of transportation. The nearest highway at Chinle, Arizona, was fifty miles distant. Keams Canyon, twenty-five miles southwest of Low Mountain, was the site of the nearest trading post, and Zah's family frequently made the two-day trip by horse and wagon to purchase such staples as coffee, sugar, and flour. The journeys were the family's only contact with the outside world, and for young Zah they were invariably special occasions. At the Keams Canyon and Piñon trading posts, Zah later recalled, he saw for the first time "how other people lived and was amazed at the 'looks' of non-Indians."[6]

Low Mountain changed little until Navajo G.I.s returned home after World War II, bringing with them stories of the progress and conveniences of American society as well as an appreciation for the value of education. While some of the old men around Low Mountain discussed the positive aspects of education, Zah remembered, the community hesitated to embrace the concept completely. In their contacts with the federal government, Navajos had seldom been asked for their opinions; most often they were told what to do. Education, many of them knew, meant that children were taken from their families and sent to distant boarding schools. Young Zah was subjected to the process, separated from his family at the age of nine and placed in a school more than one hundred miles away.[7]

Although Low Mountain Navajos remained divided about the need for education, Zah's own feelings were strongly influenced by educated relatives who worked as teachers and guidance counselors for the Bureau of Indian Affairs. Several of his aunts and uncles spent the school year at

BIA institutions in Flagstaff, Arizona; Brigham City, Utah; and Chemawa, Oregon; returning to Low Mountain during the summer months. "I dreamed of the day I would be able to do the same thing," Zah later wrote, "and I wanted to get as much education as I could and later return to the reservation to help the Navajos as my relatives were doing."[8]

Determined to pursue his dream, Zah left Low Mountain to enroll in the Phoenix Indian School, and following his graduation in 1958 continued his education at Phoenix College where he earned an associate of arts degree. In 1963 he received a bachelor's degree in education from Arizona State University. In 1964, his first job took him back to the Navajo Reservation where he worked as a vocational education instructor for the Area Redevelopment Administration at Window Rock High School. The following year, Zah was back at Arizona State University to supervise the training of volunteers for the VISTA program.

In the mid-1960s the Navajo Reservation enjoyed the benefits of a number of Lyndon Johnson's "Great Society" programs. The Office of Economic Opportunity, in particular, had a profound impact on the Navajo Nation through its various social and antipoverty programs. The tribal council authorized Navajo participation in the Community Action Program in 1964, and early the following year the Office of Economic Opportunity approved the tribe's request for funds to establish the Office of Navajo Economic Opportunity. Peter MacDonald, who had recently returned to the reservation, assumed the position of director of ONEO. Under his leadership, ONEO expanded to include programs for community development, Head Start, migrant and agricultural placement, alcoholism rehabilitation, and recreation and physical fitness, among others. ONEO's Legal Aid and Defender Society was established in 1967, and it eventually developed into an independent entity known by its initials DNA for *Dinébeiina Nahiilna Be Agaditahe.* The Navajo phrase translates as "Attorneys Who Contribute to the Economic Revitalization of the People."[9]

MacDonald used his control of ONEO to catapult himself to the center stage of Navajo political life.[10] DNA would serve a similar function for Peteson Zah, who joined the organization in May 1967 as an assistant to the director Ted Mitchell. The fledgling legal services group lacked even an office in its early days, and Zah's first task involved the acquisition of office space for the DNA staff of lawyers and court advocates.

Since a suitable structure was not available, Zah and his associates acquired lumber from local sawmills and constructed the building themselves. Despite its Spartan beginnings, DNA immediately filled an obvious need on the reservation, providing legal assistance for Navajos with an income of less than 3,500 dollars. And from the beginning, DNA was a grass-roots endeavor, as local chapters elected agency committees, who, in turn, chose the board of directors.[11]

The organization's first years were stormy ones as opposition to Mitchell's appointment entangled the legal services program in controversy that ended only with Mitchell's resignation in 1970. In addition, Tribal Chairman Raymond Nakai openly opposed DNA, and his supporters on the tribal council continually harassed the new organization. According to one DNA official, Nakai did not like the people DNA hired, and some tribal officials identified DNA with Ralph Nader's "Raiders," assuming that its employees were "summer vacation reformers." DNA also drew criticism from forces off the reservation. Irritated by its suits against reservation trading posts and the Gallup Indian Ceremonial, Sen. Barry Goldwater denigrated DNA by referring to it as a group of "young, inexperienced lawyers who have infested the Navajo Reservation." During the 1969 Senate debate on the economic opportunity program, Goldwater introduced an amendment to give the tribal council control over the legal services office. Fortunately for DNA, Senators Edward M. Kennedy and Walter Mondale successfully mobilized support to defeat the amendment.[12]

Despite such resistance, DNA could point to substantial success. It became popular with Navajos as soon as it began to assist people with their legal problems. Its offices at Shiprock, Crownpoint, Tuba City, Chinle, and Window Rock were each supplied with two attorneys, two counselors, and two interpreter-investigators. By the fall of 1968 it employed eighteen lawyers, many of them graduates of the prestigious law schools at Harvard, Yale, Columbia, Stanford, and elsewhere. Between April 1967 and July 1968, DNA served over 7,900 clients; by 1970 its case load reached nearly 12,000. Over the three years of its existence, it had been involved in 27,400 cases. Its community education programs reached over 15,000 residents at chapter, community, and school meetings, where DNA employees discussed, in Navajo and English, such topics as legal services, preventive law, and consumer and community education.[13]

Peter MacDonald's election as Navajo tribal chairman in 1970 guaranteed DNA's survival; indeed, the new chairman gave the organization his wholehearted support. Leo Haven succeeded Ted Mitchell as director and guided DNA until 1972, when Zah assumed control. Although he lacked formal legal training, Zah practiced in tribal courts and took all appellate cases for DNA. He also helped train tribal court advocates, young Navajos proficient in basic court procedures, and participated with them in complicated litigation.[14]

Among DNA's most controversial suits were those directed against operators of reservation trading posts. Few Navajos could count on a regular income, and traders had traditionally extended them credit in exchange for sheep, blankets, and other produce. Navajo customers accepted the traders' terms, usually unaware of hidden charges and powerless to combat high interest rates. Zah particularly resented the resulting "economic bondage" of Navajos to post operators. "I have a burning hate for the traders," he admitted, pointing out that "these bastards have been taking advantage of my people, the Navajos." In 1971, DNA lawyers filed a class action suit against the Piñon Trading Post and secured an out-of-court settlement for 32,500 dollars. Its personnel then helped Piñon residents organize a consumer's cooperative, the first of several such enterprises to grow up on the reservation. For Zah, the cooperative store represented a way "to cut out the traders" and allow Navajos to control their economic affairs.[15]

Outside the reservation, DNA championed consumer rights for Navajos against bordertown merchants from Gallup to Flagstaff. Among its most common activities was representation of Navajos whose vehicles had been repossessed by automobile dealers. One of DNA's suits produced a ruling that required auto dealers to obtain written consent from tribal courts before entering the reservation to repossess a vehicle, and thereafter some of the conflicts were eliminated. But as late as 1978, approximately 10 percent of all DNA cases still concerned repossessions.[16] DNA achieved its greatest victory in 1973, when the United States Supreme Court ruled in *McClanahan* v. *Arizona State Tax Commission* that Navajos were exempt from paying state income tax on wages and salaries earned on the reservation. The decision, according to Zah, was "a landmark tribal sovereignty case," not only for Navajos but for all Native Americans.[17]

DNA's success brought Zah national recognition in 1972 when the Native American Legal Defense and Education Fund selected him as its first president. Shortly afterward, he was chosen to serve on the executive committee of the National Legal Aid and Defender Association. His selection by the national organizations attested to the success of DNA and the growing reputation of its director. Under his guidance, DNA's advocacy of the rights of local Navajos had challenged tribal, state, and local governments and eventually would take on such energy companies as Exxon. The entire experience was exciting for Zah and his DNA staff, providing a unique opportunity to work with people at the local level. "I felt their needs and problems," he explained. "We really didn't care who was on the other side."[18]

In 1973, Zah and his legal services program faced the loss of OEO funding and were also challenged by a new legal organization, Lawyers for Navajos, Incorporated, which sought to supplant DNA on the reservation. Zah's organization triumphed in both instances. An out-of-court settlement with OEO secured its funding for the rest of the year, and the tribal council strongly supported DNA against the Lawyers for Navajos. With passage of the National Legal Services Bill in early 1974, DNA was assured of continued financial support, and Lawyers for Navajos simultaneously lost its bid to operate the reservation's legal services program. DNA changed its name in accordance with the new legislation, becoming DNA–Peoples' Legal Services and expanding its program to encompass legal aid to the neighboring Hopi Reservation.[19]

During the next several years, Zah was at the center of Navajo political life. In May 1976, he took leave from his DNA post to organize the "Walk for Better Government"—a protest march in response to a wave of rumors and allegations generated by a Justice Department investigation of the Navajo Housing Authority and audits of tribal finances authorized by the tribal council. In fact, the audits found no evidence of financial malfeasance, and only one member of the housing authority, Pat Chee Miller, was found guilty of any crime. But the publicity emanating from the investigations raised serious questions about the integrity of tribal government and undermined the faith of many Navajos in that institution.

On May 18, the opening of the tribal council's spring session, a column of "Navajo People Concerned for their Government" walked from the Window Rock Civic Center to the council chambers to present a list of recommendations. Speaking for the contingent, Zah told members of the council that the news stories about corruption had caused Navajos to wonder about their tribal government. Indeed, many were embarrassed by the whole affair. The source of the problem, according to Zah, was not the tribal chairman or any person but the cumbersome, ineffective governmental structure that had been established years earlier by the Bureau of Indian Affairs. "Instead of looking for a new man or a new woman to run the Tribal Government," he argued, "I think it is time to look for a new Tribal Government." The existing institution was not accountable to the Navajo people, and Zah was particularly concerned that council members had not discussed the scandals at local chapter meetings.[20]

The marchers' first recommendation called for a task force to reorganize the government. And Zah asked also for a committee to investigate the tribe's administrative organization, financial status, and current resources. In closing he warned, "We must change the whole system of government in terms of checks and balances especially in relation to policies and expenditures of the tribe."[21] The May march and Zah's address brought no immediate action from either MacDonald or the tribal council, but the affair demonstrated the extent of dissatisfaction among Navajos. Equally important, Zah emerged as an important reform advocate, and he set forth ideas about government reorganization that would surface again in a few years. In the meantime, Navajos endured another investigation of tribal affairs when a Phoenix grand jury in 1977 subpoenaed tribal chairman Peter MacDonald. Navajos in this instance rallied to the chairman's defense, and the tribal council appropriated seventy thousand dollars for his legal defense. After only a week of hearings, MacDonald was acquitted, and the Navajo Nation's era of scandals finally ended. The audits, investigations, and indictment had disrupted tribal government and clearly limited MacDonald's ability to address important issues, but he seemingly lost little of his political support. Indeed, he may have benefited politically from the ordeal of his indictment.[22]

MacDonald determined to campaign for an unprecedented third term in 1978, though a dozen candidates, including several former political allies, were ready to challenge him in the primary election. Peterson Zah's name was mentioned frequently as a possible opponent of MacDonald, but the DNA director remained determined to avoid the 1978 race. He still had goals for DNA which he hoped to fulfill, and he was also deeply committed to his family following a July 1977 fire that had destroyed their home. Evidence suggested that the fire had been caused by arson, and Zah believed that it was connected to DNA's legal battles with the tribe and energy companies.[23]

Still, Zah impressed some Navajos as MacDonald's strongest challenger. By May 1978 a campaign committee had been organized, and bumper stickers promoting his candidacy had appeared around the reservation. Zah continued to argue that he could better serve the Navajos through DNA, and in June he explicitly stated that he would not run for chairman. "I believe in better government," he remarked, "but what is the position from which to do this?" The main issue confronting Navajos according to Zah, was the need for a new system of government. And while he had spoken out frequently about the need for reorganization, he cautioned his supporters that such statements did not reflect any motivation to run for chairman.[24]

In the ensuing election, MacDonald swept by his primary opponents and went on to defeat Raymond Nakai in the November general election. Zah could afford to wait to enter tribal politics. He was only forty-one years old in 1978 and already had gained widespread recognition throughout the reservation. Several more years as director of DNA would only enhance his reputation, and conflicts over mineral development and the land dispute with the Hopis promised to involve his legal-aid network extensively.

The dispute between the Navajos and Hopis reached a critical stage in 1974 when Congress passed the Navajo-Hopi Land Settlement Act, which was followed three years later by the partition of the former Joint-Use Area between the two tribes. In 1978, estimates indicated that 4,800 Navajos living on land granted to the Hopis would have to relocate, while a small number of Hopi families would need to abandon their homes on Navajo land.[25] MacDonald had vigorously opposed the Land Settlement Act since its passage. When possible, he had sought to delay implementation of its provisions, hoping eventually to see the measure repealed. In his 1979 inaugural address he damned the "involuntary uprooting" of thousands of Navajos. "A nation that cries tears for Palestinian refugees, Cuban refugees, for Hungarian and Vietnamese refugees, for political refugees, has no business creating a class of Navajo refugees—homeless, displaced, uprooted, and sentenced to die in exile," MacDonald stated, "just because a few Congressmen and Senators have decided for their own peace of mind that the dispute must be settled now, once and for all."[26]

The intent of the Land Settlement Act had not been the creation of a new class of refugees, but Navajos understandably viewed the relocation of thousands of residents with alarm. The law provided relocation benefits for the heads of families and made provisions for replacement homes, but such measures did not make relocation more palatable. The task of overseeing the relocation process fell to a federal commission, the Navajo and Hopi Indian Relocation Commission, located in Flagstaff. By September 1978 the commission had relocated sixty-four Navajo families, most of whose members were in their thirties and had attained some education.[27] The group was hardly representative of the Navajo population in the former Joint-Use Area.

MacDonald relied on the tribe's lawyers in negotiations with the Hopis and the federal government, while he doggedly continued his attempts to have the law repealed. In reply to Representative Morris Udall's contention in 1980 that both tribes had reconciled themselves to the law, MacDonald pledged to pursue every possibility for repeal, vowing, "We will not rest, we will not be satisfied, we will not stop our efforts until the homes and lives of the Navajo people in this area have been preserved."[28] Such language was reassuring to some, but Navajos living on the contested Hopi land perceived few improvements in their situation. Earlier court decisions had ordered the reduction of livestock in the former Joint-Use Area and also required that both tribes approve of any new construction projects. The Hopis were reluctant to approve Navajo requests, and the Navajos intensely resented this "freeze" on improvements of homes, schools, and roads.[29]

DNA was one of the few tribal organizations to aid residents directly, and its lawyers challenged grazing restrictions, stock reductions, and unfair compensation payments in behalf of local stock raisers. They also assisted those who contemplated moving by helping them secure relocation benefits. A 1977 grant from the Department of Health, Education, and Welfare enabled DNA to focus some of its attention on the needs of the elderly and to provide them with assistance in coping with relocation. Through DNA's involvement in the daily lives of the area's residents, Zah and his staff acquired an extensive knowledge of the plight of Navajos throughout the former Joint-Use Area. Equally important, DNA's activities produced a measure of satisfaction for the area's frustrated residents.

The land dispute and relocation issue were particularly poignant for Zah. He had grown up in the area and still retained close family ties there. Until passage of the 1974 Land Settlement Act, Navajos and Hopis had lived peacefully, and few Hopis in the area were anxious to see Navajo residents forced to relocate. Zah maintained that the land dispute was a creation of the federal government, and not an issue precipitated by either tribe. He realized, too, that any hostility between Navajos and Hopis would benefit the energy companies, which were interested in the area's mineral deposits. Control of the deposits by the smaller and weaker Hopi Tribe could prove especially beneficial for the corporations. In either case, Zah was convinced that both tribes were being used by outside interests.[30]

Zah's connections with the former Joint-Use Area and his understanding of its special problems were important factors in his decision to enter the 1982 primary election campaign. During informal announcements at chapter houses in the area in January 1982, he argued that "a chairman with a deep understanding and concern for that area" could repair many of the damages that had been caused by the land dispute. He cited its lack of health facilities and school buildings, its inadequate roads, and its poor water and utility services as results of the government's freeze on construction projects. Zah acknowledged that Navajos had not created the problems, but he criticized the tribal government's lack of concern for the needs of the area's residents in the years following the 1977 partition of the land.[31]

Zah proposed no panacea for the complex issue, but his long, personal friendship with Ivan Sidney, the recently elected Hopi tribal chairman, offered some hope for a solution. The escalating costs of the relocation program, he added, might induce Washington to accept a solution worked out by the new tribal chairmen.[32]

Zah's friendship with Sidney and its implications for a favorable resolution of the land dispute remained a constant feature in Zah's campaign. "Two leaders who have respect for one another can start anew and afresh on an old problem," he told audiences at White Cone and Whippoorwill in February. When Zah formally announced his candidacy later in the month, he invited Sidney to attend the rally at his home chapter at Low Mountain. The Zah and Sidney families had been friends for years, and the two tribal leaders had known each other since their student days at Phoenix Indian School. The invitation caused Sidney some concern, but he eventually accepted. "From there I had an interest," he later told a reporter, adding that MacDonald's reelection would mean "a lot more fighting" over the disputed land.[33]

By the spring of 1982 the relocation of Navajos had received widespread attention from scholars, journalists, and other writers. The intense strain of relocation on older, traditional Navajos was discussed in *Land and Religion at Big Mountain* and *A Sociocultural Assessment of the Livestock Reduction Program in the Navajo-Hopi Joint Use Area*, by anthropologists at Northern Arizona University. Thayer Scudder's *No Place to Go: Effects of Compulsory Relocation on Navajos,* a study requested by the Navajo-Hopi Land Dispute Commission, appeared in 1982; and *The Second Long Walk: The Navajo-Hopi Land Dispute,* by former *Navajo Times* and Gallup *Independent* reporter Jerry Kammer, had been published two years earlier. Scudder was perhaps the strongest proponent of repealing the 1974 law, arguing that its revocation would reduce the "human costs" of relocation for some five thousand Navajos. In addition, repeal would be more consistent with United States policy concerning the Indian Self-Determination Act, and it would also eliminate the growing financial burden for the federal government.[34]

In May 1982, Roger Lewis of the Navajo and Hopi Indian Relocation Commission aroused public interest when he described relocation as a "tragic, tragic thing" and added that he sometimes felt that the commission was "as bad as the people who ran the concentration camps during World War II."[35] Lewis's comments, along with earlier descriptions of the hardships caused by relocation, provided the impetus for the new discussions that focused on transfers of land between the two tribes as a means of reducing the number of relocatees. Tribal negotiating teams, headed by MacDonald and Sidney, met in Albuquerque in June to consider boundary adjustments. But the talks collapsed abruptly when MacDonald and his aides failed to appear at a scheduled meeting with the Hopis, although the group was meeting in a nearby room. In the ensuing blast of recriminations, all hope for an immediate negotiated settlement was lost.[36]

MacDonald's indiscretion, for which he eventually apologized to Sidney, provided Zah with an opportunity to attack his opponent, and he suggested to a campaign audience that the incumbent chairman was perhaps tired, having spent a dozen years in office. "How can we resolve anything if our chairman doesn't even show up to talk, especially when the talks are about reducing the number of Navajos who must be relocated," he asked. Zah was certain of his ability to discuss issues with Sidney, he pointed out, adding that "therein lies the hope for negotiations."[37]

During the campaign, Zah also relied on his reputation as a reformer and argued forcefully for reorganization of tribal government. MacDonald, Zah maintained, had lost sight of the basic needs of Navajos in his pursuit of "power and politics." In contrast, Zah pledged to return authority to the tribal council and to local communities. He also attacked MacDonald's lack of concern for education, and proposed a uniform system of education on the reservation. Navajos, he maintained, needed to decide the direction of their children's education, and he advocated a tribal education agency to oversee the instruction of youngsters "in what is best to the Navajo people—Navajo culture and language" in a well-rounded curriculum.[38]

Like MacDonald, Zah was a proponent of Navajo self-sufficiency and viewed taxation of energy companies as a means to foster economic independence. But Zah was keenly aware of the concerns of local residents living near mining sites on the reservation. DNA had defended them over the years and had amassed an extensive stock of information about the impact of mineral exploitation on local communities. Therefore, Zah proposed that, in the future, mining companies must first confer with local landowners, "grass roots, hogan-level Navajos," before taking their proposals to the tribal government at Window Rock.[39]

Throughout the campaign, both MacDonald and Zah were affected by the dismal economic plight of the reservation. High unemployment among Navajos hampered Zah's efforts to raise money, and his campaign staff was composed largely of volunteers. MacDonald had to defend his administration against critics of the high unemployment rate, but he remained a formidable candidate. During twelve years as chairman, he had attracted an extensive following and could point to a credible record of achievement. And as the incumbent candidate he could count on additional advantages. Consequently his supporters anticipated a primary victory of several thousand votes. MacDonald finished first among the candidates in the August primary election, but his margin over Zah proved to be exceedingly thin. Zah trailed the incumbent by less than 1,000 votes—20,083 to 19,086.[40]

In the ensuing general election campaign, Zah adhered to the strategy developed in the previous months. He selected Edward Begay, a popular politician from the eastern portion of the reservation, as his running mate and also gained the support of Wilbert Willie, Jack Jackson, and Larry Isaac, all of whom had been candidates in the primary. MacDonald chose Frank Paul to run with him, and Raymond Nakai added his endorsements to their cause.

Zah continued to stress his long friendship with Ivan Sidney as a special advantage in resolving the land dispute. He also used the two months before the November general election to develop his plans for tribal government reform and reorganization. Tribal authority, he argued, needed to be decentralized. According to his plan, the agencies and chapters would receive tribal funds and staff members to take care of local needs, while larger towns on the reservation moved toward township status, supplied with sufficient tribal funds for community improvements and similar responsibilities. Reform of the tribal government at Window Rock required the establishment of separate executive, legislative, and judicial branches of government.[41]

The theme of decentralization also characterized Zah's approach to developing the tribe's mineral resources. His emphasis was on planned development, with special attention to local needs and interests. MacDonald, Zah pointed out, "likes to do big things, bring in big companies to do big things." In contrast, Zah's energy policy was designed to promote orderly use of resources. He remained committed to taxing energy companies operating on the reservation, and he pledged to use the proceeds to create employment programs, to provide aid to elderly Navajos, and to fund scholarships for students.[42]

In the primary election, Zah successfully attracted the votes of young Navajos, and he courted them again during the next two months. "I don't like the brain drain syndrome," he told a student audience at Navajo

Community College. Zah encouraged Navajos to pursue a college education but was concerned that few found jobs on the reservation. His administration, he promised, would make room for educated young men and women in tribal government. The Council for Navajo Women had supported Zah in the primary campaign, and he recognized the need to open opportunities for women in tribal government. His appointment of Claudeen Bates Arthur as his campaign policy adviser suggested that his administration would bring women into important positions in Navajo government.[43]

A particular asset for Zah was his ability to exploit the growing dissatisfaction with MacDonald's twelve-year administration. Many Navajos remembered that in 1970 MacDonald was an acknowledged grass-roots leader. "But now he's on a pedestal," one Navajo explained to a reporter. "In twelve years he has rubbed people the wrong way." Several of the candidates in the primary campaign had voiced similar criticisms. Jack Jackson, for example, complained that the tribal council seemingly operated "at the whim of one person—Peter MacDonald." Women, too, had developed grievances against the incumbent; the Council for Navajo Women, in particular, was disillusioned with his administration. Many local Navajos also resented the fact that when MacDonald visited chapter houses he was escorted by a bodyguard of tribal policemen.[44]

Zah's long association with DNA–Peoples' Legal Services was a distinct advantage. As its director he was well known throughout the reservation, and DNA had the reputation as one of the few organizations that was responsive to the needs of grass-roots Navajos. "We seem to get involved in everything that happens here," one of its officials remarked. *The Navajo Times* echoed the same sentiment, pointing out that "on the Navajo reservation just about everyone knows about DNA. Either they have been clients themselves or someone in their family has used the DNA service."[45] Zah had gained additional recognition as leader of the "Navajo People Concerned for their Government" in the 1976 confrontation with MacDonald's allegedly scandal-ridden administration.

MacDonald's advisers remained content to stress the accomplishments of his administration and worked to hold together the constituency that had worked so effectively since 1970. Occasionally, a MacDonald aide complained that the *Navajo Times* had not given the incumbent adequate coverage or that the Gallup *Independent* sought to "throw the election to

Zah." But the MacDonald camp remained generally optimistic. Zah's support in the primary had been "soft," one of MacDonald's supporters reasoned, adding that the chairman had the upper hand and the momentum to achieve an "easy victory."[46]

There would be no such victory for MacDonald in 1982. In the general election, Zah gathered widespread support throughout the reservation and put together substantial margins in the larger chapters and at the Chinle, Fort Defiance, and Shiprock agencies to upset MacDonald by five thousand votes. In chapters in the former Joint-Use Area, he recorded a narrow victory over the incumbent. Zah also attracted young voters, who turned out in large numbers for the general election. These "alienated factions," as one analyst described the youth vote, had lost all faith in MacDonald during his third term and found an exciting leader in Zah.[47]

For Zah, the victory "completed a true grass roots effort to end years of unresponsive, unbalanced government." While politicians and others puzzled over the election results, Zah moved quickly to implement the programs he had advocated for the previous ten months. Within a few weeks he had assembled a committee on government reorganization to recommend major changes in tribal government. Out of its discussions came suggestions for reform in forty areas of tribal government. Jack Jackson, a member of the reorganization committee, described its meetings as a "historic occasion," the first time that Navajos had met to discuss the kind of tribal government they wanted.[48]

Government reorganization emerged as a prominent theme in Zah's inaugural address on January 11, 1983, when he introduced the theme of a "new Navajo partnership" to meet the needs of the tribe. The new chairman envisioned a close relationship between his office and the tribal council, but authority was not to be centralized in Window Rock. "We will decentralize the government so that local issues are decided by local communities," he told the audience. The structure of tribal government was also in need of change, according to Zah, and he proposed the separation of powers among the three branches of government.[49]

Resolution of the land dispute with the Hopis required a new understanding with the neighboring tribe. Throughout the history of the conflict, Zah maintained, lawyers from the outside had exercised too much control and had caused the traditional Navajo-Hopi relationship to deteriorate. "A little feast in the shade of a tree, and a lot of understanding would have taken us further toward a positive solution," he explained. In an effort to end the dispute, he emphasized that he and Sidney were committed to working together on areas of common concern.[50]

Resource development on Navajo land also required a new approach, and Zah announced that current leases with "unrealistic royalties" would be reviewed immediately. Rather than spending millions of dollars to hire outside law firms, the new chairman adhered to a campaign pledge to employ Navajo professionals.[51] When negotiations with energy companies began in the spring of 1983, the tribe was represented by the staff of the tribe's Minerals and Resources Department and members of Zah's own office.

The optimistic inaugural address with its promises of reform reflected the euphoria of Zah's election. But his State of the Navajo Nation address on January 25 was a much more realistic assessment of conditions on the reservation. Zah acknowledged that his reforms would be difficult to accomplish because of the severe effects of the recession. High unemployment remained a problem, and the Reagan administration's budget reductions had meant a corresponding cutback in programs and grants for the reservation. At the end of 1982, the tribe was running a deficit of approximately 25 million dollars for fiscal year 1983, and Navajo Agricultural Products Industries and Navajo Forest Products Industries had accrued millions of dollars in debts. Navajo Community College needed 1.5 million dollars for the current academic year and more for the following year, and the tribe owed the U.S. Labor Department over 7 million dollars. Even the current budget was in serious jeopardy, Zah lamented.[52]

One remedy for the tribe's financial difficulties was through renegotiation of existing leases with energy companies to increase royalty payments to the tribal government. Zah had long pledged to review such unfair leases, and his administration initiated the policy in April 1983, when the tribal council rescinded agreements with Chuska Energy and Development Company and Dineh Bii Resources—both Navajo-owned companies. Leases with the companies had never gone into effect, but tribal officials were certain that they could obtain better returns for the tribe. Negotiations with other companies would soon follow, and Zah asked the tribe's Justice Department to develop plans for a severance tax to provide an additional source of tribal income.[53]

In the meantime, Zah's reform of tribal government had been elaborated. The new chairman proposed the establishment of an Office of Legislative Affairs, which included three subdivisions—an expanded Office of the Legislative Secretary, an Office of Intergovernmental Affairs, and an office devoted to writing bills for eventual presentation to the tribal council. During Peter MacDonald's administration, the tribal council agenda was circulated only on the day of the council sessions. In contrast, the Office of Legislative Affairs would have authority to print the agenda two weeks prior to council meetings, thereby encouraging representatives to discuss agenda items with local residents well before the council met. Zah's goal of establishing a close partnership with local Navajos was reflected in the department devoted to preparing bills; it was designed to allow anyone to introduce a bill on any subject in the tribal council. The Office of Intergovernmental Affairs was essentially a liaison office to coordinate communications between Window Rock, Washington, D.C., and state capitols. Shortly after the measure had been announced, Zah and Begay visited chapter houses to stimulate local participation in the new administration's policy of partnership, stressing the need for local initiative.[54]

Perhaps the most dramatic aspect of Zah's administration concerned his frequent meetings with Ivan Sidney. The talks between the two tribal leaders, even their celebrated "historic negotiations" in Albuquerque in March, provided no solution to the land dispute, and both men realized that resolution of the problem was a long-term objective. But through their cooperation and obvious mutual respect, Zah and Sidney stimulated a sense of optimism among Hopis and Navajos. "We feel that we've got 100 per cent progress when we just sit at the same table today," Sidney said of the meetings in Albuquerque. Impressed by the good will generated by the tribal leaders, several Navajo chapters passed resolutions of appreciation for Zah's efforts, and the Hopi tribal council added its endorsement of Sidney's endeavors. Their early talks led to joint efforts to improve roads connecting the reservations and a common request that the BIA cease impounding livestock in the disputed area for ninety days and allow residents to make minor improvements in their dwellings.[55]

Much of the success attributed to Zah and Sidney resulted from a basic change in Navajo policy. Jeff Begay of the Navajo Tribe's Justice Department, and a staff assistant to Zah, explained that the new approach to resolving the land dispute focused on minimizing the number of Navajos forced to relocate—"to work within the constraints and minimize the hardship impacts." By calming Hopi fears of repeal of the 1974 legislation, Zah's policy enhanced the course of negotiations and opened new areas of cooperation. By the end of March, both tribal councils had passed a joint resolution advocating construction of a road between the Hopis' Second Mesa and Black Mesa on the Navajo Reservation. BIA support for their proposal encouraged Zah and Sidney to consider additional cooperative endeavors to improve health and educational facilities.[56]

When Zah summarized his administration's accomplishments after its first one hundred days, he pointed to substantial achievements as a result of cooperation with Sidney. Congress had appropriated money for a Hopi high school at Keams Canyon to educate youngsters of both tribes, and funds had been committed for the construction of medical clinics in the disputed area for the use of Hopi and Navajo residents. The route for the Black Mesa–Second Mesa road, the "Turquoise Trail," had been approved by Arizona state authorities, and its construction eventually would benefit both tribes. Future talks, Zah hoped, would lead to Navajo-Hopi cooperation against energy companies operating on Indian land. A joint committee had been proposed to negotiate with Peabody Coal, and the Navajo chairman anticipated that continued cooperation would provide both tribes with an equitable return for exploitation of their mineral resources. Energy companies like Peabody had used the land dispute to the detriment of Navajos and Hopis, Zah stated, and consequently they paid royalties of only fifteen cents to thirty-two cents per ton of coal.[57]

Zah's administration had produced other important results as well. The North Central Accreditation Association approved the Navajo Division of Education as an accreditation agency, and the tribe received additional federal funds from the 1982 Highway Improvement Act and the Emergency Jobs Bill. But the reservation's endemic economic problems remained unsolved, and the 1983 budget deficit represented an additional burden. New, equitable royalties from energy companies might alleviate the worst of the financial crisis eventually; in the immediate future, Navajos had to accommodate themselves to additional reductions in federal programs by the Reagan administration.

No one realistically expected Zah's administration to resolve the tribe's economic problems or the land dispute in its first few months in office.

Zah acknowledged as much in his inaugural address, noting that the problems facing the Navajo Nation had taken years to create and the solutions also would require years of hard work. In his first one hundred days, however, Zah had stimulated some changes in Navajo attitudes about government. His real accomplishment had been to establish the foundation for the kind of government he had envisioned for years and described in campaign speeches and tribal council addresses. Its theme was cooperation, or "partnership"—the term Zah preferred—and reflected his own "people-oriented" approach to tribal government. Much of Zah's public career, beginning with his association with DNA, had rested on his desire to reach and meet the needs of grass-roots Navajos.

He shared with his predecessor, Peter MacDonald, an intense pride in the Navajo heritage and a willingness to foster programs to stimulate both nationalism and self-sufficiency. But his style separated him dramatically from MacDonald. Soft-spoken and articulate, he preferred to visit chapter houses and agencies, drawing ideas from all parts of the reservation. He was equally determined to attract young Navajos into service to the Navajo Nation, convinced that young Navajo professionals "possess the intellectual ability and the dedication necessary to administer the entirety of tribal government affairs."[58] Gaining respect for Navajos had influenced his tribal policies, including relations with energy companies. Zah expected to gain higher royalties from such companies, but he was equally concerned about the attitudes of corporate officials. "We are looking for people who will have in mind respect for Navajos and our land," he told a Phoenix reporter. Zah vowed not to wait long for officials to contact the tribe, pointing out that "we will actively solicit partnerships, and make our own proposals."[59]

While no definitive judgment of Zah's success can rest on a discussion of a one-hundred-day career, it appeared in the fall of 1983 that the "new Navajo partnership" was working. Relations with the Hopis were better than they had been in perhaps several decades, and his administration remained optimistic about the renegotiation of leases. The initial reform of tribal government had begun, and Zah had brought tribal government to local Navajos. Major economic problems remained, however; and those issues, it appeared, would likely determine Zah's political future and the well-being of the Navajo Nation as well.

Notes

1. Navajo Nation, Navajo Film and Media Commission, Third Term Inaugural Address of Peter MacDonald, January 9, 1979, p. 2. On MacDonald's administrations, see Peter Iverson, *The Navajo Nation* (Albuquerque, 1983).

2. *Navajo Times*, September 22, 1982.

3. *Arizona Magazine* (Phoenix *Arizona Republic*), May 8, 1983, p. 10; *Navajo Times*, November 10, 1982.

4. Gallup, New Mexico, *Independent*, November 3, 1982.

5. Robert A. Roessel, Jr., "Tragedy at Low Mountain," in *Indian Communities in Action*, ed. Robert A. Roessel, Jr. (Tempe, Ariz., 1967), p. 60; Peterson Zah, "A Personal Presentation and Evaluation of Community Development at Low Mountain," in *Indian Communities in Action*, p. 120; *Dineh: The People—A Portrait of the Navajo*, Western World Productions, 1976 (documentary film).

6. Zah, "A Personal Presentation," p. 121.

7. Ibid., pp. 121–22.

8. Ibid., pp. 122–23.

9. Peter Iverson, "Peter MacDonald," in *American Indian Leaders: Studies in Diversity*, ed. R. David Edmunds (Lincoln, Nebr., 1980), pp. 224–25.

10. Iverson, *Navajo Nation*, p. 126.

11. *New York Times*, January 14, 1983; for a discussion of DNA's early years, see Iverson, *Navajo Nation*, pp. 91–100.

12. *Navajo Times*, June 8, 1978.

13. Ibid., September 10, 1970; June 8, 1978; Iverson, *Navajo Nation*, pp. 94, 99.

14. *DNA in Action*, September 30, 1972, p. 2.

15. *Dineh;* Iverson, *Navajo Nation*, pp. 134, 171.

16. *Navajo Times*, June 8, 1978; and April 6, 1978; Gallup *Independent*, January 25, 1983.

17. *Navajo Times*, July 14, 1982.

18. *New York Times,* January 14, 1983; *DNA in Action,* January 7, 1972, p. 9.

19. *Navajo Times,* June 7, 1973; June 14, 1973; July 5, 1973; June 6, 1978; June 28, 1973.

20. Ibid., May 6, 1976; May 20, 1976; June 8, 1978.

21. Ibid., May 20, 1976.

22. Iverson, *Navajo Nation,* p. 208.

23. *Navajo Times,* July 7, 1977; October 6, 1977; *New York Times,* January 14, 1983.

24. *Navajo Times,* June 22, 1978.

25. Navajo and Hopi Indian Relocation Commission (hereafter cited as NHIRC), *Interim Progress Report* (Flagstaff, Ariz., 1978), p. 1. The number of Navajos subjected to relocation grew dramatically as the NHIRC continued its enumeration. By the end of 1980, the commission had enumerated 2,801 Navajo households, comprising 9,525 Navajos residing on Hopi land; only 109 Hopis resided on land partitioned to the Navajos. See NHIRC, *Report and Plan* (Flagstaff, Ariz., 1981), p. 3.

26. Third Term Inaugural Address of Peter MacDonald, p. 4.

27. NHIRC, *Interim Progress Report,* pp. 11, 148.

28. Quoted in Jerry Kammer, *The Second Long Walk: The Navajo-Hopi Land Dispute* (Albuquerque, 1980), p. 219.

29. NHIRC, *Interim Progress Report,* p. 9.

30. Peterson Zah, personal interview, May 7, 1983; *Dineh.*

31. *Navajo Times,* January 20, 1982.

32. Ibid.

33. Ibid., February 10, 1982; Gallup *Independent,* February 10, 1982.

34. Thayer Scudder, *No Place to Go: Effects of Compulsory Relocation on Navajos* (Philadelphia, 1982), pp. 126–27. See also John J. Wood, Walter M. Vannette, and Michael J. Andrews, *A Sociocultural Assessment of the Livestock Reduction Program in the Navajo-Hopi Joint Use Area* (Flagstaff, Ariz., 1979); and John J. Wood and Kathy M. Stemmler, *Land and Religion at Big Mountain: The Effects of the Navajo-Hopi Land Dispute on Navajo Well-Being* (Flagstaff, Ariz., 1981).

35. *Navajo Times,* May 12, 1982; *Arizona Daily Sun* (Flagstaff), May 7, 1982; May 9, 1982.

36. *Navajo Times,* June 23, 1982; June 30, 1982.

37. Ibid., June 30, 1982; July 7, 1982.

38. Ibid., February 3, 1982; May 12, 1982; June 9, 1982.

39. Ibid., July 14, 1982; June 8, 1978.

40. Gallup *Independent,* August 12, 1982; *Navajo Times,* August 18, 1982.

41. *Navajo Times,* October 6, 1982; and October 14, 1982; Gallup *Independent,* October 28, 1982.

42. Gallup *Independent,* October 28, 1982.

43. Ibid., October 21, 1982; *Navajo Times*, August 25, 1982.

44. Gallup *Independent*, August 11, 1982; *Navajo Times*, March 23, 1983; and August 25, 1982.

45. *Navajo Times*, June 8, 1978.

46. Gallup *Independent*, October 6, 1982; *Navajo Times*, October 20, 1982.

47. *New York Times*, January 14, 1983; *Navajo Times*, November 10, 1982; Gallup *Independent*, November 3, 1982; and November 4, 1982.

48. *Navajo Times*, November 4, 1982; Gallup *Independent*, December 8, 1982.

49. Peterson Zah, Inauguration Address, January 11, 1983, p. 1.

50. Ibid., p. 2.

51. Ibid.

52. Peterson Zah, State of the Navajo Nation, January 25, 1983, pp. 2–3.

53. Gallup *Independent*, April 5, 1983; Peterson Zah, Report of Peterson Zah, "The First 100 Days," pp. 6–7.

54. Gallup *Independent*, February 22, 1983; *Navajo Times*, March 2, 1983; and March 9, 1983.

55. *Navajo Times*, March 25, 1983; Gallup *Independent*, March 2, 1983; March 24, 1983; *Qua Toqti*, April 7, 1983.

56. Gallup *Independent*, March 31, 1983.

57. Zah, "First 100 Days," pp. 9–10.

58. Ibid., p. 6.

59. *Arizona Magazine*, May 8, 1983, p. 11.

THE QUEST FOR SOVEREIGNTY

Given the lawyers' definitions of Native Americans' problems and possibilities, the first step on the road to solutions seems obvious. In order to break the powerlessness cycle, regaining control of one's own affairs–i.e., self-sufficiency–is necessary. Here the concept of "tribal sovereignty" appears to the lawyers to be made to order. Though the concept is "fundamentally of Western origin,"[1] the tribes have been dealt with in such terms by Anglo society for many years. Moreover, it is a term with which lawyers are familiar and able to work. Though hundreds of pages of legal and social scientific work have been devoted to discussing, analyzing, and trying to define "sovereign," the concern here is with what it has come to mean in Native American affairs. More specifically, the activity of lawyers representing Native Americans in pursuit of tribal sovereignty will illuminate what it is by how it is practiced.

Quasi-Sovereignty

A SHORT HISTORY

In Native American legal history, the tribal sovereignty concept is actually "quasi-sovereign," because the federal government has the power to alter Native American status should it so desire.[2] Essentially, the term covers the very complicated legal status of tribal governments vis-à-vis other governmental units and citizens. With respect to the federal government and its agents, Native American units retain every right of self-government that has not been taken away or altered by congressional action.[3] As one lawyer explained it, "There is no law saying Indians could or could not do that. The rights not taken away remain with the tribe." With regard to state governments and their agents, such as cities and counties, Native American units are sovereign unless Congress has given the states the jurisdiction or power to interfere. In practice, however, states often take a more aggressive role. For example:

> Today states may assert authority over Indian tribes in the absence of Congressional prohibition, provided that there is no interference with a recognized right of tribal self-government or the exercise of federal authority.[4]

Thus tribal sovereignty has come to be the residue of self-government rights left to the tribes by Congress plus those rights which have been successfully asserted by the tribes and recognized as such by specific states.

Much of the long history of the United States' relationship with Native American tribes consists of altering tribes' legal status to accord with changing policy goals. Since the judicial branch of the federal government recognized tribes as only quasi-sovereign, Congress and the executive could tamper with the degree and nature of powers and rights left with the tribes. As is well known, federal policy has swung back and forth from assimilation and termination to separation and recognition of cultural values. Present federal policy is, at least rhetorically, supportive of Native American sovereignty (often defined as the right of self-determination, a well known phrase with which, theoretically, the United States deals with other governments as well). An example is the Jackson resolution:

> The Jackson resolution would establish that it will be the policy of the federal government to "give Indians the freedom and encouragement to develop their individual, family, and community potential and to determine their own future to the maximum extent possible." It further states that "maximizing opportunities for Indian control and self-determination shall be a major goal of our national Indian policy."[5]

This resolution is Congressional recognition of the shift in national policy expressed by President Richard Nixon in 1968.[6] If followed by action consistent with its rhetoric, it could greatly aid the movement for Native American self-determination.

From the perspective of lawyers who represent Native Americans, tribal sovereignty is more vital than our shifting national policy on the issue suggests. As one lawyer stated, "Self determination is the road to salvation. It means to be able to control their own destiny." Tribal sovereignty, with or without supporting national policy, informs activity: "Even if the doctrine . . . were a legal fiction, judicial enunciation of the doctrine has given Indians a theory today upon which to build more viable systems of self-government and economic development."[7] If Native Americans are to solve their problems, according to their lawyers, they must first be able to control their own destiny and operate like a government. For example:

> Notwithstanding the fact that there are many questions concerning the scope of Indian sovereignty, one general conclusion emerges: It is necessary for Indian tribal governments to examine past actions which have limited their sovereignty so that they may anticipate and prepare for similar actions in the future. Unless tribal governments exercise or otherwise clearly identify those powers which they still possess, they run the risk of losing what remains of tribal sovereignty—which essentially is the right of self-government.
>
> If Indians and non-Indians truly aspire to the goal of "Indian self-determination," tribal sovereignty must be recognized.[8]

From the legal viewpoint, the concept and practice of Native American tribal sovereignty must be maintained.

NECESSARY PREREQUISITES

In other words, "it is not only the theoretical power that is important, but the exercise of that power."[9] Though recognition of the concept of tribal sovereignty is helpful, by itself it is not enough. As one lawyer stated, "The legal rights have been there many years, but legal rights are not automatic. The law is not self asserting." In order for tribal sovereignty to do the job lawyers see it as capable of doing, it must be exercised through aggressive assertion and utilization of sovereignty rights on the part of the tribes. Assertion and utilization require positive action. The law of sovereign rights is truly the activity of exercising those rights. But before tribes act, they must want to do so. They must become ready and willing to take control of their own destiny. In the lawyers' words, Native Americans' political consciousness must be raised.

Simultaneously, the tribes need willing and competent legal aid in order to assert their legal rights, both in the courts and elsewhere. As one of the attorneys interviewed put it: "Lawyers have played a major role as lobbyists and legislators . . . Lawyers are a critical part of our system so if you want a major piece of legislation, you want to get a good lawyer on it." In order to translate the theory of tribal sovereignty into practice, the attorneys feel two prerequisites must be met. First, there must be clients desirous of acting. And secondly, there must be attorneys willing and able to represent such clients.

Are the clients ready? According to one lawyer, "The movement for tribal sovereignty is the biggest movement right now." He explained that, at least in Washington and most of the Pacific Northwest, fishing rights cases are the impetus for this movement. The advent of the oil discoveries in 1966 played a similar role in awakening the political consciousness of the Alaskan Indians. The catalytic factor may vary from case to case, but natural resources are almost always involved. But one lawyer argued that the change in attitude by Native Americans

> was part of a world wide system of minority assertiveness. The increasing egalitarian notions of the 50s and 60s has also hit Indian communities. It is not exactly the same and doesn't show up the same way, but it is part of the world wide egalitarian movement.

Regardless of cause, the attorneys perceive an increase in Native American political consciousness.

However, because self-determination is essentially legal, tribes need professional advice on how to proceed. In the past, competent legal representation has been unavailable to Indians "for all the old reasons, such as lack of funds, racism, lack of legal knowledge, etc." But now things are changing:

> Legal representation of Indians was very bad until about five to seven or eight years ago. Now it is markedly improved. This is true generally for all minorities but with Indians it came later. Indians are usually represented quite well to excellently now. That has combined with the assertiveness of Indians insisting on their rights and on following legal and other measures to assert those rights–it could be that assertiveness is partly a result of the lawyers–a kind of a reciprocal thing.

This combination of raised political consciousness and increasing availability of competent and willing legal counsel makes the present quest for tribal sovereignty viable.

The Components of Tribal Sovereignty

But what does sovereignty or self-determination actually mean to these lawyers? What does the activity of the pursuit of tribal sovereignty reveal? The attorneys' definition of sovereignty will become clearer by looking at the components they believe to be central and are therefore engaged in asserting and utilizing. There are presently three main areas in which lawyers are busily aiding tribes in the assertion of governmental powers: (1) jurisdictional questions involving control over Native Americans and any others who enter reservation boundaries; (2) licensing, taxing and zoning powers to maintain control over their land; and (3) the assertion of treaty rights generally relating to resources such as fish, game, water, minerals, etc. By examining each in turn, what the quest for sovereignty means in terms of activity will begin to emerge.

JURISDICTION

One of the major areas of legal concern is the expansion of sovereignty by the assertion of jurisdiction. The standard definition of "jurisdiction" is:

> 1. *Law.* The legal power, right, or authority to hear and determine a cause or causes. 2. Authority of a sovereign power to govern or legislate; control. 3. Sphere of authority.[10]

But jurisdiction has taken on a very complicated pattern on reservations over the course of the years.[11] In the criminal jurisdiction area, authority was shared for a time by the federal and tribal governments. Under the Major Crimes Act (23 Stat. 362, 385), the federal government assumed total responsibility for prosecution and punishment of several serious felonies, such as rape, murder, and kidnapping. However, this still left a large range of jurisdiction to the tribes. In 1953, in response to what Congress and some tribes saw as an inability to handle the "crime" problem (and as part of a move to terminate separate Native American entities), Public Law 280 was passed.[12] This Act gave states the power to exercise state jurisdiction on Native American land and over Native Americans, if *the state* desired to assume it. Several did, creating what is now viewed by the lawyers as a blatant invasion of tribal sovereignty. Therefore, a specific goal of many lawyers is to pass legislation to get retrocession of Public Law 280.

During the hearings regarding the Native Bill of Rights,[13] a portion of which related to the alteration of Public Law 280, testimony was almost unanimous in decrying the Act and supporting its repeal:

> Indian groups have urged repeal of Public Law 280 because it authorizes the unilateral application of State law to all tribes without their consent and regardless of their special needs and circumstances. Many tribes have also asserted that tribal laws were unnecessarily preempted by Public Law 280 and that, as a result, they could not govern their tribal communities effectively.[14]

The main argument against Public Law 280 was summarized by Senator Sam Ervin (Dem., N.C.), chairman of the committee, as "that the control by the State, the State having jurisdiction over the tribal lands, over the reservation, would have a tendency to prevent the desirable objective of having the tribe develop its capacity for self-government."[15]

Following the hearings, S. 966 was enacted, creating procedures for resumption of jurisdiction.[16] However, according to the attorneys, this still leaves too much power with the states. In order for a tribe to regain jurisdiction, the state legislature must cooperate. In Washington, lawyers representing Native Americans have not yet been able to win such cooperation. Therefore, since jurisdiction is so vitally important, legal activity continues to be directed toward returning that power to tribal governments, if not through repeal by state legislatures or the victory of a court case, then by overriding federal legislation.[17] The bill most recently presented to the Congress supports the concept of Indian self-government because it requires action solely by the tribe—no permission from the state is needed.

One of the reasons the attorneys perceive jurisdictional resumption as so important is a concern with law and order.[18] It is assumed that if the tribe is to be able to maintain internal order (as it must), then the lawmaking and enforcing authority must be within the tribal unit. Regaining jurisdiction includes the creation of a good criminal justice system.[19] One lawyer explained a portion of the tasks he performs for his Native American clients as follows:

> The law and order code business. There is a stock code. To define crimes is not too difficult. To define punishments is not too difficult. Then we have to create judges and give them responsibilities. Essentially we are making a fundamental legal system. I am presently drafting a law and order code for them.

Similarly, as part of the legal education process, law students aid in the drafting of law and order codes for the various tribes in the Seattle area. Much effort goes into drafting the codes so that each tribe will be able to assert its law and order jurisdiction. Resumption of such powers is a fundamental step in preserving tribal authority and maintaining order.

But Public Law 280 "authorized the various States to assume civil and criminal jurisdiction in the Indian country."[20] Though criminal enforcement plays an important role, civil jurisdiction is perceived to be just as vital. Areas such as adoption, domestic relations, and building and sanitation regulations, are also important areas of concern. One tribal attorney stated that the tribal government would "enforce its laws against Indians and non-Indians alike in the reservation."[21] Thus all problems and all persons should become subject to *tribal* jurisdiction.

Some tribes have adopted what is commonly called an "implied consent" ordinance. This is posted on reservation boundaries and states that all those who enter, by the act of entering, have agreed to abide by all tribal laws and accept tribal jurisdiction. One of the major recommendations of a study of tribal authority sponsored by the Law Enforcement Administration Association (LEAA) was that each tribe adopt such an implied consent law. The study included a draft model ordinance for tribes to utilize.[22] Such actions are designed to lead to complete resumption of jurisdiction—civil and criminal—over all persons, "Indian and non-Indian alike," by the tribal government. Jurisdiction—control over all within certain boundaries—is a very important component of sovereignty.

TAXING AND ZONING

To the attorneys, the power to tax and zone is synonymous with "acting like a government." Though which entity has the authority to tax and zone is a jurisdictional question, it merits special treatment because lawyers representing Native Americans direct much of their activity toward the assertion of these powers. Lawyers' very definition of sovereign includes the taxation and zoning powers.[23] Several subproblems are involved due, for example, to the fact that taxing can be a method of raising revenue or of regulation, or both. For outside governmental agencies to attempt to tax Native Americans is viewed as an invasion of tribal sovereignty. Similarly, zoning holds implications regarding the control of land, and thus, development. Though taxing and zoning are lumped together in the lawyers' minds, they involve different activities and so will be considered separately.

In Washington State, the controversy over taxing has taken a rather peculiar form. Much space is devoted in the news to the sale of cigarettes and liquor by Native Americans. Though it may seem strange to defend such shops with arms, to the Native Americans and their lawyers the issue is one of principle. It revolves around the question of the authority of the state and federal governments to tax Native Americans and their governments. Cigarette sales involve state power. Native American sellers do not pay the state taxes on cigarettes so they can sell them fairly cheaply. The state, continuing to lose revenues, continues to attempt to collect the tax. For example, in a recent legislative session, a bill was presented proposing that a duty on cigarettes be collected upon leaving reservation boundaries. During testimony, one major Native American lawyer, Robert Pirtle, "representing several Indian tribes, opposed the measure on grounds federal law clearly exempts the state from collecting the tax on cigarettes sold on Indian land."[24] If the state could tax, it could regulate or even destroy the Native American businessman.[25]

Though the Washington cases usually involve cigarettes, the principle would apply to any business. For example:

> An enrolled member of the Hoopa Tribe has brought suit in Humboldt Superior Court seeking a declaration that businesses on the reservation are not subject to county and state taxes. . . . The suit contends that the county is without authority to tax or regulate the Indian's business, as businesses on the reservation are regulated by the federal government and the state lacks taxing jurisdiction on the reservation.[26]

Obviously, the lawyers' activity is to insure that one sovereign entity (in this case the state government) cannot invade the land of another sovereign entity (the tribal government) to tax or regulate its citizens. That is a power reserved to the sovereign entity over those boundaries.

In another area, the state excise tax on vehicles, a stronger principle is being asserted. As the lawyer interviewed explained it:

> The tribe has owned vehicles for several years and each year they get a huge excise tax bill from the state. They have known for years they shouldn't have to pay that tax—why should they pay that to the state? We are a government; we shouldn't pay this. . . . The problem came up again this year. It was given to the tribal attorney [a new situation] and they called the Attorney General and the DMV [Department of Motor Vehicles] and made their case that we should have state exempt licenses just like any other government.[27]

The state, of course, did not agree. However, on their attorney's advice and assistance, in order to assert tribal sovereignty and challenge the state's taxing power, the tribe drafted and adopted its own licensing ordinance, issued tribal license plates, and refused to pay the state tax bill. Though this case is presently in the lower courts, it is expected that similar activity will not cease.

The other side of the coin is tribal power to collect taxes for the tribe's benefit. Exemption from state taxation is one vital assertion. But sovereignty also includes the positive power to do, the exercise of power. It seems to be an axiom that governments need revenue and tribal governments are no exception:[28] "Indians have been on a grant economy, and that is worrisome, but now taking control of things." For example, regarding cigarette taxation by the tribes, "tribal taxes collected on the sales are helping Indians take care of their high unemployment and social problems without going to the state for help."[29] The important fact is tribal assertion of the *exclusive* power to tax and collect such revenues for tribal benefit. Similarly, it can be expected that other forms of taxation, such as the licensing ordinance, will also be asserted beyond sovereign immunity to the positive power to tax and, in this case, issue tribal licenses and permits.

Equally important to the attorneys is the power of zoning, which includes the ability to regulate land usage and development possibilities. For example, in discussing the Alaskan case, one attorney noted: "It [the borough] also has zoning power which is *very important* because now oil is going to have to go to the municipal corporation and get permission to locate an oil well someplace, or permission to build a road, etc."[30] Because zoning gives the governing authority control over land use and development, the possibility of destruction by outsiders merely interested in quick profit is forestalled. As one attorney stated: "It [the tribe] must maintain control over the land usage on the reservation."[31]

A report on a recent zoning case deserves quoting at length, since it covers many of the issues the lawyers feel are important:

> A decision on whether the City of Palm Springs has the right to control economic development on the Agua Caliente Reservation through city zoning laws is under consideration by the Ninth Circuit Court, following a hearing here in mid-January . . . The court battles started as soon as the city began enforcing its zoning laws on Indian land. Among other arguments, the city claims that PL 280 gives the right to do this.
>
> As things now stand, both the city and the Agua Calientes have legally constituted planning commissions and separate zoning ordinances. At first it was thought the two commissions could work cooperatively but the city has consistently denied the right of the Indian commission to final approval on matters affecting Indian land . . .
>
> The primary issues the court is being asked to decide are: the legality of including trust land in the city, whether the city zoning ordinances constitute unlawful interference with tribal government, and whether application of the zoning ordinances is inconsistent with federal law . . . Simpson [tribal attorney] also maintains in his brief that the Agua Caliente Tribal Council not only has a right but a duty to control development of their land for the tribe's best interests and they are entitled to do so without state interference. He presents a strong argument that this right was not affected by PL 280. Finally, he argues that the zoning attempts are "inconsistent with performance by the United States as trustee under the supremacy clause of the Federal Constitution."[32]

With the help of expert planning consultants, lawyers engage in the very important activity of drafting zoning ordinances, building and sanitation codes, and procedures for granting zoning variances and building permits.[33] Without such power, Native American governments will lose control of reservation lands to outside encroachments (and, usually, destruction).

In sum, to the lawyers, the very essence of sovereignty lies in the power to tax and zone. Assertion and utilization of taxing and zoning powers includes both the exemption from outside interference and the positive exercise of such powers by the tribal units. To the attorneys, a government must have exclusive control over the land within its boundaries, regardless of ownership, if it is to actually be a government. That control is perceived to be best exercised through taxation and zoning powers.

TREATY RIGHTS AND ECONOMIC RESOURCES

Consistent with and underlying these components of sovereignty is the perceived need to regain control and pursue development of the economic resources of the tribes.[34] According to the attorneys, it is extremely difficult to assert and maintain sovereignty without an economic base. There is a need both for tribal resources and for employment. Political and economic development must be simultaneous. When the "economic situation [is] settled, why, some other things could take place."[35] In order to settle the economic situation, assertion of sovereignty based on treaty rights is required. Questions of jurisdiction and of taxing and zoning are vital to the attempt to increase economic resources. But the assertion of treaty rights goes beyond to the acquisition and control of the natural economic resources (such as water, minerals, timber, game and fish, etc.) available to Native American governments.

In Washington, the most visible and long running controversy centers on the extent of fishing rights.[36] Most lawyers who represent Native Americans there work on a fishing rights case at one time or another.[37] The most recent case, U.S. v. Washington, commonly called the "Boldt decision," is a great victory for the Native Americans and their lawyers.[38] The ruling expands the previously established Native American exemption from state regulation within reservation boundaries to *all* usual and accustomed fishing areas of the "treaty tribes,"[39] and guarantees Native Americans 50% of the catch (following the taking of all fish necessary for ceremonial purposes). As the chairman of the Indian Fisheries Commission stated:[40] "Judge Boldt's decision has given us an economic base where the state has not been able to do that."[41] In other words, all the activity expended in pursuit of treaty rights has been worth it. The Boldt decision has strengthened tribal sovereignty. While it was in the making, Native American political consciousness was raised and tribes were solidified. But most importantly, the prerequisite for maintaining and developing as a tribe—an economic base—is now possible.

Just as important, from the lawyers' viewpoint, is the portion of the Boldt decision which rules that the state cannot regulate any Indian fishing, on or off the reservation. The state cannot interfere with treaty rights; in other words, it must recognize Native American sovereignty in this respect: "The Judge held that the tribe, '*as a government*,' can regulate their fishermen off reservation without any regulation by the state. The real work is implementing the decision. It's ahead." As with taxing and zoning, the point is both to rid the tribe of outside interference and to exercise power positively. But it is also vital to have economic independence and resources. In the fishing rights cases, all these components were combined and won. The right to fish without state regulation and the concomitant power to make and enforce their own fishing regulations for their own members both on and off reservation is a vital recognition of tribal sovereignty. It may also provide income, an economic base which can be utilized to consolidate and further these gains.

It is not only fishing rights that are now being successfully asserted. Much legal activity is presently aimed at claiming or controlling any and all economic resources to which treaty tribes are entitled. Not all tribes have access to fish. The major point in all these cases is to remove state interference and regulation. Treaty rights are so valuable that activity is directed at maintaining them even if the underlying land has been sold or otherwise lost.[42] For example, a recent judicial decision stated that even though the Klamaths had sold their land, their right to hunt and fish in their original domain was not sacrificed.[43] The same point was pressed in a recent Puyallup case. The Court ruled that even though most of the Puyallup reservation has been sold (and is now within the city limits of Tacoma), Native Americans retain the treaty rights to that land. This includes hunting, fishing or selling untaxed cigarettes in Tacoma.[44] Presumably, following the Boldt decision, *tribal* governments would make and enforce regulations covering these treaty rights and the Native Americans engaged in exercising them.

The states, however, are not the only entities interfering with tribes' control over economic resources. Prior to the move for self-determination, the Bureau of Indian Affairs (BIA), under the Secretary of the Interior, negotiated leases with outside parties for exploitation of Native American resources and, in general, managed such resources for the "benefit" of the tribe. Sovereignty, however, requires full control. According to one lawyer, "We are taking over Bureau monies also. The tribe is taking over the local office functions." Another lawyer described one of his functions in terms of a recent issue as follows:

> We also should make sure their [Native Americans'] land is being put to the highest and best use, besides getting the money, i.e., the coal company thing at Wind River. The requirement is that the coal company must get signatures on the leases of all the interested owners, but the land is fractionated so it won't get all the signatures so the BIA would go ahead and approve it. The people find out about it later. But here the Secretary said you have to deal with the Indians. Here the Secretary took the action.

It can be safely assumed that the Secretary of the Interior did not take that action out of the goodness of his heart, but was forced to do so by the Native Americans' lawyers.[45] In line with these lawyers' emphasis on regaining complete control of resources, lease renegotiation by the tribe and its attorneys is an important activity. Here, too, the idea is not only the necessity of possessing the resource base, but tribal control of that base as well.

Economic development is not relegated solely to traditional activities, like fishing and hunting, or to lease renegotiation for better landlord terms. Lawyers are also involved in the development of new industry. For example, one lawyer put together a shake mill and was contracting with logging companies to do timber salvage. Another pointed out that all tribal owned land makes it easier to think about economic development. Since economic development is a vital part of the assertion and maintenance of sovereignty, the lawyer can assist most by performing the "function, close to the lawyer's heart, of expanding the resources available for development and the closely-related function of unraveling the legal complexities that make use of the resources almost impossible."[46] Much of the lawyer's activity, then, centers on economic expansion.

Another vital component, therefore, in the assertion of tribal sovereignty is regaining and maintaining control of economic resources. Economic development is congruent with the activities conducted to gain jurisdictional and taxing and zoning powers: like them, control over and development of economic resources emphasize the necessity for tribal entities to rid themselves of outside interference and control. All such activities in pursuit of sovereignty are perceived by the attorneys as meshing and cumulating so as to make self-determination a reality.

Sovereignty as Power

The meaning of sovereignty as seen through legal practice revolves around the concept of power. To talk about sovereignty in this context is to explore the meaning of power as practiced by the attorneys. Lawyers' activities in pursuit of sovereignty reveal power as the ability to control and to act in vital areas. Sovereignty means control over people through jurisdictional authority and over the land through taxing and zoning. It also means control over economic resources through the pursuit of treaty rights. Power therefore includes control over people, land, and resources both internally and as against others. It embodies an adversary notion which posits foes and balkiness and thus a need for enforcement mechanisms. The notion of power embodied in this practice centers around the ability to control; sovereign rights set one entity's ability to control against another's right to do so.

If sovereignty means control over people, land, and resources, then it covers both political self-determination and economic self-sufficiency. Sometimes economic self-sufficiency is presented as a prerequisite to sovereignty, however: "In order for any minority group to enjoy the full import of its 'rights' in our success-oriented society, it must first obtain economic self-sufficiency."[47] Much of the pursuit of treaty rights is for this very purpose—economic development. Similarly, the point of disputes over taxing and zoning can often be traced to the desire to acquire the ability to develop economically. On the other hand, it is very difficult to make these assertions without a strong governmental base. As one attorney wrote:

> It seems to me that the only way the Tribes are going to be successful

> in dealing with economic activity affecting the reservation, the fishing and hunting issue, or any other issue, is to take on the form of the white man's government and laws and exercise the considerable powers inherent in their own legal-governmental structures in as aggressive a way as is possible. They must push the limits of their tribal powers to govern reservation and off-reservation activities affecting them in the areas in which the reservations exist. They must be on the attack. Otherwise, the state, county, city, local flood control districts—what have you—will take on those powers and functions. The tribes will always be on the defensive—crying over spilled milk as it were—until little by little no rights of self government will exist.

In order to be "on the attack," tribes must believe themselves to be a government and act like one. In the legal mind, sovereignty, or acting like a government, centers around questions of jurisdiction and the ability to tax and zone. Sovereignty therefore requires both political self-determination and economic self-sufficiency.

The question of which comes first is irrelevant: the two go hand in hand. Political self-determination is impossible without an economic base, and economic development is impossible without a strong governmental unit. Political self-determination and economic self-sufficiency are essentially the same as well as interdependent. Their congruence extends to a point where it is difficult for the lawyers to distinguish between a business and a government. The major difference is the additional power of taxing and zoning possessed by the governing unit, making the government a more powerful business unit.

Survival through Sovereignty

Underlying the quest for sovereignty, in all its guises, is the belief that such a quest is the "road to salvation." In this case, salvation means survival of Native Americans as a people. From their lawyers' point of view, such survival is impossible without progress through economic development. One attorney stated, "you have got to develop the land." Another asserted that if Native Americans "don't go outside, learn the white tools, assert yourself, and use the land," they "will not survive." Development of the land and other resources is not possible without control of them. Therefore, sovereignty must be regained. The development of sovereignty as the power to control is necessary in order to progress, which is in turn necessary in order to survive.

Without survival, the overarching goal of a "meaningful choice" would of course be irrelevant. Therefore, the first order of business is survival, which can be accomplished by replacing powerlessness with power, which can in turn be accomplished through the resumption of tribal sovereign rights. The lawyer's part in this is summed up as follows:

> an attempt is made to define certain aspects of the economic development role that reservation lawyers must confront. First, as has been indicated, there is the basic problem, rooted in deeply-held attitudes, of assisting in the definition of the economic development goals; second, there is the function, close to the lawyer's heart, of expanding the resources available for development and the closely-related function of unraveling the legal complexities that make the use of the resources almost impossible. Third, there is the necessity of encouraging the growth of adequate managerial expertise.[48]

The first and second activities form the basis for perceiving the necessity of asserting sovereignty and attempting to gather into the tribal unit as much power as possible. The third role, developing managerial expertise, is the subject of the following chapter.

NOTES

1. "Any discussion of tribal sovereignty begins on a questionable basis because the concept of sovereignty is fundamentally of Western origin. Applying a concept of the supreme and absolute political power of a state to a stateless society such as that which existed among Indians . . . appears to lead to a contradiction in terms." National American Indian Court Judges' Association, *Justice and the American Indian,* in 5 volumes. Washington, D.C.: United States Government Printing Office, 1974, vol. 4, *Examination of the Basis of Tribal Law and Order Authority,* p. 27.

2. See "Chapter I. Sovereignty and the flow of power" in Monroe E. Price, *Law and the American Indian: Readings, Notes and Cases* (New York: Bobbs-Merrill, 1973), pp. 1-183 for the complete history.

3. "Indian tribes . . . still possess their inherent sovereignty excepting only where it has been specifically taken from them, either by treaty or by Congressional Act." IRON CROW v. OGLALA SIOUX, *et al,* 231 F. 2d 89, 94 (8th Cir., 1956) quoted in Jay Vincent White, *Taxing Those They Found Here: An Examination of the Tax Exempt Status of the American Indian* (Albuquerque, N.M.: Univ. of New Mexico for the Institute for the Development of Indian Law, 1972), p. 21.

4. Kenneth W. Johnson, "Sovereignty, citizenship and the Indian," 15 *Arizona Law Review,* 1973, pp. 973-974. This has a very familiar ring because it is the same type of

reasoning and concepts applied to the states' powers as against the federal government.

5. "Legislation permitting Indian self-determination presently awaits congressional approval," *Northwest Indian News,* July 1974, p. 9.

6. "July 8, 1970, Speech on Indian policy," *Weekly Compilation of Presidential Documents.* Washington, D.C.: United States Government Printing Office, 1970, pp. 894-896.

7. Jerry L. Bean, "The limits of tribal sovereignty: the cornucopia of inherent powers," 49 *North Dakota Law Review,* 1973, pp. 303, 331.

8. NAICJA, *Justice,* op. cit., vol. 4, *Examination,* p. 39.

9. Monroe E. Price, "Lawyers on the reservation: some implications for the legal profession," 161 *Law and the Social Order,* 1969, p. 173.

10. *Webster's New Collegiate Dictionary,* 1958 ed., s.v. "jurisdiction."

11. NAICJA, *Justice,* op. cit., vol. 5, *Federal Prosecution of Crimes Committed On Indian Reservations,* p. iii.

12. 25 U.S.C. 1321 et seq. as amended. It will be referred to herein as "Public Law 280."

13. 25 U.S.C. 1301-1331. Sections 1302-1303 are the portions devoted specifically to constitutional rights and will be covered in depth in Chapter 5. However, the name covers a wide variety of measures which were taken up at the same time and therefore are included in the term "Native Bill of Rights," which will be used herein. See Appendix A for the text of the Act.

14. *Hearings before the Subcommittee on Constitutional Rights of the Senate Committee on the Judiciary, on S. 961, S. 962, S. 966, S. 967, S. 968, and S.J. Res. 40 to Protect the Constitutional Rights of American Indians,* 89th Cong., 1st Sess., June, 1965, p. 4. See also pp. 67, 72, 77, 81, 102, and 132 for further examples.

15. Ibid., p. 107.

16. 25 U.S.C. 1321-1323.

17. "Legislation permitting Indian self-determination presently awaits congressional approval," *Northwest Indian News,* July 1974, p. 9.

18. This is not exactly the same as the political slogan, "law and order," of our recent past, but it draws on the same general belief in law in order to maintain order, deriving from the fear of chaos and echoing of the liberal context.

19. "Good" in this context, of course, pertains to the attorneys' perceptions and beliefs concerning the proper forms and methods.

20. *Hearings,* 1965, op. cit., p. 112.

21. Quinault tribal attorney at public hearing before the Grays Harbor County Planning Commission, Montesano, Washington, 8 October 1974; author's observation, no formal record.

22. NAICJA, *Justice,* op. cit., vol. 4, *Examination,* Appendix.

23. "Felix S. Cohen has written, 'One of the powers essential to the maintenance of any government is the power to levy taxes. That this power is an inherent attribute of tribal sovereignty which continues unless withdrawn or limited by treaty or by an act of Congress is a proposition which has never been successfully disputed.' . . . the tribal power to levy taxes . . . is derived from the inherent sovereignty of the Indian tribe," and "it is an essential aspect of the right of self-government for a government to determine not only the level of taxation, but also to determine that there will be no taxation at all. Therefore, a state tax against reservation Indians would constitute an infringement of an essential matter of self-government, namely, the right of the tribe *not* to levy taxes." White, op. cit., pp. 18-19 and 49, respectively.

24. Gordon Schultz, "Repeal asked for law aiding Indian sales of cigarettes," Seattle *Post Intelligencer,* 18 February 1974, p. A8.

25. As an old legal maxim states: "the power to tax is the power to destroy." McCULLOCH v. MARYLAND, 17 U.S. (4 Wheat.) 316 (1819).

26. "Indian sues for relief against taxes," *Wassaja*, April-May 1974, p. 16.

27. This story was related to me by Attorney 1; however, a short while later it was confirmed by a filler-type newspaper article regarding the arrest of a tribal member for driving a tribally licensed vehicle, a misdemeanor. Eventually, however, I am sure this issue will reach the state and federal courts since the principle involved is deemed vital by the lawyers.

28. "History aside, there is the practical need for revenue which is generated by any taxation, and this need is great both to the state and to the Indian." White, op. cit., p. 6.

29. Gordon Schultz, op. cit. Such revenue can be impressive, for example, a recent increase in tribal tax on cigarettes was expected to boost "the tribe's annual cigarette tax revenue from its average $750,000 to more than $3 million." ("Indians smoking over cigarette tax," Seattle *Post Intelligencer*, 25 August 1974, p. A9.)

30. "It" in this case is a borough, which is a municipal corporation possible under the Alaskan State Constitution. It is a very strong home-rule type of local government which must be initiated and then adopted by the people of an area. In this case, it is 95% native, as the borough the attorney was discussing was one instituted by the natives of the Alaskan North Slope. At that time, it was assumed it would always be native controlled and the strength of borough powers would work to the natives' advantage in preserving their land.

31. Quinault tribal attorney at public hearing before the Grays Harbor County Planning Commission, Montesano, Washington, 8 October 1974; author's observation, no formal record.

32. "Palm Springs Indians in court to protect rights," *Wassaja*, January-February 1975, p. 15. The Quinault Tribe is in a similar situation, leading to the hearing cited above.

33. Quinault tribal attorney, County Planning Commission Hearing.

34. This is an emphasis more blatant with the attorneys since these resources can be and often are perceived as cultural and religious artifacts. For example, the recent fishing rights decision, 384 F. Supp. 312, 520 F. 2d 676, cert. denied 96 S. Ct. 877, hereinafter called "the Boldt decision," recognizes this function in the case of salmon, so that the division for profit making purposes between non-Indians and Indians takes place *following* the taking of sufficient fish to satisfy the needs of the Indians for ceremonial purposes. In other words, these natural phenomena were perceived to be part of the social whole and *not* as an *economic* resource whose value was monetary.

35. *Hearings*, 1965, op. cit., p. 715.

36. Most treaties concluded between Native Americans of the future Washington State and the United States Government contained the following language: "The right of taking fish at all usual and accustomed grounds and stations is secured to said Indians in common with all citizens of the territory" (e.g., Charles J. Kappler, comp., *Indian Affairs: Laws and Treaties, Vol. II: Treaties*. Washington, D.C.: United States Government Printing Office, 1904, pp. 661 and 719). This phrase has been the center of controversy since that time.

37. Such work has taken a variety of forms. For example, attorneys 1, 3, 8 and 9 were involved in the bringing of earlier, preliminary fishing rights cases. Others, such as attorneys 11A-D, are doing the subsidiary work necessary under the Boldt decision to establish which tribes are "treaty tribes" and thus fall under the decision, and which geographic locations were "usual and accustomed" fishing grounds of which tribes. This obviously necessitates contact between all tribes and their attorneys as the details are worked out.

38. This case has now gone through the appeals process. See footnote for the full

citation. However, it was and is being responded to as the original trial court presented it, i.e., as the Boldt decision.

39. The determination of treaty tribes is also important for internal tribal reasons having to do with tribal enrollment. See the subsection "Civil Rights" in Chapter 5.

40. The Indian Fisheries Commission is the body established pursuant to the Boldt decision whose purpose is the regulation of the statewide Indian fishery.

41. KOMO TV, "Viewpoint." Seattle, Washington, 29 September 1974, Forrest Kinley, Chairman of the Indian Fisheries Commission, guest.

42. John Clinebell and Manuel Quintana, "Puyallup tribe: the theft of the Puyallup land base," *National Lawyers' Guild Law Student Indian Summer Project: Project Report* (Seattle, Washington, 1973), pp. 3-63, documents and describes one such case of Indian land loss.

43. "Oregon loses its case," *Wassaja,* November-December 1974, p. 6.

44. These are, at present, theoretical possibilities. The main issue was the right to fish at the mouth of the Puyallup River, which is Commencement Bay and the Port of Tacoma. See "Supreme Court settles it: Tacoma within Puyallup Reservation," *Northwest Indian News,* December 1974, p. 1.

45. See Richard Coleman, "Cheyennes favored in coal leasing dispute,"*Northwest Indian News,* July 1974, pp. 1 and 9.

46. Price, "Lawyers on the reservation," p. 183.

47. Roger L. Tuttle, "Economic development of Indian lands," 5 *University of Richmond Law Review,* 1971, p. 319.

48. Price, "Lawyers on the reservation," pp. 183-184.

Self-Determination and Subordination
The Past, Present, and Future of American Indian Governance

Rebecca L. Robbins

> [V]iewed in their totality, as one among many alternative routes that the course of Indian-white...history could have followed, the present status of [American Indians] presents an extraordinary spectacle of a variety of small cultural enclaves that have maintained better than anyone might have expected their culture, their aspirations, their land, and their autonomy after being overwhelmed by a tidal wave of invaders.
>
> Wilcomb Washburn
> Smithsonian Historian, 1985

> How do we make permanent the understanding that [American Indian nations] are political entities? We are more than just unique little cultures. We are tired of educating the Congress and the government about this basic relationship.
>
> LaDonna Harris
> Comanche, 1986

The key to understanding the social, economic, and political status of contemporary Native North America rests in determining the form by which it is governed. Traditionally, the indigenous nations of this continent were entirely autonomous and self-regulating, having perfected highly complex and sophisticated governmental forms long before the European invasion of the hemisphere.[1] Indigenous governance in the Americas was far more refined than that evidenced across the Atlantic, at least until some point well into the 19th century. Certain of the structures and principles of indigenous governance, notably those drawn from the Haudenosaunee (Iroquois) Confederacy—consisting of the Mohawk, Onondaga, Seneca, Cayuga, Oneida, and Tuscarora nations, all located within the present state of New York and adjoining areas of Canada—were so advanced that they were consciously utilized as a primary model upon which the U.S. Constitution was formulated and the federal government created.[2]

As researcher Sharon O'Brien has framed the matter:

> [S]ometime between A.D. 1000 and 1500, a great, visionary leader, Deganawidah, proposed that warring tribes form a confederacy—The Great Peace (known by whites as the Iroquois League, or Iroquois Confederacy) remains in existence. It was founded on the principles Deganewidah and his kinspeople cherished and nurtured: freedom, respect, tolerance, consensus, and brotherhood. These values contrasted sharply with the principles which underlay European governments at the time. In the 1500s, European governments were based on notions such as authoritarian rule by monarchs and the use of force and coercion to bring about unquestioning obedience.[3]

Under the terms and spirit of the *Ne Gayaneshagowa*, or "Great Binding Law," to which all parties pledged themselves:

> [T]he confederacy's constitution provided for a governing council of fifty civil chiefs, the Council of Fifty [each member of which was appointed by, and could be recalled by, elder women known as Clan Mothers]. Each of the fifty seats was named, ranked, and associated with a particular duty or responsibility...Each year the Onondagas called together the Council of Fifty to discuss matters of mutual concern and resolve differences peacefully. Matters of interest strictly to one [nation] were handled by that [nation] individually, but anything involving two or more [nations] was discussed by the Council of Fifty...[T]he Onondagas were responsible for confirming [any] decision or subjecting it to further discussion. Ideally, all decisions were unanimous. All council members were to be of "one heart, one mind, one law." The system gave all [six] nations equal power.[4]

Nor were the Iroquois the only such example. With regard to the powerful Muscogee (Creek) Confederacy of the present states of Georgia and Alabama, O'Brien delineates an extremely complex structure balancing such matters as age and gender roles, civic and insular affairs, as well as secular and spiritual matters, through a "three-tiered system of advisors" that apportioned powers and responsibilities throughout society:

> Harmony was so highly valued among the Muscogees that a special system was devised to maintain it even when a major issue could not be resolved to everyone's satisfaction. If a member or several members of a *talwa* [community] continued to disagree with the majority on a policy, they were free to move on and establish their own community, with the support—not the enmity—of those whose *talwa* they were leaving. When a dissident group established a new town (and also when a neighboring [nation] joined the Muscogee Confederacy), an ember from one of the mother [original] *talwas* was used to start the fire of the new settlement as a symbol of continuity and unity.[5]

The Lakota (Sioux) Nation of the northern Great Plains region, an entity that actually constituted a functioning confederation rather than a single homogeneous socio-political unit, developed an intricate localized structure known as the *tiyospaye* within which women exercised considerable practical influence by virtue of owning all real property and elders maintained not only an active advisory capacity with regard to the conduct of younger executives, but effective veto power over their decisions. The *tiyospaye* was manifested upward, to the national level. From there, this decentralized and inherently inclusive form of organization was inherently reflected by all seven participant nations—the Oglala, Sicangu (Brûlé), Minneconjou, Hunkpapa, Itazipco (Sans Arcs), Sihasapa (Blackfeet), and Oohinunpa (Two Kettles)—with regard to their overall participation in the confederacy.[6]

Many comparable examples of this refinement and sophistication were exhibited by traditional American Indian governments. These include the forms and structures evident among the various Pueblos of present day New Mexico and Arizona,[7] the Yaqui Confederation of the Sonoran Desert region,[8] those of the Yakimas and other nations of the Great Basin area,[9] and others. The point is that the indigenous peoples of North America required lessons in democratic governance from no one. To the contrary, their precontact attainments in this regard not only informed the establishment of the first modern democracy achieved by the European tradition (the United States), but they also exerted a noticeable influence on French Enlightenment philosophers such as Rousseau, whose thinking provided considerable impetus to the French Revolution.[10] To a certain extent at least, the same can be said with regard to such post-enlightenment European political thinkers as Karl Marx and Frederick Engels.[11]

Implications of U.S.-Indian Treaties

There can be no doubt that the United States formally recognized the fully sovereign national status and character of North American indigenous governments during the period following the American Revolution.[12] This was undoubtedly due in large part to the fact that native nations had held—and in many respects continued to hold for some time—the balance of military power all along the new republic's western border.[13] Additionally, as Vine Deloria, Jr., has pointed out, the Continental Congress, representing as it did an outlaw state, was desperate to establish its ability to comport itself responsibly and in accordance with the customs and conventions of diplomatic law.[14] Indian nations, many of which had already been formally recognized through treaties as legitimate sovereignties by various European Crowns, were in more of a position to recognize the legitimacy of the U.S. than the other way around.[15]

Correspondingly, U.S. relations with American Indians were legally restricted—in precisely the same fashion that relations were restricted with the European powers—to the level of interchange between the federal executive and various indigenous governments.[16] This is to say, the relationship was formally cast as being government-to-government in nature, a matter abundantly reflected in the fact that the U.S. Senate ratified not fewer than 371 separate treaties with Native American governments between 1778 and 1871.[17] These were complemented by a myriad of international agreements, unratified treaties, and other instruments of foreign affairs extending into the early 20th century.[18] At least as late as the Supreme Court's 1903 *Lonewolf v. Hitchcock* decision, federal authorities were still sending *de facto* treaty commissions into the field to negotiate with native leaders as the heads of nations entirely separate from the United States.[19]

Insofar as the federal government is constitutionally prohibited from entering into treaty relationships with any entity other than another fully sovereign national government, it follows that each treaty entered into by the United States with an Indian nation served the purpose of conveying formal federal recognition that the Indian nation involved was indeed a nation within the true legal and political meanings of the term. Further, given that these treaties remain on the books and thus are binding upon both parties, it follows that North American indigenous peoples continue to hold a clear legal entitlement—even under U.S. law—to conduct themselves as completely sovereign nations unless they themselves freely determine that things should be otherwise.[20] For this reason, they have been described as constituting "the nations within" the United States.[21] The native nations of North America are not presently allowed, however, to comport themselves as such.

The current reality is that American Indian governance within the United States has been converted into something very different from that which traditionally prevailed, or anything remotely resembling the exercise of national self-determination. Through the unilateral assertion of U.S. "plenary power" over Indian affairs, a doctrine forcefully articulated in the 1886 *United States v. Kagama* case, the status of indigenous national governments has been subordinated to that of the federal government. In other words, the sovereignty of native nations has been diminished without their consent to approximately the same level as that enjoyed by the states of the union. Under legislation such as Public Law 280, which emerged during the 1950s, the status of Indian nations has been in many cases again unilaterally lowered by the United States, this time to a level below that of the states, placing the indigenous governments affected by the change in approximately the same posture as counties.[22] Today, in a number of areas such as southern California, counties and even municipalities have extended jurisdictional prerogatives over indigenous people and their territories, eliminating the last pretenses that native peoples are intended to retain any residue of genuine sovereignty at all.[23]

In sum, it is accurate to observe, as has been noted elsewhere, that American Indian nations within the geography presently claimed by the United States exist in a condition of "internal colonization."[24] That is, their rights to self-government have been usurped by a foreign power, in this case one that claims their very homelands as its own, in order for that power to benefit from the resources their lands provide. Any serious effort on the part of Native Americans to change these circumstances will therefore necessarily assume the form of decolonization struggles.[25] And, as is usually the case in such situations, the process by which the colonial structure was created sheds considerable light on the means and methods that will necessarily attend such expressions of indigenous self-determination in the years ahead.

Effects of the "Indian Wars"

Once the United States had established and consolidated itself to the point where it could tip the balance of military power to its own advantage, it began a 100 year series of armed conflicts popularly known as the "Indian Wars." As Creek/Cherokee scholar Ward Churchill and others have observed, this description is a misnomer: "The term is revealing in itself. There is no historical record of any war between [Indian nations] and the United States which was initiated by the Indians. Each known outbreak of open warfare was predicated upon documentable invasion of defined (or definable) Indian lands by U.S. citizenry. The defensive nature of Indian participation in these wars is thus clear. Logically, they should thus be termed 'settler's wars' or, more accurately, 'wars of conquest.'"[26] It was mainly through this extended series of unprovoked assaults upon indigenous peoples that the United States expanded from its original territorality along the Eastern Seaboard to encompass the area now comprising the "lower forty-eight" states.

Given the intended outcomes of this warfare on the part of the aggressors, it should come as no surprise that the United States often took native governments—and leaders upon which the effective functioning of these governments were perceived as depending—as primary targets.[27] At times such tactics took the approach of contriving situations in which individuals such as the great Shawnee leader, Tecumseh, who very nearly created a confederation of indigenous nations extending along the western U.S. border from Canada to the Gulf of Mexico, could be killed in battle.[28] On other occasions, outright assassination was employed, as in the cases of the Seminole leader, Osceola, in 1838,[29] and the Lakota "recalcitrants" Tesunke Witko (Crazy Horse) and Tatanka Yatanka (Sitting Bull), in 1877 and 1890, respectively.[30]

In still other instances, Indian leaders who had opposed the U.S. were executed after they had been defeated, as when President Abraham Lincoln ordered the mass hanging of thirty-eight Santee Dakota warriors at Mankato, Minnesota, in 1862.[31] A quarter-century later this was still going on, as is witnessed by the hanging—lynching would be a better word—of Kintpuash (Captain Jack), head of the northern California Modoc resistance, in 1873.[32] In addition, the federal government adopted a policy of imprisoning those Indian leaders who refused to bow to non-Indian authority in locations far from their lands and people. In this connection, the examples of Hinmaton Yalatkit (Chief Joseph) of the Nez Percé,[33] and Gothalay (Geronimo), the Chiricahua Apache "hold-out," spring readily to mind.[34]

The purpose of physically eliminating the strongest and most effective patriots among Native American leaders in nation after nation went beyond simply undercutting these nations' abilities to engage successfully in defensive war. The United States, with an eye to the aftermath, quickly developed a concomitant policy of recognizing or appointing "Indian leaders" of its own—usually individuals with little or no authority deriving from their own people, but upon whom the federal government could rely to comply with its needs and desires—to "represent the interests" of indigenous nations.[35] Such persons—many of whom were disgraced within their own societies by virtue of having become addicted to alcohol (a conscious U.S. effort against Indians that adds up to an early experiment in chemical warfare[36]), and most of whom were bribed by federal authorities—were routinely trotted out at treaty time to "accept" terms and provisions that had either been rejected by their nations or of which the latter remained unaware until after the fact.[37] These same traitorous individuals were typically installed as "official liaisons" to Army and Bureau of Indian Affairs (BIA) officials once their respective nations had been militarily defeated and consigned to administration by "Indian Agents."[38]

Plainly, an integral aspect of U.S. prosecution of wars against the native peoples of North America was the deliberate and systematic destruction, not only of indigenous governments, but of the Indian ability to self-govern in any meaningful way. Nations defeated in war possess an inherent ability to reconstitute themselves on their own terms afterwards, unless the victorious power undertakes concrete steps to prevent this from occurring. It is customary, and in many circumstances legally required, that the former rather than latter course be followed, even when "territorial adjustment" is the basis of conflict. The U.S. approach to "Indian fighting" was all along something entirely different. From the outset, it was designed to preclude any sort of autonomous reconstitution on the part of the vanquished. Instead, it consciously set the stage for the perpetual colonial subordination of Native America to the United States.

From Sovereignty to Subordination

By the mid-1880s, virtually all American Indians within the United States had ceased military resistance against U.S. expansion in North America.[39] In most cases, the native peoples west of the Mississippi River had withdrawn into portions of their traditional homelands reserved for their exclusive use and occupancy by the provisions of treaty agreements with the federal government; those originally resident to areas east of the river had also largely been relocated to the "permanent Indian territory" of Oklahoma by that point.[40] Typically, in exchange for their agreement to cease armed resistance and legally cede the remainder of their land base, these reserved territories were guaranteed permanent protection from further abridgement by non-Indians.[41] The right to native self-governance within these residual territories was also implicit to, and sometimes spelled out within, these arrangements.[42] Under such conditions, it seems likely that many—if not most—indigenous peoples might well have recovered their equilibrium, eventually reestablishing their collective self-sufficiency and vitality in the reservation context.

In 1885, however, the United States began to move in a serious fashion to eliminate all vestiges of genuine sovereignty among indigenous nations, bringing them directly within its own polity for the first time. The process started in earnest with the "Major Crimes Act" through which the federal government unilaterally extended its jurisdiction over felonies occurring among Indians in Indian territories, displacing traditional jurisprudence in such matters.[43] This initiated a process by which the United States ultimately enacted some 5,000 separate statutes usurping native jurisdiction—both criminal and civil—on reservations at every level.[44] The Major Crimes Act was followed, in 1887, by the General Allotment Act, which unilaterally negated Indian control over land tenure patterns within the reservations, forcibly replacing the traditional mode of collective use and occupancy with the Anglo-Saxon system of individual property ownership.[45] Not only was the cohesion of indigenous society dramatically disrupted by allotment, and traditional governmental prerogatives preempted, but it led directly to the loss of some two-thirds of all acreage still held by native people at the time it was passed.

The Allotment Act set forth that each American Indian recognized as such by the federal government would receive an allotment of land according to the following formula: 160 acres for family heads, eighty acres for single persons over eighteen years of age and orphans under eighteen, and forty acres for children under eighteen. "Mixed blood" Indians received title by fee simple patent; "full bloods" were issued "trust patents," meaning they had no control over their allotted property for a period of twenty-five years. Once each person recognized by the government as belonging to a given Indian nation had received his or her allotment, the "surplus" acreage was "opened" to non-Indian homesteading or conversion into the emerging system of national parks, forests, and grasslands. Thus, the potential for a resumption of Indian self-sufficiency was largely eliminated, setting the stage for a condition of permanent economic dependency among all native people within the United States.[46]

The purpose of all this was "assimilation," as federal policymakers described their intentions, or—to put the matter more unabashedly—to bring about the destruction and disappearance of American Indian peoples as such.[47] In the words of Francis E. Leupp, Commissioner of Indian Affairs from 1905 through 1909, the Allotment Act in particular should be viewed as a "mighty pulverizing engine for breaking up the tribal mass" which stood in the way of complete Euroamerican hegemony in North America.[48] Or, to quote Indian Commissioner Charles Burke a decade later, "[I]t is not desirable or consistent with the general welfare to promote [American Indian national] characteristics and organization."[49] Hence, one little-noted aspect of the General Allotment Act was that it required each "qualified" Indian (i.e., those of "mixed blood"), in order to receive the deed to his or her parcel of land, to accept U.S. citizenship, a circumstance which served to further confuse the already garbled identities and loyalties of recipients.[50] In 1924, Congress completed this process by passing a "clean-up" measure, the Indian Citizenship Act, unilaterally conferring American citizenship upon all native people—whether they desired it or not—who had not otherwise been nationalized as part of the U.S. population.[51]

A bit earlier, during the winter of 1919-20, a team of geologists employed by the Standard Oil Corporation had been exploring a section of the Navajo Reservation in northeastern Arizona. Deciding in 1921 that local rock formations suggested the probability of oil and natural gas deposits in the area, the group requested the U.S. Bureau of Indian Affairs (BIA) superintendent on the reservation to convene the traditional Diné (Navajo) government for purposes of authorizing the drilling of test holes to determine whether and to what extent the minerals were present.[52] Much to the surprise and consternation of both Standard and the BIA, the Diné elders declined, unanimously and unequivocally. This "unacceptable" outcome was bureaucratically altered by Commissioner Burke in early 1923 through promulgation of a set of *Regulations Relating to the Navajo Tribe of Indians.* This was done, according to Burke, in order to "promote better administration of the Navajo Tribe of Indians in conformity to law and particularly as to matters in which the Navajo tribe at large is concerned, such as oil, gas, coal and other mineral deposits."

The commissioner followed up by appointing, without consulting the Diné people themselves, what he termed a "Navajo Grand Council," composed entirely of young, hand-picked, white-educated Indians, and from which the traditional Diné leadership was excluded altogether. When the new council met for the first time on July 7, 1923, it immediately acknowledged that its primary allegiance was to the U.S. rather than to its own ostensible constituency. Its first act was to sign the leasing instruments that provided a veneer of legitimacy to the federal government's bringing of major corporate interests onto the reservation for the first time, over the express objections of the traditional Diné council.[53] Thereafter, the federally created council was the only "governmental" entity with which Washington would deal directly or recognize as holding authority on the reservation, a matter that has led to sustained profits for U.S. energy corporations and environmental catastrophe for the Diné themselves.[54]

"Reorganization"

During the early 1920s, a special "Committee of One Hundred" individuals selected by the interior secretary to study the U.S. "Indian problem" because of Indians' "prominence in the nation's civic, business and scholarly life" found the ongoing existence of indigenous peoples in North America to constitute an "intolerable financial burden" upon the United States. The committee recommended that dissolution of native nations and final absorption of their members into the U.S. polity be completed as rapidly as possible, allowing only for such restraints in timing and methods as might "be imposed by humane considerations."[55] These conclusions were contradicted, in 1928, by a study conducted by Lewis Meriam and his associates at the Institute for Government Research, a private think tank, which concluded that efficient utilization of mineral resources within reservation areas—by which the country might not only "recover the costs associated with its support" of the formerly self-sufficient native peoples it had so flagrantly dispossessed while creating its own economy, but turn a tidy profit as well—was being precluded by the fragmentation of land title inherent to the allotment policy.

The Meriam Report therefore recommended quite strongly that residual Indian lands (and thus "tribes") be maintained in block form, and that they be "governed" by outright corporate boards deriving their authority from, and being answerable to, the secretary of the interior.[56] From this perspective, the council prototype developed at the Navajo Reservation revealed such promise for the "beneficial" management of Indian land and resources that Meriam suggested its essential structure be replicated on as many reservations as possible. Meriam's recommendations quickly acquired powerful endorsers, both in Washington, D.C. and throughout the U.S. financial/industrial community. This became all the more true after the 1929 collapse of the stock market and onset of the Great Depression. Consequently, in 1934, Congress passed the Indian Reorganization Act (IRA), also called the "Wheeler-Howard Act," after its sponsors, Senator Burton K. Wheeler and Representative Edgar Howard.

The IRA incorporated the Meriam council/board model of "tribal governance," and required that these be based, not in native traditions, but in "constitutions" and/or "charters" drafted by the BIA. All decisions of any consequence (in thirty-three separate areas of consideration) rendered by these "tribal councils" were made "subject to the approval of the Secretary of Interior or his delegate," the commissioner of Indian affairs. Worst of all, in some ways, the IRA decreed an electoral form of "democratic majority rule" which was and still is structurally antithetical to the consensual form of decision making and selection of leadership integral to most indigenous traditions.[57] The Reorganization Act was thus designed to undercut the unity marking traditional native societies, replacing it with a permanent divisiveness: "To vote for someone means you have to vote against somebody else," as Hopi leader David Monongye has put it.[58]

The democratic facade the federal government wished to foster through imposition of the IRA—a matter embodied in a requirement that members of each specific Indian nation be polled to determine whether or not they wished to be reorganized—caused certain problems in its implementation. Despite the allocation of an annual sum of $250,000 in "education funds" to assist the new governments in presenting an incentive to their ostensible constituents to go along with reorganization, as well as establishment of a $10 million revolving fund from which these governments might borrow for purposes of engaging in "cooperative ventures" with non-Indian corporations gearing up to do increased business in Indian Country (this was described as "economic development"), grassroots native resistance to the law was immediate, outspoken, and sustained. As the Cahuilla historian Rupert Costo recounts, after first quoting at length from the Oklahoma Quapaw traditional government rejecting the IRA and enforcement of its 1833 treaty with the United States:

> In hearings before the House of Representatives, the Flathead [of Montana asserted that] instead of new legislation they believed it would be better to insist on sovereign rights and treaty rights...On May 17, 1934, in hearings before the Senate, the...Yakima nation [of Washington], in a statement signed by their

chiefs and councilmen, said "We feel the best interests of the Indians can be preserved by the continuance of treaty laws and carried out in conformity with the treaty of 1855 entered into by the fathers of some of the undersigned chiefs and Governor Stevens of the territory of Washington." Now these are only a few of the examples of some of the testimony given by Indian witnesses and most of the tribes. Many refused to even consider the IRA and rejected it outright.[59]

As the Oneidas put it in a resolution presented to IRA sponsor Wheeler on April 17, 1934:

> The Oneida nation firmly adheres to the terms of the Treaty of Canandaigua between our nation, our confederacy, and the U.S. on November 11, 1794. [We insist] that the laws of the U.S., the acts on Congress, and the customs and usages of the Oneida nation are the controlling provisions of Oneida basic law...the exponents of such basic law and the guides for the sachems, chiefs, headmen and warriors [are all bound to comply with the treaty].[60]

Such "recalcitrance" forced Indian Commissioner John Collier, who had championed the bill, to engage in extraordinary deception and manipulation of the referendum process in order to see it "accepted" by Indian nations. "Collier was vindictive and overbearing," Costo says. "He tolerated no dissent, neither from his staff nor from the tribes. He was a rank opportunist in politics, at once espousing and then rejecting one or another proposal. He did not hesitate to use informants and the FBI against Indian opponents. He habitually tampered with the truth in his dealings with Indians."[61] Recalling the struggle over the IRA in his own southern California region, Costo observes that:

> In California, at Riverside, forty tribes were assembled. All but three voted against the proposed bill. Collier then reported [to Congress] that most of the California tribes were for [it]. The historical record was falsified...We were outraged at the provisions of the [IRA]...It is a curious fact that in all the ten meetings held with Indians across the country, in not one meeting was there a copy of the proposed legislation put before the people. We were asked to vote on the so-called explanations. The bill itself was withheld. We were told we need not vote but the meetings were only to discuss the explanations. In the end, however, we were required to vote. And I suppose you could call this maneuvering self-rule. I call it fraud.[62]

In the end, 258 separate referenda were conducted, exclusive of the Indian nations of Oklahoma and Alaska, which were reorganized *en masse* (and without consent) in an amendment to the IRA passed in 1936.[63] By 1938, 189 Indian nations (encompassing some 130,000 people) acquiesced to reorganization, while seventy-seven (representing approximately 90,000) rejected it outright, usually as a gross violation of their treaty-guaranteed sovereignty.[64] To obtain even this limited result, Collier had had to engage in a heavy-handed manipulation of the referenda themselves:

> Although the IRA seemed to provide for tribal ratification of its terms, it did so in a way that effectively negated [Indian] wishes. Tribal members could vote to

> either accept or reject the IRA, but all abstentions (that is, the "votes" of anyone who didn't vote) were counted as votes in favor of the IRA...On several reservations, such as the Nez Percé and Coeur d'Alene [in Idaho], the majority of those voting voted against the act, but since abstentions were counted as votes for the act, it was ratified. On the Hopi Reservation [in Arizona], for example, traditionalists simply refused to recognize the BIA's authority, and thus most Hopis boycotted the election. Refusing to recognize the mass abstention for what it was—absolute nonacceptance of the act—the BIA counted the Hopi vote as favoring the act. Any [native nation] that failed to hold an election automatically came under the act's provisions.[65]

On the Pine Ridge (Oglala Lakota) Reservation in South Dakota, there weren't enough abstentions to carry the day against those voting against the IRA. It was subsequently discovered that a sufficient number of dead people had cast ballots to provide a pretext for ratification. Even after this was established to have been the case, the ratification was described as "binding" upon the Oglalas.[66] The same sort of situation pertained to the reorganization of the Cheyenne River (Minneconjou and Itazipko Lakota) Reservation and elsewhere.[67] Collier's most significant setback occurred when the Navajo Nation—outraged at the ruthlessness of a stock reduction program instituted against them by the BIA under provision of the 1934 Taylor Grazing Act (48 *Stat.* 1269), another piece of legislation advocated by the Indian commissioner—voted overwhelmingly to reject reorganization.[68] The point was largely moot, however, insofar as the Navajos had already undergone de facto reorganization by virtue of the earlier Grand Council imposition.

By 1940, the prevailing system of colonial governance on American Indian reservations was largely in place. Only the outbreak of World War II slowed the pace of corporate exploitation, a matter that retarded initiation of maximal "development" activities until the early 1950s.[69] By then, the questions concerning federal and corporate planners of the IRA-orientation had become somewhat technical: what to do with those indigenous nations which had refused reorganization? How to remove the portion of Indian population on even the reorganized reservations whose sheer physical presence served as a barrier to wholesale strip mining and other profitable enterprises anticipated by the U.S. business community? Such preoccupations overlapped noticeably with the desires of politicians and other individuals and organizations who remained committed to bringing about the outright and final disappearance of native peoples as a whole.

This has led to an ongoing tension and debate in federal and corporate sectors of the U.S. elites between those (often described as "assimilators" or "terminators") who wish to see an ultimate and "uncomplicated" consolidation of the country's internal territorial and politico-economic integrity on the one hand, and those (typically referred to as "IRA liberals") who perceive advantages to maintaining Indian nations as distinct, colonized entities on the other. Neither faction allowed in any way for realization of any aspect of the long and loudly voiced desire of most Indians to resume genuine self-government and other expressions of autonomous national life. The choice offered native people was and is either to endorse their own colonization by aligning themselves with the liberals, or to risk total obliteration by engaging in what amounted to national liberation struggles.

Termination and Relocation

In December 1952, the BIA submitted a list to Congress enumerating specific American Indian nations it felt were "ready to undergo...complete termination of all federal services" and "an end to the exercise of federal trust responsibility over their affairs."[70] Promoted as a measure to "liberate American Indian tribes from federal domination," the concept of termination was really intended ultimately to "do away with tribes [and their] reservations," at least those which had not been amenable to conversion into resource and profit generators for the U.S. economy.[71] Designated by the BIA as being ripe for immediate dissolution were the Nez Percé and Coeur d'Alene, the Osage in Oklahoma, the Menominee in Wisconsin, the Salish and Kootenai (Flathead) in Idaho, the Turtle Mountain Anishinabé (Chippewa) in North Dakota, the Six Nations and others in New York, the Potawatomi and other nations in Iowa, the Klamath and other nations in Oregon, and all the nations located within western Washington, Texas, Michigan, Kansas, Nebraska, and Louisiana.[72]

The 1952 BIA proposal was nothing new. In May 1943, Oklahoma Senator Elmer Davis had introduced a report, S-310, calling for the unilateral abrogation of all treaties with Indian nations, withdrawal of federal recognition of their existence, and abolition of the BIA itself.[73] Davis was publicly joined in these sentiments by other legislators such as Senator Dennis Chavez of New Mexico and Idaho's Burton K. Wheeler, cosponsor of the IRA.[74] With the resignation of John Collier as Indian commissioner in January 1945, the search began for a replacement who would be able to carry out such a policy. This resulted, in May 1950—after trial runs with William A. Brophy (1945-49) and John Ralph Nichols (1949-50)—in the appointment of Dillon S. Myer, former head of the wartime internment program directed against Japanese Americans.[75] Myer quickly set himself to the task of reorganizing the BIA to oversee the destruction of targeted native societies, once and for all.[76]

The culmination of this process occurred with the approval of House Concurrent Resolution 108, otherwise known as the "Termination Act," on August 1, 1953. Actually, this is something of a misnomer insofar as H.C.R. 108 did not itself bring about termination. Instead it called for enactment of specific statutes that would terminate selected Indian nations.[77]

> Major [termination] legislation affecting particular [nations] came out of the second session of the Eighty-third Congress in 1954. Among the [nations] involved were the comparatively large and wealthy Menominee of Wisconsin and the Klamath of Oregon—both owners of extensive timber resources. Also passed were acts to terminate...the Indians of western Oregon, small Paiute bands in Utah, and the mixed bloods of the Uintah and Ouray Reservations. Approved, too, was legislation to transfer administrative responsibility for the Alabama and Coushatta Indians to the state of Texas...Early in the first session

of the Eighty-fourth Congress, bills were submitted to [terminate the] Wyandotte, Ottawa, and Peoria [nations] of Oklahoma. These were finally enacted early in August of 1956, a month after passage of legislation directing the Colville Confederated Tribes of Washington to come up with a termination plan of their own...During the second administration of President Dwight D. Eisenhower, Congress enacted only three termination bills relating to specific [nations] or groups. Affected by this legislation were the Choctaw of Oklahoma, for whom the termination process was never completed, the Catawba of South Carolina, and the Indians of the southern California *rancherias*.[78]

All told, 109 indigenous nations, or portions of nations, were unilaterally dissolved by congressional action between 1953 and 1958.[79] Concomitantly, Congress passed the earlier-mentioned Public Law 280 in 1954, increasingly placing unterminated reservations under state jurisdictional authority, and, in 1956, Public Law 959, known as the "Relocation Act." The latter corresponded closely to a steadily diminishing congressional allocation of funds to the meeting of federal obligations to unterminated Indians, a matter resulting in the deterioration of such things as educational and health services (already very poor) on the reservations, spiraling unemployment among reservation Indians (already the highest of any population group), and a net decline in reservation per capita income (already the lowest in North America).[80]

P.L. 959 provided funding with which to underwrite moving expenses, establishment of a new residence, and a brief period of job training to any Native American willing to relocate "voluntarily" to one of a number of federally approved urban centers. Under the circumstances, this led to a sudden mass exodus of Indians from their reserved territories, with some 35,000 being relocated to such places as Los Angeles, San Francisco, Denver, Phoenix, Minneapolis, Seattle, Boston, and Chicago during the years 1957-59 alone.[81] Despite early (and ongoing) indications that the relocation experience was a disaster, both for the individuals involved and for their respective nations, by 1980 ongoing federal pressure had resulted in the "migration" to cities of slightly over half of all American Indians (about 880,000 of the approximately 1.6 million reflected in the 1980 census).[82] As Oglala Lakota activist Gerald One Feather has put it:

> The relocation program had an impact on our...government at Pine Ridge. Many people who could have provided [our] leadership were lost because they had motivation to go off the reservation to find employment or obtain an education. Relocation drained off a lot of our potential leadership.[83]

It is not that no resistance was mounted to termination and relocation. To the contrary, it was considerable and sustained. The Blackfeet of Montana, for example, acting in consultation with attorney Felix S. Cohen—whom they'd naturalized as a citizen of their nation and who had been a key member of John Collier's Indian Bureau during the formative phases of the IRA—physically occupied their tribal buildings against BIA impoundment and successfully argued on the basis of prior litigation to prevent Myer's policies from being implemented against them.[84] Similarly, the Oglala Lakotas of Pine Ridge—in a confrontational strategy described by Myer as "Communist inspired" (the Indian commissioner caused an FBI "subversive activities" investigation into the matter)—employed Cohen's advice to bar implementation of BIA termination efforts on their reservation.[85] Despite the fact that Myer came within a hair's breadth of having "A Bill to Authorize the Indian Bureau to Make Arrests Without Warrant for Violation of Indian Bureau Regulations" passed in collaboration with reactionary Senator Pat McCarran, these sorts of stand-offs continued throughout the 1950s.[86]

More broadly, the Association of American Indian Affairs (AAIA), spearheaded by articulate and determined spokespersons such as Avery Winnemucca (Pyramid Lake Piaute), Popavi Da (San Ildefonso Pueblo), Manuel Halcomb (Santa Clara Pueblo), Rufus Wallowing and John Wooden Legs (Northern Cheyenne), William V. Creager (Laguna Pueblo), Thomas Main (Gros Ventre), Servino Martinez and Paul Bernal (Taos Pueblo), and Ben Chief (Oglala Lakota), also in consultation with Cohen, put up a fierce fight centering on concentrated public relations and lobbying efforts. As a defense against further terminations, AAIA avidly endorsed IRA colonialism. It was joined in this posture by the National Congress of American Indians (NCAI), headed by Earl Old Person (Northern Cheyenne) and assisted by Cohen's associate (and fellow IRA liberal), attorney James E. Curry.[87] This response was effective, at least insofar as, by 1958, Interior Secretary Fred Seaton was willing to assert publicly that the Eisenhower administration would no longer support legislation "to terminate tribes without their consent."[88]

The IRA liberals had won, garnering a visible and subservient base of support in Indian Country that had been absent during the period of reorganization itself. This was accomplished even while they assisted their more reactionary counterparts in "clearing away much of the dead wood" represented by native nations that had earlier rejected colonial status and engineered reservation demography to allow increased utilization of the native land base by U.S. corporations. In the context of Indian activism that emerged during the 1960s and '70s, some of the worst results of the Eisenhower-era onslaught were rolled back. For instance, after protracted struggles, federal recognition of certain terminated nations, such as the Siletz of Oregon and the Menominees, was "restored."[89] Still, incalculable damage had been done, not only to those nations that were actually terminated, but to the willingness of most remaining native governments to challenge federal authority. To reinforce the latter circumstance, HCR 108 was left dangling like a Damoclean sword over Indian national decision making for another decade, until it was negated, at least in part, by the Indian Civil Rights Act of 1968. Relocation, meanwhile, continued full-force until "the BIA in 1980 finally shut down its urban employment centers."[90]

Activism and "Self-Determination"

As the 1960s dawned, much of Indian Country was in a furor concerning the threats to the very existence of indigenous nations posed by termination and other federal policies. While those involved in IRA-style tribal governance tended to be cowed into even greater measures of "cooperation," a bold new activist sensibility began to show itself in other quarters:

> Proud of their heritage and determined to protect their political, cultural and land rights, Indian people across the country organized, demonstrated and protested. In 1961, five hundred Indians representing sixty-seven [nations] met at the University of Chicago and adopted a Declaration of Indian Purpose. Later that year several of the younger participants from the Chicago conference [notably Clyde Warrior, a Ponca university student] formed the National Indian Youth Conference (NIYC). This group demonstrated against the denial of Indian rights, staged "fish-ins" to support Northwest...fishing rights claims, published studies and newspapers, and lobbied Congress. Five years later, the native peoples of Alaska formed the Alaska Federation of Natives to protect and preserve Alaskan native culture, land and resources.[91]

By the mid-60s, under the leadership of the young Lakota activist/law student Vine Deloria, Jr., even the historically staid National Congress of American Indians (NCAI) had adopted a much more "radical" and engaged approach to politics. By the end of the decade, Deloria had published *Custer Died for Your Sins,* a book widely viewed as a cornerstone statement of native resistance, followed shortly by *We Talk, You Listen,* sometimes described as "an American Indian Declaration of Independence."[92] These broadsides coincided with the founding of the first truly militant Indian rights organization, the American Indian Movement (AIM), in Minneapolis during 1968 and the extended occupation of Alcatraz Island by a coalition organization called Indians of All Tribes during 1969-70. By 1971, not only Alcatraz, but a series of physical confrontations between the Pit River Indians of northern California and the Pacific Gas and Electric Corporation (which claimed to own the Indians' land), repeated occupations of unused portions of the Fort Lawton military facility in Washington state, and highly publicized AIM demonstrations at the Mt. Rushmore National Monument and the Mayflower Replica had drawn considerable public attention to questions of Indian rights.[93]

This upsurge in Indian activism corresponded with a more generalized breakdown—manifested in the civil rights and Black liberation movements, student power and anti-war movements, and incipient Chicano rights and women's liberation movements—of the apparent consensus that had marked U.S. society during the 1950s.[94] By 1966, President Lyndon Johnson was somewhat desperately articulating a national policy he described as the formation of a "Great Society" designed to address the demands voiced by the entire range of "dissidents." One element of Johnson's attempt to defuse the situation was a speech entitled "The Forgotten American"—delivered in the wake of the release of a study he had commissioned to examine Native American issues—in which he renounced termination policy and promised Native America that "a new period in which Indian rights will be honored" was at hand.[95] This was followed, in short order, by passage of Public Law 89-635 (80 *Stat.* 880; codified at 28 U.S.C. 1362), the first section of which provided indigenous nations a clear standing upon which to sue the federal government for the first time. The hand of native governments was thus strengthened to a certain extent, at least in terms of their being able to defend themselves in court against some federal impositions.

P.L. 89-635 was followed, in 1968, by passage of the Indian Civil Rights Act, a law that effectively disallowed termination by spelling out in some detail the expectations of Congress with regard to the future functioning of Indian governments. Although much ballyhoo about "reinforcement of Indian rights" attended enactment of the civil rights bill, its purpose was ultimately cooptive (as was most Johnson-era legislation): to further integrate IRA-type governance into the functioning of the federal hierarchy itself.[96] Any questions as to whether the Indian Civil Rights Act might signify some new degree of federal acceptance of real indigenous autonomy and self-governance were subsequently put to rest with the passage of the Alaska Native Claims Settlement Act. This law, enacted in 1971, carried the logic of the IRA much further than had been the case in 1934:

> ANCSA...organized the Alaska natives into thirteen regional corporations, incorporated under state law, and various village corporations. It implemented the settlement [of Alaska native claims to territory and the right of self-government] "without establishing any permanent racially defined institutions, rights, privileges, or obligations, without creating a reservation system or lengthy wardship or trusteeship, and without adding to the categories of property and institutions engaging in special tax privileges."[97]

Meanwhile, beginning in 1969, as part of a strategy to "chill" forces for social change more generally, the administration of Richard M. Nixon took a very proactive approach to discrediting and otherwise neutralizing the political opposition. With regard to American Indian activism, one of Nixon's major initial tactics seems to have been to channel considerable federal support to a consortium composed of IRA government figures known as the National Tribal Chairman's Association (NTCA; presently renamed the National Tribal Chairman's Fund, or NTCF), the primary purpose of which was to provide a "native voice" endorsing the status quo in Indian affairs while publicly denouncing AIM and other assorted "sovereigntists" as "irresponsible, self-styled revolutionaries...renegades...and terrorists...without visible support among their own people."[98] Such federal tactics deepened already existing divisions between IRA-oriented "tribal leaders" (or "sell-outs," as AIM described them) and the traditionalists with whom the militants aligned on reservations across the country. They also placed AIM and the government itself on an outright collision course.

The conflict emerged in sharp relief during November 1972 when a sizable contingent of Indians, largely organized by AIM and describing themselves as "The Trail of Broken Treaties," arrived in Washington, D.C. on the eve of the U.S. presidential election. They carried with them a Twenty Point Program devoted to redefining the federal-Indian relationship on terms embodying elements of real self-determination for the latter, and demanded the program be negotiated by Nixon or his representatives prior to election day. A considerable portion of the Twenty Point Program was devoted to reassertion of Indian rights to full national sovereignty as implied by their treatied relationships with the federal government. As Vine Deloria, Jr., has summarized the matter:

> The first point dealt with a restoration of constitutional treaty-making authority...The second point proposed that a new treaty commission be established within the next year which could contract a new treaty relationship with the American Indian community on a tribal, regional, or multitribal basis...The fourth point (the third point had nothing to do with treaty rights) asked for a commission to review the treaty violations of the past and present and set up procedures for review of chronic treaty violations by both the states and the federal government...The resubmission of unratified treaties to the Senate for approval was the fifth of the Twenty Points...The sixth and perhaps most fundamental point, and one that would be later prominent at Wounded Knee, was a demand that all Indians be governed by treaty relations...The seventh point asked for mandatory relief from treaty violations by state governments...The eighth and final point dealing with the treaty relationship asked for judicial recognition by the government of Indians' right to interpret treaty provisions.[99]

To emphasize the seriousness of their agenda, Trail participants occupied the BIA's central headquarters in downtown Washington for several days, until White House aide John Ehrlichman delivered a promise from the president that he would be "open to discussion." Most of the Indians then left the capitol, taking the bulk of the BIA's internal documents with them when they left.[100] The administration tried to offset the impact of the Trail of Broken Treaties by bringing in NTCA head Webster Two Hawk, serving at the time as president of the IRA government on the Rosebud Sioux Reservation, to announce that "American Indians stand with President Nixon...We are disgusted with what happened" during the BIA takeover.[101] The gambit failed, however, mainly because Two Hawk was almost immediately unseated in a runoff election for the Rosebud tribal presidency by Robert Burnette, a major Trail organizer.[102] Worse, from the federal point of view, AIM had by then become locked in a toe-to-toe confrontation with the forces of Tribal President Richard Wilson, head of the IRA government on the Pine Ridge Sioux Reservation, and was garnering sufficient grassroots support to impeach him and replace his entire regime with a reconstituted version of the traditional Lakota Council of Elders.[103]

When the Justice Department rushed a large contingent of U.S. Marshals to Pine Ridge to support Wilson while he rigged the impeachment process, they merely exacerbated the situation, precipitating a sensational seventy-one-day armed confrontation at Wounded Knee, a hamlet on the reservation known mainly as the site of an 1890 massacre of Lakotas by the 7th Cavalry.[104] In the aftermath, AIM leader Russell Means challenged Wilson for the tribal presidency during the 1974 Pine Ridge general election and appears to have won, although what the U.S. Commission on Civil Rights termed "massive voter fraud" prevented him from being seated. On many other reservations as well, what might be seen as an "AIM sensibility" of desiring to depose IRA "puppet governments" in favor of more traditional forms was rapidly gaining ground.[105] The system of colonial governance of Indian Country so carefully developed by the United States over a lengthy period was showing signs of unraveling.

Federal response to the situation was essentially two-fold. First, an outright counterinsurgency campaign was launched against AIM—which was by then being described as "the shock troops of Indian sovereignty"—on Pine Ridge and elsewhere. In some ways, this represented a return to the 19th-century policy of assassinating the most patriotic and promising native leaders, as when Oglala Sioux Civil Rights Organization head Pedro Bissonette was murdered by BIA police on Pine Ridge during October 1973.[106] Second, with the activist core of Native America thus tied up in a protracted armed struggle which left scores of their number dead or imprisoned, the government itself adopted the rhetoric of indigenous liberation.[107] As early as 1970, seeing in such semantics a means of confusing or preempting the positions of the Indian opposition, Richard Nixon had delivered a message to Congress stating that he wished to see national Indian policy advanced within a vernacular framework of "self-determination."[108] In 1975, after Nixon had been driven from office by the "excesses" of Watergate, his desire was fulfilled with passage of the Indian Self-Determination and Educational Assistance Act.

Like the Indian Civil Rights Act before it, the Indian Self-Determination Act had little to do with its title. Contrary to accepted meanings of the term in international law, the federal legislation provided no hint that native peoples in the United States would at last be allowed to "freely determine their political status and freely pursue their economic, social and cultural development."[109] Instead, it called for increased Indian participation in staffing those programs implemented to carry out policies formulated by the federal government. Moreover, it placed a particular emphasis on "education" as a main vehicle by which Indians, as a whole, might eventually be indoctrinated to accept the idea that such subordination added up to freedom.[110] As Russell Means put it, "The so-called self-determination policy of the federal government was designed and intended to bolster rather than dismantle the whole structure of BIA/IRA colonialism. Only it calls upon us to administer our own colonization to a greater extent than we have before. Instead of labeling it as a 'Self-Determination Act,' they should have called this law the Self-*Administration* Act of 1975."[111]

Federal Reaction and Native Response

Follow-up to the Self-Determination Act came in the form of the final report of an American Indian Policy Review Commission, established by Congress in 1975 to formulate a federal strategy to accompany the new legislation, on May 17, 1977: "This report generally recommended a continuation of the federal policy [initiated in 1968] of protecting and strengthening tribal governments as permanent governmental units *in the federal system* [emphasis added]."[112] This conclusion was officially opposed by the commission's vice chairperson, reactionary Washington Representative Lloyd Meeds, who in his dissent argued vociferously that resolution of "the Indian problem" resided, not in the final incorporation of native nations into the federal structure, but in the expeditious abolition of all remaining vestiges of indigenous sovereignty:

> In our Federal system, as ordained and established by the United States Constitution, there are but two sovereignties: the United States and the States. This is obvious not only from an examination of the Constitution, its structure, and its amendments, but also in the express language of the 10th amendment which provides: The powers not delegated to the United States by the Constitution, nor prohibited by it to the States, are reserved to the States respectively, or to the peoples...The blunt fact of the matter is that American Indian tribes are not a third set of governments in the American federal system. They are not sovereigns.[113]

Meeds was swiftly joined by a broad assortment of paleo-conservatives who, for a variety of reasons extending from narrow self-interest to philosophical white supremacism, wished to see termination resumed and completed:

> After 1977, the political momentum for a fundamental change in the direction of federal Indian policy became intense. Organized political groups, like Montanans Opposed to Discrimination and the Interstate Congress for Equal Rights and Responsibilities, unsuccessfully lobbied Congress to extinguish Indian rights and force Indian assimilation. Others in Congress sought to go beyond Congressman Meeds' call...In 1977 H.R.J. Res. 1 was proposed to limit Indian treaty hunting and fishing rights. Then Congressman [Jack] Cunningham of Washington introduced H.R. 13329, 95th Cong., 2d Sess. (1978), Orwellianly entitled the Native American Equal Opportunity Act. If enacted, this bill would have, *inter alia,* directed the President within one year to abrogate all treaties entered into with Indians, terminated federal [recognition]...fully subjected all Indians to state jurisdiction, compelled Indian [nations] to distribute certain tribal assets on a per capita basis to their members, eliminated the restraints on alienation and tax immunities enjoyed by [reserved] tribal lands, and abrogated treaty-protected Indian hunting and fishing rights.[114]

The response from Indian Country to this onslaught was mixed. Those within the IRA government apparatus opted largely to protect their positions from the terminators by ever more ostentatious displays of the extent to which they embraced absorption into the federal domain as mere administrative entities. The accommodationist position was perhaps best framed by Robert Burnette, who, in the aftermath of winning a tribal presidency of his own, seems to have lost the militant native rights perspective he once carried along the Trail of Broken Treaties to Washington, D.C.:

> We are part of the United States of America. We are within its jurisdiction and subject to the plenary powers of Congress. So we are not, in a sense, sovereign, except that we do have treaties and the United States has usually tried to honor those treaties. The notion of tribal sovereignty is wishful thinking on the part of...modern day [Indian] leaders.[115]

Such assertions of fealty to federal power through inversion of historical and political realities was met head on by more traditionally oriented leaders such as Onondaga subchief Oren Lyons, whose nation had rejected the IRA in 1936: "We are not going to be part [of the federal system] because we are a separate sovereign nation."[116] Lyons and others consistently articulated a coherent vision of indigenous sovereignty, but it was left once again to the American Indian Movement to force the traditionals' message into the political arena. This time the mechanism employed was a process known as "The Longest Walk," initiated by AIM leader Dennis Banks and carried out by several hundred members of his organization. After spending several well-publicized months marching across the country from San Francisco to Washington, D.C., the AIM members held a mass rally at the Washington Monument on July 25, 1978. During the rally, they delivered a manifesto throwing down the gauntlet to the forces advocating a resumption of termination, challenging the federal definition of self-determination and the entire structure of IRA colonialism, and demanding acknowledgment of the right to unfettered expressions of sovereignty for all indigenous nations. These issues, they said, would be carried before the United Nations in short order. On July 27, California Representative Ron Dellums read the entire manifesto into the *Congressional Record*.[117]

AIM was true to its word with regard to the UN. In 1974, the traditional Lakota elders had called for a major meeting on the Standing Rock Sioux Reservation to discuss taking their treaties with the United States "before the family of nations" to seek review and enforcement. The meeting ended with AIM leader Russell Means accepting responsibility for carrying not only the Lakota treaties but all U.S.-Indian treaties, and "the human rights of the indigenous peoples of the entire hemisphere" into the international arena. Means named a Cherokee AIM member, Jimmie Durham, to establish and direct the movement's "international diplomatic arm," the International Indian Treaty Council (IITC), which was headquartered at United Nations Plaza in New York City.[118]

By 1977, Durham had secured United Nations Type II (Consultative) Non-Governmental Organization (NGO) status for IITC, making it the first indigenous entity in the world to assume such a role. He had also convinced the U.N. Commission on Human Rights to schedule a major hearing on the rights of American Indians at the Palace of Nations in Geneva, Switzerland. With support from the World Council of Churches, IITC was then able to bring representatives of ninety-eight indigenous nations from North, Central, and South America to testify.[119] In 1979, the Bertrand Russell International Tribunal on Human Rights conducted comparable hearings in Rotterdam.[120] The result was the creation in 1982 of a U.N. Working Group on Indigenous Populations, mandated to monitor and report on the interactions between various states and indigenous nations, undertake global studies of the politico-economic conditions in which native peoples now find themselves and the implications of treaty relationships between indigenous nations, and draft a Universal Declaration on the Rights of Indigenous Peoples.[121]

Since its formation, the Working Group on Indigenous Populations has scheduled two sessions annually at which native delegations provide input. Although IITC eventually collapsed as a viable entity (circa 1985-86), other indigenous organizations such as NIYC, the Indian Law Resource Center, Four Directions Council, Grand Council of the Crees, and the World Council of Indigenous Peoples had by then achieved NGO status. A separate NGO, the South American Indian Council (CISA), has emerged to represent the interests of the indigenous peoples of that continent. Further, the significance of American Indian participation in U.N. forums had also been amplified by the presence of native peoples from elsewhere, notably the Inuits of the circumpolar region, Native Hawaiians, Maoris of New Zealand, Kooris and other "Aboriginals" from Australia, and the Karins of Burma. By 1989, the Working Group was considering a second draft of its proposed Declaration,[122] while the International Labor Organization (ILO)—a specialized U.N. agency—adopted a *Convention on the Rights of Indigenous and Tribal Peoples* that is open to ratification by United Nations member states at the present time.[123] In a further development during the same year, the General Assembly of the Organization of American States resolved to "request the Inter-American Commission on Human Rights to prepare a juridical instrument relative to the rights of indigenous peoples, for adoption in 1992."[124]

All in all, the success of AIM's international initiatives has proven sufficient, not only to forestall the terminationist intentions of reactionaries like Meeds and Cunningham, but to subject the entire comportment of the federal government vis-à-vis Indians to a sort of international scrutiny it has never before encountered. This has prompted policymakers to proceed with far more caution than they have in the past. The tendency is bound to increase in the years ahead as the formal elements of international law designed to ensure indigenous rights are set in place. At this juncture, even organizations such as the Boulder, Colorado-based Native American Rights Fund (NARF, a federally funded legal firm exclusively devoted to handling cases for "recognized tribal governments")—long a leading proponent of the notion that subordination to federal dominion was "the best deal Indians can get," and which openly scoffed at IITC's efforts as being "AIMsters playing diplomat"—has queued up to obtain NGO status.[125]

In effect, AIM has to some extent reversed the Nixonian principle of inducing a "chilling effect" upon its opponents. This, in turn, has allowed a much greater degree of maneuvering room during the second half of the 1980s for those indigenous governments within the United States who wish to avail themselves of it. What will come of these changed circumstances remains to be seen, but an avenue of opportunity has been opened and preliminary indications are that there will be constructive results. As former NCAI Director Suzan Shown Harjo, herself no flaming radical, has put it, "Not enough attention has been paid to the Indian activism of the 1960s and the 1970s. The American Indian Movement, the second battle at Wounded Knee, and the occupation of the BIA building brought about tremendous change in Indian country. These events changed the way Indians are viewed and the way we view ourselves."[126]

Openings

In 1983, Russell Means made another bid for the tribal presidency at Pine Ridge. His platform, drafted by Colorado AIM leader Ward Churchill, was dubbed "The TREATY Program," and delineated a comprehensive plan to, among other things, rescind the reservation's IRA constitution, reinstate the traditional Oglala Lakota elders' councils as the primary level of government, pursue recovery of lands guaranteed the Lakota Nation under the 1868 Fort Laramie Treaty as a first national priority, and implement an economic development program based on bilateral/multilateral trade agreements with other nations.[127] The response from grassroots Pine Ridge communities was such that the BIA solicited a tribal council resolution disqualifying Means from the ballot because he had been convicted under a South Dakota "anarcho-syndicalism" statute during the late 1970s (he remains the only person ever sentenced for this nebulous offense in the history of the state).[128]

Although federal interference thus for a second time prevented Means from attempting to convert a contemporary native government into a vehicle for self-determination, the TREATY plan was widely circulated, its concepts studied and adapted to other settings. Before the end of the decade, AIM members such as Ted Means (at Pine Ridge) and Larry Anderson (at Navajo) had made their way onto their respective reservations' tribal councils, carrying "militant" notions of sovereignty with them as they went.[129] Others were even more successful, as is witnessed by the elections of Wilma Mankiller to head the Cherokee Nation of Oklahoma, Twila Martin at the Turtle Mountain Reservation in North Dakota, and Rubin Snake at the Winnebago Reservation in Nebraska.

The second half of the '80s also saw a stiffening of sovereigntist resolve even among some figures long associated with IRA colonialism. A notable instance is that of Joe DeLaCruz, chairperson of the Quinalt Nation on the outer coast of the Olympic Peninsula in Washington state, who has effected a tribal self-sufficiency program based largely in the salvage of redwood and cedar stumps left behind when major non-Indian timbering concerns logged the reservation during the 1930s. The manufacture of such items as shake shingles has not only provided an employment base among the Quinalt, but the proceeds have facilitated establishment of a tribal salmon hatchery and smoking plant, as well as a land consolidation program within the reservation's boundaries that is designed to undo the negative effects of allotment earlier in the century. DeLaCruz has also been instrumental in blocking completion of Coastal Highway 1—which begins at the Mexican border, is intended to end at the Canadian, and must cross Quinalt land in order to do so—until the state of Washington agrees to a jurisdictional arrangement acceptable to the Indians.[130]

Under steadily mounting pressure brought by Indian leaders of virtually every political persuasion, increasing public attention to U.S. Indian policy,[131] and public revelations concerning gross corruption within the BIA,[132] the federal government gave ground steadily with regard to native rights to self-government as the 1990s approached. On September 15, 1988, Congress amended the Indian Self-Determination Act (Public Law 100-472 301-306) to enable a self-selected group of ten indigenous nations—Quinalt, Rosebud Sioux, Lummi and the Jamestown Band of Klallam (both on Puget Sound), Mille Lacs and Red Lake Chippewa (both in northern Minnesota), Mescalero Apache (New Mexico), Hoopa (central California), Confederated Salish and Kootenai (Idaho), and Tlingit-Haida (southeastern Alaska)—to begin serious planning for self-governance on their own terms. From the model or models they develop during the five years of their pilot effort, it is expected that a broad extrapolation of the ways and means of achieving viable expressions of contemporary indigenous sovereignty may emerge.[133]

This potential is reinforced by the activities of the Special Committee on Investigations of the Senate Select Committee on Indian Affairs, chaired by Hawaii Senator Daniel Inouye. The special committee was formed in 1987 to investigate the above-mentioned allegations of rampant mismanagement and corruption in the BIA, and to tender recommendations on how the situation might be corrected. During the course of its investigation, the select committee took testimony and conducted on-site interviews with some 2,010 Indians and non-Indians concerned with Indian policy and examined a voluminous quantity of documentary material pertaining to federal Indian affairs. In its final report, published on November 20, 1989, the select committee called for a "New Era of Agreements" between the United States and indigenous nations within its borders. This "empowerment of tribal self-governance through formal, voluntary agreements" is, as the committee put it, contingent upon "mutual acceptance of four indispensable conditions":

1. The federal government must relinquish its current paternalistic controls over tribal affairs; in turn, the tribes must assume the full responsibilities of self-government;
2. Federal assets and annual appropriations must be transferred *in toto* to the tribes;
3. Formal agreements must be negotiated by tribal governments with written constitutions that have been democratically approved by each tribe; and
4. Tribal governmental officials must be held fully accountable and subject to fundamental federal laws against corruption.[134]

While it is clear that both the recent amendment to the Indian Self-Determination Act and the Select Committee's recommendations still retain the legally groundless presumption that Indian nations are somehow inherently subordinate to the United States, they combine to move in a direction that may serve to diminish the sorts of colonial control manifested in IRA liberalism. By transferring significant decisionmaking back to native governments, along with the assets to give them meaning, the federal government consciously and tangibly strengthens the former at the expense of its own hegemony for the first time in its history. Perhaps more importantly, the Select Committee's recommendation that future U.S.-Indian relations be predicated in "formal, voluntary agreements" is tantamount in many ways to a suggestion that treaty-making be resumed in every respect but the name and procedure for federal ratification.

The last point, of course, is hardly unimportant insofar as it denies Indian peoples the formal recognition of their national sovereignty implied by treaties, *per se*. Given the openings that are increasingly apparent, however, it may well be that this obstacle too can be overcome. The negotiating positions of native governments are in any event substantially enhanced. As things stand, the Indian rights agendas set forth in the 1972 Trail of Broken Treaties Twenty Point Program and the 1978 Longest Walk Manifesto may be seen as the benchmark articulations toward which federal policy is being steered (however grudgingly). As they are consummated, ideas such as those postulated in the 1983 TREATY Program may finally begin to be realized in a "real world" reservation context. It will be a long road from here to there, but it may now be said with a degree of confidence that at least some of the crucial groundwork for the national liberation of Native North America has been laid.

The Road Ahead

Nothing can adequately compensate American Indian nations for their experience at the hands of the United States over the past 200 years. Nothing can undo the legacy of the wars of extermination and dispossession the United States has waged against native peoples. Nothing can truly mend the damage done to indigenous societies by the systematic liquidation of their best leaders, the sustained and intentional suppression of their cultural and economic structures, the imposition of alien forms of governance and legal codes. There is no taking back the unrelenting trauma and suffering undergone by generations of native people forced to live in squalor as the wealth of their assets poured into the coffers of their oppressors. Nor can the extent of the lies, the seamless web of mendacity and duplicity, to which Euroamerica has subjected Native America since the first European "boat person" set foot in this hemisphere ever be retrieved. Probably, not even the damage done to the very treaty-guaranteed land that has been so ruthlessly stripped from native nations can at this point be fixed. Things will never be as they might have been.

Still, if things cannot be set exactly right, they *can* at least be made better. Native North America can at last be accorded its fundamental human right to self-determination. This need not be understood as meaning that each and every indigenous nation will automatically secede, becoming a sovereignty separate from the United States. Rather, it means that their intrinsic right to do so must be acknowledged, formally and unequivocally, by their colonizers. Only from this position—free from a dominating power unilaterally precluding certain of their options for its own reasons—can any nation "freely determine its political, social, and economic destiny," and hence the nature of its mode of governance. Viewed in any other way, the term "self-determination" is at best meaningless, at worst a subterfuge meant to mask its exact opposite, the continuation of a relationship between colonizer and colonized.

In the event, should the United States finally and simply admit what has been true all along, that native nations are absolutely entitled to complete national sovereignty, it is likely that few (if any) American Indian peoples would elect to exercise it fully. The Navajo nation, given the scale of its land base and population and the mineral resources available to it, might opt for complete independence. Similarly, should the Lakota Nation be able to recombine its territorality and population through recovery of all or most of what was once called "The Great Sioux Reservation," it might pursue such a course. In all probability, the remaining indigenous nations would select a commonwealth status vis-à-vis the United States, comparable to that occupied by some nations of the former British empire with regard to England, or a variation of the "home rule" status accorded by Denmark to its former "possessions" Iceland and Greenland. It is also possible that certain coastal or "trans-border tribes"—nations such as Blackfeet, Mohawk, and Haida (which are bisected by the U.S.-Canadian boundary), or Yaqui and Tohono O'Odham (bisected by the U.S.-Mexican border)—might wish to pursue some type of multinational arrangement. The point is that we will have thus been able to at last *decide for ourselves* the sort of relationship we wish to have with the United States, and other countries as well.

From this, it follows that we will finally be in a position to define for ourselves, nation by nation, the forms of governance best suited to our needs. Again, it is likely that very few native peoples will attempt a literal reconstitution of their traditional forms of government. In certain cases, such as the Haudenosaunee and the Hopi, where traditional governing bodies have continued to function (at Hopi, in parallel and in conflict with its IRA "replacement") throughout the periods of conquest and colonization, there may be exceptions. In most instances, however, the enforced rupture between past and present governmental forms has been too great, too much has been lost along the way. Nonetheless, it is also true that in virtually every case some degree of recollection of how traditional governments functioned, and why they approached things as they did, remains in place. Consequently, it is quite probable that most self-determining indigenous governments will exhibit a combination of traditional and non-traditional characteristics. There are a multiplicity of conceivable options relating to jurisdiction and definition and conditions of citizenry, legal codes and trade relations, social strictures and land use patterns. The possibilities of the forms that may be assumed by autonomous native governments are virtually endless.

What is necessary is no mere gestural concession on the part of the United States, but an actual relinquishment of its pretensions to preeminent rights over the lands and lives of others, lands and lives it has long professed to believe are its own, to do with as it will. For the self-determination of Native North America to be realized, the United States must be prodded into following through with the development of the "new relationships" with indigenous nations called for by Senator Inuoye's Select Committee, but it must be compelled to honor its past treaties with those nations in concrete ways. The treaty territories, or substantial portions of them, along with the resources associated with these lands, must be returned to native control if Indian Country is to possess the economic base from which to make self-governance practicable. Given what is at stake—a literal dismemberment of what is now seen as the internal territorial and economic integrity of the United States—the struggle will undoubtedly continue to be difficult, perhaps at times bloody. But it is well underway.

Altogether, despite the hurdles which remain to be cleared, the prospects for a revitalization of American Indian self-government and other aspects of self-determination are in many ways brighter than they have been since the conclusion of the "Indian Wars." The cycle of our prolonged battle for bare survival—a resistance to extinction emblemized by the sacrifices of Tecumseh and Osceola, Crazy Horse and Geronimo, Rupert Costo and Popavi Da, Anna Mae Aquash, Russell Means, and Dennis Banks—may be coming to a much overdue conclusion. Those of us who are indigenous to this land must now accept the responsibility of seizing every opportunity and doing the hard work necessary to achieve the potential for liberation they created. No less must non-Indians—regardless of their race, gender, ethnicity, sexual preference, or the story of how they got here—accept the responsibility of assisting us to succeed. For only in this way can we transcend the bitter legacy we have mutually inherited, forging instead a new heritage of respect, cooperation, and freedom. And only in this way can we transform the America that is into the America that could be.

Notes

1. See generally, Schusky, Ernest, ed., *Political Organization of Native North Americans*, University Press of America, Washington, D.C., 1970.
2. With regard to Iroquois influence on the U.S. Constitution and structure of the corresponding republic, see Grinde, Donald A. Jr., *The Iroquois in the Founding of the American Nation*, Indian Historian Press, San Francisco, 1977; Johansen, Bruce, *Forgotten Founders: How the American Indian Helped Shape Democracy*, The Harvard Common Press, Boston, 1982; and Johansen, Bruce, and Donald A. Grinde, Jr., *Exemplars of Liberty*, American Indian Studies Program, UCLA, 1991. Also see Burton, Bruce A., "Iroquois Confederate Law and the Origins of the U.S. Constitution," *Northeast Indian Quarterly*, Vol. 3, No. 2, Fall 1986, pp. 4-9; and Barriero, José, ed., *Indian Roots of American Democracy*, American Indian Program, Cornell University, Ithaca, NY, 1989.
3. O'Brien, Sharon, *American Indian Tribal Governments*, University of Oklahoma Press, Norman, 1989, pp. 17-18. She is relying heavily upon Colden, Cadwallader, *The History of the Five Indian Nations*, Cornell University Press, Ithaca, NY, 1958; Wallace, Anthony F.C., *The Death and Rebirth of the Seneca*, Alfred A. Knopf Publishers, New York, 1969; and Wilson, Edmund, *Apologies to the Iroquois*, Vintage Books, New York, 1960. An interesting and useful companion reading is Nammack, Georgiana C., *Fraud, Politics, and the Dispossession of the Indian: The Iroquois Land Frontier in the Colonial Period*, University of Oklahoma Press, Norman, 1969.
4. O'Brien, op. cit., pp. 18-19. Also see Jacobs, Wilbur, "Wampum: The Protocol of Indian Diplomacy, *William and Mary Quarterly*, 3rd Series, No. 6, October 1949, pp. 596-604; and Miles, George, "A Brief Study of Joseph Brant's Political Career in Relation to Iroquois Political Structure," *American Indian Journal*, No. 2, December 1976, pp. 12-20.
5. O'Brien, op. cit., p. 23. She relies upon Corkran, David H., *The Creek Frontier, 1540-1783*, University of Oklahoma Press, Norman, 1967; Debo, Angie, *The Road to Disappearance: A History of the Creek Indians*, University of Oklahoma Press, Norman, 1941; Green, Donald E., *The Politics of Indian Removal: Creek Government and Society in Crisis*, University of Nebraska Press, Lincoln, 1977; and Swanton, John R., "Early History of the Creek Indians and their

Neighbors," *Bureau of American Ethnology Bulletin*, No. 73, U.S. Government Printing Office, Washington, D.C., 1922. Also see Morton, Ohland, "The Government of the Creek Indians," Parts 1 and 2, *Chronicles of Oklahoma*, No. 8, March 1930, pp. 42-64; June 1930, pp. 189-225.

6. On the Lakota, see O'Brien, op. cit., pp. 23-6. Also see Pennington, Robert, "An Analysis of the Political Structure of the Teton Dakota Tribe of North America," *North Dakota History*, No. 20, July 1953, pp. 143-55; DeMallie, Raymond, *Lakota Society*, University of Nebraska Press, Lincoln, 1982; Hassrick, Royal B., *The Sioux: Life and Customs of a Warrior Society*, University of Oklahoma Press, Norman, 1964; and Vestal, Stanley, *Warpath and Council Fire: The Plains Indians' Struggle for Survival in War and Diplomacy, 1851-1891*, Random House Publishers, New York, 1948.
7. On the Pueblos, see O'Brien, op. cit., pp. 27-9. Also see Dozier, Edward P., *The Pueblo Indians*, Holt, Rinehart and Winston Publishers, New York, 1970; Jones, Oakah L. Jr., *Pueblo Warriors and Spanish Conquest*, University of Oklahoma Press, Norman, 1966; and Ortiz, Alfonso, ed., *New Perspectives on the Pueblos*, School of American Research, University of New Mexico, Albuquerque, 1972.
8. On the Yaquis, see Hu-DeHart, Evelyn, *Yaqui Resistance and Survival*, University of Wisconsin Press, Madison, 1984.
9. On the Yakimas, see O'Brien, op. cit., pp. 29-33. Also see Daugherty, Richard, *The Yakima People*, Indian Tribal Series, Phoenix, AZ, 1973; Guie, D.H., *Tribal Days of the Yakima*, Republic Publishers, North Yakima, WA, 1937; and MacWhorter, Lucuilus, *Crime Against the Yakima*, Republic Publishers, North Yakima, WA, 1913.
10. On the influence of Iroquois and other Indians upon the thought, not only of Rousseau, but British Enlightenment thinkers such as John Locke and Thomas Hobbes, see Johnansen, op. cit., pp. 14, 120-1. Also see Cohen, Felix S., "Americanizing the White Man," *American Scholar*, Vol. 21, No. 2, Summer 1952, pp. 177-91.
11. With regard to Iroquois influence on Marx and Engels, it plainly accrued through Marx's reading, between December of 1880 and March of 1881, of anthropologist Lewis Henry Morgan's 1871 book, *Ancient Society*, based in large part upon his earlier (1851) *The League of the Hau-de-no-sau-nee or Iroquois*. Marx took at least 98 pages of handwritten notes on the topic of traditional Iroquoian governance. After Marx's death, his collaborator, Frederick Engels, inherited these notes and converted them into a book entitled *The Origin of the Family, Private Property and the State*, originally subtitled *In Light of the Researches of Lewis H. Morgan*. The Engels exposition is included in *Marx and Engels: Selected Works*, International Publishers, New York, 1960.
12. The language of Article I, Section 10 of the U.S. Constitution prohibits the federal government from entering into treaty relationships with entities other than fully sovereign nations. A treaty, once ratified by the Senate, therefore represents formal recognition by the United States of the fully sovereign national status of the other party or parties to the agreement. Between 1778 and 1871, the Senate duly ratified at least 371 treaties with various American Indian peoples.
13. An examination of this consideration may be found in Graymont, Barbara, *The Iroquois in the American Revolution*, Syracuse University Press, Syracuse, NY, 1972. A broader perspective is offered in Tebbel, John, and Keith Jennison, *The American Indian Wars*, Harper and Brothers Publishers, New York, 1960. Also see Hall, Arthur H., "The Red Stick War: Creek Indian Affairs During the War of 1812," *Chronicles of Oklahoma*, No. 12, September 1934, pp. 264-93.
14. Deloria, Vine Jr., "Sovereignty," in Roxanne Dunbar Ortiz and Larry Emerson eds., *Economic Development in American Indian Reservations*, Native American Studies Center, University of New Mexico, Albuquerque, 1979. Also see DeMallie, Raymond, "American Indian Treaty Making: Motives and Meanings," *American Indian Journal*, No. 3, January 1977, pp. 2-10.
15. See Peckman, Howard, and Charles Gibson, eds., *Attitudes of the Colonial Powers Toward the American Indian*, University of Utah Press, Salt Lake City, 1969. Also see Schaaf, Gregory, *Wampum Belts and Peace Trees: George Morgan, Native Americans and Revolutionary Diplomacy*, Fulcrum Publishers, Golden, CO, 1990.
16. See Prucha, Francis Paul, *American Indian Policy in the Formative Years: The Indian Trade and Intercourse Acts, 1790-1834*, University of Nebraska Press, Lincoln, 1970; and *Documents of United States Indian Policy*, University of Nebraska Press, Lincoln, 1975.
17. For texts and other data, see Kappler, Charles J., *Indian Treaties, 1778-1883*, Interland Publishers, New York, 1972.
18. The Sioux legal scholar Vine Deloria, Jr., has collected some 1,400 pages of such material to

date, and believes several hundred additional pages exist.

19. This was true despite a rider attached to the Indian Appropriations Act of 1871 (ch. 120, 16 *Stat.* 544, 566) formally suspending federal treaty-making with indigenous nations.
20. This principle derives from a range of sources, but is embodied quite clearly in the United Nations Declaration on the Granting of Independence to Colonial Countries and Peoples (December 14, 1960), and the International Covenant on Civil and Political Rights (March 23, 1966). For a broad view, see Bennett, Gordon, *Aboriginal Rights in International Law*, Royal Anthropological Institute, London, 1978.
21. The term was coined by Deloria, Vine Jr., and Clifford M. Lytle, *The Nations Within: The Past and Future of American Indian Sovereignty*, Pantheon Books, New York, 1984.
22. See Goldberg, Carol E., "Public Law 280: The Limits of State Law over Indian Reservations," *UCLA Law Review*, No. 22, February 1975, pp. 535-94. More generally, see Fixico, Donald L., *Termination and Relocation: Federal Indian Policy, 1945-1960*, University of New Mexico Press, Albuquerque, 1986.
23. On the southern California Indians specifically, see Shipeck, Florence Connolly, *Pushed Into the Rocks: Southern California Indian Land Tenure, 1769-1986*, University of Nebraska Press, Lincoln, 1988.
24. See, for example, Churchill, Ward, "The Indigenous Peoples of North America: A Struggle Against Internal Colonialism," *The Black Scholar*, Vol. 16, No. 1, February 1985.
25. This position is consistent with the United Nations' Declaration of the Granting of Independence to Colonial Countries and Peoples (1960): "All peoples have the right to self-determination: by virtue of that right they freely determine their political status and freely pursue their economic, social and cultural development." For the full text, see Brownlie, Ian, *Basic Documents on Human Rights*, Oxford University Press, London/New York, 1971, pp. 28-30.
26. Churchill, Ward, "The 'Trial' of Leonard Peltier," preface to Jim Messerschmidt's *The Trial of Leonard Peltier*, South End Press, Boston, 1983, p. viii.
27. This practice should be contrasted to the rules of "civilized warfare" then pertaining among the European powers, in which it was held that heads of state—and usually government functionaries more generally—were exempt from being killed by military action. That the United States subscribed to these conventions is witnessed in its treatment of, among others, President Santa Ana in the wake of the 1846 Mexican-American War, and of Confederate President Jefferson Davis at the end of the American Civil War. The kind of warfare practiced against Native America was of a wholly different sort, and patently illegal, even by the standards of the day.
28. On Tecumseh, see Sugden, John, *Tecumseh's Last Stand*, University of Oklahoma Press, Norman, 1985, especially p. 180: "Most witnesses remembered Tecumseh's body on its back...the limbs drawn up...Then on October 6 the souvenir hunters got to work, and when the warrior had been stripped of his clothing...Kentuckians tore skin from his back and thigh...[T]he rapacious soldiery so thoroughly scalped the corpse that some of them came away with fragments of skin the size of a cent piece and endowed with a mere tuft of hair. When [one of them] was interviewed in 1886 he was able to display a piece of Tecumseh's skin."
29. On the imprisonment and subsequent murder of Osceola on January 27, 1838, after he attended—under protection of a white truce flag—a peace negotiation requested by U.S. officials, see Boyd, Mark F., "Asi-Yahola or Osceola," *Florida Historical Quarterly*, Vol. XXXIII, Nos. 1-2, January/April 1955.
30. On the assassination of Crazy Horse in 1877, see Sandoz, Mari, *Crazy Horse: Strange Man of the Oglalas*, University of Nebraska Press, Lincoln, 1942. Also see Clark, Robert, ed., *The Killing of Chief Crazy Horse*, University of Nebraska Press, Lincoln, 1976. On the assassination of Sitting Bull in 1890, see Vestal, Stanley, *Sitting Bull: Champion of the Sioux*, University of Oklahoma Press, Norman, 1957.
31. On the execution of the Santees at Mankato after the so-called Little Crow's War, see Carley, Kenneth, *The Sioux Uprising of 1862*, Minnesota Historical Society, St. Paul, 1961.
32. On the execution of Captain Jack on October 3, 1873, see Murray, Keith A., *The Modocs and Their War*, University of Oklahoma Press, Norman, 1959. Also see Riddell, Jeff C., *The Indian History of the Modoc War and the Causes That Led to It*, Pine Cone Publishers, Medford, OR, 1973.
33. On the fate of Chief Joseph, see Beal, Merril, *I Will Fight No More Forever: Chief Joseph and the Nez Percé War*, University of Washington Press, Seattle, 1963.

34. On Geronimo's incarceration, first in Florida at the same prison in which Osceola had been assassinated, and subsequently at Fort Sill, Oklahoma (until his death), see Barrett, S.M., ed., *Geronimo: His Own Story*, E.P. Dutton Co., New York, 1971.
35. A classic case of this relates to U.S. interactions with the Cherokee Nation during the period leading up the the forced removal of that people from its Georgia/Carolina/Tennessee homeland, beginning in 1833. See Wilkins, Thurman, *Cherokee Tragedy: The Story of the Ridge Family and the Decimation of a People*, Macmillan Publishers, New York, 1970.
36. For an examination of this issue, see Leland, Joy, *Firewater Myths: North American Indian Drinking and Drug Addiction*, Rutgers Center for Alcohol Studies, Rutgers University, New Brunswick, NJ, 1976. Also see French, Laurence, and Jim Hornbuckle, "Alcoholism Among Native Americans: An Analysis," *Social Work*, No. 25, July 1980, pp. 275-80; and Heidenreich, C. Adrian, "Alcohol and Drug Use and Abuse Among Indian-Americans: A Review of Issues and Sources," *Journal of Drug Issues*, No. 6, Summer 1976, pp. 256-72.
37. There are numerous examples of this practice. One of the more notorious concerns the 1861 "Treaty with the Cheyenne," by which the United States claimed the latter nation had voluntarily ceded some 90 percent of the territory recognized as belonging to it under the 1851 Fort Laramie Treaty. As it turned out, the bulk of the alleged Cheyenne signatories had not attended the treaty conference at which they supposedly agreed to the new arrangement. Those who had, declined to sign. The appearance is that the United States then enlisted the services of a group of Lakotas who had assembled for other reasons—and who appear to have thought the whole thing was simply a riotous joke on their Cheyenne cousins—to sign the document "in behalf of" various Cheyenne leaders. The implications were ultimately less than humorous, however: The terms of the 1861 treaty led directly to the Sand Creek Massacre and resulting "Indian War of 1864-1865." See generally, Hoig, Stan, *The Sand Creek Massacre*, University of Oklahoma Press, Norman, 1961. The conclusion that the signatories were probably Lakotas derives from an unpublished study of the 1861 treaty process undertaken by Cheyenne/Lakota historian Richard B. Williams.
38. The contours of this policy are readily evident in Schmeckebier, Laurence, *The Office of Indian Affairs: Its History, Activities and Organization*, Johns Hopkins University Press, Baltimore, 1927.
39. See Weems, John Edward, *Death Song: The Last of the Indian Wars*, Doubleday Publishers, Garden City, NY, 1976.
40. On the forced relocation of eastern Indians to points west of the Mississippi, see Foreman, Grant, *Advancing the Frontier, 1830-1860*, University of Oklahoma Press, Norman, 1933 and *Indian Removal: The Immigration of the Five Civilized Tribes*, University of Oklahoma Press, Norman, 1953. Also see Strickland, Rennard, *The Indians in Oklahoma*, University of Oklahoma Press, Norman, 1980; and Williams, Walter, ed., *Southeastern Indians Since the Removal Era*, University of Georgia Press, Athens, 1979. A good philosophical overview of the entire process may be found in Downs, Ernest, "How the East Was Lost," *American Indian Journal*, Vol. 1, No. 2, 1975, pp. 6-10.
41. In effect, this makes the treaties the basic real estate documents by which the United States is entitled to claim rights of legal occupancy in North America. No other legal basis exists, the United States having formally foresworn "rights of conquest" *per se* in early statutes such as the 1787 Northwest Ordinance. See Cohen, Felix S., "How We Bought the United States," *Colliers*, January 19, 1946, pp. 22-3, 62.
42. An interesting examination of the implications and dimensions of this understanding in Oklahoma may be found in Applen, Allen G., "An Attempted Indian State Government: The Okmulgee Constitution in Indian Territory, 1870-1876," *Kansas Quarterly*, No. 3, Fall 1971, pp. 89-99. For exploration of the dynamics which prevented the Okmulgee experiment and others from succeeding, see Miner, H. Craig, *The Corporation and the Indian: Tribal Sovereignty and Industrial Civilization in Indian Territory, 1865-1907*, University of Missouri Press, Columbia, 1976.
43. Act of March 3, 1885, 23 *Stat.* 385, amended as 18 USCA 1153. The problems inherent to the statute are examined in Lucke, Thomas W. Jr., "Indian Law: Recognition of a Field of Values," *The Indian Historian*, No. 10, Spring 1977, pp. 43-7. A more comprehensive examination of the philosophical questions at issue will be found in Hoebel, E. Adamson, *The Law of Primitive Man: A Study in Comparative Legal Dynamics*, Harvard University Press, Cambridge, MA, 1964.
44. See Deloria, Vine Jr., "Indian Law and the Reach of History," *Journal of Contemporary Law*, No.

4, Winter 1977, pp. 1-13. For other views, see Cohen, Felix S., "Indian Rights and the Federal Courts," *Minnesota Law Review*, No. 24, January 1940, pp. 145-200; as well as Clinton, Robert N., "Development of Criminal Jurisdiction over Indian Lands: The Historical Perspective," *Arizona Law Review*, Vol. 17, No. 4, 1975, pp. 951-91 and "Criminal Jurisdiction on Reservations: A Journey Through a Jurisdictional Maze," *Arizona Law Review*, Vol. 18, No. 3, 1976, pp. 503-83.

45. Act of February 8, 1887, 24 *Stat.* 388. See Otis, D.S., *The Dawes Act and the Allotment of Indian Land*, University of Oklahoma Press, Norman, 1973.

46. On the impact of allotment, see Kickingbird, Kirk, and Karen Ducheneaux, *One Hundred Million Acres*, Macmillan Publishers, New York, 1973. Also see McDonnell, Janet A., *The Dispossession of the American Indian, 1887-1934*, Indiana University Press, Bloomington/Indianapolis, 1991.

47. To place the matter in perspective, the expression of such intentions as a matter of state policy would become a "Crime Against Humanity," the penalty for perpetration of which is death, under the Convention on Punishment and Prevention of the Crime of Genocide (1948). It should be noted that a genocide conducted by such means does not have to be completely successful in order to be illegal. Attempting or conspiring to attempt such genocidal policies are also capital crimes under the 1948 Convention. For the complete text, see Brownlie, op. cit., pp. 31-4.

48. Leupp, Francis E., *The Indian and His Problem*, Charles Scribner's Sons, New York, 1910 (rpt: Arno Press, New York, 1971), p. 93. An examination of the attitudes involved, and their practical policy implications, may be found in Jackson, Curtis E., and Marcia J. Galli, *A History of the Bureau of Indian Affairs and Its Activities Among Indians*, R&E Research Associates, San Francisco, 1977.

49. Letter, Charles Burke to William Williamson, September 16, 1921; William Williamson Papers, Box 2, File—Indian Matters, Miscellaneous, I.D. Weeks Library, University of South Dakota, Vermillion. The articulation of similar sensibilities occurs throughout the history of the BIA; see Kvasnicka, Robert M., and Herman J. Viola, eds., *The Commissioners of Indian Affairs, 1824-1977*, University of Nebraska Press, Lincoln, 1979.

50. For a sociological perspective on this phenomenon, see Yinger, Milton J., and George E. Simpson, "The Integration of Americans of Indian Descent," *The Annals (AAPS)*, 436, March 1978, pp. 131-51.

51. 18 USCA 1401 (a) (2). For a summary of at least some of the effects, see Hertzberg, Hazel W., *The Search for an American Indian Identity: Modern Pan-Indian Movements*, Syracuse University Press, Syracuse, NY, 1971.

52. The geologists were present under provision of the 1918 Metalliferous Minerals Act, which allowed for exploitation of resources on Indian land—and required payment of a 5 percent royalty on the market value of extracted ores—but which required Indian consent prior to leases being let. The last matter is what brought about the meeting of the traditional Diné government.

53. See Parlow, Anita, *Cry, Sacred Ground: Big Mountain, USA*, Christic Institute, Washington, D.C., 1988, p. 30. Also see Kelly, Laurence C., *The Navajo Indians and Federal Indian Policy, 1900-1935*, University of Arizona Press, Tucson, 1968.

54. On this topic, see Wood, John, "The Navajo: A History of Dependence and Underdevelopment," *URPE*, No. 11, Summer 1979, pp. 25-43. Also see Ruffing, Lorraine Turner, "Navajo Mineral Development," *American Indian Journal*, No. 4, September 1978, pp. 2-15; and Whitson, Hollis, and Martha Roberge, "Moving Those Indians Into the Twentieth Century," *Technology Review*, July 1986.

55. U.S. House of Representatives, Committee of One Hundred, *The Indian Problem: Resolution of the Committee of One Hundred Appointed by the Secretary of Interior and Review of the Indian Problem*, H. Doc. 149 (Serial 8392), 68th Cong., 1st Sess., U.S. Government Printing Office, Washington, DC, 1925.

56. Merriam, Lewis, et al., *The Problem of Indian Administration*, Johns Hopkins University Press, Baltimore, 1928.

57. For itemization of the Reorganization Act's contents and its legislative history, see Deloria and Lytle, op. cit. For more contemporaneous assessments, see Nash, Jay Brian, *The New Deal for Indians: A Survey of the Workings of the Indian Reorganization Act of 1934*, Academy Press, New York, 1938; and Mckeel, Scudder, "An Appraisal of the Indian Reorganization Act," *American Anthropologist*, No. 46, April-June 1944, pp. 209-17.

58. Interview with elder David Monongye, village of Hotevilla, Hopi Reservation, Arizona, May 16, 1987 (tape on file).
59. Costo, Rupert, "Federal Indian Policy, 1933-1945," in Kenneth R. Philp, ed., *Indian Self-Rule: First-Hand Accounts of Indian-White Relations from Roosevelt to Reagan*, Howe Brothers Publishers, Salt Lake City, 1986, p. 49.
60. Quoted in ibid., p. 52. The Oneidas were joined by the rest of the Six Nations in adopting this position.
61. Ibid., pp. 28-9. Costo's assessment of Collier's tactics, especially in southern California, is borne out in the investigations of the matter by Yamasee historian Donald A. Grinde, Jr.; see his "Southern California Indians' Resistance to the Indian New Deal," unpublished draft essay presented at the Western Social Science Association annual conference, Reno, NV, April 1991.
62. Ibid., pp. 50-1.
63. Wright, Peter, "John Collier and the Oklahoma Indian Welfare Act of 1936," *Chronicles of Oklahoma*, No. 50, Autumn 1972, pp. 347-51. Also see Quinton, B.T., "Oklahoma Tribes, the Great Depression and the Indian Bureau," *Mid-America*, No. 49, January 1967, pp. 29-43.
64. Of those nations that reorganized, ninety-two were provided with BIA-written "constitutions" effectively converting them into business entities. Another seventy-two ended up with corporate charters, pure and simple. See Philp, Kenneth R., "The Indian Reorganization Act Fifty Years Later," in *Indian Self-Rule*, op. cit., p. 18.
65. O'Brien, op. cit., pp. 82-83. With regard to the travesty at Hopi, see Lummis, Charles, *Bullying the Hopi*, Prescott College Press, Prescott, AZ, 1968. Also see LaFarge, Oliver, *Running Narrative of the Organization of the Hopi Tribe of Indians*, in the LaFarge Collection, University of Texas at Austin.
66. See Taylor, Graham D., *The New Deal and American Indian Tribalism: The Administration of the Indian Reorganization Act, 1934-45*, University of Nebraska Press, Lincoln, 1980. Also see Stein, Gary, "Tribal Self-Government and the Indian Reorganization Act of 1934," *Michigan Law Review*, No. 70, April 1972, pp. 955-86.
67. See Ducheneaux, Franklin, "The Indian Reorganization Act and the Cheyenne River Sioux," *American Indian Journal*, No. 2, August 1976, pp. 8-14. More generally, see Kelly, William H., ed., *Indian Affairs and the Indian Reorganization Act: The Twenty Year Record*, University of Arizona Press, Tucson, 1954.
68. Concerning Navajo rejection of the IRA and the reasons for it, see Iverson, Peter, *The Navajo Nation*, Greenwood Press, Westport, CT, 1981. Also see Boyce, George A., *"When the Navajos Had Too Many Sheep": The 1940s*, Indian Historian Press, San Francisco, 1974.
69. This is covered in passing in Zimmerman, William Jr., "The Role of the Bureau of Indian Affairs Since 1933," *Annals of the American Academy of Political and Social Science*, No. 311, May 1957, pp. 31-40.
70. U.S. House of Representatives, Committee on Indian Affairs, *Investigation of the Bureau of Indian Affairs*, House Report 2053, 82d Cong., 2d Sess., U.S. Government Printing Office, Washington, D.C., 1952, pp. 161-78.
71. See Officer, James E., "Termination as Federal Policy: An Overview," in *Indian Self-Rule*, op. cit., p. 118.
72. *Investigation of the Bureau of Indian Affairs*, op. cit., pp. 28-30.
73. U.S. Senate, S. Rep. 310, 78th Cong., 1st Sess. (1943). The report is quoted in Philp, Kenneth R., *John Collier's Crusade for Indian Reform, 1920-1954*, University of Arizona Press, Tucson, 1977, p. 208.
74. See U.S. House of Representatives, Committee on Indian Affairs, *Investigation of the Bureau of Indian Affairs*, 78th Cong., 1st Sess., U.S. Government Printing Office, Washington, D.C., 1944, pp. 28-39. Also see Koppes, Clayton R., "From New Deal to Termination: Liberalism and Indian Policy, 1933-1953," *Pacific Historical Review*, No. 46, November 1977, pp. 543-66.
75. Brophy's main job was to usher in the Indian Claims Commission in 1946. Brophy retired due to ill health until Myer could come aboard. See *The Commissioners of Indian Affairs*, op. cit.
76. By far the best handling of Myer's character and career will be found in Drinnon, Richard, *Keeper of Concentration Camps: Dillon S. Myer and American Racism*, University of California Press, Berkeley, 1987. It should be noted that Myer was aided in his task by the passage, in 1952, of Public Law 82-291, a law authorizing transfer of "Indian services" from the BIA to other federal agencies where they could be incorporated into broader social services program-

ming. See Orfield, Gary, *A Study of Termination Policy*, National Congress of American Indians, Denver, 1965.

77. The complete text of H.R. 108 appears in Part II of Spicer, Edward H., *A Short History of the United States*, Van Nostrand Rinehold Co., New York, 1969.
78. Officer, op. cit., p. 125. The most comprehensive overview of the termination and relocation policies is to be found in Fixico, *Termination and Relocation*, op. cit. Also see LaFarge, Oliver, "Termination of Federal Supervision: Disintegration and the American Indian," *Annals of the American Academy of Political and Social Science*, No. 311, May 1975, pp. 56-70; and Stefon, Frederick J., "The Irony of Termination: 1943-1958," *The Indian Historian*, Vol. 3, No. 3, Summer 1978, pp. 3-14.
79. One dissolution, that of the Oklahoma Ponca, was delayed in committee and was not consummated until 1966. See Butler, Raymond V., "The Bureau of Indian Affairs: Activities Since 1945," *Annals of the American Academy of Political and Social Science*, No. 436, 1978, pp. 50-60.
80. For assessment of reservation economic conditions in the pre-termination period, see Project Committee on Indian Affairs, Commission on Organization of the Executive Branch of Government, *Report of the Committee on Indian Affairs to the Commission on Organization of the Executive Branch of Government*, 82d Cong., 2d Sess., U.S. Government Printing Office, Washington, D.C., October 1948. Also see Zimmerman, William Jr., "Economic Status of Indians in the United States," *Journal of Religious Thought*, Summer 1950 and Sorkin, Alan L., "The Economic and Social Status of the American Indian, 1940-1970," *Nebraska Journal of Economics*, No. 22, Spring 1974, pp. 33-50.
81. See O'Brien, op. cit., p. 86. Also see Burt, Larry W., *Tribalism in Crisis: Federal Indian Policy, 1953-1961*, University of New Mexico Press, Albuquerque, 1982; Ablon, Joan, "American Indian Relocation: Problems of Dependency and Management in the City," *Phylon*, No. 26, 1965, pp. 362-71.
82. On proportion of Indian population which is urban, see U.S. Bureau of the Census, *General Population Characteristics: United States Summary*, PC80-1-B1, Pt. 1, U.S. Government Printing Office, Washington, D.C., 1983. For use of the term "migrate," see Gundlach, James H., Nelson P. Reid and Alden E. Roberts, "Native American Indian Migration and Relocation," *Pacific Sociological Review*, No. 21, 1978, pp. 117-27.
83. Quoted in *Indian Self-Rule*, op. cit., p. 171.
84. *The Blackfeet Nation v. United States*, 81 Ct. Cl. 101 (1935). The matter is thoroughly discussed in Cohen, Felix S., "The Erosion of Indian Rights, 1950-53: A Case Study in Bureaucracy," *Yale Law Journal*, No. 62, February 1953, pp. 348-90.
85. See FBI serialization number 100-378472, January 10, 1952. On Cohen overall, see Haas, Theodore H., ed., *Felix S. Cohen: A Fighter for Justice*, Alumni of the City College of New York, Washington, D.C., 1956.
86. McCarran's draft bill, S. 2543, is contained in *The Congressional Record*, January 29, 1952.
87. Concerning the AAIA/NCAI counteroffensive, and Cohen's and Curry's parts in it, see Drinnon, op. cit., pp. 188-248.
88. Quoted in Officer, op. cit., p. 125.
89. On the Menominee restoration (Public Law 93-197 (1973), 87 *Stat.* 770, codified at 25 U.S.C. 903 *et seq.)*, see Deer, Ada, "Menominee Restoration: How the Good Guys Won," *Journal of Intergroup Relations*, No. 3, 1974, pp. 41-50. Also see Shames, Deborah, ed., *Freedom With Reservation: The Menominee Struggle to Save Their Land and People*, National Committee to Save the Menominee People and Forest, Madison, WI, 1972, and Peroff, Nicholas, *Menominee DRUMS: Tribal Termination and Restoration, 1954-1974* University of Oklahoma Press, Norman, 1982. On the Siletz restoration (Public Law 95-195 (1977); 91 *Stat.* 1415, codified at 25 U.S.C. 711 *et seq.)*, see Wilkinson, Charles F., and Eric R. Biggs, "The Evolution of the Termination Policy," *American Indian Law Review*, No. 5, 1977, pp. 139-84. Other nations that were "reinstated" during the 1970s (Public Law 95-281 (1978), 92 *Stat.* 246, codified at 25 U.S.C. 861 *et seq.)* included the Wyandotte, Peoria, Ottawa, and Modoc.
90. Officer, op. cit., p. 126.
91. O'Brien, op. cit., p. 87. For details on Clyde Warrior, the founding of NIYC, and the "fish-ins," see Steiner, Stan, *The New Indians*, Harper and Row Publishers, New York, 1968. Also see Berthrong, Donald J., *The American Indian: From Pacifism to Activism*, Forum Press, St. Charles, MO, 1973.

92. Deloria, Vine Jr., *Custer Died for Your Sins: An Indian Manifesto*, Macmillan Publishers, New York, 1969; reprinted by the University of Oklahoma Press, Norman, 1988; and *We Talk, You Listen: New Tribes, New Turf*, Macmillan Publishers, New York, 1970.
93. On the founding of AIM and its early demonstrations, see Churchill, Ward, and Jim Vander Wall, *Agents of Repression: The FBI's Secret Wars Against the Black Panther Party and the American Indian Movement*, South End Press, Boston, 1988. On the Alcatraz occupation, see Blue Cloud, Peter, *Alcatraz Is Not An Island*, Wingbow Press, Berkeley, CA, 1972. On the Pit River confrontations, see Jaimes, M. Annette, "The Pit River Indian Land Claim Dispute in Northern California," *Journal of Ethnic Studies*, Vol. 14, No. 4, Winter 1987.
94. See Albert, Stewart, and Judith Clavir-Albert, eds., *The Sixties Papers: Documents of a Rebellious Decade*, Praeger Publishers, New York, 1984.
95. The study in question is Brophie, William A., and Sophie E. Aberle, *The Indian, America's Unfinished Business: Report of the Commission on Rights, Liberties and Responsibilities of the American Indian*, University of Oklahoma Press, Norman, 1966. For the text of the Johnson speech, see *Public Papers of the Presidents, 1968-1969*, U.S. Government Printing Office, Washington, D.C., 1970, p. 335. For analysis of the speech and its policy context, see Clinton, Robert M., Nell Jessup Newton, and Monroe E. Price, *American Indian Law: Cases and Materials*, The Michie Co., Charlottesville, VA, 1991, p. 159.
96. See Burnett, Donald E., "An Historical Analysis of the 1968 'Indian Civil Rights' Act," *Harvard Journal of Legislation*, No. 9, May 1972, pp. 557-626. Also see Prucha, Francis Paul, "American Indian Policy in the Twentieth Century," *Western Historical Quarterly*, No. 15, January 1984, pp. 5-18.
97. Clinton, *et al.*, op. cit., p. 159.
98. The language is from a speech delivered by NTCA President Webster Two Hawks in Washington, D.C. on November 6, 1972; quoted in the *Washington Post* the same day. It should be noted that NTCA was supported by $100,000 in federal funds each year for fiscal years 1969-73, and that Two Hawks' trip to the capitol to make the speech in question was underwritten entirely by funds provided by Nixon's Committee to Reelect the President (CREEP).
99. Deloria, Vine Jr., *Behind the Trail of Broken Treaties: An Indian Declaration of Independence*, University of Texas Press, Austin, 2nd Edition, 1984, pp. 48-52.
100. The best account of the 1972 BIA building occupation may be found in Editors, *BIA, I'm Not Your Indian Anymore*, *Akwesasne Notes*, Mohawk Nation via Rooseveltown, NY, 1973. More generally, see *Behind the Trail of Broken Treaties*, op. cit., and Burnette, Robert, with John Koster, *The Road to Wounded Knee*, Bantam Books, New York, 1974. It should be noted that AIM's "liberation" of the BIA's internal documents revealed a broad range of questionable (and previously denied) federal practices involving the leasing of Indian lands. It also exposed a secret program of involuntary sterilization targeting native women.
101. See Churchill, Ward, "'Renegades, Terrorists and Revolutionaries': The U.S. Government's Propaganda War Against the American Indian Movement," *Propaganda Review*, No. 4, Spring 1989, pp. 12-16. Also see *BIA, I'm Not Your Indian Anymore*, op. cit.
102. Burnette and Koster, op. cit.
103. The circumstances leading up to the Wounded Knee Siege are covered in Holm, Tom, "The Crisis in Tribal Government," in Vine Deloria, Jr., ed., *American Indian Policy in the Twentieth Century*, University of Oklahoma Press, Norman, 1985, pp. 135-54. Also see U.S. Senate, Committee on Insular Affairs, Subcommittee on Indian Affairs, *The Occupation of Wounded Knee: Hearings Before the Subcommittee on Indian Affairs, June 16-17, 1973*, 93rd Cong., 1st Sess., U.S. Government Printing Office, Washington, D.C., 1973.
104. For the best single account of the Wounded Knee siege, see Editors, *Voices From Wounded Knee, 1973*, *Akwesasne Notes*, Mohawk Nation via Rooseveltown, NY, 1974. Also see *Agents of Repression*, op. cit., pp. 141-77.
105. See U.S. Commission on Civil Rights, *Report of Investigation: Oglala Sioux Tribe, General Election, 1974*, Rocky Mountain Regional Office, Denver, 1974.
106. On the assassination of Pedro Bissonette, see *Agents of Repression*, op. cit., pp. 200-3.
107. In addition to works already cited, interesting assessments of the government's counterinsurgency war against AIM may be found in Johansen, Bruce, and Roberto Maestas, *Wasi'chu: The Continuing Indian Wars*, Monthly Review Press, New York, 1979; and Weyler, Rex, *Blood of the Land: The U.S. Government and Corporate War Against the American Indian Movement*, Everest House Publishers, New York, 1983.

108. Analysis of Nixon's use of the term may be obtained in Forbes, Jack D., *Native Americans and Nixon: Presidential Politics and Minority Self-Determination*, American Indian Studies Center, UCLA, 1981.
109. This formulation accrues from Point 2 of the United Nations' 1960 Declaration on the Granting of Independence to Colonial Countries and Peoples, which the U.S.—as is usually the case with elements of international law pertaining to human rights—abstained from signing. The Declaration is reproduced verbatim in Brownlie, op. cit., pp. 28-30.
110. For cogent analysis of the Act's content, see Gross, Michael P., "Indian Self-Determination and Tribal Sovereignty: An Analysis of Recent Federal Indian Policy," *Texas Law Review*, No. 56, 1978, esp. p. 1195: "Even if it were an established fact...Indian control of [such agencies as] the BIA would not substitute for self-government."
111. Speech by Russell Means, July 25, 1978 (tape on file).
112. The commission was authorized under provision of 25 U.S.C. 174. Its findings, entitled *Report: American Indian Policy Review Commission Task Force*, were published in nine volumes U.S. Government Printing Office, Washington, D.C., 1977. The quote is taken from Clinton, et al., op. cit., p. 162.
113. Meeds is quoted from *Final Report: American Indian Policy Review Commission Task Force*, op. cit., p. 573.
114. Clinton, et al., op. cit., p. 162. For analysis, see Wilkinson, Charles F., "Shall the Islands be Protected?" *American West*, No. 41, 1979. Also see Clinton, Robert N., "Isolated in Their Own Country: A Defense of Federal Protection of Indian Autonomy and Self-Government," *Stanford Law Review*, No. 33, 1981.
115. Quoted in *Indian Self-Rule*, op. cit., p. 291. The "Indian governments as part of the federal hierarchy" theory has by now been worked out in a doctrinal sense, primarily by liberal non-Indian legal scholars such as Charles F. Wilkinson. For a full-bore display of such thinking, see his *Indians, Time and Law*, Yale University Press, New Haven, CT, 1987. For an "Indian" adaptation of the principles at issue, see American Indian Lawyer Training Program, *Indian Tribes as Sovereign Governments: A Sourcebook on Federal-Tribal History, Law and Policy*, American Indian Resources Institute Press, Oakland, CA, 1985.
116. Quoted in *Indian Self-Rule*, p. 287.
117. For discussion of the Longest Walk, and the full text of its manifesto, see Robbins, Rebecca L., "American Indian Self-Determination: Comparative Analysis and Rhetorical Criticism," *Issues in Radical Therapy/New Studies on the Left*, Vol. XIII, Nos. 3 and 4, Summer-Fall 1988, pp. 48-58. Also see "The Longest Walk," *Akwesasne Notes*, Mohawk Nation via Rooseveltown, NY, Vol. 10, No. 3, Summer 1978.
118. The Standing Rock conference and formation of IITC is covered in the updated version of *Behind the Trail of Broken Treaties*, op. cit. Corroboration has been obtained by direct interview of both Jimmie Durham and Russell Means during 1991. Portions of Durham's views on the process may also be found in his *Columbus Day*, West End Press, Minneapolis, 1982.
119. *Behind the Trail of Broken Treaties*, op. cit.
120. Russell Tribunal, *The Rights of the Indians of the Americas*, Fourth Russell Tribunal, Rotterdam, Netherlands, 1980.
121. On formation of the Working Group and its mandate (E.S.C. Res. 34, U.N. ESCOR Supp. (No. 1) at 26-27, U.N. Doc. E/1982/82 (1982)), see Anaya, James S., "The Rights of Indigenous Peoples and International Law in Historical and Contemporary Perspective," in Clinton, *et al.*, op. cit., pp. 1257-76. Also see Barsh, Russel, "Indigenous North America and Contemporary International Law," *Oregon Law Review*, No. 62, 1983.
122. For the text of the revised draft of the *International Declaration on the Rights of Indigenous Peoples*, see *Report of the Working Group on Indigenous Populations*, 7th Session, Annex II, U.N. Doc. E/CN.4/sub.2/1989/36, August 25, 1989.
123. The text of the ILO Convention, approved in June 1989, appears in "Report of the Committee on Convention 107," *Provisional Record*, No. 25, 76th Sess., 1989, pp. 25-33. For interpretation of its significance, see Anaya, op. cit.
124. The proposal for a new OAS instrument on indigenous rights, approved on November 18, 1989, is described in the *Annual Report of the Inter-American Commission on Human Rights, 1988-89*, OEA/Ser.L/v/II.76, Doc. 10, September 18, 1989.
125. During the summer of 1990, Colorado AIM Codirector Glenn T. Morris received a telephone call from a NARF staff attorney soliciting advice as to how go about obtaining NGO status.

126. Quoted in *Indian Self-Rule*, op. cit., p. 280.
127. The complete text of the Churchill/Means collaboration is forthcoming under the title *TREATY: A Program for American Indian Sovereignty*, from the Fourth World Center for Indigenous Law and Politics, University of Colorado at Denver, in early 1992.
128. On Means' 1978 conviction, see Amnesty International, *Proposal for a Commission of Inquiry into the Effect of Domestic Intelligence Activities on Criminal Trials in the United States of America*, Amnesty International, New York, 1980. AI was preparing to adopt Means as a "prisoner of conscience" at the time of his release from prison in 1979. The South Dakota anarcho-syndicalism statute under which the AIM leader was convicted has been subsequently repealed.
129. Anderson was a major leader of the resistance of traditional Diné to forced relocation from the Big Mountain area of the Navajo Nation during the period 1974-1986. See Weyler, op. cit. Also see Kammer, Jerry, *The Second Long Walk: The Navajo-Hopi Land Dispute*, University of New Mexico, Albuquerque, 1980.
130. For DeLaCruz's thinking on strategies that might lead to a resumption of genuine Indian sovereignty, see his "From Self-Determination to Self-Governance," in Minugh, Carol J., Glenn T. Morris, and Rudolph C. Ryser, eds., *Indian Self-Governance: Perspectives on the Political Status of Indian Nations in the United States of America*, Center for World Indigenous Studies, Kenmore, WA, 1989, pp. 1-14. For background on the Coastal Highway dispute and related matters, see Ryser, Rudolph C., ed., *Tribes and States in Conflict: A Tribal Proposal*, Intertribal Study Group on Tribal/State Relations, Rational Island Press, Seattle, 1981.
131. See Martinez Cobo, José R., *Study of the Problem of Discrimination Against Indigenous Populations, Final Report: Conclusions, Proposals and Recommendations*, U.N./ID # E/CN.4/Sub.2/1983/21/Add.83, September 1983. Also see Independent Commission on International Humanitarian Issues, *Indigenous Peoples: A Global Quest for Justice*, Zed Press, London, 1987.
132. With regard to the revelations on BIA mismanagement and related matters, see U.S. Senate, Select Committee on Indian Affairs, *Hearings Before the Committee on Investigations, January 30 and 31, 1989*, 101st Cong., 1st Sess., U.S. Government Printing Office, Washington, D.C., February 1, 1989.
133. The text of the relevant portions of P.L. 100-472 may be found in Minugh, et al., op. cit., pp. 122-5. Analysis of the law by three of the involved nations—Quinalt, Lummi and the Jamestown Band of Klallam—may be found on pp. 117-22.
134. U.S. Senate, Select Committee on Indian Affairs, *Final Report and Legislative Recommendations: A Report of the Special Committee on Investigations*, 101st Cong., 2d Sess., U.S. Government Printing Office, Washington, D.C., November 20, 1989, p. 17.

International Law and Politics
Toward a Right to Self-Determination for Indigenous Peoples

Glenn T. Morris

We support the principles that indigenous peoples have the right to exist as distinct peoples of the world, and that they have a right to possession of their territories and the right to sovereign self-determination. We call upon the people of the world to join us in asserting that the genocide and dispossession of indigenous peoples is a matter of rightful concern to the world community, as are matters involving a consistent pattern of gross violations of the rights of the indigenous peoples and nations under principles established by international law, and that action must be taken by the world organizations and specifically the United Nations.

Statement of the Indigenous Peoples' Fourth Russell Tribunal on the Rights of the Indians of the Americas, November 28, 1980

The historical operation of a system of legal norms and standards, ordained by a handful of states, and imposed upon the overwhelming majority of the world's peoples without their consent or input, is considered perverse and unjust by most indigenous peoples. This system, pretentiously known as "The Laws of Nations," continues to operate at the threshold of the 21st century without meaningful participation by hundreds of millions of the planet's indigenous peoples. This observation is not meant to suggest that all that has been, or continues to be, recognized as "The Laws of Nations" is either unjust or unacceptable. What it *is* intended to suggest is that, as is now readily acknowledged, colonial or settler states should not possess the right to impose their particular definition of just or equitable relations between peoples on the majority of humankind and call it "law."

Only in the past fifty years, or the past thirty for over a third of the states of the world, has self-determination been realized through the recognition that colonialism is abhorrent to the desired liberty of humankind. Through the acceptance of the U.N. charter and other human-rights instruments, self-determination of peoples is a universally accepted aspiration. Unfortunately, thousands of the world's peoples have yet to realize that aspiration. Indigenous peoples from Burma to Brazil, from the Arctic to Australia, continue to be denied the right to control their affairs in any effective and meaningful manner. In many of these countries, such as Guatemala, Bolivia, Greenland, and Ecuador, indigenous peoples comprise a majority of the total state population; yet, they often remain disenfranchised and subordinated by the descendants of the original settler or colonizing classes. Despite recent and tentative advances in the recognition of the rights of indigenous peoples in such places as Nicaragua, Greenland, and Panama, and despite some progress in certain international forums, the overwhelming majority of indigenous peoples are forced to struggle for their very existence against the enormous pressure of encroaching states surrounding them.

Through the application of international legal and political norms, many peoples under colonial domination have achieved some level of political self-determination. Many representatives of indigenous peoples and nations point to the example of the decolonization of southern Africa as an example to be emulated in the case of indigenous peoples elsewhere. Just as principles of self-determination have been applied to liberate the peoples of Zimbabwe or Namibia, where the idea of Black majority rule is accepted without question, so, too, should such principles apply to all indigenous peoples. This essay is devoted to the examination of why such principles have not been applied to indigenous peoples and how the operation of European and American legal doctrines has been used to maintain their colonial condition. One particular paradox in this examination will be the recognition that even by their own legal standards, the Euroamerican colonization of the Western hemisphere (and, by extension, other indigenous peoples' lands across the globe) was unjustified.

More important, the purpose here is to indicate that through the application of contemporary principles of international law, particularly in the area of decolonization and self-determination, indigenous peoples must ultimately be entitled to decide for themselves the dimensions of their political, economic, cultural, and social conditions. It must be emphasized that the construction of this position is not based in the supposition that because indigenous peoples constitute ethnic or cultural minorities in larger societies they must be protected due to that status. Rather, the position is that since Europeans first wandered into the Western hemisphere they have acknowledged the unique status of indigenous peoples qua indigenous peoples. That status is only now being reacknowledged through the application of evolving principles of positive and customary international law.

While such assertions may seem novel and untenable at present, it should be recalled that just forty years ago, tens of millions of people languished under the rule of colonial domination; today, they are politically independent. Central to their independence was the development and acceptance of the right to self-determination under international law. Despite such developments, many colonized peoples were forced by desperate conditions to engage in armed struggle to advance their legitimate aspirations. Similarly, for many indigenous peoples few viable options remain in their quest for control of their destinies. Consequently, a majority of the current armed conflicts in the world are not between established states, but between indigenous peoples and states that seek their subordination. Armed struggle for most indigenous peoples represents a desperate and untenable strategy for their survival. Nonetheless, it may remain an unavoidable option for many of them, because if their petitions seeking recognition of their rights in international forums are ignored, many indigenous peoples, quite literally, face extermination.

Although this chapter has implications for the status of all indigenous peoples, its concentration is primarily within the United States. This is because, in several ways, the status of indigenous nations within the U.S. is unique, and the policy of the United States toward indigenous nations has frequently been emulated by other states. The fact that a treaty relationship exists between the United States and indigenous nations, and the fact that indigenous nations within the U.S. retain defined and separate land bases and continue to exercise some degree of effective self-government, may contribute to the successful application of international standards in their cases. Also, given the size and relative power of the United States in international relations, and absent the unlikely independence of a majority-indigenous nation-state such as Guatemala or Greenland, the successful application of decolonization principles to indigenous nations within the U.S. could allow the extension of such applications to indigenous peoples in other parts of the planet.

One final introductory point: Indigenous peoples, as all colonized peoples, have come to realize the importance of semantics in their quest for self-determination. Consequently, the use of several key terms in this chapter is deliberate. The terms "indigenous peoples" or "indigenous nations" are used intentionally for the reason that, if nothing else, they accurately describe the original peoples of given territories. Ideally, the specific names of indigenous nations would be (and have been) used, but for the sake of clarity and brevity, that practice has been limited here. Although the term "nation" denotes a socio-political construct of European nature, the concept carries with it considerable importance in international debates. Fortunately, among the ranks of indigenous peoples a discussion has begun that calls into question the usefulness of forcing indigenous reality into the forms developed by Europeans. Consequently, new descriptions of the historical organization of indigenous societies, as well as indigenous aspirations, are being formulated. The result may be the evolution of completely novel international relationships between and among peoples. Despite this development, the term "nation" is deliberately used in this chapter. A reasonable explanation for the use of the term was provided by Oren Lyons of the Onondaga Nation:

> We are the original people on this land. We are the land keepers. We are not a minority within our own lands. One must understand that terminology is very important. How you address yourself is very important to [Euroamericans]. If you try and change that terminology, you will find out how important it is. So we must speak of ourselves as people...If you fall into the category of "tribes" or "bands," a gaggle of geese, a herd, a group...you're more than that. It's important not to call Indians "bands." You try to change [Euroamerican]

> terminology,...they will not accept it because it is that important. That terminology is just as important to you. So, you should first of all represent yourself as what you are. Nations are not according to size, nations are according to culture. If there are twenty people left who are still representing their nation, in the eyes of our people, they are a nation. Who are we to say less?[1]

Historical Rights of Indigenous Peoples

The historical antecedents of the legal rights of indigenous peoples may be found centuries prior to the European arrival in the Western hemisphere. After the establishment of the Holy Roman Empire, but prior to the colonial travels of Europeans to the "New World," distinctions drawn by Europeans between the various peoples of the known world were generally in terms of Christians and "infidels."[2] With the expansion of Christianity, the acquisition of territory from newly discovered peoples (such as those in Asia and Africa) or from familiar peoples (particularly the Saracens and Turks) who were unwilling to accept Christian doctrines and who were therefore subject to "reconquest," was justified through the extension of the Roman legal principle, *territorium (res) nullius.*[3] Under this extension, a "discoverer" could legally occupy a territory that was already inhabited (by "infidels") and extend Christian sovereignty over it.[4]

Eventually, this principle of effective occupation was rejected in favor of the principles of conquest and effective possession. Under these new principles, justification for extension of Christian sovereignty rested upon the attitude that infidels were the enemies of Christian civilization and that non-believers could be dispossessed of their territories justifiably by subjugation through wars of conquest. They lost all rights to territorial integrity as separate and distinct peoples. Not all Christian jurists or legal theorists of the time accepted the premises upon which the principle of conquest was founded. Among the more notable defenders of the rights of non-Christians to maintain control over their territories were Thomas Aquinas (1227-1274)[5] and Sinibaldo Fiesco, who became Pope Innocent IV (1243-1254).[6] Although the theories of these theologians and legal scholars characterized non-Christians in pejorative terms, there was a fundamental acknowledgment of a difference between the natural law of human-created institutions (*summa natura)* and the divine law of God that distinguishes between the faithful and infidels. According to Aquinas, although political society should disapprove of immoral acts, i.e., spiritual infidelity, the state must make allowances for the "natural sinfulness" of human beings.[7] In this way, the higher good fostered through the promotion of a civilized, Christian society is maintained through the peaceful integration and conversion of infidels, rather than through their violent subjugation or destruction.

Spanish Colonial Law

Columbus' return to Europe after his first voyage to the Americas promoted enormous debate regarding the status of the peoples he encountered. This debate included the scope of authority of European states to extend themselves over the lands across the Atlantic. The first known European documents addressing the question of dominion over the "New World" were the Papal Bulls of Pope Alexander VI.[8] Signed on May 3 and 5, 1493, the Alexandrine Bulls acknowledged the right of the sovereigns of Castille and Aragon to acquire and Christianize the islands and *terra firma* of the new regions. The issuance of the bulls created immediate tensions between competing European powers concerning the new territories, tensions that would remain unresolved in Europe for over 300 years and that continue in the Americas today.[9] One interesting passage from the Bull *Inter Caetera* of May 4, 1493, represents the first European acknowledgment of the national character of the indigenous peoples of the New World:

> [Columbus] found certain remote islands and also mainlands, which had not been discovered before by others before [sic] in which dwell very many tribes, peacefully living, and, as it is asserted, going naked and not eating meat; and so far as your messengers are able to conjecture *these* nations living in the said islands and lands believe that there is one God and one Creator in the heavens (emphasis added).[10]

Subsequent to their initial contact with indigenous peoples in the Western hemisphere, the Europeans examined the source, depth, and legitimacy of their claims to the lands upon which they happened, vis-à-vis the nations already occupying the same lands. Ongoing discussion concerning Spanish claims in America took place in Paris in the early 16th century, primarily facilitated by John Mair (1469-1542) and his *Commentary on the Sentences of Pater Lombard.*[11] One of Mair's most prominent students was Franciscus de Victoria (1480-1546), a professor in Glasgow and Paris, widely recognized as "the father" of modern international law.[12] Mair's writings challenged the popular contention that the Pope possessed universal secular authority, suggesting instead that sovereign authority was vested in independent, secular political associations or kingdoms. Mair agreed with earlier theorists who taught that infidels (or indigenous peoples) could be subdued if they failed to convert to Christianity, but held there was no justification for conquest if conversion requirements were met. He also believed, in the Aristotelian tradition, that slavery is a natural state for some peoples, and that civilized nations have a natural right to rule the less civilized.[13]

In Spain, the development of legal doctrines regarding the lands and peoples of the Western hemisphere was stimulated by the sermons of Father Antonio de Montesinos in 1511, which castigated the Spanish for their enslavement and slaughter of the indigenous peoples of the Americas.[14] His sermons led to a convocation of legal theorists and theologians at Burgos in 1512. Two principal views emerged from the meeting, one represented by Juan López de Palacios Rubios (1450-1542) and the other by Matías de Paz (1468-1542).[15] Palacios Rubios advanced the position that the Alexandrine Bulls provided complete legal authority for the Spanish conquest of indigenous nations, since the Pope was heir to Christ's temporal and spiritual authority. According to Palacios Rubios, this authority enabled the Pope to assert control over all infidels and compelled their obedience to the rule of the Roman Catholic Church.[16] Rubios was also author of the infamous *Requirimiento*, an edict read (in Spanish) to the indigenous peoples of the Americas informing them of their obligation to convert to Roman Catholicism and to submit themselves to the sovereign authority of the Spanish Crown.[17] Failure to comply with the *Requirimiento* resulted in immediate attack by the Spaniards on recalcitrant communities and execution of resisters. It also provided the Spanish with what they believed to be legal authority to wage a "Just War" against indigenous nations and peoples.[18] This use of the *Requirimiento* as a mere rationalization has been viewed by some commentators as an "ironic, if not ridiculous, character of a formality intended to ease the conscience of the Spanish."[19]

Conversely, Matias de Paz, in his work *Concerning the Rule of the Kings of Spain Over the Indians*, was the first European scholar to repudiate the application of the Aristotelian theory of natural slavery to American Indians. While agreeing with the fundamental precept that the Pope and Church alone had authority to dominate the world, Matias went considerably further than Palacios Rubios in recognizing the humanity of non-Christians. Matias distinguished between those non-Christians who had been exposed to Christian teachings and rejected them and those, such as indigenous peoples, who had never known the "true faith." Matias de Paz suggested that American Indians, due to their ignorance of Christianity, could legally resist *any war* levied against them by the Spanish through the *Requirimiento* process. Since "wars cannot be just on both sides," either the Spanish possessed the right to levy a Just War, or the Indians had the legal right to resist.[20] Consequently, the Spanish were in his view without legal authority to enslave or dispossess indigenous nations. According to Matias de Paz, indigenous nations possessed the absolute right of self-defense, producing the logical conclusion that the Spanish wars were legally unjust and unjustifiable. Without a basis to wage a Just War, the Spanish had no legal right to dispossess indigenous nations of their lands or of their inherent sovereign authority to govern themselves.

The Burgos debates between Palacios Rubios and Matias de Paz were important for three reasons: first, they revealed dramatically divergent perspectives among European scholars regarding the rights of indigenous peoples. Second, they led to promulgation of the Laws of Burgos, theoretically regulating every aspect of Spanish colonial life in "New Spain" (in practice, of course, these laws were routinely violated or ignored). Third, they sowed the seeds for subsequent discussions of the same subject. The most critical of these subsequent debates took place at Vallodolid between Bartolomé de Las Casas (1474-1566) and Juan Ginés de Sepúlveda (1490-1573).[21]

Prior to the crucial Las Casas/Sepúlveda debates of 1550, the Spanish jurist Franciscus de Victoria authored several articles detailing the limits of papal and Spanish authority over indigenous peoples and their territories.[22] Victoria's conclusions were clear: indigenous nations of the Americas exercised

> true dominion over their property in both public and private matters, just like Christians, and...neither their princes nor private persons could be despoiled of their property on the ground of not being true owners. It would be hard to deny those who have never done any wrong, what we grant the Saracens and Jews, who are persistent enemies of Christianity. We do not deny that these latter peoples are true owners of their property, if they have not seized lands elsewhere belonging to Christians.[23]

He also concluded that because the Pope was not the lord of the entire world, there could be no exercise of papal authority over indigenous nations.[24] Further, Victoria asserted that Christians not only were without legal claim to already occupied lands of the Americas, but (as was previously recognized by Matias de Paz) they were without sufficient legal right to levy a Just War against indigenous peoples based on the claim that the new territories now belonged to Spain through papal donation, or based on the Indian's rejection of Christianity.[25] These conclusions effectively refute any European or Euro-derived claim to the Western hemisphere based on the so-called Rights of Conquest doctrine.[26]

Victoria was the first European theorist to suggest that indigenous nations in the Americas possessed the inherent sovereign power to make territorial cessions through voluntary and informed agreements in the form of international treaties. This principle was endorsed, though by no means universally, for the succeeding five centuries by various jurists, international legal scholars, and political leaders.[27] According to the noted U.S. legal theorist and historian Felix S. Cohen, the concept of treating between European states and indigenous nations, as first suggested by Victoria, was rooted in three basic assumptions:

> 1. that both parties to the treaty are sovereign powers;
> 2. that the Indian [nation] has a transferable title of some sort, to the land in question; and
> 3. that the acquisition of Indian lands could not safely be left to individual colonists, but must be controlled by government monopoly.[28]

Influenced by the writings and lectures of Victoria, Pope Paul III issued the Bull *Sublimus Deus* in 1537, instructing his Catholic subjects to view indigenous peoples as true humans. Further, he instructed European sovereigns that "the said Indians and all other people who have been or may later be discovered by Christians, are by no means to be deprived of their property, even though they be outside the faith of Jesus Christ; and that they may and should freely and legitimately enjoy their liberty and possession of their property; nor should they in any way be enslaved; should the contrary happen, it shall be null."[29] By 1540, reports of massacres of the indigenous peoples of the Americas by the Spaniards were becoming so common,[30] and were so troubling to Charles V of Spain, that he convened a council of jurists and legal scholars to discuss the rights and responsibilities of the Crown in the Western hemisphere.[31] A series of councils and debates took place in the succeeding years, culminating in the debate between Las Casas and Sepúlveda.[32] The latter, who had never traveled to the Americas, and who had seen American Indians only in the slave market in Seville, argued in favor of the Spanish conquest of indigenous peoples, whom he viewed as sub-human infidels:

> In defending the Spanish rule, Sepúlveda argued the superiority of Spaniards and the inferiority of Indians. A just war was one in which the barbarian enemy was offered an opportunity to yield peaceably, as in the *Requirimiento* procedure...He attacked the American Indians, and most particularly the Aztecs as stupid, inept, uncivilized, cruel, idolatrous and immoral. Indeed, they were "natural slaves."[33]

Las Casas, a Dominican missionary who had traveled and lived among indigenous nations throughout the Caribbean and Latin America between 1502 and 1547, argued fervently that native peoples could not be subjugated legally by the Spanish. He agreed with Victoria that the indigenous nations of the Western hemisphere were the rightful sovereigns of their territories, that Europeans had no cause to wage Just Wars, and that conquest of the region was "unlawful, tyrannical, and unjust."[34] Although the debate did not result in dramatic policy changes in Spain, the legal and political repercussions were felt in the Americas, at least temporarily. The Spanish had no intention of vacating their colonies, but the Crown did pass a number of laws, beginning in 1573, explicitly recognizing the territorial integrity of certain indigenous nations.[35] With the passage of these laws, the Spanish implicitly created a system of trusteeship for the indigenous peoples of New Spain.[36] This is not to suggest that the trust was consistently upheld, that the rights of indigenous nations were respected, or that the repression and subjugation of native peoples was diminished. It is intended, instead, to suggest that "the oppression was in defiance of, rather than pursuant to, the laws of Spain."[37] It also suggests, as the Papal Bulls and Spanish *Cedulas* themselves did, that violations of Spanish law should have rendered the extension of Spanish territorial sovereignty null and void.[38]

English Innovations

The Spanish debate concerning the rights of indigenous peoples was carried to northern Europe and influenced the legal and political practices of other European colonial powers (Spanish Catholic influence was extended to England, for instance, until 1558, when the Protestant Queen Elizabeth I ascended to the throne). English colonizing doctrines, perhaps the most enduring for indigenous peoples, were employed first on the Irish and then exported to the Western hemisphere. According to Robert Williams, this colonial style synthesized "medievally derived legal theories on the diminished status and rights of normatively divergent savage people, anti-Spanish religious and mercantile nationalism, and English innovations of Spanish colonizing practice."[39]

English justifications for the dispossession of North America from indigenous peoples derived from an Elizabethan Protestant doctrine declaring the English in covenant with God to bring "true" (as opposed to Spanish) Christianity to "heathen natives." The development of English legal doctrines regarding colonization was heavily influenced by George Peckham, who, in turn, relied on the writings of

Victoria. Peckham, however, used Victoria for his own purposes, primarily to justify English colonization under the Laws of Nations by asserting that English Christians had the lawful right to trade with indigenous peoples worldwide. According to Peckham, if infidels refused to trade, the English were then entitled to conquer the resisters and dispossess them of their lands.[40] By this reasoning, all that was required to wage a Just War was to come upon a people that was unwilling to trade or accept missionaries. The English claimed to—but probably did not—feel legally justified in conquering American Indians on this basis. In the example of the colonization of Virginia, English colonizers, cognizant of the questionable moral and legal justification for their invasion, engaged in self-deception, refusing any objective analysis of their actions:

> Instead, a strategy of silence, in order to suppress the arousal of any contrary discourse, was agreed on. The justice of the company's royally assigned title in America would operate simply on a presumption of English superior rights in America...Conquest of America itself would prove the superior right of the English to the Indians' America...By the early seventeenth century at least, Spaniards recognized as well as did the English that legal arguments had little to do with European "rights" in America.[41]

Hence, the imposition of the European presence in the Americas cannot reasonably be asserted to be the consequence of adherence to law, but rather the operation of sheer force. The *a priori* justifications of the English, while soothing to the conscience of those invaders who benefited, demand serious scrutiny because they constitute the legal cornerstone for all subsequent English settlement in the Western hemisphere. As often happens in the development of law affecting indigenous peoples, these early self-serving justifications of the English became enshrined and legitimized in legal precedent. The 1622 *Barkham's Case* held, despite contrary writings by Vattel and other legal authorities, that the legal and political authority of "heathen infidels" was necessarily abrogated when it came into contact with Christian sovereignty.[42] With such reasoning, expansion of English and U.S. colonization of indigenous peoples was inevitable.[43]

The Status of Indigenous Nations in the U.S.

The first sustained European settlements in the area now known as the United States were established in 1565 at St. Augustine, Florida; 1607 at Jamestown, Virginia; 1609 at New Amsterdam (New York) and Santa Fé, New Mexico; and 1620 at Plymouth, Massachusetts. Without exception, these colonists were greeted by native peoples with friendship and openness, as Columbus had been before them.[44] In return, indigenous nations were confronted with racism, massacres, religious bigotry, and systematic fraud.[45] As discussed above, by the time Europeans began colonizing the Americas, they had established and adhered to (at least among themselves) a number of accepted legal norms concerning territorial acquisition and possession. Among the most basic of these standards was the "right to use that which one had created, possessed or occupied without wrongfully taking [it] from another."[46] As concerns land, this principle was known as possession of *territorium nullius,* acknowledging the rights of those who had occupied territories over prolonged periods of time, under the principle of "immemorial possession."

Enforceable rights under immemorial possession were recognized by the legal theorists of the Middle Ages, as they had been by the Romans before them.[47] The doctrine of immemorial possession, combined with the recognition of the inherent sovereignty and possessory right of indigenous nations, was found to be so compelling by the Dutch that they began to negotiate treaties for land cessions from indigenous nations from their first contact with one another.[48] The Swedish soon followed the Dutch example, as did some English colonists,[49] reinforcing conclusions that the Doctrine of Discovery did not diminish the sovereign rights of indigenous peoples, but was a mechanism of controlling competing European states in their negotiations with indigenous nations regarding territorial cessions.[50]

After the 17th century, the discovery doctrine was generally understood not to limit or divest indigenous nations of any authority over their territories. The doctrine was developed as a regulatory mechanism between European sovereigns to prioritize their rights to engage in international relations with indigenous nations, and to preempt other European states from interacting with the same indigenous nation. The discovery doctrine and the limitations that Europeans knowingly placed on their claims to lands in the Americas were succinctly described by United States Supreme Court Chief Justice John Marshall:

> The principle, acknowledged by all Europeans, because it was in the self-interest of all to acknowledge it, gave to the nation making the discovery, as its inevitable consequence, the sole right of acquiring the title and of making settlements on it. It was an exclusive principle which shut out the right of competition among those who had agreed to it. It regulated rights given by discovery among the European discoverers; *but could not affect the rights of those already in possession,* either as aboriginal occupants or by virtue of discovery made before the memory of man. It gave the exclusive right of purchase, but did not found that right on a denial of the possessors to sell [emphasis added].[51]

European states fully understood the nature of their negotiations with the indigenous nations of the Americas. Indigenous governments acted as sovereigns, despite attempts to construct circumventions and rationalizations, with all the attendant authority of this status.[52] The years immediately preceding the American Revolution saw an effort, by both the British and the newly formed Continental Congress of the United States, to centralize their relations with indigenous nations.[53] This effort represented a deliberate decision to remove the power to negotiate with native nations from the individual colonies and vest it exclusively with the national government, thereby insuring the uniformity of negotiations between equal national sovereigns.[54] In an effort to enlist the support of indigenous nations for the Revolution, the Americans began to treat formally with native governments.[55] The first of these treaties[56] was later described by the U.S. Supreme Court as "the model of treaties between the crowned heads of Europe."[57]

The founding documents and laws of the United States remove any doubt that the nascent state recognized the national sovereignty of of indigenous nations; the intention to recognize indigenous sovereignty is clear.[58] Additional evidence may be obtained from the opinions of William Wirt, an early attorney general of the United States: "So long as a tribe exists and remains in possession of its lands, its title and possession are sovereign and exclusive. We treat with them as separate sovereignties, and while an Indian nation continues to exist within its acknowledged limits, we have no more right to enter upon their territory than we have to enter upon the territory of a foreign prince."[59]

> The point, then once conceded, that the Indians are independent to the purpose of treating, their independence is to that purpose as absolute as any other nation. Being competent to bind themselves by treaty, they are equally competent to bind the party who treats with them. Such party cannot take benefit of the treaty with the Indians, and then deny them the reciprocal benefits of the treaty on the grounds that they are not independent nations to all intents and purposes...Nor can it be conceded that their independence as a nation is a limited independence. *Like all other independent nations,* they have the absolute power of war and peace. *Like all other independent nations,* their territories are inviolable by any other sovereignty...As a nation, they are still free and independent. They are entirely self-governed, self-directed. They treat, or refuse to treat, at their pleasure; and there is no human power which can rightly control them in the exercise of their discretion in this respect [emphasis added].[60]

With this policy, the United States negotiated treaties with the sovereign indigenous peoples of North America. These treaties were, and continue to be, recognized under Article VI of the U.S. Constitution as the supreme law of the United States, and continue to warrant the same respect and enforcement as any other international treaty. Of equal importance is the principle of continued respect for the national sovereignty of the indigenous nations that entered into those treaties. In the previous section, evidence was advanced that European states were forced to acknowledge the objective sovereignty of indigenous nations. This recognition eventually translated into over a century of treaty-making by the governments of France, Spain, Sweden, Britain, the Netherlands, and the United States with various indigenous nations. Between 1778 and 1871, the United States entered into and ratified more than 370 treaties with indigenous peoples.[61] Between 1871 and 1902, new covenants between the governments were formalized in "agreements." As a practical matter, particularly as regards U.S. policy that continued to define indigenous nations as sovereign, the semantic difference between treaties and agreements was of limited importance.[62] The change reflected internal institutional conflicts between the U.S. Senate and House of Representatives over which would exert greater influence in the area of indigenous relations, but the overall perception of the United States toward native sovereignty was not altered.

As with all treaties, it would be reasonable to view the covenants between the United States and indigenous nations in an international context.[63] They should be reviewed in light of the norms and developments that govern all treaties in the international arena. One underlying assumption should be that treaties represent legal obligations by nations of people, entered into in good faith, the material parts of which must be honored by the parties to the accord. Treaties are, among other things, bilateral compacts between nations or states. The United States and indigenous nations entered into agreements on a co-equal legal footing, and the agreements should be accorded the same respect as other bilateral or multilateral treaties in the international community. U.S. courts have never upheld the claim that treaties between indigenous peoples and the U.S. are inferior to, or should be accorded any less respect, than any other treaty signed and ratified by the United States.

Treaties between the United States and indigenous governments remain in force, require compliance by all parties, and have not been diminished in their international character. It should be noted that the international dimensions of these treaties have been supplemented in two important respects by the courts of the United States. First, the canon of construction for these treaties requires that they are to be interpreted as the native negotiators and signatories would have understood them.[64] Second, treaties are to be interpreted liberally by the courts, with ambiguities resolved in favor of indigenous interpretations.[65] Additionally, U.S. courts will not find an implied abrogation of a treaty through subsequent treaty or legislation; the intent to abrogate the treaty must be expressly stated by the Congress.[66] Acceptance of these canons of construction in no way diminishes the nature or force of the treaties, but rather recognizes the unique character of the relationship—geographically and politically—between the United States and indigenous nations. These canons of construction also represent a recognition by the United States of the fraudulent and coercive techniques it often employed in securing indigenous agreement to the treaties.[67]

These principles notwithstanding, it has been asserted that the treaties between the United States and indigenous nations do not properly fall within the international definition of a treaty under international law.[68] Such assertions are disputed not only in U.S. case law—as Vine Deloria, Rebecca Robbins, and other contributors to this volume make abundantly clear—but they also find disfavor in principles advanced by international experts.[69] It cannot be denied that as the 20th century comes to a close many international legal scholars and jurists refuse to recognize an international status for indigenous peoples or for the treaties to which they are parties. This is at least partly a function of powerful states, the United States among them, that argue that relations between states and indigenous peoples are purely matters of internal, domestic jurisdiction. This position is shared by virtually every member state of the United Nations that is engaged in relations with indigenous peoples.

While it is true that the United States Congress has passed thousands of laws in the area of U.S.-indigenous affairs, to suggest that the unilateral acts of a legislature can diminish the national sovereignty of indigenous nations that are thousands of years old seems an unjustifiable conclusion. Although the United States claims that its national legislature possesses such rights under the "plenary power doctrine," its assertion is not unlike similar claims by other colonizing states that have maintained that their relations with colonized peoples are purely domestic issues.[70] Asserting such claims, however, does not accord them acceptance under law.[71] The roots of the assertion that the United States possesses exclusive domestic jurisdiction over its relations with indigenous nations can be found in U.S. case law and the self-serving legislation that often accompanied it.

U.S. Colonization of Indigenous Nations

Prior to the War of 1812, the military, economic, and political strength of the United States was inadequate to colonize all of the indigenous nations whose territories were found east of the Mississippi River. By the 1820s, however, the power of the United States had been consolidated considerably, to the extent that many indigenous nations were vulnerable to military invasion by U.S. forces. The expansion of the U.S. was fueled by the racist philosophy of Manifest Destiny. Under this philosophy, the Americans believed that through divine ordination and the natural superiority of the white race, they had a right (and indeed an obligation) to seize and occupy all of North America. Typical of the pronouncements from supporters of the philosophy, Senator Thomas Hart Benton proclaimed that Euroamericans "had alone received the divine command to subdue and replenish the earth," and indigenous people had no right to the land of the Americas because this land had been created for use...by the white races...according to the intentions of the Creator."[72] Several years later, racist sentiment had not tempered. On the floor of the United States Congress, the motives underlying the colonization of indigenous nations were made clear:

> Congress must apprise the Indian that he can no longer stand as a breakwater against the constant tide of civilization...An idle and thriftless race of savages cannot be permitted to stand guard at the treasure vaults of the nation which hold our gold and silver...the prospector and miner may enter and by enriching himself enrich the nation and bless the world by the result of his toil.[73]

During the 19th and 20th centuries, the philosophy of Manifest Destiny was accompanied by several pieces of legislation that accomplished under cover of law that which would not have been legally justifiable through military force. The legislation, discussed below, was invariably framed and adopted under the pretense of assistance to indigenous nations in making the transition to the U.S. brand of "civilized" society. The U.S. definition of civilization, not surprisingly, was a pungent combination of fundamentalist Christianity, unrepentant racism, and economic Darwinism. President John Adams prefaced this philosophy in a letter to Judge Tudor:

> What infinite pains have been taken and expenses incurred in treaties, presents, and stipulated sums of money, instruments of agriculture, education...to convert these poor savages to Christianity! And, alas! with how little success! The Indians are as bigoted to their religion as the Mohametans [sic] are to their Koran, the Hindoos are to their Shaster, the Chinese to Confucius, the Romans to the Saints and angels, or the Jews to Moses and the Prophets. It is a principle of religion, at bottom, which inspires the Indian with such invincible aversion both to Civilization and Christianity. The same principle has excited their perpetual hostilities against the colonists and the independent Americans.[74]

By 1848, the United States had consolidated its political, economic, and military power sufficiently to abandon any remaining subtleties in its colonization of indigenous peoples. In his report on the status of relations between the United States and indigenous nations, as well as his prescription for a successful future policy, Commissioner of Indian Affairs William Medill reported that he favored the exercise of direct colonial power over the Indian nations:

> Apathy, barbarism, and heathenism must give way to energy, civilization and Christianity...The Policy already begun and relied on to accomplish objects so momentous and so desirable...is, as rapidly as it can safely and judiciously be done, to colonize our Indian tribes...within a small district of country, so that, as the game decreases and becomes scarce, the adults will eventually be compelled to resort to agriculture and other kinds of labor to obtain a subsistence...It may be said that we have commenced the establishment of two colonies for the Indian tribes that we have been compelled to remove; one north, on the headwaters of the Mississippi, and the other on the Western borders of Missouri and Arkansas in Oklahoma Territory.[75]

By its own admission, the U.S. had thus embraced a policy of colonizing indigenous peoples, and it augmented its policy with additional legislation. Through this policy, as Ward Churchill explains in Chapter Five, on land struggles, indigenous nations were confined to enclaves a fraction of the size of their original territories. Nor did U.S. expropriation of native land holdings end, as is popularly imagined, during the early part of the 20th century. Between 1936 and 1976, over 1.8 million acres of land were removed from the control of indigenous nations by the federal government.[76] Although these seizures were usually accorded some monetary compensation, the cessions were not made voluntarily by the native peoples involved. The damage inflicted upon the remaining territorial integrity of the indigenous nations involved is unquantifiable, and, arguably, such transactions constitute breaches of international standards of behavior.[77]

Political Colonization

While all this was going on, a series of statutes including the Major Crimes Act (1885), General Allotment Act (1887), Indian Citizenship Act (1924), Indian Reorganization Act (1934), and various termination and relocation acts during the 1950s and '60s—each of them discussed in this text by Rebecca Robbins and others—were subsequently passed in order to extend absolute U.S. control over jurisdiction, land tenure, national allegiance, and governance over even the residues of indigenous territoriality. The political colonization of indigenous nations becomes more complex as the process matures. As colonial administrations become more firmly entrenched, the comprador class on reservations refuses to acknowledge the role of the United States in the colonization of indigenous peoples at all.[78] Tribal regimes, ostensibly operated by indigenous peoples, are ultimately influenced by non-indigenous decisionmakers, usually in Washington, D.C. The appearance of self-determination is nothing more than colonial self-administration. In this way, as Voltaire stated, by maintaining the illusion of freedom, volition itself is captured, and subjugation becomes complete. Despite some recent changes in the way that the federal government views its relations with indigenous nations,[79] the ultimate decisionmaker concerning the parameters of indigenous self-determination is the U.S. In language that the U.S. considers benevolent, but that must ultimately be considered stifling to indigenous peoples, the U.S. policy of administering indigenous nations has been described in the following terms:

> A [native nation] is free to maintain or establish its own form of government...[but periodically] Congress has by statute dictated the manner of choosing tribal officials or other aspects of the [Indian nation's] government...But if Congress intends to replace the authority of an established form of government, its intent must be clearly indicated and tribal authority will continue, to the extent that it can coexist with Congress' alterations.[80]

This attitude of administration resembles virtually any of the late colonial period. Certainly, it is similar to that of Portugal in its assertion of ultimate control over the governments of the colonized peoples of Angola and Mozambique.[81] Portugal also contended that the colonies were merely overseas provinces which, with Portugal itself, constituted a single, unitary state. Because, according to Portugal, the colonies were actually provinces, they were subject only to the municipal jurisdiction of Portugal. This nation-state adamantly refused to recognize the right of its colonies to independence and self-determination. Accordingly, it administered the colonies from Lisbon, allowing "self-government" only as defined by the colonial power, and ignoring the mandate of the United Nations to facilitate the independence of the colonies.[82] Portugal, like the United States and other states that must address indigenous issues, insisted that the entire matter of its relations with its colonies was purely domestic, not within the purview of international law or international organizations.

In another example with similarities to the U.S., the government of South Africa continued, until 1990, to dictate the form of government in Namibia. Just as the U.S. claims to hold indigenous lands in trust for the benefit of the various indigenous nations, so too did South Africa hold Namibia in what it called a "sacred trust." Fortunately for the Namibians, the international community saw through the self-serving pronouncements of South Africa and applied sufficient international pressure on this nation-state to insure Namibian independence.[83] The political colonization of indigenous nations within the U.S. is relatively easy to chronicle and comprehend. As with colonialism in other parts of the world, however, it represents only part of the equation. Economic colonization is not only often more insidious, but much more difficult to overcome than political subordination.

Economic Colonization

Domination can be achieved in many ways. It does not have to be the result of overt political control. If the economy of a small country is totally dependent upon a set of external factors, this is a form of domination as effective as anything that existed in classical colonial times. The effect of all economic factors adds up to a sort of cumulative *force majeure* from which there is no escape.[84] Given the multiplicity of indigenous nations in the U.S., and given the diversity of their populations, sizes, territories, and natural resource reserves, it is difficult to generalize about their economic colonization. Nevertheless, there are several common strategies that have been used by the United States to ensure the economic bondage of native peoples to the U.S. Also, some general economic statistics are useful in ascertaining the overall current economic condition of American Indians in the U.S.

Indigenous peoples are in the worst economic position of any racial or ethnic group in the U.S.[85] In 1970, President Nixon admitted that Indians were the most economically depressed of any group, a condition that has not changed to the present.[86] The economic condition of indigenous nations can be tied directly to the political and military policies of the federal government, as overseen by the Bureau of Indian Affairs (BIA) and the secretary of the interior.[87] In recent years, the BIA has become more indigenous in appearance, but ultimately, the secretary of interior makes all important decisions. To illustrate this power, the U.S. Commission on Civil Rights wrote:

> Federal law gives the Secretary of the Interior and the Commissioner for Indian Affairs [now the Assistant Secretary of Interior for Indian Affairs] broad powers over all Indian affairs and all matters arising out of Indian relations. This includes veto power over all tribal contracts. Although the Navajo Nation has an elected council, set up under non-traditional Anglo guidelines, virtually every significant action of this council must receive BIA approval before it can become law or acted upon by the the tribe. That approval process is often unnecessarily protracted and obstructionist.[88]

After years of agitation and demands by indigenous governments, some changes have been realized in this relationship, resulting in relatively greater control of decisions on Indian reservations. Nevertheless, the federal government continues to insist that it, and not native peoples, is the ultimate arbiter of the degree of sovereignty exercised by indigenous nations. The importance of the exercise of U.S. control in Indian affairs becomes increasingly clear when one understands the considerable natural resource reserves found within the territories of indigenous nations—many of which are considered strategic by the United States.[89] In this respect, native peoples of the U.S. experience similar economic invasions and controls as other indigenous peoples—be they the Yanomamis of Brazil, the Crees of Alberta, or the Penans of Sarawak. States consistently claim that it is their prerogative to exploit indigenous natural resources for the "national security," and such matters are purely domestic in nature, beyond the scope of international scrutiny or rebuke.

What makes the economic condition of indigenous peoples in the U.S. somewhat unique is the judicially-created "trust relationship" that requires the U.S. to hold native lands and resources for the benefit of indigenous nations.[90] Although this trust can apparently be breached with impunity by the U.S.,[91] some legally enforceable rights for indigenous peoples do exist if the U.S. breaches its fiduciary obligation to them.[92] Even more interesting is the fact that the United States is a fiduciary under two trust obligations: one to the indigenous peoples it has colonized and who now live within territory claimed by the U.S., and one to the peoples of the Pacific Trust Territory, whose territories were placed in trust by the United Nations, with the U.S. as trustee. A significant difference between these two trust arrangements is that the peoples of the Pacific Trust Territory possess the absolute right to exercise self-determination when and if they choose to do so.[93] No such right currently exists under international law for indigenous nations within the U.S., and the main difference in the attachment of international rights and status has to do with geographical separation from the colonizing power. This requirement, and its implications for indigenous peoples, can best be understood upon examining the evolution of the right to self-determination in international law, and the attendant decisions about to whom the right is extended.

Decolonization and the Right to Self-Determination

Discussion of the rights of colonized peoples prior to World War I took place in the abstract, but serious discussion of limitations on the right of colonial powers to administer the colonies under their control was limited.[94] At the close of World War I, political leaders in the two major ideological camps—liberal capitalist republicanism and marxist socialism—began to recognize the inevitable decline of the system of European colonialism that had enveloped the world for the previous 400 years. Each side in this ideological struggle was determined to affect the evolution of the right to self-determination according to its particular perspective of human development and according to its own agenda for the future. Among the capitalist leadership, the most vocal in support of a right of colonized peoples to exercise self-determination was President Woodrow Wilson of the United States. In an address to Congress in 1917, Wilson condemned colonialism, and implicitly condoned wars of national liberation:

> No peace can last, or ought to last, which does not recognize or accept the principle that governments derive all their just powers from the consent of the

governed and that no right anywhere exists to hand people around from sovereignty to sovereignty as if they were property.[95]

The following year, Wilson warned the colonial powers of the impending movement of colonized peoples demanding their political self-determination:

> The rights of nations to self-determination is no mere phrase, it is an imperative principle of action which will be disregarded by statesmen in the future only at their own risk.[96]

Wilson's pronouncements, although consistent with his support of liberal democracy, cannot be considered altruistic. At the time of his statements, European socialism was spreading, and Wilson was interested in ensuring that a design for self-determination that served Western interests would prevail. Simultaneously, V.I. Lenin was constructing a political model that would soon transform the ancient Russian empire into a new society more disturbing to the West than anything the czars had ever dreamed of. A central theme to Lenin's plan, and one that he was convinced would persuade colonized peoples to elaborate marxist socialism, was his definition of self-determination.[97] He realized that the socialist model of self-determination must embrace novel and expanded notions of the rights of colonized peoples not addressed by Wilson or the West. Consequently, Lenin's theory of self-determination embraced the aspirations of millions of colonized people:

> Victorious socialism must necessarily establish a full democracy and consequently, not only introduce full equality of nations, but also realize the right of oppressed nations to self determination, i.e., the right to free political separation. Socialist parties which did not show by all their activities, both now, during the revolution and after its victory, that they would liberate the enslaved nations and build up relations with them on the basis of a free union—and free union is a false phrase without the right to secede—these parties would be betraying socialism.[98]

The Bolshevik Revolution of 1917 brought with it one of the first state declarations supporting the principle of self-determination. The Decree of Peace in 1917 declared that it was illegal for the Soviet Union to annex "small or weak peoples without their clear, voluntary, express consent and desire."[99] Although nearly seventy years elapsed before the Soviet Union took seriously Lenin's rhetoric regarding the right of nations to genuine self-determination, its support for other colonized peoples advanced the debate on decolonization dramatically in the international arena.[100] Following World War I, the creation of the Mandated Territories under the League of Nations, later renamed the International Trusteeship Council under the United Nations, began the process of supervising colonial territories working toward the attainment of self-government and eventual independence. In 1950, over 20 million people lived under the UN trusteeship system in eleven territories. Today, only one such territory remains: the Trust Territory of the Pacific Islands, administered by the United States. All of the others have either attained self-governance or independence or voluntarily consolidated their territories with neighboring nations or states.[101]

The United Nations

After World War II, a number of factors converged, leading to the disintegration of the global colonial system. Among these was the improved education and exposure to democratic principles and aspirations of political independence of colonized peoples.[102] This led to discontent and turmoil in the colonies, a factor compounded by the economic hardships experienced by the colonial powers as a consequence of the War, making it increasingly difficult to maintain distant, volatile territories.[103] Analysts have suggested that the Western countries allowed the demise of colonialism after World War II because their interest would be better protected through the containment of the Soviet Union and the Eastern bloc than through the maintenance of colonialism.[104]

With the founding of the United Nations in 1945, recognition of the right to self-determination was expressed in the United Nations charter itself.[105] According to Cristescu, the effect on customary international law resulting from reference to the right to self-determination in the charter "marks...the recognition of the concept as a legal principle and a principle of contemporary law."[106] Although some debate continues about the legal consequence of the mention of the right to self-determination in the charter,[107] state practice and subsequent U.N. resolutions have provided "ample evidence that there now exists a legal right to self-determination," under international law.[108]

Subsequent to the establishment of the United Nations and the ratification of its charter by the founding members, there was considerable debate over the substance of the rights flowing from the principle of self-determination. The elements of the right to self-determination were gradually outlined in a series of General Assembly resolutions.[109] The right also received prominent attention in the *International Covenant on Economic, Social and Cultural Rights* and the *International Covenant on Civil and Political Rights.*[110] Additionally, state practice indicates an overwhelming acceptance of the principle. Of the current members of the United Nations, over 100 were previously colonies, and have achieved their independence since the end of World War II.[111] Gudmundur Alfredsson concludes:

> The extent and general uniformity of actual state practice which has characterized the speedy dismantling of the colonial empire indicates for one thing that such *opinio juris* [on the right to self-determination] exists.[112]

The actions of the General Assembly and the Security Council have also been the subject of interpretation by the International Court of Justice (ICJ). In two relatively recent advisory opinions concerning rights to self-determination for the peoples of the Western Sahara and Namibia, the Court interpreted the law of decolonization in these terms:

> [T]he subsequent development of international law in regard to non-self-governing territories, as enshrined in the Charter of the United Nations, made

the principle of self-determination applicable to all of them. The concept of the sacred trust was confirmed and expanded to all "territories whose people have not yet attained a full measure of self-government" (Article 73). Thus it clearly embraced territories under a colonial regime.[113]

This discussion indicates that through the actions of the various bodies of the United Nations and the state members themselves, and through the confirmation of those actions in scholarly writings and judicial opinions, the law of decolonization and the right to self-determination exist as established rules of international law. This question settled, another fundamentally important one remains: who constitutes the "self" in self-determination? Under the law, who are to be the beneficiaries of the right? According to Alfredsson, the U.N. resolutions previously mentioned extend the right to colonies, non-self-governing territories, and former colonial territories integrated with the administering powers.[114] Colonies are defined through three basic criteria: 1. foreign domination, 2. the presence of a political/territorial entity in the colony, and 3. geographical separation from the colonizing power.[115] The only criterion that may be problematic for indigenous peoples to satisfy is the requirement for geographical separation from the colonizer. Because of the methods used by the "settler state" form of colonialism, most indigenous nations' territories were enveloped by encroaching powers, resulting in the colonized nations' territories being contiguous with, not separate from, that of their colonizers.

Non-self-governing territories are defined in Article 73 of the U.N. charter as "territories whose people have not yet attained the full measure of self-government." Though this category is subject to future clarification, certain characteristics are indicative of the status, namely that the colony is politically, economically, socially, and educationally underdeveloped relative to the colonizing power.[116] As discussed above, indigenous nations within the U.S. satisfy each of these criteria.[117] As with colonies, the prevailing view is that non-self-governing territories must be geographically separated from the colonizing power. This perspective, known as the "salt-water" or "blue-water" thesis of decolonization, requires that colonies be separated from the colonial power by a substantial body of water, preferably an ocean. This interpretation of decolonization was challenged by Belgium through its "Belgian Thesis," which contended that decolonization should extend to all colonized peoples, even if they are bound in enclaves entirely surrounded by colonizing states. The thesis specifically mentioned the enclave conditions of indigenous peoples for remedy.[118] Despite this attempt to extend decolonization to indigenous peoples, the "salt water thesis" has predominated in international debate.

The competence of the General Assembly to define non-self-governing territories is derived from Article 10 of the charter, and has been inferred by the ICJ in its *Western Sahara* opinion, in which the Court held that Spain "could not validly object to the General Assembly's exercise of its powers to deal with the decolonization of a non-self-governing territory."[119] Consequently, it appears to be within the competence of the General Assembly to extend the definition of non-self-governing territories to enclaves of indigenous nations. Convincing arguments to persuade the General Assembly to make such an extension can be derived from the fact that other enclaves, such as Lesotho and Gambia have been recognized as independent states without disrupting the territorial integrity of the states around them.

The final category in decolonization, colonial territories that have been integrated with the administering powers, is especially pertinent to the case of indigenous nations within the United States. Similar examples of colonial powers integrating colonies in circumvention of international law have been held to be illegal. The colonial rationale for integration schemes is explained by Alfredsson:

> [T]he practice by some colonizing states of integrating their colonial territories, even though such integration in many cases was pure constitutional fiction introduced in order to avoid international supervision by sheltering these territories under an umbrella of domestic jurisdiction, implies strongly that political decolonization appeared to the colonizers as a legal force and not just political rhetoric which they could have flatly rejected or more simply ignored.[120]

Such attempts by colonial governments to create the legal and political fiction of integration of their colonies, without the informed and willful consent of the colonized, "have failed however, and the territories involved have exercised their right to political decolonization...But the attempts provide one more compelling reason for a critical supervision and scrutiny of integration cases and for a strict adherence to the standards imposed by the United Nations for guaranteeing due process and equality."[121] Arguably, indigenous nations within the geography of the United States satisfy the criteria for decolonization if their unique conditions of original sovereignty, territory, and the nature of their colonization by the United States is considered. The primary obstacle to the recognition of their rights under decolonization principles appears to be the reluctance of states to redefine the constructs of self-determination to include indigenous enclaves.

Application of Self-Determining Right to Indigenous Peoples

Appeals by indigenous nations in international forums to secure the vindication of their rights as distinct and independent peoples is not new.[122] During the late 19th century, the Maori of Aotearoa (New Zealand) and the Aborigines of Australia, as well as various indigenous nations in Canada, submitted international petitions for resolution of territorial and jurisdictional conflicts.[123] In the 1920s, leaders from the Maori and Haudenosaunee (Iroquois) confederations petitioned the League of Nations to hear their cases for recognition under international law, but both were frustrated through the operation of diplomatic procedural rulings.[124] In the case of the Haudenosaunee, their leader, Deskaheh, spent over two years attempting to persuade the international community through the League to recognize the national status of his people, but without success.[125]

Subsequently, little attention was given indigenous issues until the adoption of the so-called Convention 107 by the International Labor Organization (ILO).[126] Formally called "The Convention of Indigenous Populations of 1957," Convention 107 fell far short of recognizing an indigenous right to self-determination. Nonetheless, for its time, the convention was a significant step forward in the contemporary recognition of the rights of indigenous peoples. The ILO recognized that indigenous peoples constitute distinct and separate peoples possessing protectable interests in their lands, cultures, and political structures.[127] The convention also laid the foundation for future progress in the area of indigenous peoples' rights. After several years of deliberation, ILO Convention 107 was deemed outdated and assimilationist in its perspective. Assimilation of indigenous peoples, while acceptable in international discourse in 1957, had fallen into disfavor since that time. The ILO began revising the convention in 1986 and concluded its revisions in 1989. The new document, known as Convention 169, updated the archaic provisions of 107 but was reviled by many native peoples as ignoring the legitimate aspirations of indigenous nations and continuing to protect states in their denial of native claims for self-determination.[128]

During the 1970s, several other events brought indigenous issues into international attention. In 1971, and again in 1977, the Declarations of Barbados, documents drafted by progressive anthropologists and indigenous representatives, called on the world to re-examine the colonial condition of indigenous peoples, and recognized the necessity of a hemispheric indigenous movement led by native peoples.[129] During this period, indigenous movements were growing and demanding recognition of their historic rights. By 1974, traditional native elders in North America called upon Russell Means, a leader of the American Indian Movement (AIM),[130] one of the most militant and prominent of the new organizations, to take their issues before the United Nations. Means and Jimmie Durham organized the International Indian Treaty Council (IITC) as the international diplomatic arm of AIM, receiving non-governmental organization (NGO) status at the United Nations in 1977. Other indigenous organizations later entered the arena and began constructing a global network of peoples, nations, and movements designed to secure the attention of international bodies.[131] In 1977 and 1981, this network convened two international conferences in Geneva and Rotterdam to examine the rights of indigenous peoples.[132]

In 1974, the United Nations Sub-Commission on Prevention of Discrimination and Protection of Minorities commissioned a study on the condition of indigenous peoples worldwide. *The Study of the Problem of Discrimination Against Indigenous Populations* by Special Rapporteur José R. Martinez Cobo consisted of ten years of extensive research on the global condition of indigenous peoples.[133] As a direct result of the study and the exhaustive work of indigenous nations themselves, the Sub-Commission voted to establish a Working Group on Indigenous Populations (WGIP) to meet annually in Geneva to provide native peoples with a voice in the international arena.[134] The WGIP has been extremely important in the indigenous quest for self-determination for several reasons. As already mentioned, it provides a forum through which native peoples can articulate their needs and aspirations, including demands for self-determination. Additionally, it exposes states to evolving and expanding debates concerning individual and group rights. In this regard, the draft proposal of the Chair of the Working Group, Erica-Irene A. Daes, for a U.N. declaration on indigenous rights provides a framework through which states can be impressed with the justness and inevitability of extending internationally recognized rights to indigenous peoples.[135]

Because Daes' draft declaration proposal does not explicitly mention the right to self-determination, some indigenous delegates to the WGIP have deemed it inadequate.136 However, despite explicit omission of the term, some benefits of the right to self-determination are clearly recognizable. For example, the draft recognizes certain collective rights—to physical and cultural integrity, traditional lands, and autonomous control of internal political, economic, and social institutions—and it requires states to honor all treaties and agreements made with indigenous nations. It therefore continues to fall short of full recognition of the right of indigenous peoples to determine their own status within the international community, to be recognized as having standing under international law other than as individuals in human rights proceedings, and to bring group claims of genocide or ethnocide. It therefore continues to recognize the supremacy of states in the ultimate determination of the rights and jurisdiction of indigenous nations, and it refuses to recognize the international nature of disputes between states and indigenous nations.

Despite these shortcomings, Daes' draft declaration provides an important step in the long, often tedious, process of transforming international legal standards. In conjunction with the draft declaration provided by indigenous NGOs, and inevitable future drafts, Daes' document can be utilized by the WGIP to educate states and alter their policies toward indigenous peoples. In addition to the draft declaration, the work of the WGIP has led directly to a study on the international status of treaties between indigenous nations and states. The study, led by WGIP member Miguel Alfonso Martinez, of Cuba, may provide native peoples with the impetus necessary to allow international adjudication or arbitration of treaty violations between indigenous peoples and states. To date, indigenous peoples have been left without any legal forums in their treaty disputes with states other than the domestic courts of the state with which they are a party in the treaty. This type of self-adjudication by states, not surprisingly, has led to many unjust interpretations of treaty provisions, to the detriment of indigenous peoples.

Conclusion

The historical denial of the extension of the right of self-determination to indigenous peoples and nations is rooted in the desire of states to protect what they perceive to be their interests. This, too, was the central motivation of some states in their refusal to accept decolonization principles. Fortunately for colonized peoples who were geographically separated from the colonizing states, the international community decided that the self-determination of peoples took priority over the right of states to hold colonies. Although the adoption of this standard was disruptive to the international status quo, advancement of world peace and freedom was considered to be more important. Similarly, a transformation in the attitudes of state actors toward the rights of indigenous peoples is under way. The major obstacle to the attainment of indigenous self-determination is the perceived sacredness of the territorial integrity of states. Recent dramatic developments in the Soviet republics and other countries of the world regarding the rights of national groups to exercise self-determination, including secession, presents an unprecedented opportunity to revisit questions considered long settled.

Of particular prominence in the discussion of indigenous self-determination is the objection that indigenous peoples, wherever they are found, constitute indivisible sectors of a unitary state. To allow indigenous peoples the ultimate expression of self determination, so goes the argument, would constitute secession, and a threat to the territorial integrity of the state in clear violation of the U.N. charter. To characterize indigenous expression of self-determination as secession, it first must be conceded that a nation has been legitimately integrated into a state. If not, it can hardly be argued that the state has a lawful right to maintain that nation in bondage. Most indigenous peoples argue that because their territories have been invaded and incorporated into states without indigenous consent, self-determination does not constitute secession, but merely the exercise of inherent sovereign powers that have never been relinquished.

Even if, for the sake of argument, the ultimate expression of indigenous self-determination *were* to constitute secession, would the recognition of such a right for indigenous peoples disrupt the desire of the international community for world peace and friendly relations between peoples? On the contrary, those aspirations would be enhanced. Professor Ved Nanda's discussion of this point is helpful.[137] Although he does not advocate secession, Nanda recognizes that national self-determination for enclave nations "appears to be an irrepressible feature of the contemporary world scene."[138] Consequently, he proposes the development of international institutional mechanisms to allow the self-determination of peoples who have been denied such rights because their aspirations were considered secessionist. According to Nanda, the legitimacy of the expression of self-determination should be governed by four criteria:

- A clearly identifiable group possessing genuine national characteristics;
- Satisfaction that the nature and the scope of the claim are compelling;
- Substantiation of the underlying historical reasons for the claim; and
- Proof of substantial deprivation of human rights.[139]

Using these criteria, many, if not most, indigenous nations in the Western hemisphere would be entitled to exercise the right. This brings us to another important point. Recognition of the right to self-determination does not compel a move to national independence. In applications of the right to non-self-governing territories, peoples may choose one of three options to express their self-determination. First, they may choose to pursue sovereign independence as a state; second, they may choose a relationship of free association with an independent state; or third, they may choose integration with an independent state. The assumption by states that indigenous peoples exercising a right to self-determination would automatically choose the first option appears unfounded. Given the difficult practical political and economic difficulties facing smaller states in the world today, most indigenous peoples may very well *not* opt for complete independent state status. Many would probably choose some type of autonomy or federation with existing states, preserving rights to internal self-governance and control as members of a larger state. Some however, may choose formal integration into a state, for reasons unique to their particular situation.

Regardless of which status an indigenous nation might choose, the movement toward recognizing each nation's right to make some choice other than unconsented to domination by a colonial or settler state appears consistent with historical notions of self-determination. To apply the conclusions of Nanda to indigenous circumstances, not only would the extension of the right to self-determination to indigenous nations, even if it meant secession, promote the expansion of rights in the world, it would also promote predictable international mechanisms of resolving disputes between indigenous nations and the states around them, leading to an overall expansion of global freedom, peace, and stability.[140] Without recognition of the right, the liberation and survival of indigenous nations remains questionable, and the majority of global conflicts in the world will remain unresolved.[141]

Notes

1. Committee on Native American Struggles, *Rethinking Indian Law*, New York, 1982, IV. For an excellent discussion of the distinctions between the terms "nation," "state," and "Fourth World" (indigenous peoples), see Nietschmann, Bernard, "The Third World War," *Cultural Survival Quarterly*, Vol. 11, No. 3, 1987.
2. Nys, Ernest, *Les Origines du Droit International*, Brussels/Paris, 1984, esp. Chapter Seven.
3. Maine, Henry, ed., *Ancient Law*, 13th edition, London, 1850, p. 257.
4. Nys, op. cit.
5. Aquinas, Thomas, *Summa Theologica Secunda Secundae*, Venetiis, 1593, Quarto 11, Article 10.
6. Nys, op. cit.
7. Post, Gaines, *Studies in Medieval Legal Thought*, Princeton University Press, Princeton, NJ, 1964, pp. 532-61.
8. Gottschalk, Paul, *Earliest Diplomatic Documents of America*, New York, 1978, p. 21. Also see Deloria, Vine Jr., *Behind the Trail of Broken Treaties: An Indian Declaration of Independence*, Delacourte Press, New York, 1974, p. 87.
9. These tensions resulted in the Treaty of Tordesillas on June 7, 1494, between Spain and Portugal, putatively dividing the planet into two equal parts. Other European States, particularly England, France, and Holland, ignored or militarily resisted the pontifical donations. Ultimately, whatever legal force was vested in the Bulls was replaced by the theory of effective occupation of territories by colonial powers. See Truyol y Serra, Antonio, "The Discovery of the New World and International Law," *Toledo Law Review*, No. 43, 1971, pp. 310-1.
10. Gottschalk, op. cit., p. 21.
11. Truyol y Serra, op. cit., p. 313.
12. See notes 22-28 and accompanying text. For a contrary opinion on Victoria, see Williams, Robert A., Jr., "The Medieval and Renaissance Origins of the Status of the American Indian in Western

Legal Thought," *Southern California Law Review*, Vol. 57, No. 1, 1983, pp. 1-99.

13. Truyol y Serra, op. cit., p. 315. Also see Hanke, Lewis, *Aristotle and the American Indians: A Study in Race Prejudice in the Modern World*, Indiana University Press, Bloomington/Indianapolis, 1959, pp. 14-15.
14. Hanke, Lewis, *All Mankind Is One: A Study of the Disputation Between Bartolomé de Las Casas and Juan Ginés de Sepúlveda in 1550 on the Intellectual and Religious Capacity of the American Indians*, Northern Illinois University Press, Dekalb, 1974, pp. 4-5.
15. *Aristotle and the Indians*, op. cit., p. 15. Also see Diaz, Jorge, "Los Doctrinas de Palacios Rubios y Matias de Paz ante la Conquista de America," in *Memoria de El Colegio Nacional*, Burgos, Spain, 1950, pp. 71-94.
16. See Bullon, Lewis, *El Doctor Palacios Rubios y Sus Obras*, Madrid, 1927.
17. See Hanke, Lewis, "The 'Requirimiento' and Its Interpreters," in *Sobretiro de la Revista de la Historia de America*, No. 1, 1938, pp. 25-34. Also see *All Mankind Is One*, op. cit., pp. 35-37. In part, the *Requirimiento* admonished the indigenous hosts that if they did not agree to convert to Catholicism and submit to the Europeans, the invaders would "take you and your wives and your children, and [we] shall make slaves of them and as such shall sell and dispose of them as their Highnesses may command; and we shall take away your goods, and we shall do all the harm and damage that we can as to vassals who do not obey...and we protest that the deaths and losses which shall accrue from this are your fault, and not that of their Highnesses, or ours, nor of these gentlemen who come with us."
18. "Just War" was a concept developed in Roman law that permitted nearly any military action for the purpose of defending the *patria*. Under medieval papal law, the war was considered just if it was for the defense "of the faith and the Church." Post, op. cit., p. 437. Later, Vattel would write that Just War can be employed only in the necessity of self defense, and that if a nation takes up arms when it has received no injury, nor is threatened with any, it undertakes an unjust war. Vattel, Emer, *The Law of Nations*, Book III, VII, Sec. 26, p. 302. Accordingly, it appears that, as regards the Spanish wars against the indigenous peoples of the Americas, the only legal right to wage a Just War belonged to the indigenous nations.
19. Truyol y Serra, op. cit., pp. 317-18.
20. Vattel, op. cit., p. 315.
21. Among those supporting Las Casas have been Balthazar Ayala, who believed that sovereignty was not exclusively a Christian right; Hugo Grotius (1583-1645) agreed that the Spanish had no right to wage a Just War in the Americas based on discovery and also believed in the equality of nations. His teachings have been extended to create the foundation for the current system of international law through the United Nations, embracing Christian and non-Christian nations alike (see Taylor, Robert, *International Public Law*, Metheun Publishers, London, 1901, pp. 75, 91). Samuel Puffendorf supported the principles of Las Casas, writing that "since every man is by nature equal to every man, and consequently not subject to the dominion of others, therefore, this bare seizing by force is not enough to found a lawful sovereignty over men" (cited in Lindley, Mark Frank, *The Acquisition and Government of Backward Country in International Law: A Treatise on the Law and Practice Relating to Colonial Expansion*, Longmans, Green Publishers, London, 1926, p. 14). The German theorists, Gunther, Kliber, and Heffter, agreed that no nation, regardless of its degree of civilization, has the right to take the property of another nation, "even savages or nomads" (Ibid., pp. 14-15). The French publisher Jeze argued in favor of the absolute right of indigenous nations to territorial and political sovereignty and held that land cessions by indigenous nations must be made freely, intelligently, and according to the customs of the indigenous nation (see Jeze, Gaston, *Etude Theoretique et Pratique Sur L'occupation Comme Mode d'Acquerir les Territoires en Droit International*, Paris, 1896). Those aligning themselves with Sepúlveda in his denial of indigenous rights to territorial and political sovereignty include the relatively modern publicists Westlake, Hall, Lawrence, and Marten Ferraro (see Lindley, op. cit., pp. 18-19). All of these men agreed with the proposition that due to the superior civilization of Europe, indigenous peoples could lose their territories without their consent through Euroamerican occupation. It should not pass unnoticed that all of these theorists hailed from states which, at the time of their publication, were holding vast tracts of territory that arguably belonged to indigenous nations.
22. Nys, Ernest, ed., *Franciscus de Victoria, De Indis et de Jure Belli: Relectiones*, Oceana Publishers, New York, 1917.
23. Ibid., Section 1, Title 4, p. 120.

24. Ibid., Section 7, Title 1-6, pp. 129-37.
25. Ibid., Section 2, Title 7-16, pp. 137-49.
26. Cohen, Felix S., *Handbook of Federal Indian Law,* University of New Mexico Press, Albuquerque (reprint of 1942 U.S. Government edition), n.d., p. 47.
27. Vattel, op. cit. Also see Kinney, Jay P., *A Continent Lost—A Civilization Won: Indian Land Tenure in America,* Johns Hopkins University Press, Baltimore, 1937, pp. 11-12, for a description of negotiations between Roger Williams, founder of the state of Rhode Island, and the Narragansett Nation; and Washburn, Wilcomb, *The Indian in America,* Harper and Row Publishers, New York, 1975, pp. 84-5, for a description of the negotiations between William Penn, founder of the state of Pennsylvania, and the indigenous nations of the region.
28. Cohen, op. cit., p. 47.
29. *Papal Bull Sublimis Deus,* in MacNutt, Francis Augustus, *Bartholomew de Las Casas: His Life, His Apostolate, and His Writings,* New York, 1909, p. 429. It should be noted that Papal Bulls were not considered cursory declarations, but carried with them the full force of law, particularly upon Catholic sovereigns. See Ullman, Walter, *The Church and the Laws in the Early Middle Ages: Selected Essays,* Metheun Publishers, London, 1975, pp. 131-2.
30. Las Casas reported the slaughter of over 20 million indigenous people in the Caribbean and Mexico before 1542. Las Casas, Fray Bartolomé de, "Cruelties of the Spaniards," in Charles Gibson, ed., *The Spanish Tradition in America,* Harper and Row Publishers, New York, 1968, pp. 106-08.
31. Las Casas, Fray Bartolomé de, "Disputa con Ginés de Sepúlveda Acerca de Lictud de las Conquistas de las Indias," in *Revista de Derecho Internacional y Political Exterior,* Madrid, 1908, Chapters LIX-LXI.
32. For a chronicle of the debate, see *All Mankind Is One,* op. cit.
33. Gibson, op. cit., pp. 113-20.
34. Lindley, op. cit., p. 12. Also see Las Casas, *In Defense of the Indians,* translated by S. Poole, Oxford University Press, London/New York, 1973.
35. Land grants to Spanish subjects to the prejudice of the indigenous peoples who had historically lived in the same area were prohibited. Any grant resulting in prejudice or injury to the indigenous nation was legally null, and full restitution was mandated. Not only was this a recognition of indigenous land rights, but it was also an admission that indigenous peoples possessed land rights previous to, and not subject to, the Crown. See Law of June 11, 1594, in *Recopilacion de Leyes de Los Reynos de las Indias,* Madrid, 1861, Bk. 4, title 12, law 9. See generally Taylor, John, *Spanish Law Concerning Discoveries, Pacifications, and Settlements Among the Indians,* University of Utah Press, Salt Lake City, 1980; and Hall, George, *Laws of Mexico,* Metheun Publishers, London, 1885.
36. Felix Cohen, "The Spanish Origin of Indian Rights in the Law of the United States," *Georgetown Law Review,* Vol. 31, No. 1, 1942, pp. 14-16. Also see Hanke, Lewis, *The Spanish Struggle for Justice in the Conquest of America,* University of Pennsylvania Press, Philadelphia, 1949.
37. Cohen, op. cit., p. 13.
38. See McNutt, op. cit., and Lindley, op. cit.
39. Williams, Robert A. Jr., *The American Indian in Western Legal Thought: The Discourses of Conquest,* Oxford University Press, London/New York, 1990, p. 136.
40. Ibid., pp. 165-71.
41. Ibid., p. 204.
42. Ibid., pp. 214-6.
43. For a comprehensive overview of these foundations, see ibid., pp. 151-334.
44. In describing his arrival in the Americas, Columbus characterized the indigenous people as "simple and honest, and exceedingly liberal with all they have...They exhibit great love towards all others in preference to themselves...They are men of great deference and kindness" (*The Columbus Letter of March 14, 1493,* University of Chicago Press, Chicago, 1953, pp. 6-10). In return "he resorted to a monstrous expedient of sending hundreds of the [Indians] overseas, to the slave market in Seville...the policy and acts of Columbus for which he was responsible began the depopulation of the terrestial paradise that was Hispaniola [sic]. Of the original natives [numbering at least 3,000,000 in 1492]...in 1548 Ovieda doubted whether 500 Indians remained" (Morison, Samuel Eliot, *Admiral of the Ocean Sea: A Life of Christopher Columbus,* Little, Brown Publishers, Boston, 1942, pp. 486-7, 492-3).
45. The subject of the initial European-Indian contact has been covered extensively elsewhere. See,

for example, Vogel, Virgil J., *This Country Was Ours: A Documentary History of the American Indian*, Harper and Row Publishers, New York, 1972, pp. 27, 52; Gibson, Arrell Morgan, *The American Indian: Prehistory to the Present*, D.C. Heath and Co., Publishers, Lexington, MA, 1985, p. 247; Brotherson, Gordon, *Image of the New World: The American Continent Portrayed in Native Texts*, Oxford University Press, London/New York, 1979; and Wrone, David R., and Russell S. Nelson, Jr., eds., *Who's the Savage?* Discus Books, New York, 1973.

46. Vattel, op. cit.
47. Maine, op. cit.
48. Broadhead, John R., "Documents Relative to the Colonial History of the State of New York," in Edmund Bailey O'Callaghan, ed., *Documents Relative to the Colonial History of the State of New York*, Vol. 1: Holland Documents II, No. 27, State Historical Society of New York, Albany, 1856, p. 99; cited in *Handbook of Federal Indian Law*, op. cit., p. 53.
49. Ibid.
50. Berman, Howard R., "The Concept of Aboriginal Rights in the Early History of the United States," *Buffalo Law Review*, No. 27, 1978, pp. 637, 653.
51. *Worcester v. Georgia*, at 542-543. Also see Coulter, Robert T., "United States Denial of Indian Property Rights: A Study in Lawless Power and Racial Discrimination," in *Rethinking Indian Law*, op. cit.
52. See Vaughan, Aldin T., *The New England Frontier: Puritans and Indians 1620-1675*, Little, Brown Publishers, Boston, 1965, pp. 109-120.
53. *Handbook of Federal Indian Law*, op. cit., pp. 56-58.
54. Ibid.
55. The Continental Congress created separate departments for its diplomatic relations with indigenous nations. Commissioners were appointed to serve essentially the same function as ambassadors, and the Congress explicitly acknowledged that "securing and preserving the friendship of Indian nations appears to be a subject of utmost moment to these colonies" (*Joint Continental Congress*, No. 2, [1795], p. 175). The British fully recognized the capacity of indigenous nations to harass, or decimate if they so chose, the Colonies. See Fey, Harold Edward, and D'Arcy McNickle, *Indians and Other Americans: Two Ways of Life Meet*, Harper and Brothers Publishers, New York, (revised edition) 1959, p. 55.
56. Treaty with the Delawares, September 17, 1778, 7 Stat. 13.
57. *Worcester v. Georgia*, at 550.
58. United States Constitution, Art. I, Sec. 8, cl. 2; Art. II, Sec. 2, cl. 1; The Trade and Intercourse Acts of 1790, 1 *Stat.* 137; 1793, 1 *Stat.* 329; 1796, 1 *Stat.* 469; 1802, 2 *Stat.* 139; and 1834, 4 *Stat.* 729.
59. Opinion rendered by Attorney General William Wirt (Op. Atty. Gen.), April 26, 1821, p. 345.
60. Op. Atty. Gen., 1828, pp. 613-18, 623-33:
61. Formal treaty making with indigenous nations was halted unilaterally by the United States with the Act of March 3, 1871, Ch. 120, sec. 1, 16 *Stat.* 544, 566. The statute explicitly states that "no obligation of any treaty previously satisfied shall be hereby invalidated or impaired."
62. See Margold, Nathan R., "Introduction," in Felix S. Cohen, *Handbook of Federal Indian Law*, U.S. Department of Interior, Washington, D.C., 1942, p. vii. Also see *Washington v. Washington State Commercial Passenger Fishing Vessel Association*, 443 U.S. 658, 675 (1979); *U.S. v. Forty-Three Gallons of Whiskey*, 93 U.S. (17 Wall.) 211, 242-3 (1872); *Worcester v. Georgia*, at 559.
63. See Barsh, Russel, "Indigenous North America and International Law," *Oregon Law Review*, No. 62, 1983, pp. 114-18.
64. *Choctaw Nation v. Oklahoma*, 397 U.S. 620, 631 (1970); *U.S. v. Shoshone Tribe*, 304 U.S. 111, 116 (1938); *Tulee v. Washington*, 315 U.S. 681, 684-85 (1942).
65. *McClanahan v. Arizona State Tax Commission*, 411 U.S. 164, 174 (1973); *Carpenter v. Shaw*, 280 U.S. 363 (1930); *Winters v. United States*, 207 U.S. 564.
66. *Washington v. Fishing Vessel Association; Menominee Tribe v. United States*, 391 U.S. 404 (1968). See generally, Wilkinson, Charles F., and John M. Volkman, "Judicial Review of Indian Treaty Abrogation. As Long As the Water Flows or Grass Grows Upon the Earth—How Long a Time Is That?" *California Law Review*, No. 63, 1975, pp. 601-61.
67. Referring to the treaties which preceded the forced removal of the indigenous nations of the southeastern United States in the 1830s, Vogel (op. cit., pp. 285-6) writes: "The treaties which preceded these expulsions...were masterpieces of intimidation, bribery, threats, and fraud.

Following these efforts to produce a fig leaf of legality for the operation, Indians were hunted down like animals, bound as prisoners, and confined in stockades to await removal. The conditions of the deportation were so barbarous that about one-third of the emigres died on the journey."

68. See *Island of Palmas Case*, Permanent Court of Arbitral Awards, 1928, pp. 44-5; Scott, James Brown, *Hague Court Reports*, The Hague, 2d Series, 1932, 84 et. seq. (115-116); "Cayuga Indian Claims Case," *Annual Digest of Public International Law Cases (1925-1926)*, pp. 237-38, 22 January 1926.
69. Rosenne, Shabati, *The Law of Treaties: A Guide to the Legislative History of the Vienna Convention*, Leyden, 1970, p. 108; *Harvard Research Draft Convention on the Law of Treaties*, Harvard University Press, Cambridge, MA, 1935, pp. 686-8; Report by J.L. Brierly, Special Rapporteur on the Law of Treaties, UN Doc. A/CN.4/23, 14 April 1950 (in *Yearbook of the International Law Commission* [YBILC] 1950 II, pp. 222-48); Crandell, Samuel Benjamin, *Treaties, Their Making and Enforcement*, Columbia University Press, New York (2d ed.) 1916, p. 76; Jencks, Wilfried C., *Law in the World Community*, Oxford University Press, London/New York, 1967, p. 143. Rosenne defined a treaty as follows: "Treaty means an international agreement concluded between states in written form and governed by international law, whether embodied in a single instrument or in two or more related instruments and whatever its particular designation."
70. For example, the case of Portugal's colonies. See note 81, below.
71. Rigo Sureda, Andres, *The Evolution of the Right of Self-Determination*, Leyden, 1973, p. 66: "It is doubtful whether states can claim domestic jurisdiction, since these constitutional changes purport to affect the international status of territories with respect of which they have pledged themselves to fulfill certain obligations." In 1989, The Economic and Social Council of the United Nations authorized a full study of the international scope, character, and status of treaties between indigenous nations and states. ECOSOC Res. 1989/77, U.N. Doc. E/1989/INF/7, at 154 (1989).
72. U.S. Senate, *Congressional Globe*, Appendix, 74, 27th Cong., 2d Sess., U.S. Government Printing Office, Washington, D.C., 1846.
73. U.S. Senate, *Congressional Record* 2462, 46th Cong., 2d Sess., U.S. Government Printing Office, Washington, D.C., 1880.
74. Cited in Drinnon, Richard, *Facing West: The Metaphysics of Indian-Hating and Empire Building*, University of Minnesota Press, Minneapolis, 1980.
75. John Medill, *Annual Report of the Commissioner of Indian Affairs*, in House Executive Document No. 1, Serial 537, 30th Cong., 2d Sess., U.S. Government Printing Office, Washington, D.C., 1848, pp. 385-89.
76. Johansen, Bruce, and Roberto Maestas, *Wasi'chu: The Continuing Indian Wars*, Monthly Review Press, New York, 1979, p. 31.
77. "Whoever agrees that robbery is a crime, and that we are not allowed to take forcible possession of our neighbor's property, will acknowledge, without any other proof, that no nation has a right to expel another people from the country they inhabit in order to settle in it herself" (Vattel, op. cit., p. 168).
78. The effects of this can be seen in Churchill, Ward, and Jim Vander Wall, *Agents of Repression: The FBI's Secret War Against the Black Panther Party and the American Indian Movement*, South End Press, Boston, 1988, pp. 103-97 .
79. These changes have included the Tribal Self-Governance Demonstration Project, P.L. 100-472 (1988), through which ten indigenous nations were allowed greater control over their affairs independent of the BIA. In 1990, seven nations were continuing the project, and moving toward complete separation from the BIA in their affairs. In addition, the U.S. Senate has begun seriously to entertain the idea, advocated many years ago by the American Indian Movement (AIM), of abolishing the BIA and allowing indigenous nations to exercise a more genuine brand of self-determination. See U.S. Senate, Select Committee on Indian Affairs, *Final Report and Legislative Recommendations, Report of the Special Committee on Investigations*, 101st Cong., 1st Sess., U.S. Government Printing Office, Washington, D.C., 1989, pp. 15-23.
80. *Handbook on Federal Indian Law*, op. cit., p. 247.
81. This refers particularly to the former colonies of Angola, Mozambique, Guinea-Bissau, Cape Verde, and Sao Tomé, which have attained their independence; and East Timor, which

continues its struggle to achieve its independence—now from Indonesia, which invaded the territory after Portugal withdrew.

82. See *Everyone's United Nations*, United Nations, New York, 1978, pp. 306-12.
83. Ibid., pp. 296-303.
84. Manley, Michael, *Jamaica: Struggle in the Periphery*, Monthly Review Press, New York, 1982, p. 217.
85. For a popular exposition on this theme, see "Fraud In Indian Country" (7 part series), *Arizona Republic*, October 4-11, 1987.
86. *Message from the President Transmitting Recommendations for Indian Policy*, H.R. Doc. 363, 91st Cong., 2d Sess. (1970). According to the National Indian Youth Council and the National Congress of American Indians, in the late 1980s, 60 percent of all indigenous people living on reservations lived in abject poverty. Rural unemployment was 80 percent, and the average indigenous person earned $7,200 per year less than the average U.S. citizen. Twenty-five percent of all indigenous children had been placed in non-Indian residences. Indigenous people have the highest per capita incidence of diabetes, heart disease, and infant mortality of any group in the U.S. and die from liver disease at ten times the U.S. rate. The alcoholism rate among indigenous youth between the ages 15 to 26 is eight times higher than the U.S. average, and one-third of all indigenous people in the U.S. die before reaching the age of 45. Incidences of hepatitis and teen age suicide are higher among indigenous peoples than any other group in the U.S. See *Miami Herald*, November 24, 1989.
87. Gibson, op. cit., pp. 443-56, 489-510, 517-21, 556-58. For a specific case study of the adverse influence of the BIA and Department of the Interior (DOI) on indigenous nations, see Moore, John H., "The Muskoke National Question in Oklahoma," *Science and Society*, Vol. 52, No. 2, 1988.
88. U.S. Commission on Civil Rights, *The Navajo Nation: An American Colony*, U.S. Government Printing Office, Washington, D.C., 1975.
89. These minerals include oil shale, gilsonite, uranium, gypsum, helium, copper, iron, zinc, lead, phosphate, asbestos, and bentonite. See Churchill, Ward, "The New Genocide: A Hidden Holocaust in the State of Native American Environments," *Research in Inequality and Social Conflict* , No. 1, 1989, and Jorgensen, Joseph, ed., *Native Americans and Energy Development II*, Anthropology Resource Center/Seventh Generation Fund, Boston, 1984. Despite the creation of such organizations as the Council of Energy Resource Tribes (CERT), ostensibly founded to survey and monitor energy resource exploitation on indigenous nations' lands, the theft of resources continues.
90. *Cherokee Nation v. Georgia*, at 17: "[Indigenous nations] are in a state of pupilage; their relation to the United States resembles that of a ward to his guardian."
91. *United States v. Mitchell* (Mitchell I), 445 U.S. 535 (1980); *Nevada v. United States*, 463 U.S. 110 (1983).
92. *United States v. Mitchell* (Mitchell II), 463 U.S. 206 (1983). Despite Mitchell II, the Court has never granted damages to indigenous peoples for breach of a general fiduciary obligation, such as is enforceable in the common law of trusts. See Chambers, Reid, "Judicial Enforcement of the Federal Trust Responsibility to Indians," *Stanford Law Review*, No. 27, 1975, p. 1213.
93. Cristescu, Aureliu, *The Right to Self-Determination: Historical and Current Developments on the Basis of United Nations Instruments*, U.N. Doc. E/CN.4/Sub.2/404/Rev.l, (1981), p. 46.
94. For an extensive listing of U.N. General Assembly and Security Council resolutions on the right to self determination, see Cristescu, Aureliu, *The Historical and Current Development of the Right to Self-Determination on the Basis of the Charter of the United Nations and Other Instruments Adopted by the United Nations Organs, With Particular Reference to the Promotion and Protection of Human Rights and Fundamental Freedoms*, U.N. Doc. E/CN.4/Sub.2/404, 2 June 1978, Vol. 1, pp. 66-9. For purposes of this paper, I have adopted the definitions developed by Alfredsson concerning "decolonization" and "self-determination": "The terms of political decolonization and external self-determination are closely interrelated and have in practice been used interchangeably. A discussion of one without extensive use of the other is practically impossible. Political decolonization can either be viewed as a separate rule of international law or as a sub-category of self-determination relating to the right of colonial territories to external self-determination...[S]elf determination can contain the right of potential beneficiaries to determine their international status, to live without foreign interference inside their own boundaries and to choose their own form of government or internal political organization, to

choose their government in a democratic manner, not to be oppressed by the majority of a State population, and to pursue their social and cultural development. Most recently, self-determination has played a role in the north-south dialogue about the distribution of wealth and control over natural resources." See Alfredsson, Gudmundur, "Greenland and the Law of Political Decolonization," *German Yearbook of International Law*, No. 25, 1982.

95. Quoted in Raschhofer, Hermann, "The Right of Self-Determination from the Western Viewpoint," *International Law and Diplomacy*, No. 31, 1962, pp. 25-36.
96. Ibid. Also see Pomerance, Michla, *Self-Determination in Law and Practice*, The Hague, 1982, pp. 1-8.
97. See Connor, Walker, *The National Question in Marxist-Leninist Theory and Strategy*, Princeton University Press, Princeton, NJ, 1984, pp. 33-8.
98. Lenin, V.I., *The Right of Nations to Self-Determination*, Progress Publishers, Moscow, 1974, p. 98.
99. Strausshenko, Gyorgy, *The Principle of National Self-Determination in Soviet Foreign Policy*, Progress Publishers, Moscow, 1969, p. 88.
100. Fein, Esther B., "Gorbachev Urges Lithuania to Stay Within Soviet Union," *New York Times*, January 12, 1990, p. 1. According to Yuri Maslyukov, a member of the Soviet Politburo and an associate of Soviet President Gorbachev, "It is only natural that Lithuanians have the right to decide their fate—to be within the Soviet Union or to leave the Soviet Union."
101. *Everyone's United Nations*, op. cit., p. 278.
102. Alfredsson, op. cit., pp. 5-6.
103. Ibid.
104. Claude, Inis L. Jr., *The Changing United Nations*, Anchor Books, New York, 1967.
105. U.N. Charter, Articles 1(2) and 55; also see Articles 73 and 76.
106. *The Right to Self-Determination*, op. cit., p. 86.
107. Crawford, op. cit., pp. 89-106. He suggests that self-determination is recognized in the charter as a principle of law, and as a right only after the unit of self-determination has been determined by the application of appropriate rules.
108. Higgins, Rosalyn, *The Development of International Law Through the Political Organs of the United Nations*, Oxford University Press, London/New York, 1963, p. 104.
109. General Assembly Resolution (GA Res.) 1514 (XV), U.N. Doc A/4684 (1960), in General Assembly Official Records (GAOR), 15th Sess., Supp. 16, pp. 66-67; GA Res. 2131 (XX), U.N. Doc. A/6014 (1965), in GAOR, 20th Sess. Supp. 14, pp. 11-12; GA Res 2625 (XXV), U.N. Doc. A/8082 (1970), in GAOR 25th Sess., Supp. 28, p. 121.
110. The two covenants, known together as the *U.N. Human Rights Covenants*, were approved by the General Assembly in 1966, and have been in force since 1976. See Alfredsson, op. cit., pp. 15-16. Also see Kelly, Joseph B., "National Minorities in International Law," *Denver Journal of International Law and Politics*, No. 3, 1973, p. 267; citing Summary Records of the Sub-Commission Meeting, 1972, U.N. Doc. E/CN 4/sub.2/SR647, p. 150.
111. Alfredsson, op. cit., p. 22.
112. Ibid.
113. *ICJ Reports*, 1971, p. 31; reaffirmed in *ICJ Reports*, 1975, p. 31.
114. Alfredsson, op. cit., pp. 43-61.
115. Ibid., p. 46.
116. Ibid., p. 51.
117. See generally, Deloria, Vine, Jr., and Clifford M. Lytle, *The Nations Within: The Past and Future of American Indian Sovereignty*, Pantheon Books, New York, 1984.
118. Barsh, Russel, op. cit. Also see *The Sacred Mission of Civilization: To Which Peoples Should the Benefit be Extended? The Belgian Thesis*, Belgium Government Information Center, New York, 1953, p. 3.
119. See generally, note 70, above.
120. Alfredsson, op. cit., p. 23.
121. Ibid., p. 59.
122. For a general discussion, see Independent Commission of International Humanitarian Issues, *Indigenous Peoples: A Global Quest For Justice*, Zed Press, London, 1987.
123. Sanders, Douglas, "The Re-Emergence of Indigenous Questions in International Law," *Canadian Human Rights Yearbook*, No. 3, 1983, p. 13.
124. Ibid., p. 14.

125. Editors, *A Basic Call to Consciousness*, Akwesasne Notes, Mohawk Nation via Rooseveltown, NY, 1978, pp. 19-35.
126. Convention Concerning the Protection and Integration of Indigenous and Other Tribal and Semi-tribal Populations in Independent Countries, adopted by the General Conference of the ILO, 26 June 1957; Convention No. 107, United Nations Treaty Series (UNTS) 238, p. 247.
127. Bennet, Gordon, *Aboriginal Rights in International Law*, Royal Anthropological Institute, London, 1978, p. 7985.
128. *The Indigenous and Tribal Peoples Convention*, International Labor Conf., 76th Sess., Prov. Rec. 25 (1989).
129. Dunbar Ortiz, Roxanne, *Indians of the Americas: Human Rights and Self-Determination*, Zed Press, London, 1984, pp. 27-70.
130. Weyler, Rex, *Blood of The Land: The U.S. Government and Corporate War Against the American Indian Movement*, Everest House Publishers, New York, 1982. Also see Churchill and Vander Wall, op. cit.
131. Among the more notable actors in this movement are the Indian Law Resource Center, Inuit Circumpolar Conference, National Indian Youth Council, Australian and Islander Legal Services, South American Indian Council, International Indian Treaty Council, Four Directions Council, and the World Council of Indigenous Peoples.
132. Ismaelillo and Robin Wright, eds., *Native Peoples in Struggle*, Akwesasne Notes, Mohawk Nation via Rooseveltown, NY, 1982; *A Basic Call To Consciousness*, op. cit.
133. Martinez Cobo, José R., *Study of the Problem of Discrimination Against Indigenous Populations*, U.N. Doc. E/CN.4/Sub.2/1987/Add.4.
134. U.N. Doc. E/CN.4/Sub. 2/1983/21, August 5, 1983. Also see Sanders, Douglas, "The UN Working Group on Indigenous Populations," *Human Rights Quarterly*, No. 11, 1989.
135. E/CN.4/Sub.2/1988/25, 212, June 1988; Appendix 1.
136. E/CN.4/Sub.2/AC.4/1985/WP.5; Appendix 2.
137. Nanda, Ved, "Self-Determination Under International Law: Validity of Claims to Secede," *Case Western Reserve Journal of International Law*, No. 13, 1981, p. 57.
138. Ibid., p. 278.
139. Ibid., p. 275.
140. Ibid., p. 279.
141. Nietschmann (op. cit., p. 7) notes that the vast majority of the world's armed conflicts are between indigenous nations struggling for some level of self-determination, and states that oppose such aspirations.

The Future of Indian Nations

Self-determination and *self-government* are not equivalent terms, yet they can describe the same social reality, simply in different contexts. Neither the federal government nor the tribes have spent much time and energy distinguishing between these two concepts, and this failure to speak precisely has produced many misunderstandings and much confusion. Both terms speak of the survival of Indian people, but they point to entirely different social realities in the future. A study of the idea of self-government would not be complete if it omitted a discussion of the possibilities inherent in this idea for the future. Since Indians of all persuasions will not abandon the idea of governing themselves in communities of their own choosing, the idea will continue to be a point around which people can rally—and plan.

Given the present tribal condition, the adherents of both self-government and self-determination must cooperate if the tribe is finally to reconstitute itself. John Collier's thinking seems incomplete now, but his ideas represented about as much as both he and the Indians could realistically hope to achieve at the time. Looking at the other efforts to realize some form of municipal-national control, it is not difficult to see that in every decade of this century, given the times and perspectives of the people, the movement toward political independence was fairly successful. Self-government and self-determination were both novelties when they were introduced, hard to understand and harder to implement in a precise manner. We hope this study can make a contribution toward both understanding these concepts and helping to prepare the ground for eventual reconciliation of these divergent viewpoints.

Past efforts, successful and unsuccessful, which we have already discussed, seem to point to specific areas in which some changes can be made that will help Indians reestablish themselves. First, there must be a structural reform of tribal governing institutions that is fundamental but also permits a continuity between past and present. The search for such reform has been a constant theme in every period we have considered. Second, some kind of determined and lasting cultural renewal must take place to help resolve the question of Indian identity in the modern world; here emotional continuity must be recognized and considered seriously. Third, economic stability must be established and maintained if Indians are to survive as distinct and healthy communities; the reservation economy must be recognized as uniquely Indian, but it must also be efficient in today's world. Finally, relations between the tribe and the federal and state governments must be stabilized, and mutual respect and parity in political rights must be established.

Recommendations that attempt to speak to these particular areas of Indian life must necessarily also speak to the two points of view that we have found existing in the Indian communities. Recommendations that do not take into account the changes that occur in natural growth processes often fall into the classification formulas, and in the past the tendency of people to absolutize recommendations has meant the death of reform. Therefore, these recommendations will attempt to identify problem areas and suggest possible alternatives that might be considered, providing the consideration is done in good faith by people determined to find a solution to pressing problems.

Reform of Tribal Governments

When John Collier established the framework for tribal governments, there was little of substance that tribes could do for themselves. Consequently, representation on tribal councils was not seen as a critically important item to be considered when a constitution was adopted. Since the bureau wanted the tribes do work primarily on economic rehabilitation, tribal governments were thought to have powers that enabled them to deal effectively with reservation resources. The sociopolitical dimension of life on the reservation itself was not emphasized.

In the decades since the New Deal, reservation populations have grown considerably. Tribal rolls have increased dramatically, and this rapid increase in population of both reservations and tribal membership has caused many problems not anticipated by the people who adopted tribal constitutions a half century ago. Many tribes restrict their voting membership by requiring some kind of residency so that voting in the tribal election is not equivalent to voting to amend constitutions and to accept or reject claims awards and negotiated settlements. Tribal members are affected by both kinds of issues, but reservation residents are much more deeply affected by elections to determine tribal officers and to operate reservation programs. The difference in kinds of elections must be reconciled so that tribal members, whether living on or living off the reservation, feel they have a stake in the outcome and participate as responsible tribal citizens.

Present tribal councils are relatively small and are organized by districts. The origin of some districts goes back to the division of the reservation by agricultural agents and boss farmers, who were charged with teaching the white man's kind of agriculture to tribal members who had received allotments. Recent litigation dealing with representation on the tribal council has moved toward an equality of voting districts in much the same way that *Reynolds v. Sims*[1] redistricted state legislatures. In some instances tribes have argued against redistricting by appeal to tradition, but courts have been reluctant to recognize a tradition that has arisen so recently.

John Collier originally wanted a considerable amount of self-government given to smaller units on reservations, to villages and settlements where there was a somewhat homogenous and historically identifiable group, such as a band or clan. When Senator Wheeler eliminated title I of Collier's original proposal and he and Margold had to rely upon case law to identify tribal powers, there was not much precedent for the recognition of political and municipal powers at the level below that of the tribal entity. So one of the critical elements of tribal government—which would have helped to clarify the national status of tribes from the very beginning of self-government—was missing and could not easily be inserted in tribal constitutions without an uproar from Congress and the Indians.

As tribes increasingly call themselves nations, partially in response to traditional arguments and partially as a means of emphasizing sovereignty against state and federal government, some form of national government must be devised. After the Five Civilized Tribes moved to Oklahoma from the South, they were able to organize themselves in a national fashion, vesting powers in the town structure, which most of them brought intact when they moved. Hence the constitutional precedent is already established for tribes and reservations to adopt a different form of government that emphasizes the identification and separation of three traditional branches of government—legislative, executive, and judicial. The old council forms can also be seen as parliamentary systems in which a failure of confidence in leadership meant a replacement of executive officers and legislators and a reformation of the government. In wholly ethnic Indian terms, tribal governments must soon consider expansion of their forms of political institution.

Another argument exists, however, that relies more heavily upon the older prereservation traditions and may be suitable for consideration from the tribal point of view. Indian tribes in their original setting never attempted to govern a large number of people. Subgroupings in bands and clans was almost always a feature of the larger tribes, and apart from the difficulty of feeding a large number of people, there was another good reason for such subdividing. Indians realized that it was not good government to have leaders and representatives who did not have some kind of personal acquaintance with the people they led. If leaders were remote, people felt alienated, and it was much more difficult for a community to function. Most Indian groups did not exceed several hundred people, and a goodly number were less than a hundred people. This close correlation between the people and the leadership positions in the tribe ensured that the council represented all points of view that were regarded as important within the community.

Tribal governments should consider substantially expanding their council membership to ensure that a more intimate ratio of people to elected officials exists. At a minimum most tribal councils should be doubled—and some tripled—so that each council member represents a much smaller number of people for whom each can accept some well-defined responsibilities. An expanded council would then approach the size of a small legislature, giving the tribal government an aspect of nationhood and allowing it to perform typical legislative functions. Expansion of the council would also assist in distinguishing the executive branch from the legislative function and help to identify areas of responsibility. A much larger legislative body would provide some badly needed protection to the tribal judiciary, which is presently subjected to immense political pressure from tribal council members whenever it begins to exercise important judicial functions.

The standard response to an expanded number of elected tribal officials by the Bureau of Indian Affairs and outside agencies has been that large tribal councils cannot make decisions that need to be made if the tribe is to function. But this point is not as relevant as it might seem.

A small tribal council can easily be controlled by the bureau. When its decision-making process is short-circuited, with little time allowed for discussion and formal action expected to take place at every session of the council, the federal government can manipulate a few members of the council and force them to do its bidding. Hence, it is the tribal government's pliability that the bureau desires, not its efficiency or an understanding of its actions. A much larger tribal council would be more difficult to intimidate, and council members would tend to think more about their responsibilities to their constituents than about their standing with government bureaucrats.

The recent admission by tribal court judges of the importance and validity of traditional customs in determining cases brought in tribal courts is, as we have noted, a progressive move that suggests a process of reconciliation occurring on the reservations. More extensive development of tribal customs as the basis for a tribal court's decision will enable these institutions to draw even closer to the people. Part of the structural change necessary for tribal governments to become more independent is for the various branches of government to have their own identities. A court of elders, either approved by the tribal council or acknowledged by it, which would help to resolve domestic disputes before they become matters for tribal courts, could be a positive innovation. Much of the activity of tribal courts is the handling of domestic disputes, and courts cannot really solve family problems. A council of community elders, on the other hand, who are related to the parties in controversy and might apply other kinds of social pressures, might prove irresistible to the parties in conflict.

The old traditional ways of governing the people relied upon individual self-discipline for enforcement. Today a person is expected to know a bewildering number of rules and regulations and prudently to avoid violating standards based upon an abstract citizen who always seems to manage to obey the law. Tribal courts are being led down the road of the "reasonably prudent man" in adopting non-Indian juridical procedures, and at times this tendency is irritating to tribal peoples. Insofar as law and order can be deinstitutionalized and public behavior made a personal responsibility, a good compromise between old and new ways can be effected. This task cannot be accomplished by the federal government but only by the people on the reservations who see the practical value of such an approach.

In traditional, prereservation society the various clans and warrior societies acted as community policemen to enforce rules made for traveling, hunting, harvesting, and other activities in which the whole band or village was involved. To prevent unequal treatment of the people by the police, some tribes alternated the groups in the role of policemen. Thus, a society would not be unjust or unduly harsh in its enforcement of the rules because they would not be policemen during the next event and there might be retaliation against them. The role of tribal policemen in most tribal groups was that of peacemaker, not law enforcer. Since the Indian Reorganization Act tribal police forces have been understood as law enforcement officers. This image suggests a mistrust of the individuals living in a community and predetermines in the police officer's mind an expectation that the individuals in a community and its institutions are antagonists.

The troubles on the Pine Ridge Indian Reservation before and during the occupation of Wounded Knee give vivid evidence of the products of the law enforcement mentality. Since Wounded Knee, the emphasis of the federal presence in many of the tribes has been on the creation of SWAT teams, additional weaponry, and development of the police force toward a more paramilitary posture. At Pine Ridge itself the tribe has taken another approach. They now designate their policemen as "peace officers" and instruct them to look at their job as one of keeping the peace in the reservation communities, not in compiling impressive crime statistics. Structural recasting of the police function on reservations would significantly enhance the role of tribal government in the lives of the people and help to develop a more cooperative attitude toward both law and government. In view of the rapidly increasing costs of maintaining a modern police force, which virtually occupies a reservation community instead of policing it, this change might bear significant fruits.

The Indian Reorganization Act allowed tribes to create subsidiary institutions to conduct certain kinds of activities on the reservation. During the War on Poverty additional entities such as school boards, development corporations, housing programs, and recreation commissions were established. The degree to which tribes now have institutions that must be managed is astounding to many people. Frequently these tribal subsidiaries are more responsive to outside funding agencies and accreditation organizations than to the tribe or tribal council. By the same token, some of the agencies created by the tribal council are subject to the political whims of council members to the point where administration of programs is simply a matter of patronage distribution. Tribal governments have to find a middle ground between these two extremes. Collier thought the charter would control the creation of these groups and relied upon the sophistication of the tribal leaders to limit their scope and power. Chartering such groups by a national council instead of a smaller tribal council might provide them with a more appropriate image and status. It would not be surrendering any tribal sovereignty but exercising it in a more comprehensive manner.

Cultural Renewal

Culture is a most difficult subject to discuss. It is also the single factor that distinguishes Indians from non-Indians in the minds of both groups. John Collier appreciated Indian culture abstractly, but had a difficult time coming to practical grips with it. He fought to protect Indian religious freedom and believed self-government was a positive step toward preserving and reviving the better elements of tribal cultures. Yet he ensured the passage of the Indian Arts and Crafts Board,[2] which for most of its existence has been a sinecure for non-Indian art hobbyists and buffs and has encouraged both Indians and non-Indians to think of culture as primarily the artifacts produced by the ancestors of today's Indians. Until Indians can get a more comprehensive idea of their own regarding the content of their cultures, resolution of conflicts with the larger society will be almost impossible.

Reviewing the efforts of the federal government in the field of Indian education over the past century, we find an unmistakable trend toward public school education and the belief that education will eventually extinguish tribal cultures, assimilating Indians into the American social and cultural mainstream. Whenever the question of "Indian" education has been raised, federal representatives have suggested that courses in Indian culture be taught in public and federal schools. John Collier saw to it that some courses on Indian traditions were included in the bureau curriculum, and in the 1972 Indian Education Act there were provisions for teaching Indian culture and history. Even the best efforts in Indian education have been directed toward reducing the respective tribal traditions to an academic subject for student consumption.

Indians must begin to understand that a living culture is so much a part of a people that it is virtually incapable of recognition and formal academic transmission. Expecting schools to do the task formerly assumed spontaneously by parents, friends, relatives, and the community in concert is only to reduce tribal culture to a textbook phenomenon. Until Indians accept responsibility for preserving and enhancing their own knowledge of themselves, no institution can enable them to remain as Indians. A glance at the fate of bilingual programs on reservations offers a hopeful approach for the future of Indian education. When bilingual education was first proposed, it was assumed that there were so many Indian children speaking their native tongue as a first language that learning English as a second language was the key to improving the performance of the students.

Proposals for bilingual education were difficult to fund in Congress because most senators and congressmen held to the old idea of the melting pot. To instruct children in the language of the home was thought to be a severe handicap in helping them to adjust to the requirements of modern American life. During these years on the reservations tribal housing programs were initiated and country Indians were encouraged to move into new houses in the few settlements on the reservations. The result was that a new generation of Indian children grew up in these rural slums and learned English as a first language. When the bilingual programs were finally authorized and funded, many of them became vehicles for teaching the native language to children who had been denied the opportunity to learn it because of the location of their homes. Indians hence made a positive program that enhanced their traditions out of a program designed to further erode them. But it was a fortunate circumstance, not a deliberate effort.

Language is the first glue that links peoples together, and the major emphasis in self-determination and ultimately in self-government should be the preservation of language where it still exists and the cultivation of it where it has eroded or fallen into disuse. Although tribal peoples are hospitable, they also have an aspect of exclusivity, and language can help keep these important links alive and useful. Finally language can help to remind people working in Indian-created institutions of the heritage they possess. The nuances of meaning that the old traditions contain and the sacredness of experience can both be expressed in the native language in more comprehensible terms for tribe members than in English. Language is the key to cultural survival and cannot be considered in isolation; it is and must be the substance of self-determination.

In today's stories of mythical old Indians, one fact stands out sharply: The old Indians were in considerably better health than the Indians of today, yet they had no modern medical facilities available to them. Religious healing and proper natural diet enabled them to meet and overcome physical weaknesses and illnesses except those of a contagious nature for which they had no immunity and no period of time in which to gain an immunity. Today certain identifiable diseases, in particular diabetes, are rampant in Indian communities. With the poverty conditions existing on many reservations, junk food has become the major source of nutrition. Cultural revival would seem to include using traditional foods and medicines wherever possible. Restoration of a traditional diet might well enable the people to regain some of their natural strength in warding off diseases.

The U.S. Public Health Service, and earlier the Indian Health Service operating under the Bureau of Indian Affairs, were designed to supplant traditional health practices. During the sixties there was a concerted effort by the Public Health Service to use the traditional medicine men and healers in conjunction with their own services. In some instances, however, the Indian holy man was seen in the same role as the Protestant minister or Catholic priest—a formal religious figure called to comfort the dying and hear any words. People did not understand that it was the particular healing gifts of the holy man that were necessary, not merely his presense at the sickbed. If tribal culture is relevant to today's world, it must be seen as a vital element in the crisis situation, not as an exotic adjunct to the white man's science and knowledge.

The Indian Civil Rights Act does not guarantee religious freedom because of the objections of the Pueblos. Many tribal governments have, nevertheless, included freedom of religion in their constitutions because there are so many different religious traditions now extant on the reservation that it would be absurd to attempt to support the tribal religion as an established religion. Indeed, in some tribes the official tribal religion might well become Presbyterian, Catholic, or Baptist. Traditional tribal religions differ from the Christian denominations that have come to the reservations and gathered converts in one important aspect: The religious ceremonies of some tribes have taken on the guise of a tourist attraction. The Sun Dance at the Sioux reservations today resembles a pageant more than a religious ritual.

Freedom of religion on reservations today does not simply mean the right to practice a traditional religion. It also must include the right to practice the tribal religion seriously without the expectation by the tribal government that the ceremonies can be used for income-generating purposes. Too many tribes today use their religious traditions in the same manner as do whites—to bless sporting events and powwows and to endorse the actions to the tribal government. For a long time the exotic nature of the tribal religion was about all that could attract white tourists. Those days are declining rapidly. Since Indian Christians are not expected to hold church services as a tourist attraction, traditional Indians should not believe that they are required to do so.

Accountability is the other side of cultural integrity, and in the open society we have in America today accountability is rarely practiced in cultural matters by any group, especially by Indians. The power and viability of a culture is largely determined by the willingness of its practitioners to take themselves seriously. A parade of white imposters pretending to be Indians has become a common phenomenon in many tribes. Articulation of tribal traditions can be the province of almost anyone willing to put himself forward as an expert on these matters. Consequently, the younger generation is never certain what is acceptable tribal behavior and what is not. The majority of adult Indians feel that they have no right to ask questions of people posing as Indians or to call obvious fakes to account. Hence the tradition of many tribes has become what the most aggressive people say it is.

Self-government and self-determination are not possible in a society in which there is no set of criteria defining what behavior and beliefs constitute acceptable expressions of the tribal heritage. Traditional Indians have tended to prostitute their own knowledge by making it available to the wandering scholar, the excited groupie, and the curious filmmaker and writer. The cultural landscape is now so littered with erroneous information that it is extremely difficult for the serious Indian youngster to learn the truth about his past. If Indians are going to govern themselves with any degree of confidence, they must begin to define what is acceptable behavior and invoke the conscience of the community to maintain these standards. Otherwise, the internal substance of the tribal comunity will become solely those people who have been able to get themselves listed on the tribal roll as federally recognized Indians.

In the decades before and shortly after the Second World War, racial minorities were plagued by the burden of acting in certain predetermined ways. An individual who was a member of a minority community was expected to behave with a degree of humility and submissiveness because he or she was regarded as a representative of the racial group, and antisocial behavior was believed to be the source of derogatory stereotypes of the group. During the sixties racial minorities attacked the more vicious and degrading stereotypes that the white majority had created purporting to explain their behavior, and everyone made great effort to overcome old stereotypes. Though a great deal was accomplished, the fact nevertheless remains that irresponsible behavior by individuals of a racial minority casts aspersions on the whole group.

Part of the problem with the Indian power slogans and protests was that the movement rapidly became antiwhite instead of pro-Indian. The same was true in the other major racial minorities. As a consequence dialogue between the white majority and the various minorities became one of accusation and bitterness, which generated the backlash against all minorities. Self-determination involves having a responsible group that has pride in itself but does not generate this pride by pointing out the shortcomings of other groups.

In this particular respect a great difference exists between the tribal Indians and the ethnic Indians. Tribal Indians maintain a great respect for their own traditions and accord to others a measure of respect for their traditions and beliefs. Ethnic Indians, on the other hand, continuously use the shortcomings of the majority to gain leverage with that majority for items on their own agenda. The Kennedy Report spent a good deal of its energy on guilt-provoking accusations against past misdeeds of the Bureau of Indian Affairs and therefore was very popular with ethnic Indians. Such internal quarrels are dangerous because individuals really do represent their group to others, and racial minorities in particular cannot spend their time helping to create derogatory stereotypes of themselves.

Almost everything that can be recommended in terms of cultural revival and consolidation involves the fundamental problem of determining a contemporary expression of tribal identity and behaving according to its dictates. Obviously, the federal government cannot perform this function, nor can the American public. The cultural revival and integrity of the American Indian community depends on the cultivation of a responsible attitude and behavior patterns in the communities themselves. Collier did not seem to understand this dimension of human relations and seemed to assume that Indian culture had such obvious strengths as to be immediately attractive to everyone in the same manner as he had been attracted to it. Collier could not have changed the Indian posture toward the rest of American society, nor could any of the subsequent commissioners of Indian affairs or chairmen of the two Indian subcommittees in Congress. Inevitably, cultural self-government and cultural self-determination must precede their political and economic counterparts if developments in these latter areas are to have any substance and significance.

Economic Stability

Finding the solution to Indian economic problems is a desperate task. During the past century economic policy regarding Indians has fluctuated between developing communal assets and encouraging individual Indians to seek their fortune alone in American society. Collier's emphasis on economic development places the reforms of the New Deal squarely within the pendulum swing and enables us to equate his term as commissioner with the sixties as times when the corporate nature of economic enterprise was fostered. As far back as we can take American history, the non-Indian has been fascinated with Indian lands and resources and has demanded that they be used in the same manner as he uses his property. Since Indians have generally resisted this alternative, unless a radical change is made in the manner in which non-Indians perceive land, no lasting economic peace can ever be achieved between Indians and the rest of American society.

Land ownership has been the central legal issue involving Indians, and this century has seen the drastic erosion of the land base of the tribes. Collier's major concern while a private citizen and later as commissioner was to halt the loss of reservation lands and allotments and begin to rebuild the landholdings of the tribes. During the sixties, because there was still a feeling that termination might remain a viable solution of the Indian problem, Congress did little to assist tribes in consolidating their lands. The heirship problem continued to get worse, and the response of the Bureau of Indian Affairs was to purchase a computer to keep track of the Indian owners of allotments.

Indian reservations with allotments have a multitude of problems that unallotted reservations do not have. It is exceedingly difficult to create economic grazing or farming units on allotted reservations because quite often there are not enough allotments contiguous to one another to make up an economically feasible block of land for leasing or tribal use. Questions of ownership of the underlying minerals have plagued some tribes with allotments, and there is good precedent for the proposition that the tribe and the individual Indian owner have ownership of minerals. Water rights for allotments sometimes preclude the tribal water right in the sense that they represent the irrigable acreage on the reservation, and the tribe has to overcome previous allocations of water by the courts in order to begin new developments using their *Winters* water rights. Indians frequently sell their allotments to non-Indians and make it difficult for the tribe to consolidate tracts for its own use. Though tribes have the right to meet high bids, tribes do not always have the funds to make the purchase.

Land consolidation remains the major unsolved economic problem of Indian tribes. Until tribes are able to own their lands in one solid block, they cannot reasonably make plans for use or development of their resources. But consolidation has other implications that make it important. Civil and criminal jurisdiction depend upon the existence of trust lands. Whenever an allotment goes out of trust, the tribe loses jurisdiction over that area and must rely upon negotiated agreements with state and county governments in order to exercise jurisdiction over the area. Zoning for economic development and housing and enforcement of hunting and fishing codes is exceedingly difficult when the area under consideration is not wholly trust land.

Tribes do not have access to funds for land purchase for consolidation purposes because of a number of factors. Interest rates make investment in land prohibitive; income does not enable tribes to repay loans. Administrative costs in maintaining records of ownership on heirship lands continue to escalate, leaving less money for land purchase. Most important, the Reagan administration, in its massive reductions in domestic social programs, has forced the tribes to use their income to meet the immediate social needs of their people, foregoing any investments in activities that would help to stabilize the reservation economy. The Indian land situation is therefore becoming increasingly more serious, with no prospect of relief.

During the late sixties the bureau began to emphasize the great mineral wealth that underlay Indian reservations. Its idea was to attract large corporations for long-term leasing of the resources, thereby developing an increased income for tribes, which could be used in meeting matching requirements of federal grants and development projects. Following the Arab oil boycott, when the emphasis shifted to making America free of foreign energy sources, Indians were made to believe that they were the Arabs of the North American continent, possessing coal, oil, natural gas, and uranium in quantities sufficient to hold the American economy at ransom in exchange for considerably higher royalties on their minerals. Some tribal chairmen visualized themselves as the equals of the Saudis and began to demand respect they had not earned and did not merit.

After much debate and considerable rhetoric about Indian energy resources, a new national organization was founded—the Coalition of Energy Resource Tribes (CERT). With large grants from several federal agencies, CERT began operations as technical advisor and representative of the energy-rich Indian tribes. In the formative years of this organization refugees from Iran began to fill positions within the staff of CERT and act as consultants to the group. The men who had helped lead the Shah to disaster were now in the business of counseling the Indians on how to get the same deal for themselves. By 1983 CERT had overspent its budget and was doing drastic staff reductions. Its accomplishments were sparse to nonexistent, but it was the favorite of both the Carter and the Reagan administrations because it preached economic self-sufficiency for the reservations based upon astute use of their energy resources.

One problem with CERT was that very few Indian reservations

actually had the energy resources on which it was concentrating. On some of the reservations there was a clear choice between leasing grazing and farming lands to get at the minerals underneath or keeping the lands intact for use by tribal members for agricultural purposes. Hence energy development was not a supplement to existing reservation development; rather, it threatened to supplant existing activities and exchange economic self-sufficiency on the part of many tribal members for an expanded cash income available for programming by the tribal government. Some tribal governments therefore adopted the very methods of exploitation that had destroyed the resources of other parts of the country and made their coal and other energy minerals valuable, at least for the moment.

The economy of many reservations is a microcosm of the national economy. Large welfare rolls exist and large tracts of reservation lands have been set aside for energy development. A massive tribal bureaucracy is attempting to meet the social needs of the people, not realizing that many of these needs have been generated by the leasing of lands for mineral exploitation purposes. Generally the lands abandoned after uranium mining and strip mining of coal are not being restored to useful condition, and consequently injurious slag heaps of discarded refuse are found in many areas that were once free of contamination. The reservation has become a resource to be used and discarded, not a homeland for the tribe. The old combination of subsistence agriculture supplemented by social welfare programs and seasonal work has vanished in some areas, to be replaced by a welfare-cash economy that cannot sustain itself without massive federal assistance. Under the Reagan administration the Indians receive only strong admonitions to try harder to develop their private sector and, until lately, the accusations of James Watt about federal socialism on the reservations.

John Collier saw Indian tribal members as stockholders in a unique form of corporate enterprise. They had an expectation that as the tribal economy began to make progress, they would share in its benefits. But shifts in the federal budget deprived tribal members of the benefits they had been expecting. The development programs of the sixties in most instances created a rural slum that was as dependent upon its connections to the outside world as any suburban or urban area in the country. Housing programs clustered Indians together in small projects on many reservations, depriving them of living on and using their lands. The reservation economic structure became wholly artificial and was totally dependent upon an ever-increasing federal subsidy. Then, when it seemed there was no way to return to the old subsistence economy, and indeed inflation had made that possibility very remote, the Reagan administration simply reduced federal support, but in such absolute terms as to reduce the tribes to near bankruptcy.

Self-government is probably a farce without some steady form of tribal income to support it, and this argument prevails whenever the question is raised about leasing of Indian resources. But equally absurd are the tremendous costs of welfare and social programs that a tribe must bear when it removes its people from intimate and subsistence use of their lands and forces them to become recipients of public largess. The reservation economy of most tribes today is wholly artificial and could not survive but a few weeks without a transfusion from outside the reservation. Many Indians speak of this condition as colonialism, but it is considerably more devastating than simple colonialism. It is the final and systematic and perhaps even ruthlessly efficient destruction of Indian society.

Tribal Indians have fought back against the exploitation of tribal resources by outside non-Indian corporations. But they have not been able to articulate in comprehensible terms the implications they see in the developments that are occurring around them. Instead of raising questions about the practicality of rapid exploitation of reservation resources, they have generally phrased their opposition to projects with religious arguments and appeals to the religious mission of the tribe to protect the land—a worthy and moral stance to be certain, but unlikely to be convincing to tribal accountants charged with keeping the government solvent. They have not yet advocated a return to a natural economy derived from the sophisticated and self-sufficient use of the land, although their speeches clearly forecast the articulation of such beliefs.

The fundamental question of economic stability on the reservations revolves about the dilemma of whether the land is to be exploited, and therefore simply another corporate form of property, or to be a homeland, in which case it assumes a mystical focal point for other activities that support the economic stability of the reservation society. The Bureau of Indian Affairs naturally sees the reservation as valuable property and encourages Indians to view it in the same manner. Federal granting agencies provide funds primarily for development and use purposes, and private foundations also see the reservation as property to be used primarily for economic gain. Therefore, traditional, tribal Indians are at a severe disadvantage in articulating their point of view.

Economic stability depends at least in part on the feeling of familiarity of the people with their means of making a living. Where employment has a substantial relationship with previous activities, the people feel more comfortable and at ease with themselves and are willing to make accommodations to enable them to continue working. Thus fishing, ranching, and agriculture are all familiar and traditional in the sense of being activities in which the people have been engaged for most of this century. Industrial wage work and energy exploitation do not have roots in tribal society and produce a sense of alienation in the people. Even some forms of recreation and resort management seem strange and out of place for many Indians whose tribe has developed this kind of economic activity.

The critical factor in achieving economic stability seems to be in encouraging tribal officials to develop programs that are perceived by the people as natural extensions of things they are already doing. A natural economy maximizes the use of the land in as constructive a manner as possible, almost becoming a modern version of hunting and gathering in the sense that people have the assurance that this kind of activity will always be available to them. Some forms of industrial and wage work can take on the aura of natural economy. The Iroquois, for example, have become specialists in high steel work to the degree that it seems a natural part of their tradition, even though they must live in urban areas away from the reservation in order to engage in it. The Lummis and some of the other tribes have developed sophisticated aquacultures, and this kind of development relates directly to the tribal traditions, even though it is today expressed by and based on highly technical skills.

The Carter administration cut back economic opportunities for Indians rather drastically, but it did not articulate an economic philosophy that had sociological and cultural overtones. The Reagan administration has emphasized elitism and uncontrolled exploitation under the aegis of private enterprise, thereby creating a new divisiveness within the Indian reservation community. Further, Reagan's gospel of reliance on the private sector is absurd when applied to reservations, where the only private enterprise has been the non-Indian trader and the mixed-blood rancher or storekeeper. With the budget cutbacks it is not possible to have anything except instant misery on the reservations. Since the reservation economy can only maintain stability under the present conditions by the infusion of outside capital, the prospects, both long- and short-term, for Indian economic stability are exceedingly remote.

Federal-State Relations

Beginning with the militant rhetoric used by the Abourezk Commission to describe the status of tribal governments, the popular slogan among tribal officials is to insist on a "government-to-government relationship" with the federal government. Considering that tribal governments are closely controlled by the federal government and obtain a good deal of their administrative overhead from the federal government, this phrase has less substance than people would like to admit. If we use it to describe the *status* of tribal governments when compared with the United States and in some instances its constituent states, we have a more accurate characterization of the goal of Indians in clarifying their relationship with the United States. They believe that with some understanding and with a steady policy of support and development, there could be a more comprehensible working arrangement with other political entities that would respect the idea and practice of self-government.

Although the treaty recommendations of the Twenty Points did not receive the attention they deserved, they still remain good descriptions of the proper ongoing treaty process that would be most useful for Indian tribes. There has been some indication that among traditional people the idea of arbitration and mediation is favored in disputes with state governments and might be encouraged in the case of federal involvement. The ideology generally adopted by Republican administrations, however, makes Indians wards of the government and emphasizes the idea that Indians are citizens. Treaties are therefore anathema because they provide evidence of the fact of continuing federal responsibility to and for Indians.

Tribal courts and tribal governments have been working toward achieving a full faith and credit relationship with the states, and in view of the expectation that Indian reservations will continue into the future, this is an important area for consideration. It demands a recognition of the basic treaty relationship without making it distasteful to local legislators who often chafe at the idea of accepting tribal governments as equal political entities. There are two ways that full faith and credit can be achieved. A tribe can completely adopt the laws and procedures of a state and become virtually identical to the state in numerous areas of activity. Hunting and fishing regulations can be the same, tax policy can be similar, the tribe carefully avoiding any conflict with the state, and domestic relations laws can be made identical. Cross-deputization can be achieved, making the tribal police and the state police a nearly identical force in the reservation areas. This approach basically surrenders the flexibility of the tribal government to meet the unique needs of the people in exchange for peaceful relations with the state and its agency.

A much more difficult approach, and one favored by tribal Indians, would be comparable with the status of the Amish settlements. Reservations would develop their social relations to a degree where they earned the respect and envy of the non-Indian world. Stories abound of the old days when it was not necessary to have locks on doors on the reservation and where honesty and truthfulness was an outstanding characteristic of Indian society. In the speeches of traditional leaders in recent years, this visionary picture of a society of justice is painted in most vivid terms. The problem with the manner in which traditional people articulate this idea today is that almost all of the blame is placed on the white man for destroying this paradise and little responsibility is taken by Indians for abandoning it. In view of the present state of the reservations, this alternative remains a goal to achieve rather than an immediate condition that can be accomplished.

A middle ground between these two extremes can be found and may indeed be what both tribal leaders and traditional people have in mind as they adopt more of the ideology of self-determination and focus less on self-government. Assuming responsibility for education and various aspects of social welfare, adopting the use of customary law in tribal courts, and refusing development schemes that would injure lands beyond repair all seem to be steps toward creating a better reservation society that hints at the idyllic vision of the traditional people. As more and more individuals make conscious decisions to accept the self-discipline that traditional life imposes, we may well see a substantial change in reservation social conditions, pointing toward an internal integrity that must surely underlie a full faith and credit relationship.

A continuing problem that John Collier could not handle and subsequent generations have not solved with any degree of sophistication is claims against the federal government. Tribes have had a continuing problem getting their claims heard in court. The Indian Claims Commission did not finish its work by any means. It made the process of claims resolution so tedious and placed the tribes and federal government in an adversary position so that reasonable compromises could not be worked out and finally just exhausted the patience of Congress, which terminated it in 1978. Since the expiration of the claims commission, tribes have had to take their cases to the U.S. Court of Claims for resolution.

In recent years a new kind of claim has arisen, partially from the dereliction of the Indian Claims Commission and Bureau of Indian Affairs in fulfilling their duties under the Indian Claims Commission Act. Every Indian tribe or community was supposed to receive notice of its right to file against the federal government under the provisions of the act. Hardly any Indian tribes in the eastern United States were so notified, and it was not until the early seventies that the land claims of eastern Indians began to attract attention. The Maine tribes successfully pursued their claims and were awarded both land and money in a negotiated settlement. Other eastern Indian tribes have been pursuing their claims and are in the process of getting them resolved in agreements of a similar nature. Many Indian claims are still outstanding.

The importance of claims is that until the tribe feels it has received both justice and an accounting for its past relationship with the United States, claims prove to be a disruptive political issue within the tribe. Tribal leaders can be attacked by their opponents on the flimsy ground that they have not pursued the claim with sufficient vigor. Additionally many Indians do not want to embark on any kind of development for themselves until they get their claims money. The Sioux for almost a generation were stymied because many people thought that claims were about to be settled and refused to consider other kinds of developments and activities until the claims were finalized. Claims are both satisfying in terms of fulfilling ancient promises and disruptive in that they take an inordinate amount of time and energy away from other reservation activities that would be more profitable in the long run.

Prompt settlement of outstanding tribal claims against the United States would help to lay the past to rest with some sense of finality and enable tribes to devote their time to other things. Negotiated settlements could be effected that would involve the resolution of other problems, such as heirship lands, capital for development projects, and special funding of certain kinds of projects that would need a sustained financial support system for a period of years. The structural change that resolution of claims would involve would be the elimination of the adversarial, judicial proceeding in favor of negotiated settlements specifying the duration of leases and the exchange of particular rights and privileges.

One of John Collier's most cherished goals was the establishment of a Court of Indian Affairs. As we have already noted, he had to sacrifice this title of his omnibus reform bill in order to get Senate support for self-government. The idea of a national court to handle Indian matters should be revived and made a regular part of the federal judiciary. We already have various federal courts that deal with specific subject matter, and the justification for each of them is that they require a special knowledge and deal with a special body of law and hence relieve the regular federal courts from having to deal with technical subjects with which they might not have expertise.

No area of federal law is more complicated or requires more expertise than federal Indian law. Hundreds of treaties, thousands of statutes, and hundreds of thousands of administrative rulings and actions are involved in federal Indian law. Over six hundred separate Indian communities are dependent in some manner on the vagaries of interpretation of federal Indian law, and literally billions of dollars and the lives of over a million people are at stake in Indian cases. There is sufficient justification for such an institution in both the scope of subject matter and in the amount of money presently spent in litigation on Indian matters by the federal and state governments and Indian tribal governments.

Indians have not traditionally supported this proposal, and with good reason. Appointments to the federal judiciary have generally been regarded as political rewards to the party faithful, and so there is a danger that the Court of Indian Affairs would become dominated by individuals antagonistic to Indians. The Indian position has generally been to demand that the tribes appoint some of the judges or at least have a hand in the selection of the people who would serve in such a court. A variety of ways could be found to ensure impartiality in the decisions of the court, and we cannot take the time to elaborate the complex alternatives that might be considered. The fact remains that this court would provide a focus to litigation dealing with Indian issues and attempt to bring a consistent source of expert knowledge to the solution of issues affecting Indians.

The idea of self-government for Indians began almost as soon as Indians had fairly continuous contact with non-Indians. It has been the subject of wholly arbitrary bureaucratic action and very spontaneous Indian militant activities. Generally, the structure put in place to achieve Indian self-government is premised upon a deep mistrust by the government of the actual process of self-government. Federal officials fear a loss of control over the decisions that Indian communities might make, and therefore, although federal policy several times has declared self-government for tribes, it has not been realized to any great extent.

Indians have preserved the idea of nationhood or peoplehood throughout their period of contact with the non-Indian world but have had great difficulty communicating the essence of what they believe to the larger society. In many respects during the postwar period Indians have acted like other racial minorities in their approach to problems and in their efforts to get the attention of the federal government. But this movement to be a recognized minority group within American society has spawned an Indian traditional backlash, which seems to have directed Indian attention to a deeper appreciation of the old ways.

Apart from some structural changes, there is no good solution to the question of self-government today. Indians have few viable options open to them because they lack the substantial economic and social freedom to experiment with alternative ways of doing things. Self-government is in large part social and community growth, and this growth takes both time and realizations about the world that are not capable of being programmed. A change in perception by both Indians and federal and state officials who deal with Indians is imperative if any substantial progress is to be achieved in the future. Until Indians resolve for themselves a comfortable modern identity that can be used to energize reservation insitutions, radical changes will not be of much assistance but will only serve to confuse people.

Self-government is basically a political idea, and it has been superceded in our generation by the demand for self-determination. Indian affairs has thus moved beyond political institutions into an arena primarily cultural, religious, and sociological and there are no good guidelines for either policy or programs in this new area of activity. The old scholarship that treated political and economic activities as separate from the rest of human experience can no longer describe political and economic developments in Indian tribes without reference to the profound cultural and emotional energies that are influencing Indians today. It is probably too late to put the Indian genie back into the bottle. John Collier planned too well in his efforts to give Indians self-government. In setting the theoretical framework for reconstituting an ancient feeling of sovereignty, he prepared the ground for an entirely new expression of Indian communal and corporate existence. We are just beginning to recognize the nature of this expression.

Acknowledgments

Kickingbird, Kirke, Lynn Kickingbird, Charles J. Chibitty, Curtis Berkey. *Indian Sovereignty* (Washington: Institute for the Development of Indian Law, 1977): 1–64.

Henriksson, Markku. "Treaty Legislation." In *The Indian on Capitol Hill: Indian Legislation and the United States Congress, 1862–1907* (Helsinki: Finnish Historical Society, 1988): 62–76. Reprinted with the permission of the Finnish Historical Society.

Churchill, Ward. "Implications of Treaty Relationships Between the United States and Various Indian Nations." In *Native Americans and Public Policy*. Edited by Fremont J. Lyden and Lyman H. Legters (Pittsburgh: University of Pittsburgh Press, 1992): 149–63. Reprinted with the permission of the University of Pittsburgh Press.

Wilkins, David E. "The U.S. Supreme Court's Explication of 'Federal Plenary Power:' An Analysis of Case Law Affecting Tribal Sovereignty, 1886–1914." *American Indian Quarterly* 18 (1994): 349–68. Reprinted with the permission of the University of Nebraska Press.

Deloria, Vine, Jr. "Self-Determination and the Concept of Sovereignty." In *Economic Development in American Indian Reservations*. Edited by Roxanne Dunbar Ortiz (Albuquerque: University of New Mexico Native American Studies, 1979): 22–28. Reprinted with the permission of the University of New Mexico, Native American Studies Center.

Gross, Emma R. "The Origins of Self-Determination Ideology and Constitutional Sovereignty." In *Contemporary Federal Policy Toward American Indians* (Westport, Conn.: Greenwood Press, 1989): 31–48. Reprinted with the permission of Greenwood Publishing Group.

Barsh, Russel Lawrence. "The Challenge of Indigenous Self-Determination." *University of Michigan Journal of Law Reform* 26 (1993): 277–312. Reprinted with the permission of the University of Michigan Law School.

McCullogh, Ann. "Indian Tribal Taxation: A Cornerstone of Sovereignty." In *Native Americans and Public Policy*. Edited by Fremont J. Lyden and Lyman H. Legters (Pittsburgh: University of Pittsburgh Press, 1992): 165–89. Reprinted with the permission of the University of Pittsburgh Press.

Jaimes, M. Annette. "Federal Indian Identification Policy: A Usurpation of Indigenous Sovereignty in North America." *Policy Studies Journal* 16 (1988): 778–98. Reprinted with the permission of the Policy Studies Organization.

Harring, Sidney L. "Crazy Snake and the Creek Struggle for Sovereignty: The Native American Legal Culture and American Law." *American Journal of Legal History* 34 (1990): 365–80. Reprinted with the permission of the Temple University School of Law.

Lubick, George M. "Peterson Zah: A Progressive Outlook and a Traditional Style." In *Indian Lives: Essays on Nineteenth- and Twentieth-Century Native American Leaders*. Edited by L.G. Moses and Raymond Wilson (Albuquerque: University of New Mexico Press, 1985): 189–214. Reprinted with the permission of the University of New Mexico Press.

Medcalf, Linda. "The Quest for Sovereignty." In *Law and Identity: Lawyers, Native Americans, and Legal Practice* (Beverly Hills: Sage Publications, 1978): 47–65. Reprinted with the permission of Sage Publications.

Robbins, Rebecca L. "Self-Determination and Subordination: The Past, Present, and Future of American Indian Governance." In *The State of Native America: Genocide, Colonization, and Resistance*. Edited by M. Annette Jaimes (Boston: South End Press, 1992): 87–121. Reprinted with the permission of South End Press.

Morris, Glenn T. "International Law and Politics: Toward a Right to Self-Determination for Indigenous Peoples." In *The State of Native America: Genocide, Colonization, and Resistance*. Edited by M. Annette Jaimes (Boston: South End Press, 1992): 55–86. Reprinted with the permission of South End Press.

Deloria, Vine, Jr. and Clifford M. Lytle. "The Future of Indian Nations." In *The Nations Within: The Past and Future of American Indian Sovereignty* (New York: Pantheon Books, 1984): 244–64. Reprinted with the permission of Pantheon Books.

9 780815 336297

For Product Safety Concerns and Information please contact our EU representative GPSR@taylorandfrancis.com
Taylor & Francis Verlag GmbH, Kaufingerstraße 24, 80331 München, Germany

www.ingramcontent.com/pod-product-compliance
Lightning Source LLC
LaVergne TN
LVHW011107300926
849160LV00008B/304

* 9 7 8 0 8 1 5 3 3 6 2 9 7 *